Where Have All the Flowers Gone
A Singer's Stories, Songs, Seeds, Robberies

WHERE HAVE ALL THE FLOWERS GONE
A Singer's Stories, Songs, Seeds, Robberies

by Pete Seeger

edited by Peter Blood

A Sing Out Publication

Editor: **Peter Blood**
Publications Director: **Eric Nemeyer**
Art Director: **Kristen P. Morgan**
Executive Director: **Mark Moss**
Text layout, music typesetting: **John Roberts**
Cover illustration: **Eric Von Schmidt**
Interior line drawings: **Pete Seeger** (unless otherwise noted)
Bibliography, Discography, and Indexes: **Peter Blood**

ISBN: 1-881322-01-7

Library of Congress Cataloging-in-Publication Data

Seeger, Pete, 1919-

    Where have all the flowers gone: a singer's stories, songs, seeds, robberies / by Pete Seeger, edited by Peter Blood.
    p. cm.
    Includes bibliographical references and indexes.
    Discography: p.
    ISBN 1-881322-01-7
    1. Seeger, Pete, 1919- 2. Folk singers--United States--Biography 3. Folk songs 4. Popular music
    I. Blood, Peter.
ML420.S445A3 1993
782.42162'0092--dc20
[B]

                                                        93-8352
                                                        CIP
                                                         MN

Orders and inquiries should be directed to the publisher:
Sing Out Corporation, P.O. Box 5253, Bethlehem, PA 18015-0253   (215) 865-5366

To Toshi

TABLE OF CONTENTS

Chapter 5: New Tunes to Others' Words 85

Chapter 6: New Words to Others' Tunes 117

Chapter 7: The Vietnam War 147

Chapter 8: From the Great Old Book 171

Chapter 9: Think Globally, Sing Locally 201

Chapter 10: Time, Home, Family, Friends 227

ACKNOWLEDGEMENTS

"**I have drunk from wells I did not dig, been warmed by fires I did not build**" *

This book would not be in your hands but for the work of thousands of people. Here's thanks to them all.

Papermakers, printers, truckers, salespersons.

Editors: Peter Blood, Eric Nemeyer, Mark Moss of *Sing Out!* And typists: Linda Beatty, Andra Sramek, Debbie Schwartz. Page Layouts by Kristen P. Morgan. Proofreader Jackie Alper.

For music advice, as well as music computing, I was lucky to get the help of singer John Roberts through long months of re-writing and revisions. See John's picture on page 241.

Thanks to songwriters and publishers who allowed me to reprint copyrighted songs. © Copyright information is in small type under each song. I also thank unknown thousands of musicians and poets whose work I have built on in some way.

Thanks to artists and photographers whose works have been used. I don't know all your names. Write me; I'll give proper credit in future printings. Likewise, any reader who spots any mistake: write.

Thanks to the archives of *The Peoples Weekly World* and The Fellowship of Reconciliation for help in locating pictures, also Gene Shay, Joe Hickerson, Harold Leventhal, Joy Graeme, Judy Bell, and Toshi Seeger for locating many things.

Thanks to friends on several continents who took the trouble to read earlier drafts and make suggestions:

Rick Abrams	Joy Graeme	Gretchen Reed
Greg Artzner	Fred Hellerman	Larry Richmond
Antoon Aukes	Greg Landau	Will Schmidt
Judy Bell	Terry Leonino	Steve Sedberry
Bob Bossin	Harold Leventhal	Rod Sinclair
Oscar Brand	Reuben Musgrove	Michael Skuppin
Geoff Brown	Lillebjørn Nilsen	Joe Stead
Suman Chatterjee	Shari Nilsen	Dario Toccacelli
Tica Da Costa	Ruth Pelham	Kan Yazawa
Bill Goodman	Vladimir Pozner	

I couldn't take everyone's advice, but I took a lot of it. The book is better, thanks to you all. But I send it to the printer now with misgivings. Every project I've ever worked on (songs, houses, boats, organizations) needed changes and amendments. What if a few months from now it's obvious I made a big mistake?

But right now I don't want to make the mistake of delaying longer. Or the mistake of staying silent. Ready or not, here 'tis.

* Thanks Harvard Magazine

Theme from "The Goofing-Off Suite"

In my family I get a favored role. If I'm lying on the bed playing the banjo or guitar while there's lots of other work to be done, my family says, "Grandpa's practicing." So it was that 35 years ago Folkways issued an LP called *The Goofing-Off Suite*, and a few years later, it was even published. This melody and its accompaniment are so simple that it seems presumptuous to call it a song. Yet it lingers in the memory. I start this book with it.

Originally titled "Opening Theme"
By Pete Seeger (1956)
© 1959 (renewed) by Sanga Music Inc.

Chapter I All Mixed Up

This book tells the story of one person's attempts, over a long lifetime, to put together new songs. Sometimes changing old songs slightly, adding new words to old melodies, or new melodies to old words. Combining traditions from many lands. "Something old, something new, something borrowed and something blue," like the bride's wedding dress. If you're looking for songs, skip ahead. Ignore the personal chit-chat between the songs. But if you're curious about the life of a musician in 20th century America, here goes.

On both sides of my family, I come from people used to putting pen to paper. Letters, diaries, speeches, essays, journalism, occasionally poems or books. So as a kid, I occasionally wrote poems.

Forbidden

I saw a frightened child
Peering through a crack
Which looked out on the courtyard of the world.
His mind was full of wonder,
Trying hard to comprehend
The forbidden, secret, good things that he saw.
But voices of guardians,
The secret, silent guardians,
Came floating down the hallway, and he fled.
    I saw him again
    And he'd brought along a chisel
    Trying, trying, to see more clearly.
    But once again the guardians,
    The stealthy, ghostly guardians
    Came gliding down the passageway.
    Again he fled.
"That's forbidden."
"That's not right."
"Run and save yourself
Before you fall to hell."
And then, very satisfied,
They walked slowly back
With their rusty, unused keys
In their mouths.
    I've never seen him since,
    For he stayed
    Where all good children should.
    But he's dropped his chisel.
    Let's pick it up.

By Pete Seeger (1934)
TRO - © 1993 Melody Trails, Inc., New York, NY.

I was 15, in junior year at prep school. Don't know where the idea came from — I was able to read well and widely. No one had me locked up. I had a laissez-faire upbringing.

My mother was a violinist;[1] my father lectured on music theory, history, and composition. Both dedicated professional musicians, teaching at Juilliard Institute, New York City. It was a world of high ideals, long training, great discipline. But early in life I learned that rules were made to be broken. Henry Cowell, the modern composer, was a family friend. When I was six, I remember him playing the piano with his fists.

My mother had hoped that one of her children would play the violin. She bought miniature fiddles for my two older brothers. But they rebelled. When I came along my father said, "Oh, let Peter enjoy himself." I remember having fun at age four or five making a racket on a wide variety of instruments: autoharp, pennywhistle, marimba, a pull-push accordion, a piano, a pump organ. All by ear.

Age eight I was given a ukelele. Started picking out chords, learning their names. Plunk, plunk. My father was researching some of the few collections of folk music available in those days. I learned from him that there were often different versions of the same song. People change words, melody, made up new verses. This was an important lesson: you can choose the version of the song you want to sing.

[1] Constance DeClyvver Edson (1886-1975) was ⅜ English descent, ¼ French, ¼ Irish, ⅛ Dutch. My father, Charles Louis Seeger (1886-1978), was ⅛ German and the rest English settlers in Massachusetts. So far as I know. One never knows what went on between the sheets. We're all distant cousins, all 6(?) billion of us. A grandfather and a great-grandmother played piano, another could rattle the bones, another loved to sing and dance, into her 70's.

Age 17, I met the folksong collector Alan Lomax, who showed me thousands of songs I never knew my country had. Through Alan, I also met Leadbelly, Aunt Molly Jackson, Jim Garland and Sara Ogan, all southern singers and makers of songs, who turned my teen-age mind around, politically as well as musically.

And at age 20, I met Woody Guthrie, the most prolific songwriter of them all. He, too, used a standard technique of putting new words to old tunes (see p. 85). One can make up a new song by changing around an old song. Who cares if it is not completely original? The aim in this world is to do a good job, not to try and prove how original one can be. I had long been acquainted with the jazz technique of taking over a pop melody and changing it a bit. So when I heard Woody sing Jimmie Rodgers' yodeling blues "T for Texas," just having registered for the draft (October 1940) it inspired me to put together this "new" song:

C for Conscription

Well it's C_____ for Con-
(yodel)
scription,_____ C for Cap-i-tol Hill._____
C for Con-scrip-tion, C for Cap-i-tol Hill,_____
(falsetto)
hey, hey, hey._____ And it's C for the
Con-gress that passed that god-dam bill. Yo-del-
lay- ee Yeow! hoo, hoo, hoo,— hoo._____

Words by Pete Seeger (1940) Music adapted from a traditional blues
© 1993 by Stormking Music Inc.

Two years later I was willingly in uniform for three and a half years, helping to defeat the "Axis powers," Germany, Italy, and Japan. Occasionally these days, I find myself singing peace songs and soldier songs side by side.

For 50 years I was able to make a living standing on a platform, with a microphone to help, and for an hour or two, exploring a wide range of old songs and new songs, sometimes circling around a subject. "The truth is a rabbit in a bramble patch. One can rarely put one's hand upon it.

One can only circle around and point, saying 'It's somewhere in there.'" (CLS)[2]

I once sang more stories of long ago and far away. Within recent decades I've sung more stories of far away and not so much of long ago. And in recent times, one of the main purposes of my own singing is to persuade other people to sing together. It is fun to sing together. It is fun to learn how to harmonize. It is fun to learn how to play with the rhythm.

In a program of 20 or 30 songs or more, I'll usually find myself singing at least one or two that I've helped to put together. I've rarely tried to do a whole program out of just songs that I've helped compose. More often some other songwriter or some old song can carry the program forward better.

Nevertheless, in this particular volume I decided to explore my own experiments. Originally the book was to be called *The Songwriter As a Joiner.*

This was partly a pun, because through my life at various times I've joined others in some kind of an organization, consciously or unconsciously, reluctant or enthusiastic: family, school, choir, performing group, student union, Communist Party, U.S. Army, marriage, *Sing Out!* magazine, Sloop *Clearwater*, musicians union, Unitarian church, volunteer fire department, veteran's organization, etc.

But also I was thinking of Beethoven, who once said, "I am a joiner," referring to a cabinetmaker who joins and fits pieces of wood together.

Speaking of Beethoven, my father once spent an evening discussing with other musicologists how much of a Beethoven symphony was original Beethoven, and how much was inherited from tradition and from other composers. At first it seemed that it might be 50–50.

But as they talked, they recognized that Beethoven used major and minor scales invented centuries earlier and the symphonic form developed by Haydn and Mozart. He used musical instruments from many parts of the world. They concluded that about 10 percent of a Beethoven symphony could be said to be original Beethoven. About 90

Photo by Daniel Seeger

---

[2] Throughout this volume, I'll try to give credit where credit is due. All my life I've quoted my musicologist father (above), so if you see (CLS), you will know it refers to something he said or wrote.

ALAN LOMAX, WOODY GUTHRIE & LEADBELLY, JIM GARLAND; AT BOTTOM: AUNT MOLLY JACKSON, SARAH OGAN

percent was tradition, or inherited from other composers.

Of course, Beethoven was able to put together great music no one else had been able to put together before or since. So, we don't belittle his genius any more than we belittle Shakespeare for getting plots for his plays from old sources.

At one time I had hoped to have drawings, sketches of the people who had helped put together these songs: a sketch of Lee Hays, who wrote the words of "If I Had A Hammer." A sketch of Peter, Paul & Mary, who changed my melody of that song (and only then did it "take off"). A sketch of some Don Cossack soldiers of 100 or more years ago singing an old Russian song, "Koloda Duda," whose verses inspired "Where Have All The Flowers Gone" (see pp.166–169).

A picture of the women and men in a congregation in a black church in the 1870's or the 1880's for the song "Jacob's Ladder."

A picture of some tough, frowning intellectual. Bearded, sandaled, with a traditional Hebrew robe. That would be Ecclesiastes, who wrote most of the words of "Turn, Turn, Turn."

Such pictures were too ambitious an idea. Eric Von Schmidt put most of 'em on the cover. Besides, how could we picture all the numberless, nameless people who invented the harmony, rhythms, scales which we use? Some of these folks might have lived within the last few hundred years, but most of them lived long ago. Likewise, how would we picture the people on several different continents who put together the instruments I play and the variety of language I speak and write in? Impossible.

Thousands of years ago our ancestors, wherever they lived on this earth, knew only to trust their own tribe, and struggle to the death against any other tribe entering their hunting grounds. Then clever folks learned how to use boats, horses, wheels. They learned how to use symbols, language, numbers. Now we've spread over all the earth, and find ourselves jammed in cities, competing for crumbs from the rich man's table.

My guess is that if there's a human race still here in a hundred years it will be because we've learned to value Survival over $uccess, to live and learn, to grin and bear it. We'll use our new tools of communication to reach out to our cousins, hard-working folks in every single corner of this globe. A worldwide search for justice.

In trying to find ways we can work together, we'll use sports, arts, humor of many kinds. I've tried to combine old, old songs with brand new ones. Tried singing in different languages. Tried working with little kids, and with old folks. And above all urged folks to participate, in politics, in music, in all life.

For example, on the next page you'll find a song put together over 30 years ago. I swiped a Caribbean melody and a Caribbean beat. If you read music, see what you can make of it.

All Mixed Up

Words & music by Pete Seeger (1960)
© 1965 (renewed) by Stormking Music Inc.

1. You know, this language that we speak
   Is part <u>Ger</u>man, part Latin, and part Greek,
   With some <u>Cel</u>tic and Arabic and Scandinavian*
      all in the heap,
   —Well amended by the people in the street.
   <u>Choc</u>taw gave us the word "okay," **
   "Vam<u>oose</u>" is a word from Mexico way,
   And <u>all</u> of this is a hint, I suspect,
   —Of what comes next:

CHORUS (AFTER EACH VERSE):
I think that this whole world
Soon, mama, my whole wide world
Soon, mama, my whole world,
Soon gonna be get mixed up.

(THE RHYTHM KEEPS ON, BUT I SPEAK SLOW AND CLEAR):
"Soon, mama, my whole world
Soon, mama, my whole wide world
Soon, mama, my whole world
Soon, gonna be get mixed up."
(SING):
Soon, mama, my whole world
Soon, mama, my whole wide world
Soon, mama, my whole world
Soon gonna be get mixed up.

2. I like <u>Pol</u>ish sausage, I like Spanish rice
   —Pizza pie is also nice
   <u>Corn</u> and beans from the Indians here
   <u>Washed</u> down by some German beer
   <u>Mar</u>co Polo travelled by camel and pony
   —Brought to Italy the first macaroni
   And <u>you</u> and I, as well as we're able
   —Put it all on the table.***

3. There <u>were</u> no redheaded Irishmen
   Before the <u>Vik</u>ings landed in Ireland.
   <u>How</u> many Romans had dark curly hair
   Bef<u>ore</u> they brought slaves from Africa?
   No <u>race</u> on earth is completely pure;
   Nor is <u>any</u> one's mind and that's for sure.
   The <u>winds</u> mix the dust of every land,
   And <u>so</u> will woman and man.***

4. Oh, <u>this</u> doesn't mean we will all be the same.
   We'll have <u>dif</u>ferent faces and different names.
   <u>Long</u> live many different kinds of races
   And <u>dif</u>ference of opinion; that makes horse races.
   Just re<u>mem</u>ber The Rule About Rules, brother:
   "What's <u>right</u> with one is wrong with another."
   <u>And</u> take a tip from La Belle France
   —"Vive la difference." ***

* This irregularity, a 6/4 measure, is only in the first verse.
  The rest of the verses hold to 4/4 time.
**Still argued about. See p. 88.

*** Variant melodies in verses 2, 3, 4:

(v. 2) put it all on the ta - ble

(v. 3) And so will wo - man and man

(v. 4) "Vi - va la diff - rawhns"_____

Although I put this song together over 30 years ago, only within the last five years did I realize how effective it could be as an audience singalong. After the first verse and first chorus I simply say the words clearly: "Soon, mama, my whole world. Soon, mama, my whole wide world. Soon, mama, my whole world. Soon gonna be get mixed up." Then with arm gestures I encourage the crowd to sing, making sure they get the crisp effect of the four ungrammatical syllables at the end.

After the second verse's chorus I'll call out "Sing it again!" right while the crowd is singing those last four syllables. Then to give a little relief from all this talking and teaching and singing, I'll whistle a verse, improvising as well as I can. It's a fun rhythm. Now the third and fourth verses come, with not a second's pause before starting the fourth verse. And at the end it's good to even repeat the chorus a third time, ending abruptly. You'll be rewarded with a moment of dead silence after the word "up."

Guitarists may like to try playing this chorus. I do it in "Dropped D tuning," that is, a lowered bass string. For an explanation of this, and TAB (tablature) see the Appendix.

Where did I get this tune and rhythm from? In 1932 I first got bitten by the Caribbean music bug. "The Peanut Vendor" from Cuba was on all the airwaves. Sixty years later I'm still captivated by the rhythms, the agile melodies. In 1991 I discovered that it was Louise Bennett, Jamaican folklorist, who in 1952 sang me a song which is almost identical to this melody: "Woman Tawry Lang."

Maybe Americans have found it easier to latch on to new traditions because we are uprooted people, and have few deep roots. But as compensation, we've often developed the ability to put down new roots very quickly.

If I'm encouraging people to mix things up, what happens to the International Copyright Law?

First, consider the overall picture:

"Judge the musicality of a nation not by the presence of virtuosos, but by the general level of the population which knows how to make music." (CLS) This quote from my father is roughly the equivalent of what was said by the African-American scholar, W.E. DuBois, "I would judge the wealth of a nation not by the presence of millionaires but by the absence of poverty."

I think they're both right, yet our technology and our economic system seem to produce the present bad situation: millions of people feel themselves poor and powerless; millions feel that music is something to be made only by experts. I have spent a life "borrowing" others' ideas. I really can't object if people borrow some of mine. I am glad if someone can improve my song.

If people simply want to sing my songs their own way I usually say hooray. Bernice Reagon heard me sing "Oh, Had I a Golden Thread" with a fast banjo accompaniment. I heard her sing it unaccompanied with a changed melody (see p. 67).

When I complimented her on her new melody, she said in surprise, "I didn't know I had made up a new melody. I was just singing it more or less as I could remember you singing it." That's the folk process.

However, I'm grateful to the International Copyright Convention (CISAC) rules. There are commercial type folks who would love to make new words to these songs and use them as singing commercials, were they not stopped by the copyright law. Even so, some songs have been nearly massacred by pop translators. In Italy there was a hit record, "If I had a hammer, I'd hit you on the head/ Because you stole my man, you so-and-so." And in France it took the young political radicals to force a publisher to withdraw a version of Guantanamera, which had the usual "Baby, I love you" lyrics. They said to the publisher, "You cannot do that to José Marti's great international poetry."

Here's a possible compromise. I hope that people will try and improve my songs, but if they're going to go ahead and make tape recordings to sell, or make some other commercial use of one of my songs, I hope they'll write me and give me a chance to say yes or no. I've done this numerous times already with the children's story "Abiyoyo." Over the last 30 years, dozens of people have made slightly different versions of the story. But one person made such big changes, I suggested that she retitle it almost anything singable, perhaps, "Amiyaya," so that there wouldn't be any confusion in people's minds.

In general, one can say: go ahead, improvise. Add or subtract words, music — as long as you're doing it non-commercially. But if you're doing your changed version on network TV or recording it for sale — get permission first. Admittedly, in between is a large gray area — which keeps lawyers in business.

So sing, change. Add to. Subtract.

But beware multiplying. If you record and start making hundreds of tapes, watch out. Write a letter first. Get permission.

Not all multiplying is commercial. If you want to teach any of the songs in this book to your family or friends or to a choir, I say make photocopies. Enlarge the copy of the song so it's easier to read. Re-paste it so it fits the page better. Long live copying machines!

It all boils down to what I would most like to do as a musician. Put songs on people's lips instead of just in their ear.

While I don't wish my publishers ill — (I'm a lucky songwriter to be working with several honest and hard-working publishers) — my main hope in putting together this book is that I can encourage other singers and songwriters in various places and times to write songs. To adapt and rewrite other songs. To use songs not to get rich or famous, but to help this world survive. I wish I could live long enough to see more people singing again, either solo or in groups. For recreation. For reverence. For learning and laughter. For struggle. For hope, for understanding.

I know I won't live that long, but if this world survives, I believe that modern industrialized people will learn to sing again.

A word about the term "folk song." It was invented by European scholars in the mid-19th century to mean the music of the peasant class, ancient and anonymous. In the U.S.A. it was used by people like John Lomax who collected songs of cowboys and lumberjacks, coal miners and prisoners on southern chaingangs. Along came balladmaker Woody Guthrie and a string of people following him, and all of us get called "folksingers" if we are professionally singing for a living using an acoustic guitar.

By this definition, a grandmother in a rocking chair singing a 400-year-old song to a baby in her lap is not a folksinger because she's not on a platform with a guitar in her hand and a microphone in front of her.

By this definition a black man singing a 100-year-old traditional blues is not a folksinger if he's using an electric guitar to answer vocal phrases, as in so much African-American music. Likewise the call-and-response singing in tens of thousands of black churches, in the

south and north, is not thought of as folk music. Nor the songs in hundreds of different languages still sung by people who have recently landed on these shores or whose ancestors lived here long before Columbus. Though their songs are ancient and anonymous. And they are folks, too.

No, according to the pop definition, to be a "folksinger" you have to be a (white) person on stage with an acoustic guitar singing a song in English. A song you just made up. That's a folksong.

A silly misuse of the term "folk music." I use it as little as possible now. Call me a river singer.

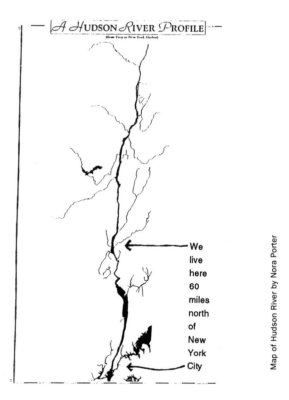

— A HUDSON RIVER PROFILE —
(from Troy to New York Harbor)

We live here 60 miles north of New York City

Map of Hudson River by Nora Porter

If you can't read music, this volume alone will probably be of limited use. Take a look at the Appendix. But within a year we hope to have demonstration tape cassettes available giving at least first verse and chorus of every song in the book. Write *Sing Out!* magazine, Box 5253, Bethlehem, PA 18015. See p.168.

And for many songs, commercial recordings are still available. See the Discography. In any case, remember that each singer has to make up her/his mind how to fit the words to the melody, and in what key to sing it. How fast or slow.

Now that you've got the general idea of what this book is about, I'll ramble on. In general my advice to a reader is to skim quickly through the book to see what its scope is, then turn back to some song you might like to get better acquainted with. Spend a little time with it.

Some chapters are roughly chronological. Other chapters try to group the songs in other ways. But to put songs in categories is like trying to categorize people. One can be fooled.

Chapter II

I dropped out of college in 1938, aged 19. Looked for a job as a reporter on a newspaper. No luck. Studied watercolor painting for a short while. Spent a summer bicycling, camping, painting pictures of farmers' houses in return for food.

In the winter of 1939 I was a member of a young artists group in New York City. It was a branch of the Young Communist League. We met weekly, 25 to 50 of us, in a loft near 14th Street. Come spring I helped build a set of puppets. Come summer I joined three others giving puppet shows in the small towns of upstate New York. In August 20,000 dairy farmers went on strike against Bordens and Sheffields, the big companies that dictated the price of milk. Farmers were getting 2¢ a quart ($1 for a 48-qt. can), when milk was selling for 10-12¢ a quart in stores.

Our puppet show went from strike meeting to strike meeting. I played the part of a cow who tells the farmer he's foolish not to get together with other farmers to demand a decent return for their labor. Between acts I sang "The Farmer Is the Man That Feeds Them All" in front of the stage. And it wasn't hard to change the 1920 cotton farmers' song, "Seven cent cotton and forty cent meat, How in the world can a poor man eat," to sing it to dairy farmers as "One Dollar Milk and 40 Cent Meat." I also changed "Pretty Polly," a Kentucky ballad about seduction and murder, into "Mister Farmer," telling how they were seduced and cheated by the big-money boys.

Writing songs was a heady experience. The folk process was working for me. In the fall I was persuaded by Alan Lomax to quit looking for a job on a newspaper and come to Washington to help him go through stacks of old country music records looking for interesting songs. In those days the country music business was just getting started. Singers came out of the hills singing old English ballads and hard times blues.

And in February 1940 Woody Guthrie hitched from California to the New York Island, and my life was never the same again.

Woody must have liked my banjo picking, because everything else about me must have seemed pretty strange to him. I didn't drink or smoke or chase girls.

Alan Lomax had spent five years putting together a great collection of protest songs collected from farmers, coal-miners, textile workers, etc.— men and women mainly in the southern and western states. He gave us a big stack of disks and paper and said, "Why don't you two finish working all this into a book?" I transcribed tunes and words; Woody wrote introductions; friends in New York, Elizabeth Higgins and sculptor Harold Ambellan, let us camp in their studio. Elizabeth saved a carbon copy of the manuscript, *Hard Hitting Songs For Hard Hit People* (I suggested the name). Thanks to her saving a copy, it finally did get published in 1967; but in 1940, no luck. In June, Woody let me tag along with him to visit his wife Mary and their three little kids in the Texas panhandle. Along the way I found I could make up a new tune if someone else did the words.

Here's Woody's introduction to the song, "66 Highway Blues."

You built that Highway and they can put you in jail for thumbing a ride on it. You built that railroad and they boot you off, shake you down, search your pockets and make you spend your last red cent to buy a ticket in to the next town. Then the watchmen and cops in the town shove you out. They get you all rounded up like a herd of sheep heading for the sledge hammer and drive you off down the road saying, "Take warning, boys, and don't ever show yourself in this town again..."

In McAlester, Okla., in Haileyville, Okla., in Amarillo, Texas, in Deming, Tucson, Phoenix, Yuma, Needles,

Los Angeles, Frisco, Tracy, Bakersfield, almost everywhere you can think of, they chase you off the trains and make you hit the Highway. Sometimes a hundred or more of you, sometimes fifty or sixty out of a single box car. That means walk. Root, hog, or die.

I had part of this tune in my head, but couldn't get no front end for it. Pete fixed that up. He furnished the engine, and me the cars, and then we loaded in the words and we whistled out of the yards from New York City to Oklahoma City, and when we got there we took down our banjo and git-fiddle and chugged her off just like you see here. She's a high roller, an easy rider, a flat wheel bouncer and a tight brake baby with a whiskey driver.

66 Highway Blues

1. There is a high-way from coast to the coast, New York to Los An-gel-es,— I'm a-go-in' down that road with trou-bles on my mind, I got them Six-ty-Six High-way blues.——

Words by Woody Guthrie Music by Pete Seeger (1940)
© 1966 by Stormking Music Inc.

1. There is a highway from coast to the coast,
   New York to Los Angeles.
   I'm a-goin' down that road with troubles on my mind
   I got them 66 Highway Blues.

2. Every old town that I ramble 'round,
   Down that Lonesome Road,
   The police in yo' town they shove me around,
   I got them 66 Highway Blues.

3. Makes me no difference wherever I ramble,
   Lord, wherever I go,
   I don't wanna be pushed around by th' police in
       yo' town,
   I got them 66 Highway Blues.

4. Been on this road for a mighty long time,
   Ten million men like me,
   You drive us from yo' town, we ramble around,
   And got them 66 Highway Blues.

5. Sometimes I think I'll blow down a cop,
   Lord, you treat me so mean,
   I done lost my gal, I ain't got a dime,
   I got them 66 Highway Blues.

6. Sometimes I think I'll get me a gun,
   Thirty eight or big forty fo',
   But a number for a name and a big 99,
   Is worse than 66 Highway Blues.

7. I'm gonna start me a hungry man's union,
   Ain'ta gonna charge no dues,
   Gonna march down that road to the
       Wall Street Walls
   A-singin' those 66 Highway Blues.

WOODY AND PETE AT HIGHLANDER, 1940

Later in 1940 I cut out on my own to continue my education. Hitchhiking and riding freights. Woody taught me half a dozen well-known commercial country songs worth a quarter in any Western bar.

"Pete, you go into a bar with your banjo on your back and buy a nickel beer. Sip it real slow. Sooner or later someone will say, 'Kid, can you play that thing?'

"Don't be too eager. Say, 'Maybe. A little.' Keep sipping your beer. Finally someone will say, 'I got a quarter for you if you'll pick us a tune.' *Now* you swing it around and play something."

I worked my way to Butte, Montana, back to Chicago, then down to Alabama, visiting the family of Joe Gelders, heroic left-wing professor. On October 16th, I registered for the draft in Scottsboro, Alabama. Visited the Harlan County, Kentucky coal country. Visited a construction camp in north Florida, textile towns in North Carolina. Back north, decided to hitchhike through my old homeland of New England. It was December. Almost froze. Back to New York. Heard about a man named Lee Hays

AMERICAN YOUTH CONGRESS RALLY AT THE WHITE HOUSE, 1940

who was also trying to get a book of union songs published. It seemed sensible to get together. I knocked on his door, met his roommate, Mill Lampell, too. A few weeks later the three of us were singing for left-wing fundraising parties around the Five Boroughs. "The Subway Circuit," we called it. By February we knew we had to choose us a name. I read aloud to Lee from Woody's introductions to *Hard Hitting Songs* and came across the word "Almanac."

"Hold on," said Lee. "Back where I come from, a family had two books. The Bible, to help 'em to the next world. The Almanac, to help 'em through the present world. We've got an Almanac. Of course, most Congressmen can't read it."

We became the Almanac Singers.

These were the days of Hitler's aerial blitz of Britain, the Russian invasion of Finland. A large section of the American (and English and French) establishment was still hoping to sic Hitler on Russia, the way they'd stopped "dangerous leftism" in Spain by helping General Franco. Harry Truman, then in Congress (ten years later, U.S. President), is supposed to have said that we should try to get Hitler and Stalin fighting each other and then help the one that's losing. Then they'd both finish each other off. Conservative Republicans spoke at "America First" rallies.

A large section of the left remembered World War I and didn't want to help the old imperialist Churchill.

Woody had written a song about the American Youth Congress going to Washington in February, 1940.

I persuaded Woody to put the song, "Why Do You Stand There in the Rain?" in the book *Hard Hitting Songs*. This is his introduction for it:

A few days before the 6,000 members of the American Youth Congress took their trip to Washington to ask the President for jobs and peace, I hoboed in from Galveston, Texas, up to the Missouri line. Rode to Pittsburgh, then hit the road a-walking again from Pittsburgh to New York in the snow.

It was snowing all of the way from Texas. Mississippi River was froze up worse than a Montana Well Digger; the Susquehannah River was six foot of solid ice, wind a-blowin' like a Republican promise, and colder'n a Wall Street kiss. But I got to town.

I hadn't been here but a couple or three days til I picked up a noise-paper and it said there that the 6,000 had been over to call on Roosevelt at his Whitehouse — and he called their trip and their stuff that they stood for 'twaddle.' It come up a big soaking rain and he made the kids a 30-minute speech in it.

Wrote up this little song about it. Ain't nothing fancy about it. Lots of better ones in this book made up by folks that was fightin' and dyin' on Picket Lines, but — anyhow, would like to dedicate this song to them 6,000 kids, and about 130 million others in this country that got soaked the same day.

Why Do You Stand There in the Rain?

Words & music by Woody Guthrie (1940)
© 1966 Stormking Music Inc.

1. It was raining might hard in that old capitol yard,
   When the young folks gathered at the
   White House gate,
   And the president raised his head and to the
   young folk said:
   Tell me, why do you stand there in the rain?

CHORUS (AFTER EACH VERSE):
Why do you stand there in the rain?
Why do you stand there in the rain?
These are strange carryings on
On the White House Capitol lawn,
Tell me, why do you stand there in the rain?

2. My dear children don't you know that unless by law
      you go,
   That your journey here must all be walked in vain.
   You gotta make your resolution by the
      U.S. Constitution,
   Then you won't get left a-standing in the rain.

3. Well they tell me they've got lands where they will not
      let your stand
   In the rain and ask for jobs upon the lawn,
   Thank God, in the U.S.A. you can stand there
      every day,
   But I would not guarantee they'd take you on.

4. Then, the President's voice did ring, why, this is the
      silliest thing
   I have heard in all my 58 years of life
   But it all just stands to reason as he passes
      another season
   He'll be smarter by the time he's 59.

5. Now, before this storm could break, Mr. John L. Lewis
      spake,
   And he said you asked for jobs; what did you get?
   A kid of seventeen, he was pretty smart, it seemed,
   Said we went there for a job, but we got wet.

6. Now, the guns in Europe roar as they have
      so oft before
   And the warlords play the same old game again,
   While they butcher and they kill, Uncle Sam
      foots the bill
   With his own dear children standing in the rain.

* Woody hated to use fancy chords, and used B7 here, though most of
  us would use F#7 because of the A# in the melody in the next measure.

LEE HAYS & PETE SEEGER, N.Y.C., 1946

Mill Lampell and Lee wrote a far nastier song. We Almanacs were singing it all over New York, for left-wing gatherings. This is just the chorus.

Ballad of October 16th

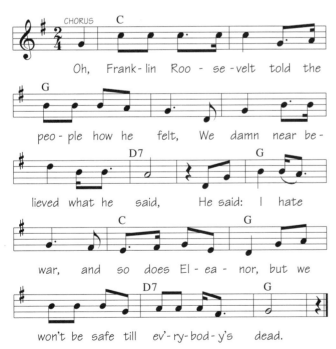

Oh, Frank-lin Roo - se-velt told the peo-ple how he felt, We damn near be-lieved what he said, He said: I hate war, and so does El - ea - nor, but we won't be safe till ev'-ry-bod-y's dead.

Words & music by Millard Lampell & Lee Hays (1940)
© 1993 by Stormking Music Inc.

Lee and Mill heard me sing a North Carolina ditty, "The Young Man Who Wouldn't Hoe Corn,"

I'll sing you a song and it's not very long
It's about a young man who wouldn't hoe corn
The reason why I cannot tell,
This young man was always well.

Soon Mill made up a new song using the same tune. Short. Effective. I still get requests for it. It should be sung dead pan, ending abruptly. Lee always marvelled at the dead silence that followed me singing it. The deadly serious ending, after the cheerful plunk, plunk of the banjo.

Strange Death of John Doe

I'll sing you a song and it's not ver-y long. It's a-bout a young man who nev-er did wrong; Sud-den-ly he died one day. The rea-son why, No one would say.

Words by Lee Hays, Pete Seeger & Millard Lampell (1941)
Music: traditional ("The Young Man Who Wouldn't Hoe Corn")
© 1950 (renewed) by Stormking Music Inc.

1. I'll sing you a song and it's not very long.
   It's about a young man who never did wrong;
   Suddenly he died one day.
   The reason why, No one would say.

2. He was tall and long and his arms were strong,
   And this is the strange part of my song;
   He was always well from foot to head,
   And then one day they found him dead.

3. They found him dead so I've been told,
   His eyes were closed, his heart was cold;
   Only one clue to how he died—
   A bayonet sticking in his side.

Lee said to me, "If we made up some more peace songs, we'd have enough to get a record album out." He and I spent an evening at the home of Helen Simon (she's Helen Travis now) and in four short hours wrote four songs. Here's one (new melody, too):

Plow Under

Words & music by Lee Hays & Pete Seeger (1941)
© 1993 by Stormking Music Inc.

Helen lives in California now. Wrote me: "You're really undertaking quite a task: tracing the transition from 'Plow Under' to 'Reuben James' etc. I remain convinced that it *was* a phony war at the outset. However we lefties weren't hep enough to note how it had changed when popular resistance to the German onslaught began in Yugoslavia ... before the invasion of the USSR."

In April a house party in Greenwich Village raised $300 (equivalent of $5,000 in 1993) and the album *Songs for John Doe* came out a month later on a little independent label. Josh White helped us make it. I'd knocked on his door, and on 24 hours' notice he contributed his voice and guitar. The album, three 78 RPM shellac discs, was distributed by left-wing bookstores across the country. The poet Archibald MacLeish, Librarian of Congress, played it for Roosevelt. "Can't we forbid this?" says the President (I later heard). "Not unless you want to ignore the First Amendment," says MacLeish.

"Well, only a few left-wingers will ever hear it," said Roosevelt, and he was right. But for history's sake, here are the words of another song. Tune of the fast banjo tune "Ida Red."

Franklin D...

Franklin D., listen to me
You ain't gonna send me 'cross the sea
    'Cross the sea, 'cross the sea
    You ain't gonna send me across the sea

Lafayette, we are here
We're gonna stay right over here
    Over here, over here
    We're gonna stay right over here

J.P. Morgan's big and plump
Eighty-four inches 'round and plump
    'Round and plump, 'round and plump
    Eighty-four inches 'round and plump

Marcantonio* is the best
But I wouldn't give a nickel for all the rest
    All the rest, all the rest.
    I wouldn't give a nickel for all the rest

(And there were more deathless verses)

Words by Millard Lampell, Lee Hays & Pete Seeger
Music: traditional banjo tune ("Ida Red") (1941)
© 1993 by Stormking Music Inc.

* U.S. Congressman from Manhattan, NYC.

Should I apologize for all this? I think so. How *should* Hitler have been stopped? Litvinov, the Soviet delegate to the League of Nations, in '36 proposed a worldwide quarantine, but got no takers. For more on those times check out pacifist Dave Dellinger's book *From Yale to Jail* (see bibliography). At any rate, today I'll apologize for a number of things, such as thinking that Stalin was simply a "hard driver" and not a supremely cruel misleader. I guess anyone who calls himself or herself a Christian should be prepared to apologize for the Inquisition, the burning of heretics by Protestants, the slaughter of Jews and Moslems by Crusaders. White people in the U.S.A. could consider apologizing for stealing land from Native Americans and enslaving blacks. Europeans could apologize for worldwide conquests, Mongolians for Genghis Khan. And supporters of Roosevelt could apologize for his support of Somoza, of Southern white Democrats, of Franco Spain, for putting Japanese-Americans in concentration camps. Who should my granddaughter Moraya apologize to? She's part African, part European, part Chinese, part Japanese, part Native American.

Let's look ahead.

The Almanacs one month later recorded six union songs and called the album *Talking Union*. In the mid-fifties Folkways records reissued it; it's still available and used 50 years later. Here's the title song, a 1941 rap song!

Talking Union

If you want high-er wag-es, let me
tell you what to do: You got to talk to the
work-ers in the shop with you;— You got to
build you a un-ion, got to make it strong,
But if you all stick to-geth-er, folks,
'twon't be long,— You get short-er hours,—
Bet-ter work-ing con-di-tions.
Va - ca-tions with pay,——
Take your kids to the sea-shore.

Words by Millard Lampell, Lee Hays & Pete Seeger (1941)
Music: traditional ("talking blues")
© 1947 (renewed) by Stormking Music Inc.

If you want higher wages, let me tell you what to do;
You got to talk to the workers in the shop with you;
You got to build you a union, got to make it strong,
But if you all stick together, now, 'twont be long.
   You get shorter hours,
   Better working conditions.
   Vacations with pay,
   Take the kids to the seashore.

It ain't quite this simple, so I better explain
Just why you got to ride on the union train;
'Cause if you wait for the boss to raise your pay,
We'll all be waiting till Judgement Day;
   We'll all be buried—gone to Heaven—
   Saint Peter'll be the straw boss then.

Now, you know you're underpaid, but the boss says you ain't;
He speeds up the work till you're 'bout to faint,
You may be down and out, but you ain't beaten,
Pass out a leaflet and call a meetin'—
   Talk it over—speak your mind—
   Decide to do something about it.

'Course, the boss may persuade some poor damn fool
To go to your meeting and act like a stool;
But you can always tell a stool, though—that's a fact;
He's got a rotten streak a-running down his back;
   He doesn't have to stool—he makes a good living
   On what he takes out of blind men's cups.

You got a union now; you're sitting pretty;
Put some people on the steering committee.
The boss won't listen when just one squawks,
But he's got to listen when the union talks.
   He better—
   He'll be mighty lonely one of these days.

Suppose they're working you so hard it's just outrageous,
They're paying you all starvation wages;
You go to the boss, and the boss would yell,
"Before I raise your pay I'd see you all in Hell."
Well, he's puffing a big see-gar and feeling mighty slick,
He thinks he's got your union licked.
He looks out the window, and what does he see
But a thousand pickets, and they all agree
   He's a bastard—unfair—slave driver—
   Bet he beats his own wife.

Now, folks, you've come to the hardest time;
The boss will try to bust your picket line.
He'll call out the police, the National Guard;
They'll tell you it's a crime to have a union card.
They'll raid your meeting, hit you on the head.
Call every one of you a doggone Red—
   Unpatriotic— Moscow agents—
   Bomb throwers, even the kids.

But out in Detroit here's what they found,
And out in Frisco here's what they found,
And out in Pittsburgh here's what they found,
And down in Bethlehem here's what they found,
That if you don't let Red-baiting break you up,
If you don't let stool pigeons break you up,
If you don't let vigilantes break you up,
And if you don't let race hatred break you up—
   You'll win. What I mean,
   Take it easy—but take it.

Mill and Lee wrote most of those verses, with a little help from me. Then for a couple weeks we were stymied. Sitting on the roof one spring day, I got inspired to write the last ten lines. (In the 1980's I cleaned up this song. I once assumed that I was singing to an all-male work force. As printed here, it's less sexist than it used to be.)

The "talking blues" verse form we'd learned from Woody. In some ways it's a better form than the sonnet. Vern Partlow wrote "Talking Atom." Woody's "Talking Dustbowl" is a classic. He learned the talking blues from records of Robert Land, who did the "original" verses on the Grand Ole Opry. And of course Land must have got the form from African-Americans. Who? Where? Here's some of Land's verses.

If you want to go to heaven let me tell you what to do.
Got to grease your feet in a little mutton stew.
Slide out of the devil's hand.
Ooze over to the promised land.
   Take it easy,
   Go greasy.

Ain't no use me working so hard.
I got a gal in the rich folks' yard.
They kill a chicken—she sends me the head.
Thinks I'm working, I'm a-laying up in bed.
   Dreaming about her.
   And three other women.

Down in the hen house on my knees,
I thought I heard a chicken sneeze.
It was only the rooster saying his prayers,
Giving out thanks to the hens upstairs.
   Rooster preaching.
   Hens a-singing.
   Little young pullets doing the best they could.

Authors unknown
Traditional African-American

Whereas modern rap songs can have a whole electric band to accompany them, the "talking blues" of 60 years ago used just a guitar, or in my case a banjo. I'd use it to decorate the space between some of the verses.

HARRY BRIDGES

The album *Talking Union* turned out so well that a month later the Almanacs were asked by the Harry Bridges Defense Committee to compose a song and record it. (Harry Bridges was a West Coast union leader.) In a few hours Millard Lampell and Lee Hays, again with a little help from me, got the job done. Six weeks later, after Woody joined us, we sang it in the San Francisco longshoreman's union hall, with Bridges present, and got a standing ovation.

The Ballad of Harry Bridges

1. Let me tell you of a sailor, Harry Bridges is his name,
An honest union leader whom the bosses tried to frame,
He left home in Australia, to sail the seas around,
He sailed across the ocean to land in Frisco town.

2. There was only a company union, the bosses had
their way.
A worker had to stand in line for a lousy dollar a day.
When up spoke Harry Bridges, "Us workers got to
get wise.
Our wives and kids will starve to death if we don't
get organized."

CHORUS (AFTER MOST OR ALL VERSES):
Oh, the FBI is worried, the bosses they are scared
They can't deport six million men they know.
And we're not going to let them send Harry over the seas,
We'll fight for Harry Bridges and build the CIO.

3. They built a big bonfire by the Matson Line that night.
They threw their fink books in it and they said we're
going to fight.
You've got to pay a living wage or we're going to take
a walk.
They told it to the bosses but the bosses wouldn't talk.

4. They said there's only one way left to get that
contract signed.
And all around the waterfront they threw their
picket line.
They called it Bloody Thursday, the fifth day of July,
Four hundred men were wounded and two were left to die.

5. Now that was seven years ago and in the time since then
Harry's organized thousands more and made them
union men.
"We must try to bribe him," the shipping bosses said,
"And if he won't accept the bribe, we'll say that he's
a red."

6. The bosses brought a trial to deport him over the seas,
But the judge said, "He's a honest man, I got to set
him free,"
Then they brought another trial to frame him if they can.
But right by Harry Bridges stands every working man.

Words by Lee Hays, Millard Lampell & Pete Seeger (1941)
Music: traditional ("The Great American Folk Melody")
© 1966 by Stormking Music Inc.

Gary Huck, United Electrical Workers/
Huck-Conopacki

In June '41 Woody quit his job writing songs for the Bonneville Power Administration ("Roll On, Columbia" and lots more) and hitchhiked east. I think he arrived about a day or two after Hitler invaded the USSR. He walked in the door of the Almanac House and with a wry grin said, "Well, I guess we won't be singing any more peace songs for a while."

I said, "You mean I have to support Churchill?"

"Why, Churchill said, 'All support to the gallant Soviet allies!'"

"Is this the same guy who said 20 years ago, 'We must strangle the Bolshevik infant in its cradle!'?"

"Yep. Churchill's changed. We got to."

Woody was right. Anti-communists ridiculed our "great flip flop." The Almanacs sang union songs to the West Coast and back, and then made up a string of win-the-war ballads which were recorded soon after Pearl Harbor. Woody's "Reuben James" was the most longlasting of these songs.

Reuben James
(The Sinking of the Reuben James)

Words & music by Woody Guthrie (1941)
© 1942 (renewed) by MCA Music Publishing, a division of MCA Inc.,
1755 Broadway, New York, NY 10019. International copyright secured.
All rights reserved.

1. Have you heard of a ship called the good
     Reuben James
   Manned by hard fighting men both of honor and
     fame.
   She flew the stars and stripes of the land of
     the free,
   But now she's in her grave at the bottom of the sea.

CHORUS (AFTER EACH VERSE):
Tell me what were their names?
Tell me what were their names?
Did you have a friend on the good Reuben James?
Tell me what were their names?
Tell me what were their names?
Did you have a friend on the good Reuben James?

2. It was there in the dark of that uncertain night,
   That we watched for the U-boat and waited for
     a fight;
   Then a whine and a rock and a great explosion
     roared,
   And they laid the Reuben James on the cold
     ocean floor.

3. One hundred men went down in that dark watery
     grave;
   When that good ship went down only forty-four
     were saved.
   'Twas the last day of October that we saved
     the forty-four
   From the cold icy waters off that cold Iceland shore.

4. Now tonight there are lights in our country so bright
   In the farms and in the cities they are telling of
     this fight,
   And now our mighty battleships will steam the
     bounding main,
   And remember the name of the good Reuben James.

(Guitarists: Capo up if you want, and use G chords. Tenors can ring out fine in the key of C.)

See p. 86 for details on how Woody put this song together. In the 1950's Fred Hellerman of the Weavers made a good new verse.

5. Now many years have passed since those brave men
    are gone
   In those cold icy waters are still and they're calm.
   Now many years have passed and I still wonder why.
   The worst of men must fight and the best of men
    must die.

I stopped singing "Talking Union." Made up a new talking blues. Sang it through World War II, in Southern training camps and in the Western Pacific. The Communist Party had influence in the labor movement then, and pushed it to a no-strike pledge for the duration.

Dear Mr. President

Dear Mr. President, I set me down,
To send you greetings from my home town,
And send you best wishes from all the friends I know
In Texas, Alabama, Ohio,
    And affiliated places. Brooklyn, Mississippi.

I'm an ordinary guy, worked most of my life,
Sometime I'll settle down with my kids and wife,
And I like to see a movie or take a little drink.
I like being free to say what I think,
    Sort of runs in the family…
    My grandpa crossed the ocean for the same reason.

Now I hate Hitler and I can tell you why,
He's caused lots of good folks to suffer and die.
He's got a way of shoving folks around,
I figure it's about time we slapped him down,
    Give him a dose of his own medicine…
    Lead poisoning.

Now Mr. President, we haven't always agreed in the past,
    I know,
But that ain't at all important, now,
What is important is what we got to do,
We got to lick Mr. Hitler, and until we do,
    Other things can wait,
    In other words, first we got a skunk to skin.

War means overtime and higher prices,
But we're all willing to make sacrifices,
Hell, I'd even stop fighting with my mother-in-law,
'Cause we need her too, to win the war…
    Old battle axe.

Now as I think of our great land,
Of the cities and towns and farming land,
There's so many good people working every day,
I know it ain't perfect but it will be some day,
    Just give us a little time.

This is the reason that I want to fight,
Not because everything's perfect or everything's right.
    No. it's just the opposite… I'm fighting because I want
A better America with better laws,
And better homes and jobs and schools,
And no more Jim Crow and no more rules,
    Like you can't ride on this train 'cause you're a Negro,
    You can't live here 'cause you're a Jew
    You can't work here 'cause you're a union man.

There's a line keeps running through my head,
I think it was something Joe Louis* once said,
    Said, "There's lots of things wrong,
    But Hitler won't help 'em."

Now Mr. President, you're commander-in-chief of our
    armed forces,
Ships and planes, and the tanks and horses.
I guess you know best just where I can fight,
All I want to be is situated right…
    To do the most damage.

I never was one to try and shirk,
And let the other fellow do all the work,
So when the time comes, I'll be on hand,
And make good use of these two hands.
    Quit playing this banjo around with the boys,
    And exchange it for something that makes more noise.

So Mr. President, we've got this one big job to do,
That's lick Mr. Hitler and when we're through,
Let no one else ever take his place,
To trample down the human race.
    So what I want is you to give me a gun,
    So we can hurry up and get the job done.

* World heavyweight boxing champion; African-American.

And we Almanacs even (briefly) got on the air with new words to "Old Joe Clark," the old fiddle tune.

Round and Round Hitler's Grave

1. I wish I had a bush-el, I wish I had a peck, I wish I had a rope to tie a-round old Hit-ler's neck. Hey!

Round and round Hit-ler's grave, Round and round we'll go. Gon-na lay that poor boy down. He won't get up no more.

Words by Woody Guthrie, Millard Lampell & Pete Seeger (1941)
Music adapted by Woody Guthrie from the traditional song "Old Joe Clark"
© 1958 (renewed) by Woody Guthrie Publications. All rights reserved.

1. I wish I had a bushel,
   I wish I had a peck,
   I wish I had a rope to tie
   Around old Hitler's neck.

CHORUS (AFTER EACH VERSE):
Hey! Round and round Hitler's grave,
Round and round we'll go.
Gonna lay that poor boy down.
He won't get up no more.

2. Mussolini won't last long
   Tell you the reason why
   We're a-gonna salt his beef
   And hang it up to dry.

3. I'm a-going to Berlin
   To Mister Hitler's town
   I'm gonna take my forty-four
   And blow his playhouse down.

4. The German Army general staff
   I guess they missed connections.
   They went a hundred miles a day
   But in the wrong direction.

5. Hitler went to Russia
   In search of Russian oil,
   But the only oil he'll find there
   Is a pot in which he'll boil.

6. Mister Hitler's traveling mighty fast
   But he's on a single track,
   He started down that Moscow road
   But now he's coming back.

We got to sing the song January '42, on a nationwide CBS broadcast, "This Is War." But the next day a headline in a major New York newspaper said "Commie Singers Try To Infiltrate Radio," and that was the last job we got.

We did make a record album (three 78 RPM discs), but they didn't sell outside left circles. "Reuben James," "Dear Mr. President," "Belt Line Girl" (by Sis Cunningham, who had joined the Almanacs in October) and the song "Deliver the Goods," which Oscar Brand still sings, with more peaceful words.

Deliver The Goods

1. It's gon-na take ev'-ry-bod-y to win this war: The butch-er, the bak-er and the clerk in the store,— The guys who run the ships, and the guys who run the trains, And the farm-er rais-ing wheat up-on the Kan-sas plains. The butch-er, the bak-er, the tin-ker and the tai-lor, We'll

Words & music by Pete Seeger (1942)
© 1993 by Stormking Music Inc.

CHORUS (AFTER EACH VERSE):
The butcher, the baker, the tinker and the tailor,
We'll all work behind the soldier and sailor,
We're working in the cities, we're working in the woods,
We'll all work together to deliver the goods.

1. It's gonna take everybody to win this war,
    The butcher and the baker and the clerk in the store,
    The guys who sail the ships and the guys who run
       the trains,
    And the farmer raising wheat upon the
       Kansas plains.

2. I got a new job and I'm working overtime,
    Turning out tanks on the assembly line,
    Got to crank up the factories like the president said,
    Damn the torpedoes, full speed ahead.

3. I bet this tank will look mighty fine,
    Punching holes in Mr. Hitler's line,
    And if Adolf wakes up after the raid,
    He'll find every piece of shrapnel says "Union made."

4. From New York City to 'Frisco Bay,
    We're speeding up production every day,
    And every time a wheel goes 'round,
    It carries Mr. Hitler to the burying ground.

5. Now me and my boss we never did agree,
    If a thing helped him, then it didn't help me,
    But when a burglar tries to bust into your house,
    You stop fighting with the landlord and throw
       him out.

THE ALMANAC SINGERS, GREENWICH VILLAGE, JANUARY, 1942
WOODY GUTHRIE, MILLARD LAMPELL, BESS HAWES, PETE SEEGER, ARTHUR STERN, SIS CUNNINGHAM

Of course, life was not all "politics." Lots of dancing, eating, joking, loving. Once after a session accompanying Woody playing some popular Mexican folk songs, I tried to play a blues. It came out sounding Mexican. It's not truly Mexican nor truly a blues. Woody tried making up words, but nothing stuck. It is still a tune wanting lyrics. I titled it "Mexican Blues." Leaf past these two pages if you are not a guitar picker.

Mexican Blues

By Pete Seeger (1941)
© 1959 (renewed) by Sanga Music Inc.

* The tremolo here is played by the right index finger, bringing it back and forth lightly over the top strings. See p. 122.

PETE SEEGER & ELEANOR ROOSEVELT
AT A SERVICEMEN'S CLUB IN WASHINGTON, D.C., 1944

I was drafted in July '42. At Keesler Field, Mississippi, learning the hydraulic system of the B-24 bomber, I used "Lincoln and Liberty Too" (a 4/4 version of "Rosin the Beau") to make a song for my fellow mechanics-in-training.

Aircraft Mechanic Song

You have heard of the pi - lot so dar - ing, As he grace-ful-ly floats through the air. But with - out all the boys in the hang - ar He wouldn't be fly - ing up there.

Words by Pete Seeger (1942)
Music: traditional ("Lincoln & Liberty Too")
© 1993 by Stormking Music Inc.

But, I'm ashamed to say, I wrote hardly any songs the next three years in service. Except a nasty ditty about officers, predicting their postwar demotion: "He'll go back to selling shoes." Unfair. To shoe salesmen.

I stayed at Keesler Field an extra six months because Military Intelligence got to investigating my left-wing opinions, first opening my mail, then later calling me in for questioning. But finally in '44 I was permitted to go overseas as a musician. I ended up in charge of hospital entertainment on the island of Saipan, north of Guam, Western Pacific. I was still a private. At staff headquarters we called ourselves the "Chairborne Infantry," "Paragraph Troops." I tell people I was in the U.S. Army for three and a half years in WWII — but what did I mainly do? Play the banjo.

Before I went overseas though, the main event for me in 1943 was getting married to Toshi-Aline Ohta, age 21. We'd met a few years earlier in New York when square dancing, found we had much in common. Her parents were both extraordinary people. We were all very close. Her mother, descended from old Virginny (slave owners), had declared her independence from that racist part of her tradition, moved to Greenwich Village, married a Japanese who was in political exile, as militarists were taking over his homeland. He did important and dangerous work for the U.S. Army in W.W. II.

On my first furlough Toshi and I made it legal. Daily letters flew back and forth between us for three and a half years. Hooray for the U.S. Army postal system.

In '45 the war ended. Lee Hays and I corresponded. "After the war we'll need an organization for people like us to keep in touch — a newsletter. New songs. Old songs. Songs to support the United Nations, to support labor, to oppose racists." FDR was dead. We'd oppose the reactionaries who'd repeal the New Deal.

I was mustered out December '45. In January '46 the first copies of the *People's Songs* bulletin came off the mimeograph machine. I found myself trying to be an organizer as well as a singer.

But the Cold War took over. Most unions kicked out us "reds." We suffered one defeat after another. Nevertheless, some fine songs were first published by our little 16-page *People's Songs*. In 1947 we printed a song called "We Will Overcome." I started singing it to audiences up north and out west, with my banjo accompaniment, oomp-chinka, oomp-chinka.

I'm only one of thousands of people who have added verses to this now-world-famous song. Here's some of its disputed history. First I give you a song written by the gospel songwriter Rev. Charles Tindley of Philadelphia in 1903.

Rev. Tindley led a large church in Philadelphia at the turn of the century. He wrote many famous hymns, including, "We'll Understand It Better Bye and Bye," which includes the use of the word, "overcome," without saying who or what is overcome: "...We will tell the story of how we overcome and we'll understand it better bye and bye."

He published a book, *Gospel Pearls*, in 1921. Soon the term "gospel songs" was used to describe the new religious songs being written by him and others.

CHARLES TINDLEY

I'll Overcome Some Day

Words & music by Rev. Charles Tindley (1903)

Tindley's song has by and large been forgotten. It's rarely sung today except by the members of Tindley's old church in Philadelphia. But next I show you a very well-known up-tempo gospel song, with similar words, but different music.

I'll Be All Right

Briskly

1. I'll be all right,— I'll be all right,— I'll be all
2. I'll be like Him,— I'll be like Him,— I'll be like
3. I'll o-ver-come,— I'll o-ver-come,— I'll o-ver-

right some day.———— Deep in my heart,
Him some day.———— Deep in my heart,
come some day.———— Deep in my heart,

I do be- lieve, I'll be all right some day.———
I do be- lieve, I'll be like Him some day.———
I do be- lieve, I'll o-ver- come some day.———

Traditional African-American gospel hymn

The spirit of this song comes when you clap on the 2nd and 4th eighth notes of every measure:

Which song came first?

I have friends who have spent a life researching African-American religious songs, and they are convinced that Tindley wrote his more European-style song with its four verses after hearing an older folk "spiritual."

But others are certain that Tindley's song came first, and that perhaps in a spirited prayer service someone improvised "I'll be all right,".

Which is right? I don't know that field of music well enough to say, except that down through musical history, borrowing has been a two-way street.

In any case, we do know the next step in the story. In 1946 several hundred employees of the American Tobacco Company in Charleston, S.C., were on strike. Most were women, most African-Americans. To keep their spirits up, they often sang hymns on the picket line. Lucille Simmons especially liked to sing this song, but she sang it very, very slowly ("long meter style") On the picket line people would see her coming, and say "Here comes Lucille! Now we're going to hear that song sung slower than anyone ever heard it before." And Lucille changed one important word, from "I" to "we."

Zilphia Horton, a white woman, learned it when a group of strikers visited the Highlander Folk School, the labor education center in Tennessee. Zilphia also had a beautiful alto voice, and she also sang it very slowly.

Freely—no rhythm

We shall o - ver - come,————

ZILPHIA HORTON; FRANK HAMILTON; GUY CARAWAN; THE NASHVILLE QUARTET; THE MONTGOMERY TRIO

DR. BERNICE JOHNSON REAGON; SEPTIMA CLARKE & ROSA PARKS;
DR. MARTIN LUTHER KING JR., PETE SEEGER, CHARIS HORTON (ZILPHIA'S DAUGHTER), ROSA PARKS, REV. RALPH ABERNATHY, HIGHLANDER, 1957

It became her favorite song. She taught it to me. So we published it as "We Will Overcome" in our little song newsletter, *People's Songs*. I sang it medium tempo, with a banjo rhythm in back of it. I didn't have her voice.

In 1952 I taught it to Guy Carawan and Frank Hamilton in California.

Zilphia Horton died in '56. In '59 Guy Carawan came to work at Highlander as a songleader. In 1960 he organized an "all-South" workshop for some 70 young people to talk and explore "singing in the movement." They latched on to the song immediately, but during the next year, as it moved into the deep South, it took on a more pronounced rhythm, dividing each of the slow beats into three short beats, much as I do in the song "Jacob's Ladder" (p. 198).

Three weeks later these young people and Guy introduced the song to the founding convention of SNCC (Student Non-Violent Coordinating Committee) at Raleigh, N.C. A few months later across the entire South, it was not "a" song. It was "the" song.

In the early '60's our publishers said to us, "If you don't copyright this now, some Hollywood types will have a version out next year like "Come on Baby, We shall overcome tonight." So Guy, Frank, and I signed a "songwriter's contract." At that time we didn't know Lucille Simmons' name. Now we try to credit the African-American people, as you see here. And someone should murmur a word of thanks to the great little Food and Tobacco Workers Union of the 1940's and '50's.

All royalties and income from the song go to a non-profit fund, the We Shall Overcome Fund, which annually gives grants to further African-American music in the South.

No one is certain who changed "will" to "shall." It could have been me with my Harvard education. But Septima Clarke, a Charleston schoolteacher (who was director of education at Highlander and after the Civil Rights Movement was elected year after year to the Charleston, S.C. Board of Education) always preferred "shall." It sings better.

We Shall Overcome

Slow, steady beat

1. We shall o-ver-come,_____ We shall o-ver-come,_____ We shall o-ver-come some day._____ Oh,_____ deep in my heart, (I know that) I do be-lieve, (Ohh)_____ We shall o-ver-come some day._____

(Songleader gives words for next verse)

Musical & lyrical adaptation by Zilphia Horton, Frank Hamilton, Guy Carawan & Pete Seeger. Inspired by African-American gospel singing, members of the Food & Tobacco Workers Union, Charleston, SC, and the souxthern Civil Rights Movement.
TRO - © 1960 (renewed) & 1963 (renewed) Ludlow Music, Inc., New York, NY. Royalties derived from this composition are being contributed to the We Shall Overcome Fund and the Freedom Movement under the trusteeship of the writers.

No two people sing the exact same verses. A songleader may start out, and later someone in the group of singers will start off with a favorite verse. Rarely is only one verse to the song sung; more often it will be sung for four or five verses or more, usually ending with a repeat of the first verse. Here's some of the verses most often sung, including a couple that I made up.

We shall overcome, we shall overcome,
We shall overcome someday.
Deep in my heart, I do believe,
We shall overcome someday.

1. *We'll walk hand in hand, we'll walk hand in hand,*
   We'll walk hand in hand someday.
   Oh, deep in my heart, I do believe,
   We shall overcome someday.

2. *We shall live in peace, (3x)*
   We shall overcome someday.

3. *We shall all be free…*
4. *We are not afraid… (TODAY!)*
5. *We shall be like "Him,"…*
6. *We shall stand together …*
7. *We shall work together… (NOW!)*
8. *The Lord will see us through…*
9. *We shall end Jim Crow…*
10. *The truth will set us free…*
11. *The whole wide world around…*
12. *Black and White together… (NOW!)*
13. *Love will see us through…*
14. *We shall stand together… (NOW!)*
15. *We shall overcome…*

Now it's been sung around the world in Europe, Asia, Africa, Latin America (where it's sometimes sung "Todos venceremos").

Incidentally, not everyone has been enthusiastic about the song. Lillian Hellman once scornfully remarked to me, "… overcome *someday, someday*?" But Bernice Reagon, when I told her this, replied, "If we said 'next week,' what would we sing the week after next?"

Waldemar Hille, editing the *People's Songs* bulletin in 1948, once showed me two short verses he found when researching U.S. labor history.

Step by step the longest march
Can be won, can be won.
Many stones can form an arch,
Singly none, singly none,
   And by union, what we will
   Can be accomplished still
   Drops of water turn a mill
   Singly none, singly none.

It was printed in the preamble to the constitution of an early coal miners' union. Says Wally, "Good verse." Says I, "What's the tune?"

"I don't know," says Wally, "I suppose some old Irish tune might fit it. Like the song from the Irish famine of the 1840's. 'The Praties They Grow Small.'"

"Let's try it," says I. It fit. And has been sung to that melody ever since.

Step By Step

Words: author unknown. From the preamble to the constitution of the American Mineworkers Association (1863)
Music arranged & adapted by Waldemar Hills & Pete Seeger (1948)
from the traditional Irish song "The Praties They Grow Small"
© 1991 by Sanga Music Inc.

Forty years later Peter Baird and the Sacramento Labor Chorus have carried the song a step further. Long live bilingualism!

Paso a paso al caminar
Vencera, vencera.
Piedras, arcos formaran,
Solas nada haran.
Y con solidaridad
El sueno se cumplira.
Gotas de agua moveran,
Solas nada haran.

People's Songs (Inc., non-profit), put on some inspiring hootenannies, had branches out west, helped put on a great singing presidential campaign for Henry Wallace, but went broke in February '49. Lee Hays, Ronnie Gilbert, Fred Hellerman, and I started a singing group. After four months we picked a name: the Weavers. One of our first records was a 78 rpm single, a ballad recounting the Klu Klux Klan-inspired attack on an outdoor concert by Paul Robeson in September '49.

Hold the Line

1. Let me tell you the story of a line that was held,
    And many brave men and women whose courage we
        know well,
    How we held the line at Peekskill on that long
        September day!
    We will hold the line forever till the people have
        their way.

CHORUS (AFTER EACH VERSE):
Hold the line!
Hold the line!
As we held the line at Peekskill
We will hold it everywhere.
Hold the line!
Hold the line!
We will hold the line forever
Till there's freedom ev'rywhere.

2. There was music, there was singing, people listened
        everywhere;
    The people they were smiling, so happy to be there—
    While on the road behind us, the fascists
        waited there,
    Their curses could not drown out the music in
        the air.

3. The grounds were all surrounded by a band of
        gallant men,
    Shoulder to shoulder, no fascist could get in,
    The music of the people was heard for miles around,
    Well guarded by the workers, their courage made us
        proud.

4. When the music all was over, we started to go home,
    We did not know the trouble and the pain that was
        to come,
    We got into our buses and drove out through
        the gate,
    And saw the gangster police, their faces filled
        with hate.

5. Then without any warning the rocks began to come,
    The cops and troopers laughed to see the damage
        that was done,
    They ran us through a gauntlet, to their
        everlasting shame,
    And the cowards there attacked us, damnation to
        their name.

6. All across the nation the people heard the tale,
    And marvelled at the concert, and knew we
        had not failed,
    We shed our blood at Peekskill, and suffered many
        a pain,
    But we beat back the fascists and we'll beat them
        back again!

Words by Lee Hays   Music by Pete Seeger (1949)
© 1959 (renewed) by Sanga Music Inc.

In the Weavers as in the Almanacs, my main contribution was as an accompanist, a singer, an arranger. A finder of songs more than a writer of songs. But Lee kept writing lyrics and asking me to try and find melodies for them.

THE WEAVERS, 1949

Tomorrow is a Highway

Moderately

To- mor-row— is a— high-way— broad and fair_____ And we____ are the man-y who'll trav-el there._____ To- mor-row— is a— high-way— broad and fair, And we— are the work-ers who'll build it— there; And we— will build it there.

Words by Lee Hays   Music by Pete Seeger (1949)
TRO - © 1950 (renewed) Folkways Music Publishers, Inc., New York, NY.
Used by permission.

1. Tomorrow is a highway broad and fair,
   And we are the many who'll travel there.
   Tomorrow is a highway broad and fair,
   And we are the workers who'll build it there;
   And we will build it there.

2. Come, let us build a way for all mankind.
   A way to leave this evil year behind,
   To travel onward to a better year
   Where love is, and there will be no fear,
   Where love is, and no fear.

3. Now is the shadowed year when evil men,
   When men of evil thunder war again.
   Shall tyrants once again be free to tread,
   Above our most brave and honored dead?
   Our brave and honored dead.

4. O, comrades, come and travel on with me,
   We'll go to our new year of liberty.
   Come, walk upright, along the people's way,
   From darkness, unto the people's day.
   From dark, to sunlit day.

5. Tomorrow is a highway broad and fair
   And hate and greed shall never travel there
   But only they who've learned the peaceful way
   Of brotherhood, to greet the coming day.
   We hail the coming day.

Artist Unknown

THE WEAVERS, 1980

In January '49, we wrought better than we thought.

It was printed on the cover of the very first issue of *Sing Out!* magazine, the successor to *People's Songs.* Turn the page.

"If I Had a Hammer"
Words by Lee Hays Music by Pete Seeger (1949)
TRO - © 1958 (renewed) & 1962 (renewed)
Ludlow Music, Inc., New York, NY.

Us Weavers recorded it this way in the fall of '49, for a microscopic label, Charter Records. Lee Hays used to say, "It was a collector's item — nobody but collectors ever bought it." A year later, when the Weavers were temporarily "on the charts," our then-manager wouldn't let us perform it ("I'm trying to cool down the blacklisters; that song would encourage them.") But nine years later three young friends formed a trio, Peter, Paul and Mary, and had a surprise hit with the song. Their re-arrangement, which swept the world, is on pp. 40–41.

PETER YARROW, NOEL PAUL STOOKEY, MARY TRAVERS

Photo by Joe Alper

It was a young radical activist, Libby Frank, in 1952 who insisted on singing "my brothers and my sisters" instead of "all of my brothers." Lee resisted the change at first. "It doesn't ripple off the tongue as well. How about 'all of my siblings?'" He finally gave in. It was sung in Europe and elsewhere in the '50's, sometimes with variant melodies, sometimes with added verses, "If I Had A Drum; If I Had A Trumpet," etc.

Victor Jara, the great protest singer of Chile, made up a version in Spanish.

El Martillo

1. Si tu viera un martillo
   Porquearia en la mañana
   Porquearia en la noche
   Por todo el paiz.

CHORUS:
A relte el pelligro
De vemos unir nos
Para defender
La paz.

2. Si tu viera una campaña
   Tocaria en la mañana
   Tocaria en la nocke
   Por todo el paiz.

3. Si tu viera una cancion
   Cantaria la mañana
   Cantaria en la noche
   Por todo el paiz.

4. Ahora tengo un martillo
   Y tengo una campaña
   Y tengo una cancion que cantar
   Por todo el paiz.
   Martillo de justicia
   Campaña de libertad
   Y una cancion
   De paz.

DENNIS THE MENACE *Hank Ketcham*

We gave him a hammer. He hammers in the morning, he hammers in the evening all over this land!

"Dennis the Menace"® Used by Permission of Hank Ketcham © 1992 North America Syndicate

For the last 25 or more years, I've sung a composite version (see p. 42). In the '90's, I'm mostly a songleader shouting the words, with the crowd doing the singing. But I found chords and a bass line I really like; I play it in Dropped D tuning, but my 12-string guitar is tuned low, so it comes out sounding in C.

When I get a crowd singing, I sometimes joke that one can sing the melody as I wrote it, or as various others have changed it, all at the same time. Somehow they all harmonize with each other.

There's a good moral here, for the world.

If I Had A Hammer

(as sung by Peter, Paul and Mary)

Words by Lee Hays   Music by Pete Seeger (1949)
TRO - © 1958 (renewed) & 1962 (renewed) Ludlow Music, Inc., New York, NY.

1. If I had a hammer,
   I'd hammer in the mornin',
   I'd hammer in the evenin',
     All over this land.
   I'd hammer out danger,
   I'd hammer out a warning,
   I'd hammer out love between
   My brothers and my sisters,
     All over this land.

2. If I had a bell,
   I'd ring it in the mornin',
   I'd ring it in the evenin',
     All over this land.
   I'd ring out danger,
   I'd ring out a warning,
   I'd ring out love between
   My brothers and my sisters,
     All over this land.

3. If I
   had a
   song…
   (etc.)

4. Well, I got a hammer,
   And I got a bell
   And I got a song—to—sing
     All over this land
   It's the hammer of justice,
   It's the bell of freedom,
   It's the song about love between
   My brothers and my sisters,
     All over this land.

If I Had A Hammer
(A Songleader's Version)

Words by Lee Hays   Music by Pete Seeger (1949 & on)

Life changes a little at a time. Only two words changed in the next lyric.

Back in the late '30's a wonderful Communist humorist and writer named Mike Quin wrote three short verses titled "How Much For Spain?" as a collection speech for medical aid to Spain. The elected government there had been attacked by General Francisco Franco and was desperately trying to survive. Corporations in the USA were trying to help Franco. After all, he was fighting Communism, wasn't he? I found in the 1940's that Mike's poem is still one of the best collection speeches anyone could make. I've only changed two words from Mike's original.

MIKE QUIN WITH WIFE MARY & BABY

How Much?

The long collection speech is done
And now the felt hat goes
From hand to hand its hopeful way
Along the restless rows.

In purse and pocket finger feel
And count the coins by touch.
Minds ponder what they can afford
And hesitate: How much?

In that brief jostled moment
When the battered hat arrives
Try, friends,* to remember that
Some folks* put in their lives.

By Mike Quin (1937), adapted by Pete Seeger (1947)
© Mike Quin. Used by permission.

* Originally "brothers" and "men."

In November of '49 the Weavers made up some campaign songs attempting to elect Vito Marcantonio mayor of New York City and re-elect African-American Communist Ben Davis to the City Council. Both lost, but for years Lee Hays and I used to laugh to think that one of the most rhythmically successful verses we ever put together was sung only once. At a Madison Square Garden rally.

The basic tune was "New York City," a blues stomp Leadbelly had put together in 1935. It had been a favorite of the Almanac Singers. We liked to improvise verses.

Here We Are in Madison Square

Words by Ronnie Gilbert, Lee Hays, Fred Hellerman & Pete Seeger (1949)
Music adapted from the song "New York City" by Huddie Ledbetter
TRO - © 1992 & 1993 Folkways Music Publishers, Inc., New York, NY.
Used by permission.

In December '49 four of us, the Weavers, were about to go our separate ways. We wanted to sing for working folks, for the left-wing types. But McCarthyism was coming in. We had no offers of jobs.

As a last resort (fate worse than death) we took a job in a tiny Greenwich Village nightclub, the Village Vanguard. Microscopic pay. There, lightning struck, as it occasionally does in the music business. The well-known band leader, Gordon Jenkins, fell in love with our work, got us a Decca recording contract.

For me the Village Vanguard was an education. Into it came a wider range of folks than I'd expected, including Hillel and Aviva, two young Israeli musicians fascinated by us mixed-up Americans singing songs in Yiddish and Hebrew ("Tzena Tzena").

Hillel (his name now is Ilka Raveh) taught me to make and play the open-ended reed flute called "chalil" in Hebrew and "nai" in Arabic. He learned from Arab shepherds how to play it, and he gets an incredible soft tone from it. A Bedouin friend listening to him once, said "That's not music. That's talking to God."

For Ilka and his Arab friend I made up a melody I put at the end of this book, p. 260. I call it "How Soon?" As I play it, I wonder how long before peace comes to that region. And to our world. As it must, sooner or later. With or without people.

> Keep away
> from the wisdom which doesn't cry
> the philosophy which doesn't laugh
> and the greatness which doesn't bow
> before children.
>
> Khalil Gibran

In 1949 Toshi and I were fortunate to find a few acres for sale on a wooded mountainside overlooking the Hudson, 60 miles north of the Big City. Only $100 an acre!

For two summers Toshi cooked over an open fire, helped me build a log cabin. The third summer we moved in permanently. For two winters I toured with the Weavers, then as the blacklist put us out of business, we took a sabbatical in '52. Lee said it turned into a Mondical and a Tuesdical. I started teaching in a small "alternative" school in New York City one day a week, and on the weekend picked up a few dollars singing somewhere.

The so-called "folk music scene" hardly existed at the time, but it was building.

People's Songs had folded in '49 but with an "Interim Newsletter" I kept a few of us in touch. *Sing Out!* magazine started up in 1950.

Moses Asch had me record one album after another for his tiny company, Folkways. It encouraged me to explore a variety of old traditions and to experiment with songwriting as well.

Our kids were little then. I'm certainly not the first versifier inspired by small children. Most of the songs or stories in this chapter would not have been put together without the existence of three small people now all grown up, with kids of their own. Danny, Mika, Tinya. They taught me so much. I'm still learning from their mother. The Clearwater[1] knows Toshi Seeger as an ace organizer. After having to organize me for 50 years, no wonder. But she's the wisest person I know: Perspicacious. Peppery. A Paradigm with Pots and Pans.[2] And we are both proud to be parents of those three.

[1] See Chapter IX.
[2] See "A Little a' This 'n' That" on p. 256. I'm good at washing 'em.

Crawly Creepy Little Mousie

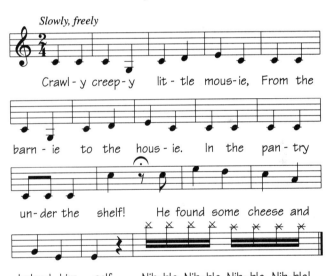

Slowly, freely

Crawl-y creep-y lit-tle mous-ie, From the barn-ie to the hous-ie. In the pan-try un-der the shelf! He found some cheese and helped him-self. Nib-ble Nib-ble Nib-ble Nib-ble!

Words traditional (nursery rhyme)
Music adapted & arranged by Pete Seeger (1959) based on the song "Doodle Dandy" collected, adpated & arranged by Frank Warner
TRO - © Copyright 1971, 1984 & 1993 Melody Trails, Inc., New York, NY.

There's no accompaniment to this song. You sit a baby or small child in your lap. Start your fingers walking up their leg, arm, or back, always ending tickling under the chin.

I read the words, an old Scottish or English nursery game, in a book. Put a tune to it. Only 30(!) years later did I realize that I swiped the tune from a marching song of 1776, which I heard Frank Warner sing:

Doodle Dandy

Doo - dle doo - dle doo - dle Dan - dy,

Corn - stalk rum and - a home - made bran - dy,

In - dian pud - ding and pump - kin pie,

That will make the Yan - kees fly! (banjo)

Traditional song (U.S., 1783) Collected, adapted & arranged by Frank Warner
TRO - © Copyright 1971 & 1984 Melody Trails, Inc., New York, NY.
From *Traditional American Folk Songs from the Anne & Frank Warner Collection*,
Syracuse University Press, 1984.

If any money ever comes in for "Crawly Creepy," 50 percent will go to the estate of Frank Warner, and if I ever locate the author or the collector of nursery rhymes where I learned the rhyme, they should get the other 50 percent. I was just the matchmaker — brought 'em together.

In the early 1920's my father was at a low point in his life. Fired as a professor for making speeches against imperialistic war. Tried to take "good music" out to people in small towns, with his family living in a homemade trailer pulled by a Model T Ford. Failed. Marriage breaking up. He decided he might as well enjoy his children while they were still children. All summer, every summer for ten years we lived in a barn 200 feet from his parents' comfortable home. In our barn no telephone, no electricity, no plumbing. One summer we all made model boats, another summer model airplanes. On trips to the beach and back, my brother John and I would harmonize all the way.

And at night my father would improvise bedtime stories for me, which I found hilarious. Twenty-five years later I tried to recollect some of them for my own children. This one ended getting on record and in print. The song was well-known early in this century as "May Irwin's[3] Frog Song" and had verses. Here I start and end with whistling. Accompaniment is not necessary.

[3] Oscar Brand just told me that May Irwin also wrote "Take Me Out To The Ball Game."

The Foolish Frog

(WHISTLING IS HEARD. A SASSY LITTLE TUNE.)

Whistling

There was once a farmer, walking down the road, whistling a tune to himself. He said, "Dog-gone, I wish I had some words to that song. But all I've got is the melody."

Just then he came to a little bridge. He leaned on the railing, looking down at the brook. There was a big old bullfrog, hopping from bank to bank. (SOUND EFFECTS). Well, the bullfrog looked up, and saw the farmer, and decided to show off. He took an extra special big hop.

Z-z-z-z-z-ztt! He landed, splash! in the water, and got himself all wet. The farmer laughed and laughed and started singing:

Way down south in the yank - e - ty yank

bull - frog jumped from bank to bank_ Just be -

cause he'd no - thing bet - ter for to do_

He stubbed his toe and fell in the wa - ter You could

hear him hol - ler for a mile and a quar - ter Just be -

cause he'd no - thing bet - ter for to do!_

Now, the farmer went walking down the road, feeling mighty proud of himself for making up a song. He went down to the corner store, bought himself some groceries, and a pair of work gloves, and a plug of chewing tobacco, and said:

"Oh, before I go, I have to sing you my new song."

"Go on home," says the storekeeper. "I'm busy here. See all these customers."

"I won't pay you my money unless you let me sing my song!"

"Well, sing it and get it over with," says the storekeeper.

The farmer started singing, and the man in the store cried out, "That's a wo-o-onderful song. Gather 'round everybody, we'll have a party!" And he passed around the free Coca-Colas and the free soda crackers, and everybody was stamping on the floor.

Meanwhile, all the wives and children back home were sitting down to supper, and — where's father? The mothers said, "Children, you better run down to the corner store and fetch your old man. He's probably down there wasting his time as usual."

So all the children run down the road. They run inside the corner store. You know, they heard that music, they forgot about coming home. The children started singing. (THE SONG IS REPEATED IN A HIGH VOICE). And they were passing around the free Coca-Colas and stamping on the floor...

In every farmhouse it was the same situation. The mothers said, "Do they expect us to work all day and nobody show up?" They started down the road waving their frying pans. Well, they get near, and hear that music, and they forget about being mad. They drop the frying pans in the gutter, walk in the store, and the mothers start singing! "Way down south in the yankety-yank, a bullfrog jumped from bank to bank..." And they were passing around the free Coca-Colas and the free soda crackers, and everybody was stamping on the floor!

Meanwhile, out in the barns, all the cows started talking. "Where is everybody? We're supposed to be milked; it's getting mighty uncomfortable!" The cows left their stalls: wobbled out of the barn and down the road right into the corner store. The cows started singing: "Moo, moo, moo, moo. Moo, moo, moo, moo. Moo-moo, moo-moo, moo-moo, mooooo." And the cows' tails were swishing out the windows, and they were stamping on the floor, and drinking the free Coca-Colas and eating the free soda crackers.

Out in the barnyard all the chickens said, "Where is everybody? We're supposed to be fed; we're getting hungry." The chickens hopped over the fence, hopped down the road, hopped into the store. The chickens started. (CHICKEN IMITATION) —P'k, P'k, P'k. And the chickens were stamping on the floor and drinking the free Coca-Co...

Meanwhile all the barns started talking to each other. "We feel mighty empty," they said, "without any cows, or any chickens. I guess we'll have to go find them." So the barns picked themselves off their foundations, galumped down the road, and s-q-u-e-e-z-e-d themselves into that corner store, believe it or not. Did you ever hear a rusty hinge on a barn door? That's the way the barns sang:

"Eeeeeee, eeeeee, errrrrrrrrrrrrrrrrrr."

Out in the fields, all the grass says: "Where is everybody? The cows are supposed to come and eat us. I guess we'll have to go find them." The grass picked itself up and swished off down the road, and swished right into the store, and the grass started:

"Whsh-whsh-sh-sh-sh. Sh-sh-sh-sh-sh-shhh. Sh-sh-sh-sh-sh-sh-sh-sh-shhhhh."

Of course, when the grass was gone, the fields were gone. The brook said: "I don't have any banks to flow between." The brook bubbled down the road. It bubbled right into the corner store.

"Bublbublbublbublbublbublbublbublbublbublbublbub!"

The brook was bubbling up and down the stairway! The grass was growing out the chimney! Feathers flying through the air! Cows' tails swishing out the windows! Everybody stamping on the floor and drinking the FREE Coca-Colas and eating the FREE soda crackers!

Meanwhile, there's the bullfrog in mid-air.

He looks down. There's nothing underneath him. He looks over. There's no bank to land on. (FROG VOICE) "Where am I?" And he starts hopping down the road. The road rolled itself up behind him like a roll of toilet paper. (BANJO MAKES SOUND OF HOPPING).

"Hey, what's that racket down at the corner store?" says the frog.

"Why...They're singing! They're singing about ME!" And he was so proud he puffed himself up with pride!

And he puffed, and he puffed, and he POOM!!!

He exploded. Cows, barns, chickens, houses, farmers, wives, children — the whole corner store went up in the air. And then everybody floated down. They landed right where they were supposed to have been the whole time. Sat down eating supper feeling kind of foolish for themselves.

Next day they went out to find the frog. They looked high, they looked low. Coca-Cola bottles and soda crackers in all directions. But no frog. So all there is left of the frog is the song. We might as well sing 'er once again.

(SING TUNE THROUGH)

Can you whistle?

(WHISTLE IT THROUGH, FOR AN ENDING)

Song by May Irwin (19th c.), adapted by Pete Seeger
Story by Charles Seeger (1924) & Pete Seeger

Sweepy, Sweepy, Sweepy

1. Sweep-y sweep-y sweep-y,
Sweep-y sweep-y sweep-y, Sweep-y sweep-y
sweep-y, Sweep-ing up the floor.
Sweep-y sweep-y sweep-y, Sweep-y sweep-y
sweep-y, Sweep-y sweep-y sweep-y, till there
ain't no more. 2. Dust-y dust-y
dust-y, Dust-y dust-y dust-y,
Dust-y dust-y dust-y, dust-ing up the
shelf. Dust-y dust-y dust-y,
Dust-y dust-y dust-y dust-y, Dust-y dust-y
dust-y, Do-ing it my-self.

Words & music by Pete Seeger & Mika Salter Seeger (1954)
TRO - © 1957 (renewed) & 1965 (renewed) Ludlow Music, Inc., New York, NY.

1. Sweepy, sweepy, sweepy
    Sweepy, sweepy, sweepy
    Sweepy, sweepy, sweepy
    Sweepin' up the floor
    Sweepy, sweepy, sweepy
    Sweepy, sweepy, sweepy
    Sweepy, sweepy, sweepy
    'Til there ain't no more!

2. Dusty, dusty, dusty (3x)
    Dustin' up the shelf
    Dusty, dusty, dusty (3x)
    Doin' it my self!

3. Putty, putty, putty (3x)
    Puttin' things away
    Putty, putty, putty (3x)
    Then go out and play!

4. Moppy, moppy, moppy (3x)
    Moppin' up the room
    Moppy, moppy, moppy (3x)
    Foom! Foom! Foom!

5. Cleany, cleany, cleany (3x)
    Clean the window panes
    Cleany, cleany, cleany (3x)
    'Til you see through again!

6. Throwy, throwy, throwy (3x)
    Throwin' things away
    Throwy, throwy, throwy (3x)
    Far away!

7. Makey, makey, makey (3x)
    Makin' up the bed
    Makey, makey, makey (3x)
    That's what I said!

8. Shakey, shakey, shakey (3x)
    Shakin' out the sheet
    Shakey, shakey, shakey (3x)
    'Til the two ends meet!

9. Washy, washy, washy (3x)
    Washin' up the dishes
    Washy, washy, washy (3x)
    And the soap suds squishes!

REPEAT FIRST VERSE

Mika was age seven or eight, I think. We were in the middle of a big house cleaning. Neither of us can remember who made up what verses.

DANNY & MIKA SEEGER, 1953

I Wonder, I Wonder, I Wonder

1. I wonder, I wonder, I wonder
   What Tinya* can possibly do?
   I wonder, I wonder, I wonder
   What Tinya can possibly do?

2. She can play with her blocks,
   Or go throw some rocks,
   Or climb a tree and look at the view.
   I wonder, I wonder, I wonder
   What Tinya can possibly do

3. I see someone's hand,
   I see someone's hair,
   I hear someone go peek-a-boo.
   I wonder, I wonder, I wonder
   What Tinya can possibly do.

4. She crawls on the floors,
   She looks 'round the door,
   She's tryin' to wear my shoe.
   I wonder, I wonder, I wonder
   What Tinya can possibly do.

5. I see someone's hair,
   I see someone's toe,
   But I can't guess possibly who.
   I wonder, I wonder, I wonder
   What Tinya can possibly do.

REPEAT FIRST VERSE

* Of course you put into a song the name of the child you are singing it
to. My stepmother, Ruth Crawford Seeger, gave me the idea to do this
when she put out the book *American Folksongs For Children* in 1949.

Words & music by Pete Seeger (1956)
© 1970 by Stormking Music Inc.

TINYA SEEGER, 1956

CHINA, 1972

To Everyone In All the World

To ev-'ry-one in all the world— I
reach my hand, I shake their hand.— To
ev-'ry-one in all the world— I
shake my hand like this. All, all to-
geth-er, the whole wide world a-round. I
may not know your lin-go, but I can say, By
jin-go, No mat-ter where you
live, we can shake hands.

Words & music by Pete Seeger (1956)
© 1990 by Stormking Music Inc.

This French translation is by Raffi, who has spread the song across Canada. Thank you, Raffi!

A tous et chacun dans le monde
Je tends la main, j'leur donne la main.
A tous et chacun dans le monde
Je donne la main comme ça.

Tous, tous ensemble,
Au monde entier je chante.
C'est très facile entre humains,
Avec une poignée de main,
N'importe où dans le monde,
On peut s'en tendre.

Now's a good time to thank folklorist Alan Lomax for not only teaching me, but teaching the USA a lot of its best music. The 20th Century revival of interest in "American Folk Music" is due more to the work of this man than any other person. His father, John Lomax, started collecting cowboy songs in the year 1900. Most folklore collectors tend to dig up bones from one graveyard and bury them in another (in libraries). But old John wanted to make a nation aware of its own great songs. He got President Theodore Roosevelt to write an introduction for his book *Cowboy Songs* in 1908. Other collections followed.

THREE GENERATIONS OF JOHN A. LOMAXES

In the mid-1930's his son Alan was put in charge of the Archives of Folk Song at the Library of Congress, and in a few short years of energetic work accomplished what others might have taken a lifetime to do. I and others picked up the songs Alan taught us and made a living singing them ever since. Many tunes we take for granted today, like "House of the Rising Sun" and "Home On the Range," would not be known today had they not been collected and published by his father, John A. Lomax, or by him.

The inspiration for the next song was an African-American children's song, "Little Bird, Little Bird Fly Through My Window," which the Lomaxes collected. The irregular 5/4 measure is part of its charm.

Little Girl See Through My Window

Words by Pete Seeger (1956)
Tune: "Little Bird, Go Through My Window" collected, adapted & arranged by
John A. & Alan Lomax
Additional words by Terry Leonino and Greg Artzner
TRO - © 1941 (renewed) & 1970 Ludlow Music, Inc. & Stormking Music Inc. NY, NY.

CHORUS:
Little girl, little girl,
See through my window.
Little girl, little girl,
See through my window.
Little girl, little girl,
See through my window.
See what you can see.

1. I <u>see</u> the ships and the <u>airy</u>-o-planes,
   I <u>see</u> the cars and the <u>choo</u> choo trains
   A<u>round</u> the ring-o <u>world</u>-o.*

2. I <u>see</u> the rich, I <u>see</u> the poor
   <u>I</u> see millions, <u>millions</u> more
   Around the ring-o world-o.

3. I <u>see</u> the clever, I <u>see</u> the smart,
   I <u>see</u> the folks who <u>have</u> no heart
   Around the ring-o world-o.

4. I <u>see</u> a world where <u>them</u> and me
   Can <u>dwell</u> in sweet <u>sereni</u>ty
   Around the ring-o world-o.

5. I <u>see</u> the chains and the <u>prisons</u> too,
   I <u>see</u> the hammers to <u>break</u> 'em through
   Around the ring-o world-o.

6. I <u>see</u> the waters <u>and</u> the lands
   Just <u>waiting</u> for a <u>helping</u> hand
   Around the ring-o world-o.

* You can sing each verse twice so your audience can join in.

Terry Leonino and Greg Artzner, who sing under the name "Magpie" made up a raft of new verses in the 1980's. They started where I left off.

CHORUS:
Little bird, little bird
Fly Through my window, (REPEAT 3 TIMES)
See what you can see.

I see the waters and the lands
Just waiting for a helping hand
   Around the ring-o world, O.

I see the rivers, streams and lakes
And trouble that pollution makes

I see the rivers, lakes and streams
Teeming with life and flowing clean

I see the people everywhere
All healing water, land and air

I see recycling and such
So we don't have to waste so much

I see the dumps all filled complete
And soon becoming obsolete

I see the spotted owl so small
Thriving among the timbers tall

I see the wolf and the grizzly bear
The spotted eagle in the air

I see the forests growing tall
Provide for creatures great and small

I see mountains no longer mined
Respected by all humankind

I see the people find the worth
In taking care of Mother Earth

I see the people of all lands
All reaching out and joining hands

One Grain of Sand

One grain of sand,——

One grain of sand—— in

all the world, One grain of sand,——

One lit - tle boy, one lit-tle girl.——

Words & music by Pete Seeger (1955)
TRO - © 1957 (renewed) & 1965 (renewed) Ludlow Music, Inc., New York, NY.

1. One grain of sand,
   One grain of sand, in all the world,
   One grain of sand,
   One little boy, one little girl.

2. One grain of sand,
   One lonely star up in the blue,*
   One grain of sand,
   One little me, one little you.

3. One grain of sand,
   One drop of water in the sea,
   One grain of sand,
   One little you, one little me.

4. One grain of sand,
   One leaf of grass upon a plain,
   One grain of sand,
   I'll sing it now again and again, again
   And again, again and again.**

5. One grain of sand,
   One grain of sand in all the world,
   One grain of sand,
   One little boy, one little girl.

6. One grain of sand,
   One grain of sand is all my joy,
   One grain of sand,
   One little girl, one little boy.

7. One grain of sand,
   One lonely star up in the sky,
   One grain of sand,
   One little you, one little I.

8. One leaf of grass,
   One leaf of grass upon the plain,
   One leaf of grass,
   We come and go again and again.

9. The sun will rise,
   The sun will rise and then go down,
   The sun will rise,
   One little world goes round and round and round
   And round, and round and round and round
   and round.***

10. So close your eyes,
    So close your eyes and go to sleep,
    So close your eyes,
    One little smile, one little weep.

11. One grain of sand,
    One grain of sand on an endless shore
    One grain of sand,
    One little life, who'd ask for more.

12. One grain of sand.
    One drop of water in the sea,
    One grain of sand,
    One little you, one little me.

13. One grain of sand,
    One grain of sand is all my own,
    One grain of sand,
    One grain of sand is home sweet home.

14. So go to sleep,
    So go to sleep by the endless sea,
    So go to sleep,
    I'll hold you close, so close to me.

REPEAT FIRST VERSE

* Verse 2

One lone-ly star—— up in the blue,

** Verse 3 similar to Verse 9 below
*** Verse 9

One lit-tle world goes round and round and. round and

round and round and— round and round and round.

This can be a long song. It all depends how sleepy the baby is. But you know, some of my most successful singing has been when 100 percent of my audience goes to sleep on me.

Sweet-a-Little Baby

Very ryhthmically, No accompaniment needed

Sweet - a lit - tle ba - by,

sweet-a lit - tle ba - by, sweet-a lit - tle

ba - by, be-longs___ to eve - ry - bod - y.

Sweet-a lit - tle ba - by, sweet-a lit - tle

ba - by mine.___

1. Sum - mer is a - com - ing and the

win - ter is gone.___ Spring - time's a -

flower - ing all day long.___

Hm___

Words & music by Pete Seeger (1955)
TRO - © 1957 (renewed) & 1965 (renewed) Ludlow Music, Inc., New York, NY.

(Perhaps this should have been written in 6/8 time. The first of each two eighth notes is strongly accented.)

CHORUS (AFTER EACH VERSE):
Sweet-a little baby, sweet-a little baby,
Sweet-a little baby belongs to ev'rybody!
Sweet-a little baby, sweet-a little baby mine.

1. Summer is a-comin' and the winter is gone.
Springtime's a-flowerin' all day long.
Summer is a-comin' and the winter is gone,
Springtime's a-flowerin' all day long. Hm—

2. She's got a sister and a brother, too,
And someday she'll be a big girl, too.
She's got a sister and a brother, too,
And some day she'll be a big girl, too. Hm—

3. She's got a mama and a papa so tall,
Her mama's so pretty and that ain't all.
She's got a mama and a papa so tall,
Her mama's so pretty and that ain't all. Hm—

4. Winter is a-comin' and the north wind blows,
And everybody in the house gets sniffles in
their nose.
Winter is a-comin' and the north wind blows,
And everybody in the house gets sniffles in their
nose. Hm—

5. She's got two bright eyes and a snub, snub nose,
And where she got 'em Lord only knows.
She's got two bright eyes and a snub, snub nose,
And where she got 'em Lord only knows. Hm—

6. She's getting sleepy, now, close your eyes,
Now don't I wish you'd stay this size.
She's getting sleepy, now, close your eyes,
Now don't I wish you'd stay this size. Hm—

MOSES ASCH

Most of these children's songs here just popped out when I was playing with my kids back in the 1950's. At the time I could wander into the office of Moe Asch (Folkways Records) almost any time, on little or no notice. He'd prop up a mike in front of me, and I'd sing the latest songs I'd learned or made up. A half hour later I'd be on my way. A few months later he might have included some of the songs in a new Folkways LP he was showing school teachers at some educational convention. The sales of these records were microscopic by any commercial standard. Hardly a single record store bothered to carry Folkways. But little by little we all grew and learned.

Where's My Pajamas

1. Where's my pa - ja - mas? Where's my pa -
ja - mas? Where's my pa - ja - mas? She
hol - lered 'round the room, Hey! Where's my pa -
ja - mas? Where's my pa - ja - mas?
Where's my pa - ja - mas? A - round the room!

Words & music by Pete Seeger (1957)
© 1985 by Stormking Music Inc.

1. Where's my pajamas? (3x)
   She hollered 'round the room, Hey!
   Where's my pajamas? (3x)
   Around the room.

2. Where's my pillow? (3x)
   She hollered 'round the room, Hey!
   Where's my pillow? (3x)
   Around the room.

3. Where's my blanket? (3x)
   She hollered 'round the room…etc.

4. Where's my Teddy? (3x)
   She hollered 'round the room…etc.

5. Where's my kisses? (3x)
   She hollered 'round the room…etc.

All these songs don't mean I was a particularly good father. Half the time I was away singing some place. One year Toshi counted the days I was home: 90 out of the year's 365. That might have been the year after I was sentenced to jail for a year, for not cooperating with the House Committee on Un-American Activities. We accepted almost every job offered, on the assumption that most of them would be cancelled. But none of them were. The Court of Appeals acquitted me. It was a horrendously busy year. Toshi said, "Never again. Next time no appeal. Let him go to jail."

As for me, I'll never sing these songs without seeing in my mind's eye certain little children. Something good that has happened can never be made to unhappen. And never is a long time.

Now there are grandchildren.

TINYA SEEGER WITH SON KITAMA, 1981

Little Fat Baby

Some - day you'll be a - ble to walk.
Some - day you'll be a - ble to talk.
No more will you poop in your pants.
You'll be a - ble to sing and dance.
And_ then, oh_ then, oh_ then, oh then,_
I'll wish I had that lit - tle fat ba - by
in my arms a - gain._

Words & music by Pete Seeger (1982) © 1993 by Sanga Music Inc.

TAO RODRIGUEZ & CASSIE SEEGER WITH THEIR GRANDFATHER, 1974

You'll Sing to Me Too

Words & music by Pete Seeger (1973)   © 1993 by Sanga Music Inc.

1.   I don't know where I'll go
     But we're here, and we're near
     So I'll sing to you and someday you'll sing to me too.

CHORUS:
I will sing to you, I will sing to you
I will sing to you and someday you'll sing to me too.

2.   We don't know where we'll go
     But we're here, and we're near
     So I'll sing to you and someday you'll sing to me too.

3.   I don't know, where I'll go
     But we're here and we're near
     So I'll sing to you and someday you'll sing to me too.

LAST CHORUS:
You'll sing to me too, You'll sing to me too.
I will sing to you and someday you'll sing to me too.

And we do sing together.

TAO & PETE, NEW YORK CITY, 1992

As long as I've put down on paper the last three songs, I include a couple more never sung outside home. The first, to the tune of "John B. Sails," was made up when we moved the small family up to the country from New York.

Load Up the Moving Van

So load up the mov-ing van,

Here comes the mov-ing man,

Leave New York Cit-y far be-hind.—

Good-bye, good-bye, good-bye, good-bye,

Leave Green-wich Vil-lage a

long—— way be-hind.——

Words & music adaptation by Pete Seeger (1949)
Original tune ("The Wreck of the John B.") adapted by Lee Hays from a collection by Carl Sandburg. (Bahamian author unknown.)
TRO - © 1951 (renewed) & 1993 Folkways Music Publishers, Inc. & Melody Trails, Inc., New York, NY.

Chronologically, this song belongs 20 pages back, when my inlaws got a job as caretakers of a summer camp to be near their grandchildren. The only verse I can remember started:

O Grandma, she got drunk,
After packing all the trunks...

Toshi's mother was deeply religious in her own way, but also had a fine sense of humor, and put up with my diabolical materialism. I include the song because it's still a usable chorus. As in many songs for children, here is a potential song for *any* family having to move, who can afford a moving van.

The next song's improvised verses go to a usable tune and chorus I made up years ago and never could think of any other use for. You can change them to suit the details of your trip.

We'll Keep Rolling On

Pough- keep- sie's eight-y- six miles a-way,— But

we're get-ting hun-gry now.— Let's pull o-ver at the

next stop, and all of us get some chow?—

When we're rest-ed, when we're full,—

we can take off a-gain.—

I can take a turn— at the driv-ing, and

you can get some shut-eye then.— And

We'll keep roll-ing on,— We'll keep

roll-ing on,— We'll keep roll-ing— and a-

long a-bout dark— we ought-a be there.

Words & music by Pete Seeger (1989)
TRO - © 1993 Melody Trails, Inc., New York, NY.

As I put together this chapter, I realize that I've rarely performed most of these songs on stage, although I've had occasional requests for them, probably from children or parents who heard them on a Folkways recording.

If I'm singing for kids, at a school or a camp. I'll stick to surefire songs: "Skip to My Lou," "She'll Be Comin' Round The Mountain," "Green and Yeller," "Let's Go On a Bear Hunt," "The Old Lady That Swallowed a Fly," and Larry Penn's "I'm a Little Cookie." And for real toddlers, "Eensy Weensy Spider," and "The Wheels On the Bus Go 'Round And 'Round." Oh, and "The Green Grass Grows All Around," And if I can find colored chalk and an easel, "I Had a Rooster, And The Rooster Pleased Me." (I draw pictures for this one.)

What's a good song for a six-year-old is often looked down on by a ten-year-old. Sometimes I try to handle the problem by asking "Do you have a baby brother or sister back home? Try doing this with them." And then I teach them all "Crawlie Creepy Little Mousie."

And similarly for adult audiences I've told "Abiyoyo" and the "Foolish Frog" story, as well as other stories. Folklorist Alan Lomax believes that the best of the old English ballads survived because they could be appreciated on several different levels, by people of different ages, when they were sung around the fireplace by a grandmother.

In this television age will family singing survive? It may not be as common as it used to be, but I'm sure it will. It would help if concerts for children, whether at school or camp or anywhere, were thought of as teaching sessions, to show kids some good songs they could take home. Recordings are handy tools, as are paper and print. But let's not allow them to replace people.

In the back of my mind are two contradictory thoughts: 1) Someone once said "Every society faces the task of civilizing an onrushing horde of barbarians — its own children."

And, 2) Woody Guthrie said he didn't want to make children like grownups. He'd like to see grown-ups more like kids.

My older brother's second wife Judith was bubbling her six-months-old baby when I was visiting, and we made up the next song. My niece now has a baby of her own.

The Baby Burping Song

Words & music by Pete Seeger & Judith Seeger (1966)
© 1966, 1968 by Sanga Music Inc.

START EACH VERSE:
As long as I am singing
I will sing you one (two, three, etc. to ten)

1. One for the baby that sucks its thumb,
   And one for the bubble that's soon to come.
2. Two for the love of me for you. (TO 1.)
3. Three for the loves of my babes and me. (TO 2.)
4. Four for the world outside my door. (TO 3.)
5. Five for the joys of being alive. (TO 4.)
6. Six for the baby that plays and kicks. (TO 5.)
7. Seven for a great big upstairs heaven. (TO 6.)
8. Eight for the things for which we wait. (TO 7.)
9. Nine for the Lord that made you mine. (TO 8.)
10. Ten's for the songs we sing again. (TO 9.)

Hush Little Baby
(The Hambone Lesson)

Many know these words sung slowly as a lullaby, but I've found it a great game song when speeded up. The songleader does not sing the last word, the one that rhymes each couplet. The listeners, two — or two thousand — do that.

I first demonstrate a simplified version of what many children in the south know as "the Hambone." This is the "accompaniment." No banjo, no guitar. I learned it from Sonny Terry's nephew, J.C. Burris. Who knows? The idea could have started off in Africa thousands of years ago.

The songleader either sits or goes into a slight crouch. Feet pat two times each measure, while hands pat eight times to each measure. Later, when the hands accentuate every third pat (see accents P over the music), the feet help keep it all together — the "basic beat."

Left and right hands alternate. Rock-steady tempo throughout.

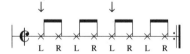

The arrows above the notes show the conventional downbeats emphasized by the voice. In the column at right you'll see all sorts of syncopated off beats emphasized when you pat on the back of your hands, your chest, etc. — it's not something you can learn in a few minutes.

The above rhythm, hopefully picked up by others learning from you, continues while you talk:

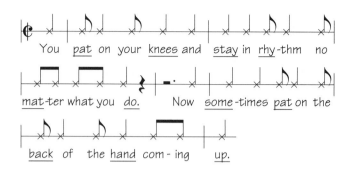

The letter P shows when the left hand pats the back of the right hand.

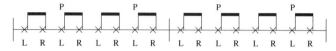

Demonstrate this—over and over.

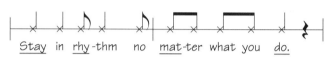

When they have this, give them a variation.

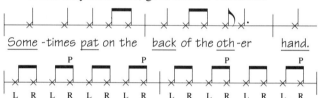

Note the accents showing when the right hand pats the back of the left hand.

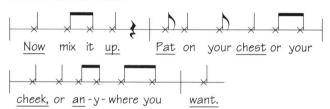

Only a few will be able to keep up with you, but it's fun to try. Whether you pat on the backs of of your hands, or your chest or cheeks, these accented beats are now sounding every *third* eighth note. Keep your feet patting the basic 4/4 time or you'll be confused yourself. Your hands are emphasizing every *third* eighth note.

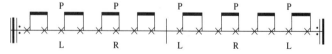

Without stopping, start the chant:

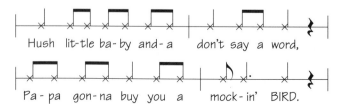

The capitalized word at the end of every other line is supposed to be said by the listeners, not the songleader. The rhyme usually cues them in, even if they never heard the chant before.

Sometimes I either point at the listener(s), or cup an ear to indicate that they are supposed to call out rhyming words.

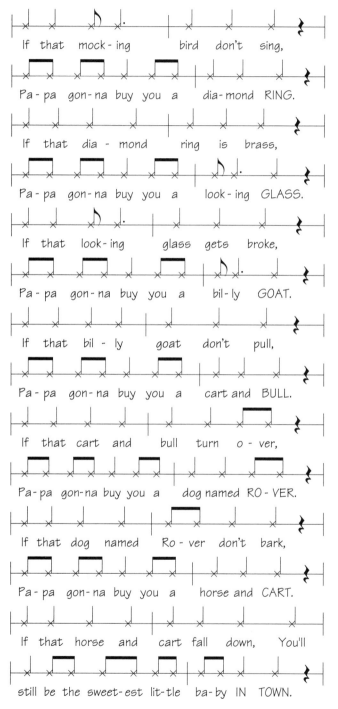

Collected, adapted & arranged by John A. Lomax & Alan Lomax
New musical arrangement by Pete Seeger (1993)
TRO - © 1941 (renewed) & 1993 Ludlow Music, Inc. & Melody Trails, Inc., New York, NY.

And you end it abruptly. By now everyone gets the word "TOWN."

A Five-Part Handslap

As a kid I invented my own way of handslapping. It had a five-rhythm, 5/8 if you want to get technical. So no one picked it up from me. You stand in a bit of a crouch, so your hands can slap the side of your leg a little above the knee:

1) With the right hand (R) coming up, slap the right leg
2) With the left hand (L) slap the left leg, coming up
3) Slap (SL) the two hands together by coming down with the right hand while the left is still coming up
4) The right hand slaps the right leg, going down and past it
5) The left hand slaps the left leg, going down and past it.

One the way down you slap the front of the leg. On the way up you slap the side of the leg.

I got so I could do it so fast my hands were a blur. At various times in my life I remembered the "skill" but never knew what to do with it. In the last 20 years I realized that if I patted my feet on every *fourth* pat or slap, the slap of the two hands together came out differently each time. Sometimes on the downbeat, sometimes on the upbeat. It's fun! So now I hand this useless skill on to you to waste your time with. I never saw anyone else do it.

See if you can decipher the following:

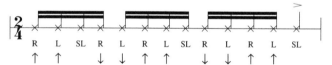

Stand in a slight crouch. Pat down with both toes twice each measure. See T below. T for toes. Here's some variations on the pattern.

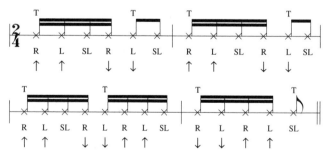

Of course you can simply do it over and over without stopping at the end of a measure. Start slow. Get faster. Keep the beats regular. Or play some fast 2/4 dance music — fiddle tunes are good. Or marches. Just try and keep in rhythm with whatever you play, slow or fast. You'll gradually learn to keep it all smooth. Over a period of time. Get the skill into your hands and out of your head.

Skip Rope Chant

Nixon was a liar
North was too
Pretty soon the White House
Better be Fu-fu-

Fumigated, expurgated
Opened up to all
But before that time comes
We gotta grow tall

Tall not in centimeters
Tall not in inches
But tall in knowing
How the Big Shoe pinches

Tall in knowing
All the how's and the why's
'Cause then we can learn
To expose the lies

Before _____ is a liar
And _____ is too
And if you don't know why
Then out goes y—o—u

By Pete Seeger (1986)
© 1993 by Sanga Music Inc.

Who was Nixon? Who was North? The politics of the 1970's and '80's are long past and gone. But you could update it and give it new life. Fill in the blanks.

In a book of African folk tunes notated by J.N. Maselwa and Rev. H.C.N. Smith, I came across a lullaby. A footnote explained that it was sung as part of a story about a monster. "The parents get the giant dancing, and when it falls down in a fit, it is dispatched by the parents." From that hint, I improvised a new story for my own children, not realizing at the time how closely the symbolism hit home.

Abiyoyo

(START BY SINGING THE SONG.)

Once upon a time there was a little boy, who played a ukelele. He'd go around town: plonk! plonk! plonk! The grownups would say:

"Take that thing out of here." (KICKING MOTION)

CLEARWATER FESTIVAL, 1981

Not only that. The boy's father would get in trouble. The father was a magician. He had a magic wand. He could go Zoop! and make things disappear. But the father was a terrible practical joker. He'd come up to someone doing a hard job of work — (MAKE MOTIONS OF SAWING WITH A HANDSAW) *zzt, zzt, zzt. Up comes the father: Zoop! The saw would disappear. He'd come up to someone just about to drink a nice glass of…something. Zoop! The glass would disappear. He'd come up to someone just about to sit down after a hard day's work, and zoop! no chair.*

People got tired of this. They said to the father: "You get out of here. Take your magic wand and your practical jokes and you and your son…"
(POINT TO THE SIDE. MAKE MOTION OF KICKING.)

The boy and his father were ostracized. That means, they made 'em live on the outskirts of town.
(BANJO STARTS A LOW, MENACING STRUM ON THE LOWEST STRING)

Now, in this town they used to tell stories. The old people used to tell stories about the monsters and giants that lived in the old days! They used to tell a story about Abiyoyo. They said he was as tall as a tree, and could eat…people…up. Of course, nobody believed it, but they told the stories anyway.

But one day, one day, the sun rose, blood red over the hill. And the first people that got up and looked out of their window — they saw a great big shadow in front of the sun. And they could feel the whole ground shake.
(STOMP, STOMP.)

Women screamed. (RESPONSE) *Strong men fainted.* (UGH). *Run for your lives! Abiyoyo's coming!*

Down through the fields he came. He came to the sheep pasture and grabs a whole sheep. Yeowp! He eats it down in one bite. He comes to the cow pasture. Yuhk!

Just then the boy and his father woke up. I think they'd been up late the night before at a party. The boy rubbed his eyes.

"Hey, paw, what's coming over the fields?"

"Oh, son. It's Abiyoyo. Oh, if only I could get him to lie down. I could make him disappear."

The boy said, "Come with me, father." He grabbed his father by one hand. The father grabbed the magic wand, and the boy grabbed his ukelele. Over the fields they went, right up to where Abiyoyo was.

People screamed "Don't go near him! He'll eat you alive!"

There was Abiyoyo (ARMS OUTSTRETCHED). *He had long fingernails, 'cause he never cut 'em. He had slobbery teeth, 'cause he never brushed them. Matted hair, 'cause he never combed it. Stinking feet, 'cause he never washed them. He was just about to come down with his claws, when the boy whipped out his ukelele.*

(SINGING:)
Abiyoyo, Abiyoyo
Abiyoyo, Abiyoyo
Abiyoyo, yo yoyo yo yoyo
Abiyoyo, yo yoyo yo yoyo…

Well, the giant had never heard a song about himself before; a foolish grin spread across his face. He started to dance.

ABIYOYO, ABIYOYO,

The boy went faster (DANCE AROUND).

ABIYOYO, YO YOYO, YO YOYO
ABIYOYO, YO YOYO…

The giant got out of breath. He staggered. He fell down flat on the ground.
Zoop, zoop! (POINT DOWN).
People looked out of their windows. "Abiyoyo disappeared!" They ran across the fields, lifted the boy and his father up on their shoulders.
"Come on back to town. Bring your damn ukelele." And they all sang:

Abiyoyo, Abiyoyo
Abiyoyo, Abiyoyo
Abiyoyo, yo yoyo yo yoyo
Abiyoyo, yo yoyo yo yoyo.

Story by Pete Seeger (1952) Song: traditional South African lullaby
© 1963 (renewed) Fall River Music Inc.

The folk process in summer camps has produced new versions of it. I urge any parent reading this to try telling stories by ear instead of always relying on the printed page. After retelling the old favorites, reshape stories from anywhere and everywhere (movies, novels, the Bible, TV shows, anecdotes and riddles). Before long you'll be making up brand new stories. How? Start thinking, "What would happen *if*…?"

© Len Munnik, Amsterdam

About age nine I discovered a great song to sing while on a swing — the length of the chain or ropes holding the seat should be about six or seven feet. If they are too long, the song goes too slowly. The underlined words should be sung when leaning back and trying to make your toes touch the clouds.

Oh, How He Lied

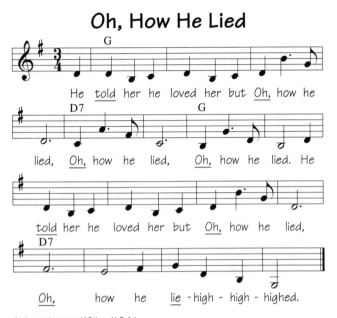

He told her he loved her but Oh, how he lied, Oh, how he lied, Oh, how he lied. He told her he loved her but Oh, how he lied, Oh, how he lie-high-high-highed.

Author unkwnown (19th c. U.S.A.)

1. He <u>told</u> her he loved her, but
    <u>Oh</u> how he lied, <u>oh</u> how he lied, <u>oh</u> how he lied.
    He <u>told</u> her he loved her, but <u>oh</u> how he lied,
    <u>Oh</u> how he <u>lie</u>-high-high-highed.

2. They <u>were</u> to be married, but
    <u>She</u> up and died, <u>she</u> up and died, <u>she</u> up and died
    They <u>were</u> to be married, but <u>she</u> up and died.
    <u>She</u>-up-and-<u>die</u>-high-high-highed.

3. He went to the fun-er-al but
    Just for the ride (3x)
    He went to the fun-er-al but just for the ride,
    Just-for-the-<u>ri</u>-high-high-highed.

4. She went to heaven and
    Flip-flop she flied (3x)
    She went to heaven and flip-flop she flied,
    Flip-flop she <u>fly</u>-high-high-highed.

5. He went the other way and
    Frizzled and fried (3x)
    He went the other way and frizzled and fried,
    Frizzled and <u>fry</u>-high-high-highed.

Now in the 90's I realize that many songwriting friends regularly write songs with children on schools. Sandy Byer in *Sing Out!* magazine (Vol. XXXVI, #1) wrote it up in detail.

Songwriting is something that I consider a birthright of everyone…

At a workshop during the January gathering of the Children's Music Network, the participants gave many good reasons for giving children the opportunity to write songs. Here's a sampling: "It provides a chance for empowerment… It's an activity in which they can all be a success… It can be accomplished by all age levels and abilities… It brings children together creating a community in harmony… We encourage drawing, why not the creation of music?… Most children's music is created and chosen by adults. Participation returns music back to our children and shows respect for what they have to say." …

For young children you might want to begin with zipper songs.[4] "The More We Get Together" as done by Ella Jenkins is an example of a zipper song. You can ask the children what else they can do besides "get together."…

You could expand this process by using zipper songs that require a longer response. A song like "Aiken Drum" is a good example. Students can make up phrases like, "and his hair was made of spaghetti," or "his hands were made of pizza," or "his ears were made of lettuce," etc.…

When working with one class at a time, some performers and teachers like to use written templates to include all the students. Rosalie Sorrels' song, "I'm Gonna Tell" seems to be a popular choice. The students are each given a page on which is written

> "I'm gonna tell _____,
> I'm gonna tell _____,
> I'm gonna tell _____,
> I'm gonna tell on you."

The students then write in their suggestions, making sure that the last word of the third line rhymes with "you." For example, "I'm gonna tell that you hit me on the head, I'm gonna tell that you threw up in bed, I'm gonna tell why our cat is now blue, I'm gonna tell on you." Then the class can sing back all the verses they made up…

Laura Berkson, from Kingston, RI, had her high school students make up a song collage just like video artists make visual collages. Her high school students actually made a video of their song, which was a chronicle of the last thirty years of American music …

Sandy suggested people contact Sarah Pirtle at 54 Thayer Road, Greenfield, MA 01301, or the Children's Music Network, Box 307, Montvale, NJ 07645-0307, (617) 899-5053 (East Coast), (213)460-4387 (West Coast). Writes Sandy: "Most performers agree that in group songwriting one needs to choose… a topic." Bob Reid of Santa Cruz, CA says, "…everyone should come away with a sense that songwriting is fun and easy, not boring and difficult."

[4] Lee Hays gave the name "zipper song" to any song that could get a new verse by zipping in one new word.

Chapter IV
Some Love Songs. Some Music Without Words

Love songs? In much of 18th and 19th century rural America there were two kinds of music: church music and "love songs," which meant sinful songs. All the old English ballads were called "love songs." But once I put out an LP record *Love Songs for Friends and Foes* claiming that most of the songs I sing are love songs — love of home, family, country, world, etc. In this chapter my definition is (only) a bit restricted.

In the mid-1950's I was blacklisted from radio and TV work and "night club" work. But across the river from where I live, in the foothills of the Catskills, were some resorts which didn't think much of the blacklist; and every summer I'd get a few weekend jobs where I could sing my brand of old American folk songs, union songs, peace songs, and songs from other countries.

Driving home late at night over the Shawangunk Mountains and rolling farmland I found myself putting new words to a simple but great old Irish air. It was once a love song, but I knew it best with words from the 1916 Easter Rebellion — the last line went

> "…And Britannia's sons
> With their long range guns
> Sailed…in…through the foggy dew…"

Over the Hills

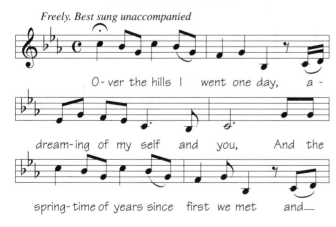

Freely. Best sung unaccompanied

O-ver the hills I went one day, a-
dream-ing of my self and you, And the
spring-time of years since first we met and—

all— that— we've been through. May I
not with de-light still— dream of the years of the
sum - mer and fall— to be? And the
man-y man-y ver-ses— still to be sung in the
bal - lad of you and me.

Words by Pete Seeger (1954) Music: Traditional Irish folk tune ("The Foggy Dew")
TRO - © 1958 (renewed) & 1965 (renewed) Ludlow Music, Inc., New York, NY.

A love song I've sung more often is "Kisses Sweeter Than Wine." Interesting story behind it. Leadbelly (Huddie Ledbetter) was living in New York in the 1940's. (For more about this extraordinary man and musician, see the biography of Leadbelly by Wolfe and Lornell, Harper Collins Publishers.) Once singing at a Greenwich Village party he heard an Irish artist, Sam Kennedy, singing a lonesome old Irish song, "Drimmin Down ."

> A sorrowful ditty I'll tell ye right now,
> Of an old man that had but one cow.
> He took her to the field to be fed,
> And all of a sudden poor Drimmer dropped dead,
> Oh — mush-a sweeter than thou.*

Traditional (Irish)

* I don't know what it means, either.

Leadbelly liked the tune, but he wanted to sing it his own way. Some time later, at another crowded Greenwich Village party, he took Sam Kennedy aside into the bathroom, the only quiet place they could find. He said, "Sam, I'd like to sing your song, but I'm changing it a little, and I wonder if it is O.K. with you." Sam was very polite. He said, "Leadbelly, it's an old, old song. Everybody's got a right to sing it the way they want to. You sing it your way; I'll sing it my way." Leadbelly changed the rhythm. Also garbled the words.

Once, I was humming through the melody as Leadbelly sang it. I was intrigued by the unusual chords Leadbelly used to accompany it. He'd played A major 7th chords, but sang it in A minor.

But I couldn't remember his words. I found myself singing, "Oh-oh, kisses sweeter than wine."

I knew it was a good idea for a chorus, but I wasn't skilled enough to figure what the heck to do with the rest of the song. I jotted the idea on a scrap of paper and dropped it in a file labeled "song ideas 1949."

It's a year later. Us four Weavers (Lee, Ronnie, Fred and me) found ourselves in a most unexpected situation. Thanks to the enthusiasm of bandleader Gordon Jenkins, we'd recorded one of the songs of Leadbelly, who'd died penniless the year before.

"Goodnight Irene" sold more records than any other pop song since WWII. In the summer of 1950 you couldn't escape it. A waltz yet! In a roadside diner we heard someone say, "Turn that jukebox off! I've heard that song 50 times this week."

And the Weavers found ourselves on tour going from one expensive nightspot to another — the Thunderbird Hotel in Las Vegas, Ciro's in Hollywood. In Houston's Shamrock Hotel we were sitting around a swimming pool contemplating a letter from our manager, "Decca Records wants to record some new songs. Please start rehearsing them."

Lee says, "Pete, get out your folder of song ideas; let's go through them, see if there's something we can work on."

I'm humming this idea and that as I leaf through scraps of paper. I come to this. Lee said, "Hold on, let me try it."

Next morning he came back with about six or seven verses. As I remember we pared them down to five. Sometimes I only sing four verses and get away with it. It was a mild seller back in 1950 — a much better seller a few years later when country singer Jimmy Rodgers did it. But what makes me really happy is that it has become a standard with many people. The songwriter as a matchmaker!

Now, who should one credit on this song? The Irish, certainly. Sam Kennedy, who taught it to us. Leadbelly, for adding rhythm and blues chords. Me, for two new words for the refrain. Lee, who wrote seven verses. Fred and Ronnie for paring them down to five. I know the song

publisher, The Richmond Organization, cares. I guess folks whom TRO allows to reprint the song, (like Sing Out!, the publisher of this book) care about this too.

Kisses Sweeter than Wine

Words by Ronnie Gilbert, Lee Hays, Fred Hellerman & Pete Seeger (1950)
Music by Huddie Ledbetter
TRO - © 1951 (renewed) & 1958 (renewed) Folkways Music Publishers, Inc., NY, NY.

1. When I was a young man* and never been kissed
    I got to thinking over what I had missed.
    I got me a girl, I kissed her and then
    Oh Lord, I kissed her again.

CHORUS (AFTER EACH VERSE):
Oh, kisses sweeter than wine,
Oh, kisses sweeter than wine.

2. He asked me to marry and be his sweet wife,
    And we would be so happy all of our life,
    He begged and he pleaded like a natural man,
      and then
    Oh Lord, I gave him my hand.

3. I worked mighty hard and so did my wife,
    Workin' hand in hand, to make a good life.
    With corn in the field and wheat in the bin, I was,
    Oh Lord, the father of twins.

4. Our children numbered just about four,
   They all had sweethearts a-knockin' at the door.
   They all got married and they didn't hesitate; I was,
   Oh Lord, the grandfather of eight.

5. Now we are old, gettin' ready to go,
   We get to thinkin' what happened a long time ago.
   Had a lot of kids, trouble and pain, but,
   Oh Lord, we'd do it again.

* Adjust words throughout depending if the verses are sung by a man or woman.

When I sang this song last year at the wedding of Dave Bernz and Mai Jacobs (she's Walter Lowenfels' granddaughter), I got the crowd to sing the chorus over and over. They sang better each time. I'd call out:

"Oh, sing it again"
"Let's hear just the women"
"Let's hear just the men"
"How about just the grandparents"
"Hey, let's sing it for all the great grandparents, they
    live in our memory, hey, for all the ancestors"
Pause.

"Let's sing it for all those who never had any children but who left us things we use: the word-makers, the picture makers, the inventors of things and recipes, the bridgemakers, the liberators, the peacemakers."
Pause.

"One more time. For all the generations to come."

Oh__ oo__ kisses sweeter than wine.
Oh__ oo__ kisses__ sweeter__ than wine......

Four children? Eight grandchildren? This is certainly the most subversive song I've ever sung. Subversive to a stable world, certainly. Use a little arithmetic:

We each had 2 parents, 4 grandparents, 8 great-grandparents. Unless someone married a 1st cousin or 2nd cousin. Right? So 10 generations ago, say 330 years, each of us had 1024 ancestors somewhere in the world. Or slightly less, because almost certainly now there's been some coupling between distant cousins.

Go back a mere 1330 years and we each could have had over 1,000,000,000,000 (one thousand billion) ancestors except that we're sure there were less than one billion people on earth at that time.

So most of us 5.6 billion humans on earth now are distant cousins of each other, if you go back enough thousands of years, before our omnivorous ancestors migrated to different continents or islands.

Look into the future. If the average person today had only 2 children, in a century they'd have 8 descendants, and in 1330 years they (we) could have 1,000,000,000,000 de-

scendants, which is a lot more population than this old world could take. In a few thousand years it will be a rare person who can claim *not* to have been descended, more or less, from most of us—all 5.6 billion of us, alive today. Kisses sweeter than wine.

Use your math. $2^2 = 4$, $2^3 = 8$,
$2^{10} = 2x2x2x2x2x2x2x2x2x2 = 1024$,
2^{40} = one thousand billion
    (usually called "one trillion").
Subversive. Race mixing. See "We'll All Be A-Doubling," p. 207.

MARIACHI COCULENSE, MEXICO.

During WWII, a Mexican-American fellow soldier sang me a beautiful Mexican pop song "La Feria de las Flores." It was originally in 3/4 time, and supposed to be sung in two-part harmony.

One day in the '50's, I found myself humming the melody (top notes) to a Tennessee-type strummed banjo rhythm, 2/4 time. All of a sudden these words came out. I don't sing them often. Us New England types are kind of shy, you know. Good song, though.

Try singing my lyrics either to Mungo's original rhythm or to my new banjo melody which follows. (Indented verses use the "B" melody).

Note the asterisks. They indicate places you can add beats if you want to. Why? It's a Mexican tradition. The 3/4 rhythm stays steady. One guitar might play 3/8. One guitar may improvise on the top strings, another simultaneously on the bass strings. These asterisks show places where instrumental musicians can have fun, putting in instrumental runs or decorations, as is customary with Mariachi bands. After you get to know the melody, you too can improvise, adding or subtracting beats. You can even add full measures if you wish. But keep the tempo constant.

La Feria de las Flores

Words & music by Chucho Mungo

Festival of Flowers

1. One sudden warm day in June,
   We drove far out in the country,
   We parked our car along the highway,
   And strolled across the meadows.

2. Just two of us hand in hand,
   Gathering armfuls of flowers,
   The sun rose high above us,
   We left our cares behind us.

3. There was a pool of clear water,
   Between the meadow and the forest,
   We stripped and bathed all over,
   And stretched out in the sunlight.

4. I'll remember this day forever—
   Our festival of flowers.
   Those short moments in our lifetime
   When we were one with nature.

5. Just two of us, hand in hand,
   Spending a few precious hours
   The sun rose high above us,
   In our festival of flowers.

Here's how I sing it with the banjo.

Words by Pete Seeger Music by Chucho Mungo

Years ago, visiting Marxist friends in Denver, I found these words to the next song, when fooling around on a guitar.

I thought I'd made up a good tune. Years later realized I'd swiped the idea from "Nearer My God To Thee."

Oh, Had I A Golden Thread

Words & music by Pete Seeger (1958)
© 1959 by Stormking Music Inc.

1. Oh, had I a golden thread
    And needle so fine
    I'd weave a magic strand
    Of rainbow design
    Of rainbow design.

2. In it I'd weave the bravery
    Of women giving birth,
    In it I would weave the innocence
    Of children over all the earth,
    Children of all earth.

3. Far over the waters
    I'd reach my magic band
    Through foreign cities,
    To every single land,
    To every land.

4. Show my brothers and sisters
    My rainbow design,
    Bind up this sorry world
    With hand and heart and mind,
    Hand and heart and mind.

5. Far over the waters
    I'd reach my magic band
    To every human being
    So they would understand,
    So they'd understand.

REPEAT FIRST VERSE

Well, my guess is that if a person likes a song well enough to want to keep it going longer, they'll make up new verses.

I'd weave an end to guns and bombs,
Bury them under concrete floors
The days of anger end
And there be no more wars
There be no more wars.

(BILL GOODMAN, CHICAGO)

I'd weave a land of parks
Where people can be at peace
The land will be sparkling clean
And there be a clear breeze
And there be a clear breeze.

In it I'd weave the dignity
Of folks in every land
In it I'd weave justice
To strengthen every strand
Every strand.

(PAULA BELSEY, OREGON)

As I told you in the first chapter, Bernice Reagon made up a good new version of the melody.

How Does A Melody Get Made Up? #1

When you're having fun with music. For years I've amused myself putting short melodies to highway signs, to advertisements, to newspaper headlines.

It helps to be able to write down a good tune so you don't forget it. Malvina Reynolds in her mid-forties went to school, brushed up on music notation just so she could do this.

Consider: playing guitar or piano doesn't necessarily help. It can hinder. Some of the greatest melodies have come from parts of the world where melodies are sung unaccompanied. They have to be good enough to stand up by themselves, without a sea of harmony supporting them.

Someone asked me once, what does repeating the last line of a verse do for a song? I don't really know. Many song traditions do it. What does any repetition do? Perhaps it gives one time to savor different meanings in the words. Or time to think: "What the heck is the next verse?"

Maybe it reinforces an idea. Often it encourages a listener to join in. The blues form tends to repeat the first line, as do some old European songs.

In the musical *Hair*, they repeated the last line of one song so many times it became a song itself, "Let the sun, let the sun, let the sun-shine in." In a Washington, D.C. peace rally in '69, I heard 50,000 sing it for five or 10 minutes.

Why do ideas come to one at odd hours? The brain works in odd ways. Unexpected connections get made when you're relaxed. The Shakers said the angels guided their pen. Bob Dylan said he didn't know where the ideas came from. Arlo Guthrie believes there's a stream of song ideas flowing past us all the time, and we just have to know how to reach out and grab one. "I'm just glad I don't live down-stream of Bob Dylan," says Arlo.

I suspect there's more to it than this. Thomas Edison said, "Genius is 5 percent inspiration and 95 percent perspiration." And a famous painter said, "The test of an artist is to finish a work, long after the original moment of inspiration has passed." See pp. 89 and 258.

Here's ways to start writing melodies. Change old melodies slightly at first, altering their character with only a note or two. Don't just improvise aimlessly. Imagine you have to make a march into a blues, or vice versa. Try changing "Yankee Doodle" as it would be sung by three very different people.

I'm Gonna Sing Me A Love Song

Slow blues time

1. I'm gon-na sing me a love song just in hopes you might be— pass-ing by,

I'm gon-na sing me a love song just in hopes you might be pass-ing by, *(falsetto)*

And if you're not too bu-sy,

Per-haps I might catch you on the fly.—

Words & music by Pete Seeger (1954)
TRO - © 1967 Melody Trails, Inc., New York, NY.

TOSHI-ALINE OHTA & PETE SEEGER, 1943

Photo by Berenice Abbott

Next, a love song for overly busy people. In this technological world it seems like half of us are trying to do three jobs, and the other half are unemployed.

1. I'm gonna sing me a love song
   just in hopes you might be passing by.
   I'm gonna sing me a love song
   just in hopes you might be passing by.
   And if you're not too busy,
   perhaps I might catch you on the fly.

2. Oh, come along with me down by the spring,
   Won't you come along with me down by the spring,
   To see the waters gliding,
   and hear the nightingales sing.

3. What I got to say's so personal,
   can't say it to no one but you,
   What I got to say's so personal,
   can't say it to no one but you,
   It's just mm, mm, mm, ooh, ooh, ooh, ooh, ooh.

4. Now my song is over, but the melody lingers on,
   Now my song is over, but the melody lingers on,
   And should I ever leave you, remember when I'm gone.

TOSHI & PETE SEEGER, 1992

People who know a "real blues" would dismiss this song. Yet I've sung it on and off for 40 years. Even had requests for it.

Next, a story I've told on stage. It's a ragtime tune, hence the piano part.

This Old Car

A friend of mine, we'll call him Joe, was driving home. He lives in New Jersey about an hour's drive from New York City. He was going up the West Side Highway. He was thinking of his old car, seven years old. Pretty soon he's going to have to turn it in, but he hoped he could hold out for another year.

He was thinking of his wife, Molly, who always sees that it's greased and oiled every 3,000 miles, and so on. If it wasn't for Molly, the car would have broken down long before. Before he got to the George Washington Bridge, he finished the verse:

I been many a mile in this old car
And I hope I got many more
All — because little Molly
Sees that it's well cared for
The spark plugs spark, The carburetor carbs
The pistons do what they're supposed to do.
Oh — and little Molly
Keeps it lubricated all the time

Well you know as Joe went over the Washington Bridge he was feeling rather proud of himself for making up this song. He gaily gave the man in the booth his dollar and jammed his foot on the floor and brought up the clutch too quickly. He was stuck in high gear. He couldn't get the old fashioned stick shift out of high. By using the clutch very carefully, he got started and drove home that whole way. He figured, well if you have to go through life stuck in one gear, it's better to be stuck in high gear than low. Right? Well, he sung the song to himself all the way home.

He couldn't get up the hill to his home though. He drove downtown to the garage and said, "Bill, you have to help me here. I can't get out of third gear." His friend at the garage simply raised the hood — about ten seconds later he said, "Try her now." Son of a gun, it worked perfectly. Joe got the gear-shift into neutral — no trouble.

Bill, the mechanic, he says, "The parts are just getting a little worn down there. If it happens again, you just reach down and give it a little jiggle." So as Joe was driving home, he thought of a second verse:

Now if things get a little out of kilter
Here's how to fix it right away
Reach down and give a little jiggle
Everything will be okay
The spark plugs spark, The caburetor carbs
The pistons do what they're supposed to do.
Oh — and little Molly
Keeps it lubricated all the time

Well, that's how a folk song gets made up. I asked Joe what did his wife think of it. He said with a smile, "Oh, she let me know she appreciated it."

(SING BOTH VERSES THROUGH)

This Old Car

2. Now if things get a lit-tle out of kil-ter, Here's how to fix it right a-way,

Reach down and give a lit-tle jig-gle, Ev-'ry-thing will be o-kay;_____ The

spark plugs spark, the car-bu-re-tor carbs, the pis-ton-'ll do what it's sup-posed to do,— Oh—

_____ and lit-tle Mol-ly keeps it lu-bri-cat-ed all the time._____

Words & music by Pete Seeger (1962) Piano arrangement by Joe Levin

Lee Hays was a tall man, a good bass singer, and off and on an extremely good songwriter. He would play this tune on the piano occasionally. Said he got the idea for it back in Arkansas from two wayward young women who enjoyed playing something like it. He couldn't remember their song, and ended up making his own. But he couldn't complete it. By gosh, I came along and put together a "bridge" ("money, money," etc.).

Empty Pockets Blues

Also known as "Barrel of Money Blues"
Words & music by Lee Hays & Pete Seeger (1930's-1950's)
© 1958 (renewed) by Sanga Music Inc.

1. I never had a pocket full of money,
   I never had a ruby red ring,
   All I ever had was you, babe,
   To sit and listen to me sing I've got those blues,
   Those empty pockets blues.

2. I never had a pocket full of money,
   I never had a big Cadillac,
   All I ever had was you, babe,
   And that's a fact I've got those blues,
   Those empty pockets blues.

   BRIDGE:
   Oh, money, money, money, money
   When will I make the grade?
   I'm so broke that a dollar bill
   Looks big as a window shade.

3. Now some say the blues are sorrowful,
   Some say the blues are sad,
   But when I sing the blues to you,
   They come out feeling glad, I've got the blues,
   The empty pockets blues.

Incidentally, I sing the song in the key of A. Gets a nice diminished chord, with the A# bass note.

Money, Money, Money

The last line of the "bridge" is from a country blues I heard sung by a teenager in Alabama in 1940, and never forgot. "Traditional" blues? Joseph Shabalala, leader of Ladysmith Black Mambazo, told a friend of mine, "I have learned something in the last few years. When they want to steal money, they use the word 'traditional'!"

When a copy of this book is sold, where does the money go? About 40% to the bookstore, another 10 or 15% to the distributor, another 15% or so to the printer. Let's hope all workers involved got union pay. Of the remainder, if the book sells enough, *Sing Out!* will get back its investment and the book will help keep the magazine and the Resource Center going. *Sing Out!* is a not-for-profit corporation. Copyright owners of the songs in the book all get a token fee. The writer, yours truly, for whom these pages have been a labor of love or vanity depending on how you want to look at it, has decided to give the author's royalties to a music school being started by Joseph Shabalala. In his homeland, from which so much and so many has/have been stolen.

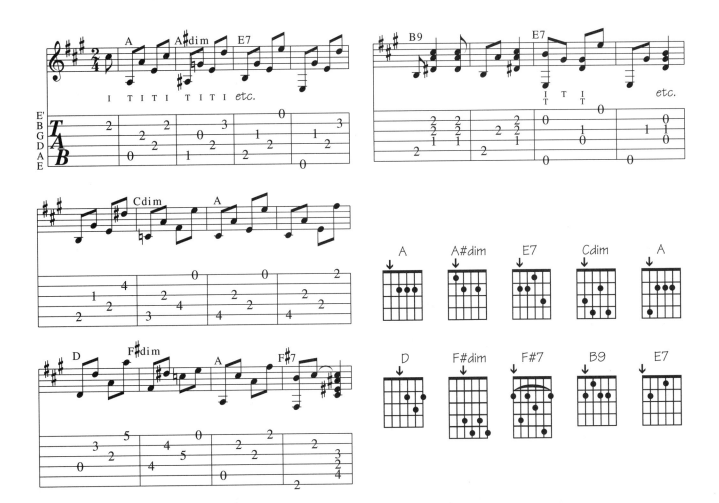

LEE HAYS PLAYING "EMPTY POCKETS BLUES," 1946

E. B. White, one of the great writers of the 20th century, spent most of his life writing short anonymous essays for the weekly magazine, *The New Yorker*. He and his wife Katherine lived in Maine. This poem he once wrote her as a birthday gift; it was published years after he died.

The Spider's Web
(original title: "Natural History")

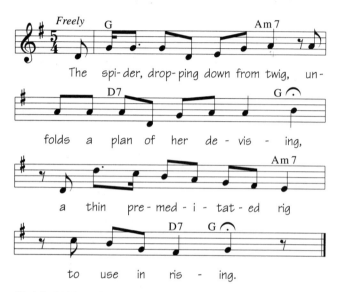

Words by E.B.White (1929) Music by Pete Seeger (1982)
Text © 1976 by E.B.White. Music © 1993 by Stormking Music Inc.

1. The spider, dropping down from twig,
   Unfolds a plan of her devising,
   A thin premeditated rig
   To use in rising.

2. And all that journey down through space,
   In cool descent and loyal hearted,
   She spins a ladder to the place
   From where she started.

3. Thus I, gone forth as spiders do
   In spider's web a truth discerning,
   Attach one silken thread to you
   For my return—ing.

I'm not the first songwriter to use the same tune for different sets of words. (George M. Cohan did it too.) Unwittingly, I put approximately the same tune to a famous 19th Century verse.

Flower in the Crannied Wall

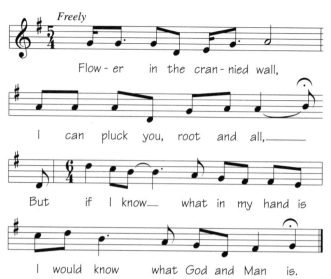

Words: Alfred Tennyson (1869) Music by Pete Seeger (1991)
© 1993 by Sanga Music Inc.

As long as we're into short songs, let me say that I think a better treatment of the same subject is an old English nursery rhyme. Some saucy young woman added a sprightly second verse.

Oats, Peas, Beans and Barley Grow

Traditional (English)

1. Oats, peas, beans and barley grow,
   Oats, peas, beans and barley grow,
   Nor you nor I nor anyone knows
   How oats, peas, beans and barley grow.

2. Now you're married you must obey,
   You must be true in all you say,
   You must be kind, you must be good,
   And make your husband chop the wood.

Starlight, Starbright

Star - light, star - bright, first star I see to-night,___ I wish I may,___ I wish I might___ have the wish I wish to-night,___ That al - ways may your love be shin - ing bright,___ Just like that first star that I see to - night.

Words (original verse): traditional
Music & additional verses by Pete Seeger (1951)
TRO - © 1962 (renewed) & 1965 (renewed) Ludlow Music, Inc., New York, NY.

1. Starlight, starbright, first star I see tonight,
   I wish I may, I wish I might, have the wish I wish
   tonight.
   That always may your love be shining bright
   Just like that first star that I see tonight.

2. Star peace, green peace, surely the wars will cease.
   We'll find a way, there'll come a day,
   when people every where will say
   Forever let us put an end to war
   Upon this one world that we're working for.

3. Star song, love song, I hope it won't be long
   Before you're home and in my arms;
   then we'll both be safe from harm
   And then we'll know our love is shining bright
   Just like that first star that I see tonight.

REPEAT FIRST VERSE

This next song is part of a TV playscript I once wrote—never performed. But it's a usable song. What a great melody! The tune is "Shoals of Herring" by the late Ewan MacColl.

Once again I ask myself: how does one make up a melody? Ewan, a great singer of Scottish ballads, made up songs all his life, without thinking anything of it, borrowing old melodies and changing them a bit, to fit his new lyrics.

Read his autobiography, *Journeyman*, Sidgwick and Jackson, Publishers, England, 1990. Fascinating.

EWAN MACCOLL & PEGGY SEEGER WITH THEIR SON NEILL, CA. 1960

In the Stillness of My Heart

In the still-ness of my heart I know It's with you my life I would be shar-ing, And if I know you'll be com-ing home,___ I would fol-low deeds of love and dar-ing.

Words by Pete Seeger (1972) Music by Ewan MacColl ("Shoals of Herring")
© 1962 (renewed) & 1993 by Stormking Music Inc.

Copyrights & Robberies, Part 2

Canadian singer Alan Mills was in London and visited Cecil Sharp House, headquarters of the English Folk Song and Dance Society.

"Oh, so you are Alan Mills, the man who claims to have written "The Old Woman Who Swallowed a Fly."

"But I did. I read the words in a magazine, put together by a woman who'd based her verses on an old children's rhyme. I added some verses and put a tune to it."

"Well, we've got a field recording in our library of an old man in Yorkshire singing it."

"Let me hear that recording," said Alan.

They checked. The man in Yorkshire was recorded one year after Burl Ives had a record out of the song — and Burl had learned the song a year earlier from Alan. The two versions were identical. It was obvious that the man in Yorkshire had somehow learned it from Burl's record.

When George Wein (founder of Newport Jazz Festival and Folk Festival) heard I'd listed "the Ballad of Barbara Allen" as P.D. (Public Domain—that is, not copyrighted), he emphatically said "You're wrong, Pete. You're giving money to Columbia Records. Columbia didn't write that song."

I can see his point. And in a social system where everything has to be owned and accounted for, to leave something "un-owned" means to simply abandon it and allow it to be mistreated.

Look what's happened to the air and water.

Someone called bluesman Muddy Waters long distance from London to Chicago when he heard Eric Clapton play some of Muddy's riffs. Muddy's voice came back very relaxed, over the wire. "Oh, that's fine. When you steal, steal with taste."

Lee Hays pointed out a great melody in Carl Sandburg's *The American Songbag*, (1927), which only had one partly-usable verse. He and I both worked on it through the years. Hey, check out the guitar part.

Times A-Getting Hard, Boys

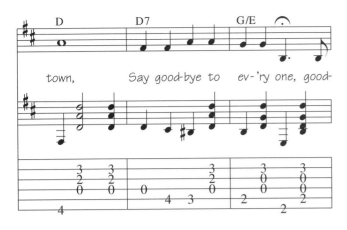

town,   Say good-bye to   ev-'ry one, good-

bye to ev-'ry one.

After changing individual notes in this guitar arrangement several times, I realized that I never play it twice the same. Neither should you.

2. Look-ing for the prom-ised land, some-

where be-yond the blue,   When I did-n't

find it, I came back to you.——

When I looked in - to your eyes, I

knew that I was home. When I looked in -

to your eyes, I knew that I was home.

New words & new music arrangement by Lee Hays. Second verse by Pete Seeger (1959)
TRO - © 1950 (renewed), 1977 & 1993 Folkways Music Publishers, Inc., New York, NY.

Perhaps a melody without words is as good a love song as any.

THE SEEGER HOME, 1950–88

"Living in the Country," the guitar piece on the next page, is one of the half dozen "compositions" in this book which have been interesting enough to be picked up and sung or played by others. Leo Kottke plays it quite fast. George Winston made a best-selling piano recording of it. The accent marks in the first few measures indicate that hidden in all these notes is a syncopated melody.

The piece came to me 35 years ago after listening to my younger sister Peggy sing and play a song collected by folklorists from African-American dockworkers off the coast of Georgia 60 years ago.

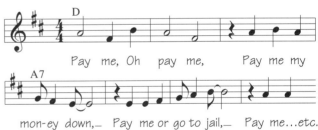

Pay me, Oh pay me,   Pay me my

mon-ey down,— Pay me or go to jail,— Pay me...etc.

If you analyze it, that's an Africanized version of one of the 19th century's most famous English sea chanteys, "Blow the Man Down."

Blow the man down, bul-lies, blow the man down,

After I heard my sister, I found myself fooling around on the guitar, and developing variations. Before the week was out, I had a new piece of music. Like the "original," it starts on the fifth note of the scale, has mainly descending phrases, except for the third phrase in each section, which tends to go up.

Check the Appendix if you want to puzzle out the tablature. Or listen to some of the recordings. (See Discography).

Living in the Country

By Pete Seeger (1958)   © 1962, 1963 (renewed) by Fall River Music Inc.

Why do I put the song in this chapter? Because of a beautiful counter melody made up by Frank Hamilton when we recorded it on two guitars for Folkways Records. It's *made* for a love song.

(My guitar melody)

(Frank's back-up guitar melody)

(More of Frank's melody)

Sooner or later someone will put words to it. Try these lyrics to Frank's "backup melody" above:

> If you would be patient and teach me
> I think that I could learn to dance (REPEAT THESE LINES)
> Who knows what then we might improvise?
> Who knows, who knows? We might improvise.

And who knows what other counter melodies may be improvised? Folk music is a very long chain.

Pete's 12-string guitar made by Bruce Taylor of Weston, CT. based on an earlier design by Stanley Francis of Liverpool, England.

Now comes an old Irish-American courting song. I made some sparkling banjo notes to introduce it.

The Leatherwing Bat

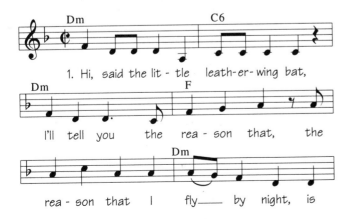

1. Hi, said the lit-tle leath-er-wing bat,

I'll tell you the rea-son that, the

rea-son that I fly—— by night, is

'cause I've lost my heart's de-light.——

CHORUS

Ow-dy dow—— a-did-dle-o day,

Ow-dy dow—— a-did-dle-o day,

Ow-dy dow—— a-did-dle-o day, and a

hey lee lee—— lee li lee-lo.

Collected, adapted & arranged by John A. Lomax & Alan Lomax
TRO - © 1947 (renewed) Ludlow Music, Inc., New York, NY.

1. Hi, said the little leatherwing bat
   I'll tell you the reason that
   The reason that I fly by night
   Is 'cause I've lost my heart's delight.

CHORUS (AFTER EACH VERSE):
Owdy dow a-diddle-o day
Owdy dow a-diddle-o day
Owdy dow a-diddle-o day
And a hey lee lee__ lee li lee-lo.

2. Hi, said the woodpecker settin' on a fence
   Once I courted a handsome wench
   But she got saucy and from me fled
   Ever since then my head's been red.

3. Hi, said the little bird so blue
   If I'd 'a' been a young man I'd 'a' had two
   So if one got saucy and wanted to go
   I'd have me a new__ string to my bow.

4. Hi, said the owl with head so white
   A lonesome day and a lonesome night
   I thought I heard some pretty girl say
   Court all night and sleep all day.

5. Hi, said the lonesome turtle dove
   I'll show you how to gain her love
   Keep her up both night and day
   Never give her time to say "go away."

I put this little banjo run together four decades ago and never figured a way to use it, except before and after singing the Leatherwing Bat. It should go lightning fast. It's an example of something you can do on a 5-string banjo.

The D Minor Flourish

Tuning—GCGBD capoed up to ADAC#E

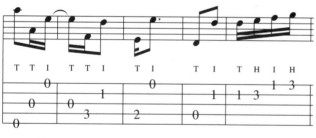

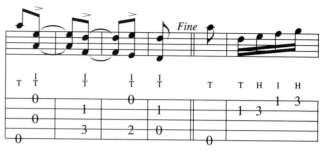

By Pete Seeger (1955)
TRO - © 1993 Melody Trails, Inc., New York, NY.

Sections #1, #2, and #3 can be juggled inter-change-ably. I played 'em for 40 years without analyzing what I was doing. Now it took me a whole day to try and write it down — still not correctly. For example, the three < < < accented notes in 2 should be more like triplets. Or maybe the four notes spread out over three short measures should be equal. I realize that as I play it, I'm still fooling around with the rhythm. It's fun to play.

The next one I thought I made up. I worked it out 30 years ago on the top strings of a guitar, and kept asking Irish friends if they knew what the melody was. No-one knew. I concluded that I must have made it up. The very month this book goes to press, friend Ernie Marrs identi-fied it: "The Memory of the Dead" or "Who Fears to Speak of 'Ninety-Eight," in Patrick Galvin's book *Irish Songs of Resistance*. Here's the 19th Century melody. It was written in 1843, words by John Kells Ingram, music by William Elliot Hudson.

The Memory Of The Dead

My version is only a little changed. I put it in this chapter because it has something of the yearning which Irish "slow airs" have. Here it is in the singable key of D.

An Irish Air

...and who'd_____ be-lieve I'd feel so good_____
_____ to dis-cov-er that I'd been wrong._____

Music by Pete Seeger (1975) derived from "The Memory of the Dead" ("Who Fears to Speak of '98") by William Elliot Hudson (1843)
New words added by Pete Seeger (1993)
TRO - © 1993 Melody Trails, Inc., New York, NY.

As you see, I had a few ideas for words to it but so far have lacked the inspiration or perspiration to complete them. I liked the way the end of the second line led into the beginning of the third line, and I liked even better the way the last note of the third line literally became the first note of the last line. If one used an ABAB rhyme pattern, you'd need a first line to rhyme with "who'd" (rude? food? lewd?) and a second line to rhyme with "wrong" (song? long? See next page). Such technicalities. They destroy the spirit of love.

Well, here's the tune as I originally made it up, for guitar in the unsingable (for me) key of A.

The tune returns to me at odd times — when I'm looking at something beautiful, or in bed half asleep, or I find myself with guitar in hand and nobody around. I think now that what I'm looking for — what so many writers look for — is the right story. It's probably lying in wait somewhere, hiding, wondering if I'll find it. Meanwhile I get distracted by jokes, such as the following. I read in the '70's about a bill proposed in Congress by Senator Fong of Hawaii, to try and stop the importing of counterfeit pop records from Hong Kong — not paying money to publishers nor anyone else who created the original hit record. Senator Fong wanted the bill co-sponsored by Senator Long of Louisiana and Senator Spong of Virginia, so it could be called the Long-Fong-Spong Hong Kong Song Bill.

There. Try writing a love song after that. But perhaps someone somewhere will find the right story. If I'm still around, let me know. I've told my publishers not to object if people want to sing their own words, even on the air — unless they are racist, sexist, violent, or otherwise stupid. But not let the song be recorded, at least not right away. Eventually there might be several sets of words floating around. Good.

I do better writing tunes for other people's words.

Some other love songs in this book are not in this chapter. Such as "False From True" (p.151). "A Little 'a' This 'n' That" (p. 256) is my best love song to Toshi. I usually dedicate it to all the cooks in the world.

I confess I don't like to categorize songs closely. How do you separate love of home, country, kids, love of O.F. (Old Forever)? The last song in this chapter is another kind of love song. A love song for the earth.

TOSHI SEEGER, 1965

This was written in 1967. I'd just returned from a tour in Japan. Early a.m., in a Hollywood motel, I pick up a copy of *Variety*, the entertainment business bible, famous for headlines like "Stix nix hix pix."

I leaf through it, see an ad from Yamaha, "Win a free trip to Japan! World song contest! Fill out these music staves with your song and mail it in to us!"

There was a page of blank music staves. I wrote this song and mailed it in. Never heard from them. But I won a prize — a song I've sung ever since. Here's a choral arrangement of it.

My Rainbow Race

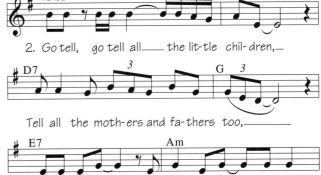

Words & music by Pete Seeger (1967)
© 1970 by Sanga Music Inc.

CHORUS:
One blue sky above us
One ocean lapping all our shore
One earth so green and round
Who could ask for more
And because I love you
I'll give it one more try
To show my rainbow race
It's too soon to die.

1. Some folks want to be like an ostrich,
    Bury their heads in the sand.
    Some hope that plastic dreams
    Can unclench all those greedy hands.
    Some hope to take the easy way:
    Poisons, bombs. They think we need 'em.
    Don't you know you can't kill all the unbelievers?
    There's no shortcut to freedom.

(REPEAT CHORUS)

2. Go tell, go tell all the little children.
    Tell all the mothers and fathers too.
    Now's our last chance to learn to share
    What's been given to me and you.

(REPEAT CHORUS ONE AND A HALF TIMES)

* I usually call out the phrases from now on, so the audience can sing
the chorus.

The Purposes of Music

(Charles Seeger was a bureaucrat in Washington 50 years ago, working for the WPA music project. He assigned a young musician, Margaret Valiant, to a community organizing job in the South with these words. I've put my own comments in italics. He wrote before the Walkman Revolution.)

1) Music, as any art, is not an end in itself, but is a means for achieving larger ends; *But many artists create for their own happiness.*

2) To *make* music is the essential thing — to listen to it is accessory; *But a mother sings, a baby listens.*

3) Music as a group activity is more important than music as an individual accomplishment.

4) Every person is musical; music can be associated with most human activity, to the advantage of both parties to the association.

5) The musical culture of the nation is, then, to be estimated upon the extent of participation of the whole population rather than upon the extent of the virtuosity of a fraction of it. *Many participate by dancing to the music. Perhaps others dance in their minds?*

6) The basis for musical culture is the vernacular of the broad mass of the people — its traditional (often called "folk") idiom; popular music and professional music are elaborate superstructures built upon the common base.

CHARLES LOUIS SEEGER

Photo by Robert Krones

7) There is no ground for the quarrel between the various idioms and styles, provided proper relationship between them is maintained — pop need not be scorned nor professional music artificially stimulated, nor folk music stamped out or sentimentalized.

8) The point of departure for any worker new to a community should be the tastes and capacities actually existent in the group; and the direction of the activities introduced should be more toward the development of local leadership than toward dependence upon outside help.

9) The main question, then, should be not "is it good music?" but "what is the music good for?"; and if it bids fair to aid in the welding of the people into more independent, capable and democratic action, it must be approved.

10) With these larger ends ever in view, musicians will frequently find themselves engaged in other kinds of activity, among them the other arts; this, however, promotes a well-rounded social function for them and ensures opportunity to make music serve a well-rounded function in the community.

You can see we're in little danger of getting overly sentimental in this chapter on love songs. Here's a story: Ammon Hennacy was a cheerful anarchist I met back in the 1950's. In the '60's, he ran a "halfway house" in Salt Lake City, called the Joe Hill House. I've quoted many times these next few sentences of his.

"Love. Courage. Wisdom. You need all three. Love alone is sentimentality, as in the average churchgoer. Courage alone is foolhardiness, as in the average soldier. Wisdom alone is cowardice, as in the average intellectual. You need all three."

Chapter V   New Tunes to Other's Words

Two hundred years ago in Scotland an old woman saw a man writing down the ballad she was singing, "Och, now ye've killed the song," she said. "Ye've wrote it down."

I'm glad to say she was wrong. Print and paper have sometimes crippled the folk process, but they haven't been able to kill it. What is this "folk process?" It is a process which has been going on for thousands of years. Ordinary people changing old things to fit new situations. Cooks translate old recipes to fit new stomachs. Lawyers translate old laws to fit new citizens. No, in spite of priest and politician, change goes on. In spite of tape, disc and computer, change goes on. And my hope is that if you like music (melodies, harmonies, rhythms) and if you enjoy using words, knowing that they also are slippery, changeable, unreliable things, you will enjoy using these songs to help build a world free of poverty, a world of peace, a world free of pollution. (Realizing too that the last 18 words can mean 18 different things to different people.)

Tradition! The show *Fiddler on the Roof* had a whole song about it. Some traditions should live: our love for working together, playing, singing together. Some traditions deserve to live only in history books: the idea that you should put to death someone you think you hate.

When Woody Guthrie made up a song, more often than not he put new words to an old melody, often without thinking of what the old song was. He'd be thinking of his new words. In the back of his mind were a bunch of good old melodies floating around; he'd reach up, pull one down and try it out. In Oregon, in '41 he wrote:

I said to him, Woody, isn't that almost the same tune as Leadbelly's "Irene"? He said "Sure 'nuff. Hadn't noticed it."

Brownie McGhee remembers singing with Woody an old gospel hymn:

Which is possibly where he got the tune for "This Land is Your Land." On the other hand, he might have been inspired by a similar song elsewhere. A half-dozen other songs have similar melodies.

Woody's "Union Maid" used the melody of "Red Wing" (whose 1907 author may have heard Schubert's "The Happy Plowman.")

Woody heard Burl Ives sing "The Blue Tailed Fly" (which Alan Lomax taught to Burl).

Jim-my Crack Corn, and I don't care

And not one, but several of Woody's children's songs are based on this tune:

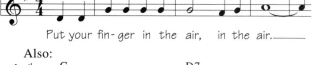

Put your fin-ger in the air, in the air.___

Also:

Jig, jig-a-jig-jig, Jig-a-long home,

"Put Your Finger in the Air" by Woody Guthrie TRO © 1954 (renewed) Folkways Music Publishers, Inc.
"Jig Along Home" by Woody Guthrie TRO © 1951 (renewed) Ludlow Music, Inc.

"Reuben James" might have been inspired by the tune of "Wildwood Flower," recorded by the Carter Family.

I will twine with my ring-lets of wav-y brown hair.

But Woody's tune is more than a bit different.

Have you heard of a

ship called the good Reu-ben James?

"Reuben James" by Woody Guthrie © 1942 (renewed) MCA Music Publishing.

Woody once joked about another songwriter, "Oh, he just steals from me. But I steal from everybody. I'm the biggest song-stealer there ever was."

Nearly always he would change the old tune slightly to make it fit his words better. Sometimes he'd sing an old song and gradually change the earlier tune. He heard the record of Blind Lemon Jefferson's "One Dime Blues."

I'm broke and I ain't___ got a dime!

I'm broke and I ain't got a dime___

After a year of Woody's singing, it came out more like:

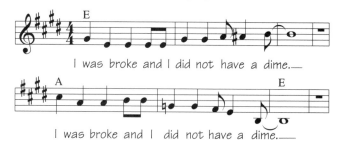

I was broke and I did not have a dime.___

I was broke and I did not have a dime.___

And then he made up some new verses. It ended up like a new song. He changed it to a four-line blues; the new first verse he'd sing like this:

Stand-ing down in New York Town one day,___

Stand-ing down in New York Town one day.___

Stand-ing down in New York Town___ one

day,___ Well, it's hey, hey, hey, hey.

"New York Town" by Woody Guthrie TRO © 1961 (renewed) & 1964 (renewed) Ludlow Music, Inc.

Woody wrote the verses of "So Long, It's Been Good to Know You," using the melody of Carson Robinson's "Ballad of Billy the Kid." Then he created a great chorus using some elements of that melody, but adding some wonderful new notes.

Same way with "Reuben James." He wrote about 10 or 15 verses telling the names of all 40 men who were drowned when the ship was sunk. The rest of the Almanac Singers, including me, complained that nobody but him would sing it that way. "Give us a chorus we can join in on." And he obliged, building his great singing chorus on some of the melodic elements of the verses (see p. 26).

Leadbelly did the same thing. Every song he ever sang he remolded to fit his voice and his 12-string guitar. Check p. 64, "Kisses Sweeter Than Wine."

After many decades and becoming slightly acquainted with the music traditions of several continents, I realized that some traditions assume that improvisation and change are the normal way to make music.

But keep in mind: some other traditions pride themselves on changing the music or words as little as possible. "I'm passing this song on to you exactly as I learned it. Don't you change it." And this is good too.

Forty years ago I learned the Seneca canoe song "Ka-yo-wa-ji-neh," from Tehanetorens (Ray Fadden). I have tried to teach it to others exactly as I learned it.

Kayowajineh

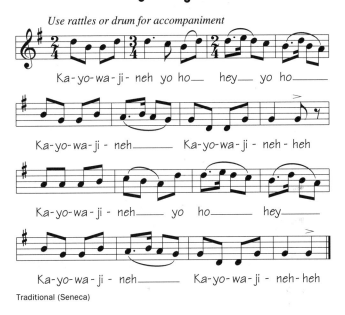

Traditional (Seneca)

Sometimes I'll play a melody on the recorder, knowing I'll never be able to sing the "original" words, but trying to play it (as near as I can remember) just as I heard it. Here's a "slow air" from Ireland or Scotland. A Catskill lumberman, George Edwards, remembered his mother singing it. He called it:

The Hills of Glenshee

Traditional

And here's a slow air from Ireland as I heard Canadian Ed McCurdy sing it. (Old friend Ed in 1949 wrote the anti-war classic "Last Night I Had the Strangest Dream.")

My Lagan Love

Traditional (Irish)

I feel the melody is far greater than any words put to it, but here's some of the old words Ed sings.

> Where Lagan stream sings lullaby
> There grows a lily fair
> The twilight gleam is in her eye
> the night is on her hair…
>
> …There on the cricket singing stone
> She stirs the bog wood fire
> And hums in sad sweet undertone
> The song of heart's desire

What does "freely" (at upper left) mean? An imperiodic rhythm (CLS). Some notes unexpectedly held longer or shorter than strict rhythm would have them. In other words, the notes never have twice exactly the same time value or meter. The time value of the notes can change — but beware changing more. *Don't* tap your foot.

Do you know any recorder players? Show them this. That's why I put it up in such a high key — for soprano or tenor recorders. Same fingering on an alto recorder gives you the key of A — much easier to sing in.

Here's another slow melody from halfway 'round the world. Unless you are familiar with Japanese traditions, again I'd suggest not changing it. (On the other hand as I was pasting this book together I heard a Led Zeppelin tape on which guitarist Jimmy Page improvised for six and a half minutes on the Irish air "She Moved Through the Fair." So maybe my theories are all wet.)

Nevertheless I've enjoyed playing "Kuroda Bushi" for a third of a century without wanting to change a note. It's a 400-year-old song, I'm told.

Kuroda Bushi

Traditional (Japanese)

When in Japan I asked them why they didn't ever try putting new words to some of their old melodies, they were shocked at the idea. I related this to my father. He replied, "You see, for them the old is so very old, and the new is so very new."

I think this is not the whole reason. It's also that the "old" songs for many people are regarded like religion. You tend to accept a religion or reject it; you don't try to change it. Except nowadays. Hooray for the folk process in religion. Politics, too.

In early times human beings lived in separate tribes with separate languages and folkways. It was unthinkable to adopt another tribe's way of dressing, eating, singing. But several thousand years ago around the Mediterranean Sea, different cultures started borrowing from each other on a large scale. Words, architecture, foods. From Africa, from Asia. After the Roman Empire fell, the tradition of borrowing continued in Europe. The windmill came to Holland from Persia in the 11th century. Soon after, gypsies brought the guitar to Spain. Genghis Khan's warriors brought the fiddle, and perhaps pasta, though Marco Polo, 90 (80?) years later, is usually credited with this.

So now you can see what led to the song on p. 14 ("All Mixed Up"). One line in the song is disputed. "The stories behind the word 'Okay' are as varied as the imaginations of the lexicographers who penned them. A native American contender: In the Choctaw language 'oke' meant 'it is' or 'it is so.' The Choctaw language served as the trade language in the Southeast and 'oke' signified that the two parties were in agreement." (Jack Weatherford in *Native Roots*, © Crown Publishers).

At any rate, credit that old racist, President Andrew Jackson, (he'd spent years in the Southeast Indian Wars), for signing state papers "O.K., Andrew Jackson" and starting its career as the world's most famous word.

Sometimes the folkways are so different that the people despise each other for centuries. (No. *Millennia*.) Irish poet Shaemas O'Sheel was infuriated by Beethoven's arrangements of Irish tunes. "That damn German stamping music! They never should have let him near those delicate Celtic melodies." In the years 300–600 A.D. the Celts fought the invading Angles and Saxons every inch of the way. The invaders must have despised the Celts too. There are only a few dozen Gaelic words in the English language ("Hooligan" is one).

I had an Irish great-great-grandmother, and a German great-great-grandfather. Long live Romeo and Juliet.

I met Alex Comfort in London, 1959. Yes, the same guy who 15 years later wrote *The Joy of Sex*. He's a mathematician too. Another cheerful anarchist. Wrote some hilarious songs when part of the Campaign For Nuclear Disarmament led by Bertrand Russell in the 1950's. Described himself as a longtime writer of verses-sung-in-the-bathroom. Lo and behold, a year or so later I got these verses from him, asking if I could make up a tune. It's still sung, although not always with the same exact words, as you'll see.

Nina Simone started singing this next song in the '60's and still sings it the way Alex Comfort wrote it. "One man's hands can't tear a prison down/Two men's hands can't tear a prison down/but if two and two...etc." Today I make so bold as to keep Alex's great three-syllable title but amend the rest of the words.

Of course you can switch things around as you want when you (I mean *you*) sing it. You might also consider

Alan Lomax's opinion that the American vowel "a" as in "cat" and "hat" is the most important vowel in American folksong — more than "oo" or "ee," which many lyricists aim at. ("June-Moon-croon-spoon" — also "thee, me, lea, sea.") Alan feels it's no accident that "This <u>land</u> is your <u>land</u>" proved so popular. And John Henry died with a <u>hammer</u> in his <u>hand</u>.

Editor:

In the October 1990 issue of this Magazine, pg. 262, the American folksinger Pete Seeger's "If two and two and fifty make a million" is followed by a suggestion for "readers...to try." Perhaps it is as simple as one-two-three: indeed 1, 2, 3 are exponents in the product $2^1 \times 2^2 \times 50^3$ which equals an exact million.

Prem N. Bajaj
Wichita State University

One Man's Hands

Original lyrics by Alex Comfort
Music (1961) by Pete Seeger Lyrics adapted by Staughton Lynd
© 1962 Fall River Music Inc.

1. Just my hands can't tear a prison down
   Just your hands can't tear a prison down
   CHORUS (AFTER EACH VERSE):
   But if two and two and fifty make a million
   We'll see that day come round
   We'll see that day come round.

2. Just my voice can't shout to make them hear
   Just your voice...etc.

3. Just my strength can't ban the atom bomb...

4. Just my strength can't break the color bar...

5. Just my strength can't roll the union on...

6. Just my feet can't walk across the land...

7. Just my eyes can't see the future clear...

REPEAT FIRST VERSE

Melodies #2

How *does* one think up a tune? Here's a few "melody games" you might try playing:

1) Try improvising variations on any tune you know, or are listening to. This is no more than any jazz musician does. Try imagining you are a musician from a different tradition or a different part of the world. How would *they* change that tune?

2) Try slowing a tune down, or speeding it up. Put it in a different "mode," major or minor. Start by changing one or two notes in the beginning, middle, or end. Then change whole phrases. You don't need to have accompaniment. Try it when driving a car, improvising changes in tunes you know. Of course, more often than not you'll decide the original tune was better. But you'll soon find what a different effect you get by just changing a few notes.

3) Here's a game I've often played when driving a car: put tunes to words on highway billboards. Pretend it's a singing commercial you hear on the air. You can play the same game leafing through magazines or newspapers. Sing the headlines. What you'll decide is what the world's best composers have long known: it's easy to make up a half-good melody. But to make up an unforgettable one takes luck, and for all anyone knows, help from The Great Unknown. Nevertheless, I agree with Thomas Edison. (Genius is 5 percent inspiration and 95 percent perspiration.) Practice may not make perfect, but it sure as hell makes for improvement.

Wimoweh
(Mbube)

I've been guilty many times in my life of not passing on a song quite correctly. Here's an example.

In 1949 I was in bed with a bad cold. Alan Lomax came in with a dozen 78 RPM records. "Pete, you might like to listen to these. Up at Decca Records they were going to throw them out, they're commercial records from South Africa."

What an ear-opener! No drums, no instrumental accompaniment. Choirs. Vocal quartets, quintets. Beautiful rocking rhythm. Rich harmonies.

With nothing to do but stay in bed and get over a cold, I listened to them over and over, transcribed the music on to staff notation and wrote down the African words as best I could. Found one song which had only a single word. I taught the song to the Weavers. Two years later I met an official of the Gallo Record Company in New York trying to drum up business. I asked him what the word meant.

"The lion is sleeping, the lion, the lion," says he.

"Do Africans ever try to put political words in their songs?" I asked.

"Oh, they try it all the time, but we weed it out."

A year or two later I read a book by a Swedish missionary, deploring the South African churches which had seceded from the missions. "The dangerous nationalistic tendencies in the native churches can be seen by the fact that one of the leading native churches is named the 'Zulu Chaka Church.' Chaka, known as 'the lion,' was the last great king of the Zulus, 150 years ago, and when he died the legend arose that the Lion was not dead; he was only sleeping, and would some day wake up."

It's easy to see, here's another song of hope, sung by an oppressed people, in spite of commercial censorship.

Then in 1980 I met a group of young South African exiles, living in New York City, and learned from them that at one point on the original recording, Solomon Linda calls out "*You are the lion! You are a lion!*"

If you want to hear how Solomon Linda did it, you can hear his 1940's hit record on Rounder Records. And Ladysmith Black Mambazo also sings it. And the old Weavers version is still available. (See Discography).

What did I do wrong? For one thing, I didn't sing the words of the bass part correctly. I sang:

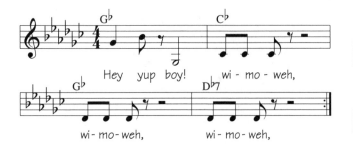

I sang, "Hey yup boy!" It should have been "M-bu-be wo!" And, not knowing Zulu, I omitted completely Solomon Linda's beautiful slow, introduction to the song, where he calls to the people, "You are a lion!"

Nowadays I can no longer hit the high notes, but I've found a way choruses can get an audience singing with them. Pitch it higher, up in A, so *all* the men in the audience can sing the great bass part. These are the correct Zulu words:

And now's a good time to point out the importance of the 1/8 rest, ⅞ . It's "wim," not "weem." *Don't* sing it this way:

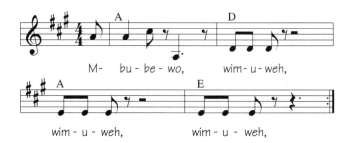

After three or four repetitions, all the men in the audience know it. Then teach *all* the women on one side of the audience the low tenor part. Although it's a high note for men's voices, it's a low note for women to sing. The South African "B" is so soft it's like an English "W."

After the women on one side learn it, teach all the women on the other side of the audience a higher tenor part.

Get the two groups of women singing their parts together a few times. Add the men's part, the bass.

The above three parts never stop. They continue throughout the entire song.

With the help of a few altos and basses in your chorus, keep the audience singing these three parts throughout the song. Now comes the excitement. There are two high parts, each four measures long — repeated for a total of eight measures — which alternate. Have the sopranos in your chorus sing the part which Solomon Linda would do in his falsetto.

Oo——————————— (voices break to open tone)

Then let them rest their voices for eight measures, while some open-voice altos take the other high part. Solomon Linda would do this in his "open" voice, not falsetto. Again, twice through, eight measures. If there's a tenor who thinks he can sing this high note, let him join the altos. Watch he doesn't strain his voice, though. Linda lost his voice. I did, too.

Ah,—— Ah,—— Ah,—— Ah,—— Ah,—

————————————— (all open tones)

Now while the altos rest their voices, the sopranos do their part twice again.

After these two lead parts have alternated three or four times, then comes a lovely countermelody which altos and sopranos can sing together (Solomon Linda sang it falsetto).

Oo——————————

oo—————— (stay in falsetto, men)

Please don't sing it the way the American pop record had it: "In the jungle, the mighty jungle, the lion sleeps tonight…" etc.

This trivializes a song of great historical importance. There's no jungle around Johannesburg, and never was. This song will be sung for centuries — by the entire world.

How to end it? I'd let both the high parts sing at once. At the end have a slight ritard. The whole chorus sings the one word slowly. Wi-mo-wehhh…! swooping to a couple of final low notes.

(open tone, not falsetto)

Ah,— Ah,— Ah,— Ah,— Ah,— Ah,— Ah,

(entire chorus and audience) Wi - mo- weh.

Words & music by Solomon Linda (early 1940's)
Arranged & adapted by Ronnie Gilbert, Lee Hays, Fred Hellerman & Pete Seeger (1949)
TRO - © 1951 (renewed) & 1952 (renewed) Folkways Music Publishers, Inc., NY, NY.

SOLOMON LINDA & THE EVENING BIRDS

In '64, in Dar Es Salaam, East Africa, I sang for a group of exiled South Africans, and felt much honored when they asked me to sing this song. "I don't know the right words." "That's okay; you have the rhythm" And as they sang along, they put their arms around each other's shoulders and did a simple dance — a few steps forward, a few steps back.

They didn't want me to stop. I sang it for eight minutes. Was hoarse for a week.

You'll be glad to know that Solomon Linda's family still receives royalties for the song. (Though in 1992 George Weiss of The Tokens won a court action giving him the right to collect royalties for the song when the recording uses his words "In the Jungle..." etc.)

But in 1951 there was a check for about $1,000 royalties because of the Weavers' recording of the song. I told the N.Y. publisher "Don't send it to Gallo Records; Linda won't get a cent."

"Get Linda's address; we'll send the check directly to him." said Al Brackman.

Through a friend in South Africa, I contacted Harry Bloom, a lawyer who had defended Africans in Civil Rights cases. "I can't promise anything, but I'll try," wrote Bloom.

Four months later he found Linda. He'd lost his voice — probably sang "Mbube" too many times without a microphone — and was working as a stock clerk for Gallo, for a few pounds a week.

Coincidentally, a Union of South African Artists was being formed to get better contracts from recording companies. The check was presented to Linda at a grand opening celebration.

There's more to the story. In the course of trying to find Linda, Bloom met a number of musicians, including Hugh Masekela. Bloom said "I've got an idea for an opera. Can you do the music for it?"

The resulting show, about a prizefighter nicknamed *King Kong*, was a hit and ran for two years in Johannesburg. The female lead was a hitherto unknown singer named Miriam Makeba.

In the '60's Bloom had to flee the land of apartheid. I met him in London. He told me a story I'll not forget as long as I live. Once an African friend burst into his office, out of breath and in great agitation. Harry said, "What's the matter? Catch your breath. Can I do anything to help?" Finally his friend got his breath.

"No, there's nothing anyone can do...But something terrible has happened...I was on that long escalator in the department store across the street...Just ahead of me was an elderly woman. She put her hand to her face and closed her eyes. I said to myself, that woman is going to faint. I put my hand out to steady her, and saw my black hand next to her white skin, and thought 'What if she should scream?' There would be no help for me. I looked around. There

was no one else on the escalator. I withdrew my hand. And she did faint.

"And she tumbled, tumbled, tumbled, all the way to the bottom."

And this is the problem for you, for me, for every soul. In a world of hate, doing a good deed may endanger your life.

The next song was written at the request of Moses Asch, head of Folkways Records. In 1950 he had paid Woody Guthrie a small stipend to go up to Massachusetts, do some investigating, and write songs about the famous Sacco-Vanzetti case. Two Italian anarchists were charged with murder, framed and executed in 1927. After Woody returned to New York Moe asked me, "Do you think you could put a tune to this? It's a letter from Nicola Sacco to his 12-year-old son."

NICOLA SACCO & FAMILY, 1922

By omitting a word here and there, or adding one, I found I could make it scan, if not rhyme. I recorded it for Moe, and he added the song to the record of Woody's about the Sacco-Vanzetti case. Almost 30 years later a couple in Maryland, Terry Leonino and Greg Artzner, who sing as a duo called "Magpie," started singing it. I heard them rehearsing it at the People's Music Weekend one January. To my surprise and delight I realized what an Italian-type melody I'd put together; they sang it in two-part harmony, which I give here. The melody is on the bottom, that is, the lower of the two notes given. It's not so hard as it looks. Just keep the rhythm steady.

Sacco's Letter To His Son
(as sung by Magpie)

Words by Niccola Sacco (1927)   Music by Pete Seeger (1951)
Harmony by Greg Artzner and Terry Leonino
Transcription by Marcia Diehl and Greg Artzner
© 1960 (renewed) by Stormking Music Inc.

* Add or subtract notes in the melody to fit the syllables in the verses.
The asterisks show where the underlined syllables will fall.

**Here are examples of where extra beats are needed to fit the lyrics.

1. If nothing happens they will electrocute us right after midnight
   Therefore here I am, right with you, with love** and with open heart,
   As I was yesterday.
   Don't cry, Dante, for many, many tears have been wasted,
   As your mother's tears have been already wasted for seven years,
   And never did any good.
   > So son, instead of crying, be strong, be brave
   > So as to be able to comfort your mother.

2. And when you want to distract her from the discouraging soleness
   You take her for a long walk in the quiet countryside,
   Gathering flowers here and there.
   And resting under the shade of trees, beside the music of the waters,
   The peacefulness of nature, she will enjoy it very much,
   As you will surely too.
   > But son, you must remember: Don't use all yourself.
   > But down yourself, just one** step, to help the weak ones at your side.

3. The weaker ones, that cry for help, the persecuted and the victim.
   They are your friends, friends of yours and mine, they are the comrades that fight,
   Yes, and sometimes fall.
   Just as your father, your father and Bartolo have fallen,
   Have fought and fell, yesterday, for the conquest of joy,
   Of freedom for all.
   > In the struggle of life you'll find, you'll find more love.
   > And in the struggle, you will be loved also.

For 40 years Lee Hays (1913-1981) and I knew each other, sang together off and on, tried making up songs together occasionally. This next poem of his I've often recited at concerts. I tried putting a tune to it; decided it was better simply recited as a poem.

To Know Good Will

If I should one day die by violence,
Please take this as my written will;
And in the name of simple common sense
Treat my killer only as one ill,
As one who needs far more than I could give,
As one who never really learned to live
In charity and peace and love for life,
But was diseased and plagued by hate and strife.
My vanished life might have some meaning still
When my destroyer learns to know good will.

By Lee Hays
© 1987 by Sanga Music Inc.

LEE HAYS, 1980

I'm glad I was able to find a singable melody for this next gem of Lee's. He sent it as a letter to my wife, also a gardener.

In Dead Earnest
(Lee's Compost Song)

Words by Lee Hays (1979)   Music by Pete Seeger (1979)
© 1981, 1982 by Sanga Music Inc.
* I find I can omit the last two lines.

If I should die before I wake,
All my bone and sinew take
Put me in the compost pile
To decompose me for a while
   Worms, water, sun, will have their way,
   Returning me to common clay
   All that I am will feed the trees
   And little fishies in the seas.
When radishes and corn you munch,
You may be having me for lunch
And then excrete me with a grin,
Chortling, "There goes Lee again."
   'Twill be my happiest destiny
   To die and live eternally.

Lee was raised in Arkansas, son of a Methodist preacher. A great story teller. In the mid-'30's Lee taught at Commonwealth College, a small Arkansas labor school.

It was forced to close by the Klu Klux Klan. A good biography of Lee, *Lonesome Traveller*, by Doris Kaplan, was published by W. W. Norton, reissued by the University of Nebraska Press. I used to think he was cantankerous. Now I think he was some kind of genius.

Lee Hays and I had a long friendship with Walter and Lillian Lowenfels of Philadelphia. Walter had been an expatriate avant-garde poet in Paris in the 1920's. Shared a poetry prize with e. e. cummings. Returned home a communist, spent 15 years editing the Pennsylvania edition of *The Daily Worker*. In his last years went back to poetry, put out some wonderful books, such as *Walt Whitman's Civil War*, and *Letters to My Twelve Grandchildren*.

Business

English translation by Walter Lowenfels (from the French of Guillevic)
Music by Pete Seeger (1961)
© 1963 (renewed) by Stormking Music Inc.

Two million bushels of North African grain
Resold to Germany for Swiss francs,
Paid for by a consortium of banks
With a deal in futures that the Stock Exchange
Unloads for coffee from Brazilian uplands
Destined for Paris. Before the whole deal sinks,
The checks written in indelible inks
Outrace Atlantic's winter hurricanes.

    At last the coffee arrives, also the wheat,
    Needless to say, the deal was a success.
    Who can deny that all of us have gained?
    Our benefactors? Three trusts. They compete
    For honor, glory, power and of course,
    Profits, where all happiness is contained.

WALTER LOWENFELS IN THE 1940'S

Touring Japan in 1967 I met a young professor, Yuzuru Katagiri, publishing a literary magazine in English (!). I'm a magazinaholic; I subscribed. Shortly after, I read this poem. I got permission to record it back then for Columbia Records. Don't be scared off because it looks like a long song; it's got four short verses, each slightly different from the other.

When I Was Most Beautiful

Words by Noriko Ibaragi (1957) Music by Pete Seeger (1967)
TRO - © 1968 & 1970 Melody Trails, Inc., New York, NY.

1. When I__ was most beautiful,
   Cities were falling
   And from unexpected places
   Blue sky was seen
   When I__ was most beautiful
   People around me were killed
   And for paint and powder
   I lost the chance__

2. When I __ was most beautiful
   Nobody gave me kind gifts.
   Men knew only to salute
   And went away.
   When I__ was most beautiful
   My country lost the war
   I paraded the main street
   With my blouse sleeves rolled high__

3. When I__ was most beautiful
   (IN TEMPO) Jazz overflowed the radio;
   I broke the prohibition against smoking;
   Sweet music of another land!
   (FREELY) When I__ was most beautiful
   I was most unhappy__
   I was quite absurd__
   I was quite lonely__

4. That's why I decided to live long
   Like Monsieur Rouault,
   Who was a
   Very old man,
   When he painted such terribly beautiful pictures,
   You see_____
   _____
   _____?

I accompany this in "Dropped D" tuning, and capo up so I'm really playing in F. Here's how the words to the 2nd and 3rd verses fit to the music:

In case some reader knows Japanese, here's the original poem.

My guess is that no two people will accompany it in the same way — though I hope they won't tamper with the words. I make the accompaniment more rhythmical in the beginning of the third verse, where the words are about jazz. Sometimes I whistle an interlude between verses.

I'm told that the words are very good in Japanese — but I doubt they fit this melody. Noriko Ibaragi is now a well-known poet. She wrote this when she was 31. Her publishers are Shicho-sha, 3-15, Sadohara-cho Ichigaya, Shinjuku-ku, Tokyo, Japan. In 1984 on another tour, she came to my concert, recited the original poem in Japanese, and then I sang this afterwards.

Incidentally, most of my life I've been prejudiced against high endings. But this one works. Pianissimo.

The poem is a good answer to the English poet (male) who tossed off the line, "Women are. Men do."

NORIKO IBARAGI

Idris Davies, a coal miner in Wales, was a friend of Dylan Thomas. I came across his poem reprinted in one of Thomas' essays. After the failure of the British general strike of 1926, Idris Davies, then a teenager, determined to leave coal mining. He studied nights for four years, and finally passed his examination to Nottingham University. After graduation, he became a school teacher in London, and published three slim volumes of poetry. Died of cancer at the young age of 44.

In 1960 Toshi and I were able to visit Mrs. Davies, Idris's mother, still living in Rhymney — a typical coal mine town: 50 yards wide and one mile long. Caerphilly is nearby, famous for a type of cheese. Cardiff and Newport are on the Bay of Bristol. Wye is a more prosperous valley 50 miles east.

Bells of Rhymney

3. Throw the vandals in court, say the bells of New-port. All would be well if if if if if if, cry the green bells of Car-diff, Why so wor-ried, sis-ters, why?— sang the sil-ver bells of Wye.— And what will you give me? — say the sad bells of Rhym-ney.

Coda—Keep the rhythm going to the end

(whistle)

Words from *Gwalia Deserta* by Idris Davies (written ca. 1927, pub. 1938)
Music by Pete Seeger (1959)
TRO - © 1959 (renewed) & 1964 (renewed) Ludlow Music, Inc., New York, NY.

Map by Peter Blood

IDRIS DAVIES

1. Oh what will you give me?
   Say the sad bells of Rhymney
   Is there hope for the future?
   Cry the brown bells of Merthyr.
   Who made the mine owner?
   Say the black bells of Rhondda.
   And who robbed the miner?
   Cry the grim bells of Blaina.

2. They will plunder willy-nilly,
   Cry the bells of Caerphilly.
   They have fangs, they have teeth,
   Shout the loud bells of Neath.
   Even God is uneasy,
   Say the moist bells of Swansea.
   And what will you give me,
   Say the sad bells of Rhymney.

3. Throw the vandals in court
   Say the bells of Newport.
   All would be well if, if, if,
   Cry the green bells of Cardiff.
   Why so worried, sisters why?
   Sang the silver bells of Wye.
   And what will you give me?
   Say the sad bells of Rhymney.

The tune came to me once on tour, in Montreal. Thanks to my pocket notebook I had the rest of the words at hand. That night I stuck the words to the microphone and tried them out.

Pronounce Rhymney more like "Rhuhmney," Caerphilly like "Caffilly," and Swansea like "Swanzy." The "r's" tend to be rolled. Rhondda sounds more like "Rhundtha."

Here's tablature for the accompaniment:

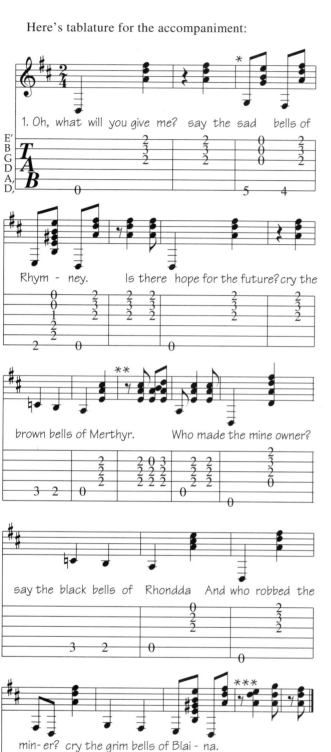

The accents are to remind you that these syncopated notes are the ones which really sound out.

Then I strike some full chords up the neck:

Oh,...what...

After singing all three verses I usually break into a regular rhythm, thumb on bass strings, index finger on top strings.

At first you see a rhythmic version of the pattern given in the chord diagrams on the next page (***).

Continue this rhythmic pattern while repeating all or some of the three verses again. You can add or subtract beats as you want, while keeping the rhythm steady. I usually end by whistling a few measures against the pounding guitar.

My accompaniment for "The Bells of Rhymney" was worked out on a 12-string guitar, which is customarily tuned lower than a 6-string. Thus D position turned out to sound B flat, a comfortable key for me to sing the song. On a 6-stringer, you either have to sing in a tenor range, or re-tune strings, or else capo way up (to sing it in G, for example). Or else figure out a new accompaniment. Here are my chords. Tuning: DADGBE.

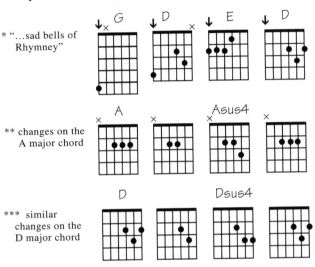

* "...sad bells of Rhymney"

** changes on the A major chord

*** similar changes on the D major chord

As a teenager I had a scholarship in an unusual prep school, Avon Old Farms, near Hartford, Connecticut. Ninety students. Best thing about it, for me, was 3,000 acres of woodland, with a small river. I could explore, camp out, snowshoe in winter. It also had some unusual teachers, including Harold Lewis Cook, poet and a friend of other poets like Edna St. Vincent Millay and Max Eastman. In Cook's English classes we'd spend three months reading and discussing in depth one Shakespeare play. One year it might be *Hamlet, Macbeth*, another year *Romeo and Juliet*, or *The Tempest*. Occasionally today I find myself rereading World Famous Will, impatient sometimes with his archaic language, his wordiness, but rewarded with some fantastic lines: "...to sleep,...perchance to dream...aye, there's the rub..." (Hamlet is contemplating suicide.)

In 1965 I stole his phrase for another idea:

To fight, perchance to win, aye, there's the rub
For victory brings power and prestige
And the children of the children of the fighters
Take all for granted, and in turn, oppress.

Around 1955, singing at another prep school, in Woodstock, Vermont, I found myself at another English class, with teacher Buffy Dunker. Together we put a tune to the song of Ariel in *The Tempest*. I'm sure other musicians have tried also; I don't know how this tune compares. It has worked for me.

Full Fathom Five

Words by William Shakespeare (1611, from "The Tempest")
Music by Pete Seeger & students of Woodstock School (1954)
© 1962, 1963 (renewed) by Fall River Music Inc.

Full fathom five thy father lies;
   Of his bones are coral made:
Those are pearls that were his eyes:
   Nothing of him that doth fade,
But doth suffer a sea-change
Into something rich and strange.
Sea-nymphs hourly ring his knell: Ding-dong.
Hark! now I hear them — ding-dong, bell.

World Savers have to guard against being unremittingly serious, but in nearly every concert program I give, I try to put in one deadly serious song. This is one. The words were given me in the spring of '74. An English translation of the last poem by Victor Jara, killed by Chilean fascists in September, 1973.[1]

VICTOR & JOAN JARA WITH THEIR DAUGHTERS

Victor was singing for students at the university when the whole area was surrounded. All within were taken prisoner and marched to a large indoor soccer stadium, Estadio Chile. For three days it was a scene of horror. Torture, executions.

An officer thought he recognized Victor, pointed at him with a questioning look and motioning as if strumming a guitar. Victor nodded. He was seized, taken to the center of the stadium and told to put his hands on a table. While his friends watched in horror, rifle butts beat his hands to bloody pulp.

"All right, sing for us now, you ——," shouted the officer. Victor staggered to his feet, faced the stands.

"Compañeros, let's sing for el commandante."

Waving his bloody stumps, he led them in the anthem of Salvador Allende's Popular Unity Party. Other prisoners hesitantly joined in.

RAT-TAT-TAT-TAT.

The guards sprayed him and the stands with machine guns.

This last poem of his was smuggled out of Chile, in several different versions. This translation was given to me by a woman at a Chicago concert in 1974. A few minutes later I stuck the words on a mike stand and improvised a guitar accompaniment as I recited them. Over a week of reciting, the chords took the form given here. (Dropped D tuning: DADGBE).

---

[1] On this date General Pinochet, with the assistance of the CIA and the ITT Corporation, took over the government of Chile, bombing the presidential palace of elected socialist Salvador Allende, and murdering him.

After reciting this, any applause is impossible.

I usually swing right into an upbeat song like "Guantanamera," which everyone can sing with me.

Years later I got Victor's original words. Mine are much shorter, as you see. I wish I knew who made the translation I was given. Gracias, anónima amiga! If you read this, get in touch.

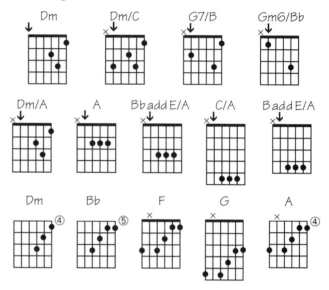

Estadio Chile

Spoken poem with guitar accompaniment.
Exact timing of the words would have to be improvised,
or learned from the recording.

Sample accompaniment, verse:

We_____   are five thousand...

Accompaniment, bridge:

The military   carry out their

plans with precision   Blood   is...

Later:

O my God   Is this the world you created?...

Words by Victor Jara (1973)   Musical setting by Pete Seeger (1974)
© 1975 Mighty Oak Music Ltd., London, England
TRO - Cheshire Music, Inc., New York, controls all publication rights for the USA & Canada.

```
     Dm              Dm/C
1.  We are 5,000__ here in this little part of the city
     G7/B                    Gm6/Bb
    We are 5,000__ how many more will there be?

            Dm/A                    A
    In the whole city, and the country 10,000 hands
     BbaddE/A                    C/A
    Which could seed the fields, make run the factories.

          BaddE/A              BbaddE/A
    How much humanity__ now with hunger, pain, panic
                           A
        and terror?


     Dm                        Dm/C
2.  There are six of us__ lost in space among the  stars,
         G7/B               Gm6/Bb
    One dead, one beaten like I never believed a human

        could be so beaten.
            Dm/A                      A
    The other four wanting to leave all the terror,
                 BbaddE/A                C/Bb
    One leaping into space, others beating their heads

        against the wall
     BaddE/A        BbaddE/A      A
    All__ with gazes__ fixed on death.


 Dm                        Bb/D   Bb/A
        The military__ carry out their plans with precision;
 Dm                       Bb/D   Bb/A
        Blood is medals for them, Slaughter is the badge

        of heroism.
                  F           G
        Oh my God. Is this the world you created?
               A         (tacit)
        Was it for this, the seven days, of amazement

        and toil?


 Dm              Dm/C              G7/B
3.  The blood__ of compañero Presidente__ is stronger
                  Gm6/Bb
        than bombs, is stronger than machine guns.

     Dm                        A
    O you song, you come out so badly when I must
     BbaddE/A    C/A
    sing_____ the terror!
          BaddE/A              BbaddE/A
    What I see I never saw.  What I have felt, and what I
        (tacit)
        feel, must come out!
     BbaddE/A
    "Hará brotar el momento!  Hará brotar

        el  momento!"*          * The moment will bloom
```

1. Somos cinco mil
   en esta pequeña parte de la ciudad.
   Somos cinco mil
   ¿Cuántos seremos en total
   en las ciudades y en todo el país?
   Solo aquí,
   diez mil manos que siembran
   y hacen andar las fábricas.
   ¡Cuánta humanidad
   con hambre, frío, pánico, dolor,
   presión moral, terror y locura!

2. Seis de los nuestros se perdieron
   en el espacio de las estrellas.
   Un muerto, un golpeado como jamás creí
   se podría golpear a un ser humano.
   Los otros cuatro quisieron quitarse todos los
       temores uno saltando al vacío,
   otro golpeándose la cabeza contra el muro,
   pero todos con la mirada fija de la muerte.

3. ¡Qué espanto causa el rostro del fascismo!
   Llevan a cabo sus planes con precisión artera
       sin emportarles nada.
   La sangre para ellos son medallas.
   La matanza es acto de heroísmo.
   ¿Es este el mundo que creaste, dios mío?
   ¿Para esto tus siete días de asombro y de trabajo?
   En estas cuatro murallas sólo existe un
       número que no progresa,
   que lentamente querrá más la muerte.

   Pero de pronto me golpea la conciencia
   y veo esta marea sin latido,
   pero con el pulso de las máquinas
   y los militares mostrando su rostro de matrona
       lleno de dulzura.

   ¿Y México, Cuba y el mundo?
   ¡Que griten esta ignominia!
   Somos diez mil manos menos
   que no producen.
   ¿Cuántos somos en toda la Patria?

4. La sangre del compañero Presidente
   golpea más fuerte que bombas y metrallas.
   Así golpeará nuestro puño nuevamente.

   ¡Canto qué mal me sales
   cuando tengo que cantar espanto!
   Espanto como el que vivo
   como el que muero, espanto.
   De verme entre tanto y tantos
   momentos del infinito
   en que el silencio y el grito
   son las metas de este canto.
   Lo que veo nunca ví,
   lo que he sentido y lo que siento
   hará brotar el momento...

As long as we're into deadly serious songs, here's another, which I sang when Marilyn Monroe killed herself with an overdose of pills. I read the poem in *Life* magazine, put a tune to it. Later on, met the author, got his permission. He knew Marilyn well; she was known as Norma Jean (her original name) to her friends.

I've written it all out, because though it has only two short melodies, there are important little variations in each verse.

MARILYN MONROE & NORMAN ROSTEN

Who Killed Norma Jean?

1. Who killed— Nor-ma Jean? I, said the Cit-y,

As a civ-ic du-ty, I killed Nor-ma Jean.

2. Who saw her die? I, said the Night,—

And a bed-room light,— We— saw her die.

3. Who'll catch her blood? I, said the Fan,

With my lit-tle pan, I'll catch her blood.

4. Who'll make her shroud? I, said the Lov-er,

My guilt to cov-er, I'll— make her shroud.

5. Who'll dig her grave? The tour-ist will come and

join in the fun, He'll dig her grave.

6. Who'll be chief mourn-ers? We who rep-re-sent,— And

lose our ten per-cent.— We'll be the chief mourn-ers.

7. Who'll bear the pall? We, said the Press,— In

pain and dis-tress,— We'll— bear the pall.

8. Who'll toll the bell? I, screamed the moth-er,

Locked in her tow-er, I'll pull the bell.

9. Who'll soon for-get? I, said the Page,— Be-

gin-ning to fade,— I'll be first to for-get.

Words by Norman Rosten   Music by Pete Seeger
TRO © 1963 (renewed) & 1964 (renewed) Ludlow Music, NY, NY.

1. Who killed Norma Jean?
   I, said the City, as a civic duty,
   I killed Norma Jean.

2. Who saw her die?
   I, said the Night, and a bedroom light,
   We saw her die.

   3. Who'll catch her blood?
      I, said the Fan, with my little pan,
      I'll catch her blood.

4. Who'll make her shroud?
   I, said the Lover, my guilt to cover,
   I'll make her shroud.

5. Who'll dig her grave?
   The tourist will come and join in the fun,
   He'll dig her grave.

6. Who'll be chief mourners?
   We who represent, and lose our ten percent.
   We'll be the chief mourners.

7. Who'll bear the pall?
   We, said the Press, in pain and distress,
   We'll bear the pall.

   8. Who'll toll the bell?
      I, screamed the mother, locked in her tower,
      I'll pull the bell.

9. Who'll soon forget?
   I, said the Page, beginning to fade,
   I'll be first to forget.

NAZIM HIKMET

"It's difficult to write about Marilyn Monroe now that she is gone. The past tense just doesn't suit her somehow; she was too acutely alive. I knew her and was very fond of her. She was a strange, tormented, endearing girl, full of fun — a bravado fun, as though daring death to strike her down. Well, it did, finally. What can we say who saw her living in that shadowland of loveless Hollywood? She who had such love in her heart — love for people, animals, birds, trees — had to die for lack of it!

Who to blame? I thought of blame, even though it's always too late. My poem tried to say it for myself, anyway…for whatever it's worth for others."

—Norman Rosten

In the late '50's I got a letter: "Dear Pete Seeger: I've made what I think is a singable translation of a poem by the Turkish poet, Nazim Hikmet. Do you think you could make a tune for it? (Signed), Jeanette Turner."

I tried for a week. Failed. Meanwhile I couldn't get out of my head an extraordinary melody put together by an Massachusetts Institute of Technology student who had put a new tune to a mystical ballad "The Great Silkie" from the Shetland Islands north of Scotland.

Without his permission I used his melody for Hikmet's words. It was wrong of me. I should have gotten his permission.

But it worked. The Byrds made a good recording of it, electric guitars and all.

I'll never forget 6,000 young people in Lisbon, Portugal, in '84, singing it with me. The English words were on a screen. I played the melody first on a recorder, then with the help of some expert Portuguese back-up musicians, we sang the whole song through, all 6,000 of us.

I never met Jeanette Turner, who was a volunteer with a New York peace organization. She died soon after she wrote me. Bless your memory, Jeanette. And Hikmet, the Turkish Communist poet imprisoned for so many years.

And thank you, James Waters, now a professor in Vermont. Your melody is one of the world's greatest. I hope you will someday forgive me for using it without permission.

I Come and Stand At Every Door
(Girl of Hiroshima)

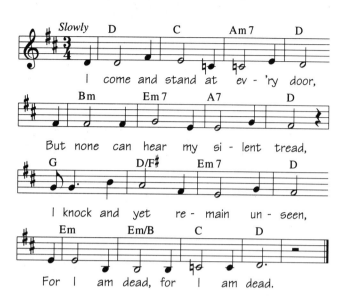

I come and stand at ev-'ry door,

But none can hear my si-lent tread,

I knock and yet re-main un-seen,

For I am dead, for I am dead.

Original Turkish poem by Nazim Hikmet   English translation by Jeanette Turner
Music by James Waters ("The Great Silkie")   Adaptation by Pete Seeger (1962)
Text © 1966 by Stormking Music Inc. Music © 1966 Folk Legacy Records.
All rights reserved.

1. I come and stand at every door
   But none can hear my silent tread
   I knock and yet remain unseen
   For I am dead, for I am dead.

2. I'm only seven, although I died
   In Hiroshima long ago.
   I'm seven now as I was then—
   When children die, they do not grow.

3. My hair was scorched by swirling flame;
   My eyes grew dim, my eyes grew blind.
   Death came and turned my bones to dust,
   And that was scattered by the wind.

4. I need no fruit, I need no rice.
   I need no sweets, or even bread;
   I ask for nothing for myself,
   For I am dead, for I am dead.

5. All that I ask is that for peace
   You fight today, you fight today.
   So that the children of the world
   May live and grow and laugh and play!

The opening three notes can be sung several different ways:

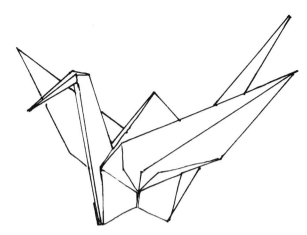

And, to try to make up to James Waters, here's the words to "Great Silkie" for which he originally wrote the melody. A "silkie" is a seal. A "nouris" is a nursing mother.

The Great Silkie

1. An earthly nouris sits and sings,
   And aye she sings, ba lily wean
   And little ken I my bairnie's father
   Far less the land that he dwells in.

2. For he came one night to my bed feet
   And a grumlie guest I'm sure was he,
   Saying, Here am I , thy bairnie's father,
   Although I be not com-e-lie.

3. I am a man upon the land
   As I am a silkie on the sea
   And when I'm far, and far frae land
   My home is in the Sule Skerrie.

4. It wasna' well, quo' the maiden fair,
   It wasna' well, indeed quo' she
   That the grey silkie of Sule Skerrie
   Should come and take my babe from me.

5. Now he has ta'en a purse of gold
   And he has placed it on her knee,
   Saying, give to me my little young son
   And take thee of thy nouris' fee.

6. And it shall come to pass on a summer's day
   When the sun shines bright on every stone
   I'll come and fetch my little wee son
   And teach him how to swim the foam.

7. And ye shall marry a gunner good
   And a right good gunner I'm sure he'll be
   And the very first shot that e'er he shoots
   Shall kill both my young son and me.

Traditional Scottish ballad

This has been a somber chapter. Now we cheer up.

I was lucky to have been acquainted with Malvina Reynolds, another of the great songwriters of this century. I am only sorry that because we lived on opposite sides of the continent, we didn't see each other often. Here's six of her songs.

Some song collaborators are close. Husband-and-wife teams. Some don't get along personally. Gilbert and Sullivan. A good many musicians work with people at long distance, as chance gets them together.

Mal and I agreed philosophically on most things. I usually deferred to her judgment, but not always.

I met her in the summer of 1947. I was 28 years old; she was 45, with beautiful white hair. She asked me if she could speak with me for a few minutes and perhaps give her some advice on the general subject of getting started as a singer and writer of songs. I usually make a practice of not discouraging people, but I have to confess that when I first met her, I didn't perceive her genius. I think I had in the back of my mind a feeling, "Gosh, she's pretty old to want to get started as a musician." I had a lot to learn.

I don't know if the advice I told her was any good or not. I probably described how I sang for a wide variety of community organizations and left-wing causes. For schools, churches, movements, and most anybody who called up. And how, if I ever was lucky to get a song written, I made copies of it; but I didn't expect any publisher to want to pay me for them nor print them and distribute them. I probably told her how Woody mimeographed the words of his songs and sold them for a few cents a copy. And I told her about our song magazine, *People's Songs*, in New York.

From time to time over the next 30 years I would receive copies of her new songs in the mail. She had bought one of those early office copying machines which could print up to 50 copies in purplish ink. And occasionally she would do me the honor of asking me to try writing a melody to her lyrics. Here are a few that I worked on. What a wonderful person. How I miss her. I'm only one of millions who have benefited from her wisdom and stick-to-it-iveness. Before she died, friends in Berkeley made a movie of her, *Love It Like a Fool*. It can still be rented from New Day Films, 121 W. 27 St., #902, New York, NY 10011, (212) 645-8210.

And a full-length biography of her is being written by Ellen Stekert.

Her life should be an inspiration to many people in many places. She refused to be discouraged, and if she thought she had a song worthy of being sung somewhere, she'd get on the telephone and ask to sing. She would not be put down, even though some people called her "pushy."

I once joked that she made up a new song before breakfast every morning. She looked at me severely and said, "You *know* it's not that easy."

Because I recorded her song "Little Boxes," in 1963 and it was even on the Top 40 very briefly, some people thought I had written it. But all I did was sing it like she wrote it.

Little Boxes

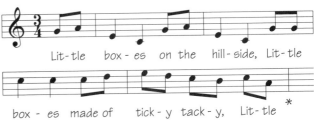

Lit-tle box-es on the hill-side, Lit-tle box-es made of tick-y tack-y, Lit-tle *

By Malvina Reynolds © 1962 (renewed) by Schroder Music Co.

She made up "Little Boxes" when she was driving to Palo Alto to sing for the P.T.A. Driving past Daly City south of San Francisco, she looked up at the hill-side, and said to her husband, "Bud, take the wheel. I feel a song coming on." When she got to Palo Alto, she had the song ready to sing.

Bud was a great guy, too. When I first knew him, he was working as a carpenter. In his early days, he'd been one of the heroic organizers of the automobile workers' union in Detroit. Later on he was an organizer for the Communist Party in Omaha. What a wonderful pair.

Photo by Joe Alper

BUD & MALVINA REYNOLDS AT NEWPORT, 1963

* Oh, a lot of readers will cuss me out for not printing all of this great song here. But I really hope people will write and get books with lots of Malvina's songs. She wisely set up a small publishing company named after the character in the comic strip Peanuts. Her friend Ruth Pohlman still runs it and mails out copies of any song you order. She even has a fax number! (510) 528-9342.
Schroder Music, 1450 6th Street, Berkeley, CA 94710-1343.
Don't forget to ask for her children's songs, *Tweedles and Foodles for Young Noodles.*

From Way Up Here

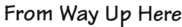

Words by Malvina Reynolds   Music by Pete Seeger and Pete Tchaikovsky
© 1962 (renewed) by Abigail Music Co. All rights reserved.

From way up here the earth looks very small,
It's just a little ball of rock and sea and sand,
No bigger than my hand.

From way up here the earth looks very small,
They shouldn't fight at all
   down there upon that little sphere.
Their time is short, a life is just a day,
You think they'd find a way.
You think they'd get along
   and fill their sunlit days with song.

From way up here the earth is very small,
It's just a little ball, so small, so beautiful and dear.
Their time is short, a life is just a day,
Must be a better way
To use the time that runs among the distant suns.

From way up here the earth is very small,
It's just a little ball, so small, so beautiful and dear.

Lovers of ballet will recognize that the notes whistled between the verses are the ones that I swiped from Tchaikovsky.

Seventy Miles

CHORUS (AND AFTER EACH VERSE):
Seventy miles of wind and spray,
Seventy miles of water,
Seventy miles of open bay—
It's a garbage dump.

1. What's that stinky creek out there,
    Down behind the slum's back stair—
    Sludgy puddle, sad and gray?
    Why man, that's San Francisco Bay!

2. Big Solano and the Montecell',
    Ferry boats, I knew them well,
    Creak and groan in their muddy graves,
    Remembering old San Francisco Bay.

3. Joe Ortega and the Spanish crew
    Sailed across the ocean blue,
    Came into this mighty Bay,
    Stood on the decks and cried, "Olé!"

4. Fill it there, fill it here,
    Docks and tidelands disappear,
    Shaky houses on the quakey ground,
    The builder, he's Las Vegas bound.

5. "Dump the garbage in the Bay?"
    City fathers say, "Okay.
    When cries of anguish fill the air
    He'll be off on the Rivière."

Words by Malvina Reynolds   Music by Pete Seeger

Mrs. Clara Sullivan's Letter

Dear Mis-ter Ed-i-tor, if you choose, Please
send me a cop-y of the la-bor news;
I've got a son in the In-fan-try, And
he'd be might-y glad to see That
some-one, some-where, now and then,
Thinks a-bout the lives of the min-ing men,
In Per-ry Coun-ty.

Words by Malvina Reynolds   Music by Pete Seeger

1. Dear Mister Editor, if you choose,
    Please send me a copy of the labor news;
    I've got a son in the Infantry,
    And he'd be mighty glad to see
    That someone, somewhere, now and then
    Thinks about the lives of the mining men,
        In Perry County.

2. In Perry County and thereabout
    We miners simply had to go out.
    It was long hours, substandard pay,
    Then they took our contract away.
    Fourteen months is a mighty long time
    To face the goons on the picket line
        In Perry County.

3. I'm twenty-six years a miner's wife,
    There's nothing harder than a miner's life,
    But there's no better man than a mining man,
    Couldn't find better in all this land.
    The deal they get is a rotten deal,
    Mountain greens and gravy meal,
        In Perry County.

4. We live in barns that the rain comes in
    While operators live high as sin,
    Ride Cadillac cars and drink like a fool
    While our kids lack clothes to go to school
    Sheriff Combs he has it fine,
    He runs the law and owns a mine
        In Perry County.

5. What operator would go dig coal
    For even fifty a day on the mine pay-roll!
    Why, after work my man comes in
    With his wet clothes frozen to his skin,
    Been digging coal so the world can run
    And operators can have their fun
        In Perry County.

6. When folks sent money to the Hazard Press
    To help the strikers in distress,
    They gave that money, yours and mine,
    To the scabs who crossed the picket line,
    And the state militia and F.B.I.
    Just look on while miners die
        In Perry County.

7. I believe the truth will out some day
    That we're fighting for jobs at decent pay.
    We're just tired of doing without,
    And that's what the strike is all about,
    And it helps to know that folks like you
    Are telling the story straight and true,
        About Perry County.

To see what a poet can do changing prose to verse, contrast Mal's words, above, with the original letter.

Scuddy, Kentucky
January 21, 1963

Dear Editor:

I recently read a magazine of yours about the labor unrest in Perry county and surrounding counties. I would like very much to get one of these magazines to send to my son in the service. I don't have any money to send you for it, but would you please send me one anyway?

I am a coal miner's wife. I have been married 26 years to a coal miner and you can't find a harder worker than a coal miner. We have been treated so unfair by our leaders from the sheriff up to the president. I know what it is to be hungry.

My husband has been out of work for 14 months. He worked at a union mine at Leatherwood. Now the company has terminated the union contract (UMWA) and plans to go back to work with scab workers. It isn't just here that all this is happening. The company will say they have to close as they are going in the hole. Then they will

Photo by Alejandro Stuart

MALVINA REYNOLDS

re-open with scab laborers that will work for practically nothing as long as the boss smiles at them and gives them a pat on the back. These men just don't realize the amount of people they are hurting or just don't care.

The operators have the money and the miner doesn't have anything but a bad name. You couldn't find better people anywhere in the whole world. But we have our pride too. We are tired of doing without. The operators have beautiful homes, Cadillacs and aeroplanes to enjoy, and our homes (camp houses, by the way) look like barns.

We don't want what the operators have. All we want is a decent wage and good insurance that will help our families. Is this too much to ask?

The operators wouldn't go in a mine for $50 a day. I've seen my husband come home from work with his clothes frozen to his body from working in the water. I have sat down at a table where we didn't have anything to eat but wild greens picked from the mountain side. There are three families around me, that each family of seven only had plain white gravy and bread for a week is true. Is this progress or what? I just can't understand it.

I have two sons that go to school and they don't even have decent clothes to wear. No one knows our feelings and I'm quite sure the coal operators don't care as long as they get that almighty dollar. Of all the things that were sent here to the Helping Fund (Editor's Note: This is the "relief" fund administered by the Hazard newspaper. See story, January PL.) not one of these needy families received a thing nor did anyone here in camp. Where did it all go? Somebody got a real good vacation with it I suppose. All the newspapers are against us because of political pressure, but our day is coming.

The government talks of re-training. My husband went into the mines in Alabama at the age of 11 with only the second grade of schooling. How could he retrain now, and him 52? It is silly to even think this will help the older miner. All the state thinks about is building up the tourist trade. How will that help us? It would just put more money in the big shots' pockets — not ours. No one would want to spend money to come here for a vacation to see the desolate mine camps and ravaged hills.

Happy A.B. Chandler lost his election by siding against the laboring class of people; by sending the State Militia and State Police (by Don Steirgill, then head of the State Police) in here to use as strikebreakers in 1959. Wilson Wyatt lost because of Governor Combs doing the same thing, only in a more subtle way. How can he hope to get elected to the Senate? How does he think Ed Breathitt will fare by endorsing him?

The truth will out someday. I'm sorry I have rambled on like this. It just seems so unjust, especially to the poor.

Please, sir, could you send me a magazine?

Thank you sincerely,

Mrs. Clara Sullivan
Scuddy, Kentucky
Perry County

You can make up a song out of many an item you read in the newspaper. The journalist has already done half your job for you. Woody made up "Reuben James," "Deportees" and "Isaac Woodward" from seeing short items in some paper. Malvina Reynolds was similarly helped to write "Andorra." It was a three-inch item in the *New York Times*. Years later I met the newspaper reporter in Andorra. He knew just what he was doing.

Andorra

Words by Malvina Reynolds
Music & final two verses by Pete Seeger

CHORUS (AFTER EACH VERSE):
I want to go to Andorra, Andorra, Andorra,
I want to go to Andorra, it's a place that I adore,
They spent four dollars and ninety cents
On armaments and their defense,
Did you ever hear of such confidence?
Andorra, hip hurrah!

1. In the mountains of the Pyrenees
   There's an independent state,
   Its population five thousand souls,
   And I think they're simply great.
       One hundred and seventy square miles big
       And it's awf'lly dear to me.
       Spends less than five dollars on armaments,
       And this I've got to see.

2. It's governed by a council,
   All gentle souls and wise,
   They've only five dollars for armaments
   And the rest for cakes and pies.
       They didn't invest in a tommy gun
       Or a plane to sweep the sky,
       But they bought some blanks for their cap pistols
       To shoot on their Fourtha July*

3. They live by the arts of farm and field
   And by making shoes and hats,
   And they haven't got room in their tiny land
   For a horde of diplomats;
       They haven't got room in their tiny land
       For armies to march about,
       And if anyone comes with a war budget
       They throw the rascals out.

Here's two verses I added:

4. I wandered down by the Pentagon
   This newspaper clipping in hand
   I said, "I want to see everyone
   In McNamara's band." **
       I said, "Look what they did in Andorra,
       They put us all to shame.
       The least is first, the biggest is last,
       Let's get there just the same."

5. The general said, "My dear boy,
   You just don't understand.
   We need these things to feel secure
   In our great and wealthy land."
       I said, "If security's what you need
       I'll buy a couch for you,
       A headshrinker is cheaper and quicker
       And a damn site safer too."

* On *their* independence day, not ours, of course.
**Robert McNamara, Secretary of Defense, 1962

It's 1991. The folk process continues. Am I proud. And I think Malvina would be proud too, to know that Charlie King of Connecticut made up a new ballad, using some of her old song. Charlie also had a news item to start him.

Factories With Amenities Hinder Poland's Stark Turn to Capitalism

By STEPHEN ENGELBERG
Special to The New York Times

KEDZIERZYN KOZLE, Poland — Prime Minister Jan Krzysztof Bielecki recently visited the sprawling Azoty chemical works here, and what he saw chilled him to his free-market bones.

More than a year after the Government began its pioneering program to dismantle the centrally managed socialist economy, this state-run company seems frozen in an earlier time, when profits did not matter much and companies typically took on the role of municipal governments.

"It still conducts functions so typical for a socialist enterprise," Mr. Bielecki lamented in an interview. "They have an indoor skating rink, a very nice swimming pool, culture center, soft drink bottling plant and a very nice laundry. They maintain 1,000 free factory apartments, heat 80 percent of the town and still make a profit."

He continued: "This company has entered an international market and holds 5 percent of world production, yet it doesn't work at all on marketing, and the name of the enterprise" — Zakladv Nawozowo-Azotowe w Kedzierzynie Kozlu — "is not pronounceable by anyone who doesn't speak Polish."

The factory, and its relationship to this squat, working-class town several hundred miles southwest of Warsaw, is a microcosm of the difficulties Poland faces in dismantling an encrusted system. In the last few weeks, Mr. Bielecki has repeatedly cited Azoty (ah-ZOH-teh), the 22d-largest enterprise in Poland, as a symbol of resistance to change.

I Want To go To Azoty

There's a factory in Silesia, in Poland's troubled land
5,000 working people and I think they're simply grand
They run the plant the old fashioned way—
socialistically
And they're doing just fine on the bottom line, now this
I got to see.

CHORUS:

I want to go to Azoty (ah-ZOH-teh), Azoty, Azoty
I want to go to Azoty, it's a fact'ry I admire
Azoty people seem content—a job for all, free heat,
free rent
While turning a profit of 10%, Azoty, hip hoorah!

It's governed by a council, employees kind and wise
They've a tiny budget for marketing, the rest for cakes
and pies
There's a beautiful pool to swim in, a wonderful rink
to skate
A theater for concerts and dances and plays and I just
think it's great!

The fact'ry churns out plastic for squirt guns, blocks
and tops
There's a laundry to wash their working clothes
and a shop for bottling pop
When they see something go to waste they try to plow
it back
So they pipe steam down to heat the town that used to
go up the stack.

It's all for one and one for all, they've lived that way
for years
They haven't got room in their tiny town for the new
free-marketeers
They haven't got room for prophets of doom or Wall
Street eagle scouts
The Prime Minister came to play that game and they
threw the rascal out.

Let's send a delegation and see if we take the hint
The Labor Czar, the Head o' the Fed, and maybe the
Mayor of Flint
Tell 'em "Look what they do in Azoty, they put us all to
shame,
It's wrong, it's Red, it's s'posed to be dead, let's try it
all the same!"

New words by Charlie King
(adapted from the song "Andorra" by Malvina Reynolds & Pete Seeger)
© 1962 (renewed) & 1993 Amadeo-Brio Music Inc., PO Box 1770,
Hendersonville TN 37077. Used by permission.

It's a well-known trick of wordsmiths to write parodies of well-known tunes. But I would not call this song of Charlie's a parody. A parody usually satirizes or at least subtly comments on the "original" song. See "Ole Time Religion," p. 136. But a song which stands on its own two feet I don't consider a parody.

Ring Like a Bell

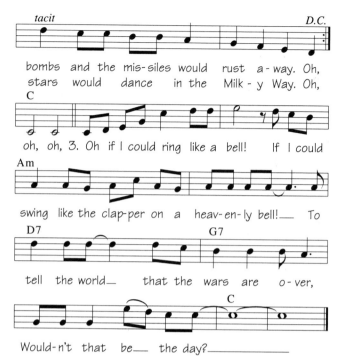

1. Oh, if I could ring like a bell!
   If I could swing like a clapper on a bell!
   To tell the world that the wars are over,
   Wouldn't that be the day?

2. Oh, if I could sound like the thunder!
   If I could sing out the glory and the wonder
   To tell the world that the wars are over,
   Wouldn't that be the day!

   BRIDGE # 1:
   Wouldn't that be the morning!
   Wouldn't that be the day!
   The faces of men would smile again
   And the bombs and the missiles would rust away.

   REPEAT VERSES 1 AND 2

   BRIDGE # 2:
   Wouldn't that be the morning!
   Wouldn't that be the day!
   The news would sound the world a-round
   And the stars would dance in the Milky Way,
      Oh, oh, oh,

3. Oh, if I could ring like a bell!
   If I could swing the clapper on a heavenly bell
   To tell the world that the wars are over
   Wouldn't that be the day.

I urge all songwriters to do what Malvina Reynolds did — send out lead sheets of words, at least, or words and melody, if possible, or a tape. Don't send a lot of songs;

send one or two at a time, but send them to a number of people.

Above all, try singing the songs for family and friends and neighbors of all sorts. These will give you your best response. Woody Guthrie used to say that he'd try out his new songs on the folks in the local bar. If it wasn't good enough for them, then he'd go back and try again to improve it.

The words for this last song were found among Mal's papers after she died. I put a tune to them and we sang it at a memorial concert for her.

No Closing Chord

Words by Malvina Reynolds (ca.1976)   Music by Pete Seeger (1976)

1. Don't play that closing chord for me, baby ba-by.
   I want a wake to wake the dead.
   Some rolling sounds with drums and rocking bass,
   And my good comrades dancing...all around
       the place.

2. Don't play that closing chord for me, baby, ba-by.
   I want rejoicing when I go.
   Celebrate my advent and that I had my day,
   With a roving melody to...send me on my way.

BRIDGE: Don't play that closing chord for me, baby ba-by,
               Lugubrious is not my style.
               I favored grins and laughs, with loving on the side.
               So do a Moog type version of "Here comes
                   the bride."

3. Don't play that closing chord for me, baby, ba-by,
   I'll bless the ground from whence I came,
   I'll make some daisy shine (daisy shine)
   Some grass grow green (grass grow green).
   And leave a sneaky dandelion to decorate the scene.

Some Proverbs

Before this chapter is over, some fragments. Every songwriter must have fragments floating around in his or her brain. Most of these are proverbs.

Eas-y come, eas-y go.

I know I'm in a melodic rut, but I found myself using the same phrase for other old sayings:

Out of sight, out of mind.

A stitch in time, saves___ nine

Another melodic phrase I'm stuck on:

Bet-ter late than nev-er___

No fool___ like an old fool

No news___ is good news

If it ain't one thing it's an-oth-er

The next two I got from Carl Sandburg's novel *Remembrance Rock.*

There's lots more to a mar-riage than four bare legs in a bed.

To the storms to come, and to the stars that fol-low the storm.

And I suspect this is an old blues:

Don't you know life is an on-ion, when you peel it you have___ to cry.___

This line I read 35 years ago. Wish the author would get in touch. What a great metaphor!

The larg-er the is-land of know-ledge,___ the long-er the shore-line of won - der.

For the above songs, all: Words by unknown authors   Music by Pete Seeger
© 1993 by Fall River Music Inc.

Chapter VI   New Words to Others' Tunes

Robert Frost was once asked, "Mr. Frost, what is your definition of poetry?"

The great poet looks skyward, pauses, purses his lips.

"Poetry is — what gets lost in the translation."

And this is why some of the world's greatest songs may never be sung outside the language area where they were created.

Nevertheless, translation is not always impossible. Edward Fitzgerald, who translated the Rubaiyat of Omar Khayam said, "Better a live sparrow than a dead eagle." In a sense, we all try to translate. Cooks translate old recipes for young stomachs. Lawyers translate old laws for new citizens. The Irish people have translated and found English words for some of their great melodies. Some European melodies have found new life in Japan and Korea. For example, the melody most of us know as "Auld Lang Syne" is known in Japan by a quite different name. It is the most popular song to sing when one is saying farewell at school graduations, at the end of a party, or when a ferryboat is pulling away and the relatives onshore wave to their friends on the boat until they can see them no more.

Max Coplet's German translation of "Where Have All The Flowers Gone" sings better than my original: "Sag mir wo die Blumen sind" (See p. 169).

Hardest to translate into English are songs in some variety of the English language which cannot be easily understood, or people will misinterpret if you try and pronounce the original way. They might think you're making fun of "dialect." Some of my favorite songs, Scottish, or West Indian, I don't ever sing in public because the original pronunciation makes them unintelligible,

and they are no longer such good songs translated into another kind of English.

I've urged people *not* to try to put English words to great songs like "Guantanamera," "De Colores," and "Amanece." It's only a matter of time before the USA, like most of the world, is some sort of a bilingual country. Learning songs in Spanish will hasten the day. And if a song is not too difficult, I urge people to try to learn the original, no matter what the country. "To learn a bit of another people's language is to get a glimpse of their soul." (Rockwell Kent).

I've been able to make only a few singable translations in my life. Here's one of them.

I learned the song in 1947, when I was singing for the Communist-led fraternal organization, the IWO (International Workers' Order) in and around Pittsburgh.

One evening after I sang, a man came up to me and said, "When I was young, we used to make up songs too."

I asked him if he would teach one of the songs to me.

"Oh, it wouldn't mean anything to you. It's all in Slovakian."

Fortunately, a friend of mine, Dr. Jacob Evanson, who was at that time the Superintendent of Music for the schools of Pittsburgh, was accompanying me, even though he mistrusted my politics. He immediately took the man aside and wrote down this song, music and words. The man's name was Andrew Kovaly; after he died I found out from his son that he had written many poems.

I didn't try to rhyme. You'll see that I simply took the literal meaning and tried to find syllables that were good to sing.

He Lies in the American Land

Freely—Drone bass—No chords

1. Ah,_____ my God! What is this land of A-mer-i-ca?_____
So_ man-y peo-ple trav-el-ing there.—
I will go_ too, for I am still young.
God, the Lord will grant me_ good luck there.

Original Slovak words & music by Andrew Kovaly (early 20th c.)
Transcribed by Jacob Evanson
English lyrics by Pete Seeger (1951)
© 1983, 1993 by Fall River Music Inc.

1. Ah, my God! What is this land of America?
    So many people traveling there.
    I will go too, for I am still young.
    God, the Lord will grant me good luck there.

2. You, my wife, stay here till you hear from me.
    When you get my letter, put everything in order.
    Mount a raven-black steed, a horse like the wind.
    Fly across the ocean to join me here.

3. Ah, but when she arrived in this strange land,
    Here in McKeesport, this valley, this valley of fire,
    Only his grave, his blood, his blood did she find.
    Over it bitterly—she cried:

4. "Ah, ah, ah, my husband,
        what have you done to this family of yours?"
    "What can you say to these children,
        these children you've orphaned?"
    "Tell them, my wife, not to wait, not to wait,
        not to wait for me."
    "Tell them I lie here! In the American Land!"

This is how the melody fits the 3rd and 4th verses.

3. Ah,_____ but when she ar-rived in_ this strange land,_____
Here in Mc-Kees-port, this val-ley, this val-ley of fire,
On-ly his grave,_ his blood, his blood did she find.
O-ver it bit-ter-ly - she cried.

4. "Ah, ah, ah, my hus-band, what have you done to this fam-'ly of yours?" "What can you say_ to these chil-dren, these chil-dren you've or-phaned?" "Tell them, my wife,_ not to wait, not to wait, not to wait for me." "Tell them I lie_ here! In the A-mer-i-can Land!"

Here's the original, from *Pennsylvania Songs and Legends*, University of Pennsylvania Press. Don't attempt it unless you get a Slovakian to coach you.

1. Ej Božemoj cotej Ameriki!
    Idze doňej narod preveliki,
    Ija pojdzem, šak som mladi ešče.
    Dami Panboh tam dajake scesce.

2. Jaše vracim kecme nezabije,
    lem ti čekaj odomňe novinu.
    Jak ot domňe novinu dostanes,
    šicko sebe doporjatku prines
    sama šedneš navraneho koňa,
    atak pridzeš draha dušo moja.

3. Ajak vona do McKeesport prišla,
    to uš muža živoho nenašla;
    lem totu krev co znoho kapkala
    atak nadnu, prehorko plakala.

4. "Ej mužumoj co žeši ucinil,
    žesi tote dzeci osirocil!"
    "Povic ženo tej mojej siroce,
    žeja ležim utej Americe;
    povic ženo najme nečekaju,
    boja ležim v Americkim kraju."

The original of the next can be found in *Norwegian Emigrant Songs and Ballads*, by Blegen and Ruud (Arno Press, New York). It was a famous drinking song both in Norway and among Norwegian-American men. The story behind it? In the 1840's, the famous Norwegian violinist Ole Bull toured the USA. Some real estate agents sold him 120,000 acres in northwest Pennsylvania, and when he returned home he announced there was free land for Norwegian emigrants. But the first settlers found it was mostly rocks. No good for farming. They headed west to places like Wisconsin. This satirical ballad was written in 1853 by Ditmar Meidel, a Norwegian newspaper editor. It had several dozen verses.

The tune is one more variant of what we know best as "Twinkle, Twinkle, Little Star," a melody with hundreds of different versions throughout Europe and the Americas. A slow, minor-key version is "Hatikvah," the national anthem of Israel. The gospel song "Come By Here" (Kumbaya) incorporates it. I suspect the tune was known by our cave-dwelling ancestors.

Oleanna

Norwegian words & music by Ditmar Meidel (1853)
English lyrics by Pete Seeger (1953)
TRO - © 1958 (renewed) Ludlow Music, Inc., New York, NY.

1. Oh, to be in Oleanna,
   That's where I'd like to be,
   Than be bound in Norway
   To drag the chains of slavery,

CHORUS:
Ole, Ole-anna,
Ole, Ole-anna,
Ole, Ole, Ole, Ole,
Ole, Oleanna

2. In Oleanna land is free,
   The wheat and corn just plant themselves,
   Then grow four feet a day,
   While on your bed you rest yourself.

3. Beer as sweet as Münchener
   Springs from the ground and flows away,
   The cows all like to milk themselves
   And hens lay eggs ten times a day.

4. Little roasted piggies
   Rush about the city streets,
   Inquiring so politely if
   A slice of ham you'd like to eat.

(SPOKEN:) *"The moon is always full. I am observing it now, with a bottle for a telescope."*

(SPOKEN:) *"In Oleanna the women do all the work! If she doesn't work hard enough She takes a stick and gives herself a beating!"* *

5. Aye, if you'd begin to live,
   To Oleanna you must go,
   The poorest wretch in Norway
   Becomes a Duke in a year or so.

* This is a joke? In 1853.

For a recording of the original Norwegian, write: Scandisk Music, 7616 Lyndale Ave. South, Mpls, MN, 55423-4028.

Here's some of the original verses.

I Oleana der er det godt at være,
I Norge vil jeg inte Slavelænken bære!
   Ole - Ole - Ole oh! Oleana!
   Ole - Ole - Ole oh! Oleana!

I Oleana der faar jeg Jord for Intet,
Af Jorden voxer Kornet, og det gaar gesvint det.

Ja Bayerøl saa godt, som han Ytteborg kan brygge,
det risler i Bækkene til Fattigmandens Hygge.

Aa brunstegte Griser de løber om saa flinke
Aa forespør sig høfligt, om Nogen vil ha' Skinke.

Kronarbejde findes ej — nej det var saa ligt da!
Jeg sad nok ikke ellersen saa frisk her aa digta.

Aa Kjærringa maa brase aa styre aa stelle —
Aa blir hu sint, saa banker hu sig sjelv — skal jeg
    fortælle.

Ja rejs til Oleana, saa skal Du vel leve,
den fattigste Stymper herover er Greve!

Drawing by Eric Von Schmidt

The old Russian folksong, "Stenka Razin," had a beautiful melody, but the words deserve to stay on the library
shelf. About a legendary Cossack chief. He is rowing
across the Volga with his band of warriors, and his bride,
a Persian princess. He hears them grumble, "Ah, Stenka
Razin has become a sissy; he's got married." Stenka Razin
roars, "I'll show you who's a sissy. Mother Volga, see
what a sacrifice I make for you!" He picks up his bride,
throws her in the Volga and drowns her. So much for
folklore. I put together some new words in 1950, while
chopping trees along the banks of the Hudson.

River Of My People

Slow, sing unaccompanied

Words by Pete Seeger   Music: traditional Russian ("Stenka Razin")
© 1953 by Stormking Music Inc.

1. There's a river of my people
    And its flow is swift and strong,
    Flowing to some mighty ocean,
    Though its course is deep and long,
        Flowing to some mighty ocean,
        Though its course is deep and long.

2. Many rocks and reefs and mountains
    Seek to bar it from its way.
    But relentlessly this river
    Seeks its brothers in the sea. *
        But relentlessly this river
        Seeks its sisters in the sea.

3. You will find us in the mainstream,
    Steering surely through the foam,
    Far beyond the raging waters
    We can see our certain home.
        Far beyond the raging waters
        I can see our certain home.

4. For we have mapped this river **
    And we know its mighty force
    And the courage that this gives us
    Will hold us to our course.
        And the courage that this gives us
        Will hold us to our course.

5. Oh, river of my people,
    Together we must go,
    Hasten onward to that meeting
    Where my brothers wait I know,
        Hasten onward to that meeting
        Where my sisters wait I know.

* If a group of men and women sing this, have them sing different lines.
**We didn't map human history as well as we thought.

So there's another song repeating the last line. There's
even more repetition in the next song. What's the purpose
of repetition? I see at least five possible reasons:
- It gives listeners a chance to join in.
- It imprints an important phrase.
- It gives the singer a chance to gather her/his
    thoughts ("what the heck *is* the next verse?").
- It gives a first time listener time to savor and digest
    a thought.
- Even those who've heard the song before can ponder
    other meanings of the words.

I found this next song in *The Treasury of Jewish Folk
Song*, edited by Ruth Rubin back in the 1940's. She had
Jewish songs from Israel, from Eastern Europe of the old
days, from New York City of the old days ("Tumbalalaika"). And she also had songs from the Soviet Union.
This song, as you'll see, was made up on a Jewish collective farm in the Crimea.

Djankoye

1. Az men fort kain Se - vas - to - pol

Iz nit vait fun Sim-fer-o-pol Dor-tn iz a

stan-tzi - ye fa - ran. Ver darf zu-chn

na - ye gli-kn S'iz a stan-tziye an an-ti-kl

In Djan-ko-ye, Djan, djan, djan.

CHORUS

Hey, Djan, hey Djan-ko-ye, Hey Djan-vi-li,

hey Djan-ko-ye, Hey Djan-ko-ye, Djan, djan,

1. djan._____ 2. djan._____

English lyrics by Pete Seeger (1947)
Original Yiddish words & music: author unknown (Crimea, 1926)
© 1947 (renewed) by Stormking Music Inc.

1. Az men fort kain Sevastopol
   Iz nit vait fun Simferopol
   Dortn iz a stantziye faran.
   Ver darf zuchn naye glikn
   S'iz a stantziye an antikl
   In Djankoye, Djan, djan, djan.

CHORUS (AFTER EACH VERSE):
Hey Djan, Hey Djankoye,
Hey Djanvili, Hey Djankoye,
Hey Djankoye, Djan, djan, djan.

2. When you go from Sevastopol
   On the way to Simferopol,
   Just you go a little farther down.
   There's a little railroad depot
   Known quite well by all the people
   Called Djankoye Djan, djan, djan.

3. Enfert Yidn oif main kashe
   Vu'z main bruder, vu'z Abrashe
   'Sgayt bai im der traktor vi a ban.
   Di mume Laye bai der kosilke
   Bayle bai der molotilke
   In Djankoye, Djan, djan, djan.

4. Ver zogt az yidn kenen nor handlen,
   Esn fete yoich mit mandlen
   Nor nit zain kain arbetzman?
   Dos kenen zogn nur di sonim
   Yidn, shpait zay on im ponim!
   Tut a kuk oif Djan, djan, djan.

5. There's Abrasha drives the tractor
   Grandma runs the cream extractor
   While we work we all can sing our songs,
   Who says that Jews cannot be farmers?
   Spit in his eye, who would so harm us.
   Tell him of Djankoye, djan.

In 1964, years later, my family and I were in the Crimea. I was singing in nearby Simferopol when I found that "Dzhankoy" was nearby, a city of about 20,000 people. I asked to visit it, went first to the newspaper office. The editor, a man in his 30's, said, "I'm not Jewish, but there are a lot of Jewish people who work here at the newspaper, and we're about to have lunch. Why don't you speak to them during lunch hour?" While I waited, I looked at the pictures around the room. Typical of socialist countries, they had awards to various workers for their good efforts, and I noticed names like Fagin and Cohen. At lunchtime there were over a dozen workers with their lunchboxes eating around a big table and chatting with each other when the editor introduced me.

I said, "I've sung this song now for 15 years and gotten audiences in the United States and other countries to sing it with me, but I'm curious to know if any of you know this song."

One woman raised her hand. She said that she didn't know the song herself, but she remembers hearing people sing it. As a matter of fact she said there was once a record out with this song on it. One of the other people at the table said, "It was probably made up on the Sholem Aleichem Collective Farm. That's now part of Rosseeya." (This is how the word "Russia" is pronounced in Russian.)

Said I, "I want to investigate the song. I've been told by friends now that Stalin's anti-semitism has been exposed, this song is a fake and should not be sung."

Laughter. Yes, laughter. They were not angry. They were a little incredulous. One said, "You go down to Rosseeya. See for yourself." And after lunch our car sped us five or 10 miles away. The manager of Rosseeya, a tall business-like fellow, shook hands. "We have 50,000 people, and thousands of hectares. We make wine, cognac, brandy."

"About 1/3 of Rosseeya is Ukrainian. A little over 1/3 are Jewish. A little less than 1/3 are Russian. I have to know all three languages. Why don't you wait a moment and I'll see if I can find one of the Jewish farmers." And a few minutes later a man in his 50's was introduced to us. It was his lunch hour now, but he took a few minutes to speak to us:

"Yes, I remember. It was about 1926. There was a crowd of young people who liked to make up songs then. During the terrible war, every Jew who was physically able was fighting. The women and children and old people were evacuated to the east to places like Tashkent, and some people never came back to live here again. There was not much to come back to. Everything destroyed. The only building left standing was the Stantsiya, the railroad station mentioned in the song. But we have a good life here."

The man sang the song to me with only very slight changes from the way I'd learned it out of Ruth's book.

(The above words were written decades ago, reprinted here. In '93 I wish I were able again to visit Djankoy. It's part of Ukraine now. I still sing the song. Mixing languages works.)

For a banjo to attempt a tune written for a symphony is a kind of translation. For a half-century I've played, mainly for my own amazement, a couple of Beethoven melodies. Here's four measures from one of them.

Ode to Joy

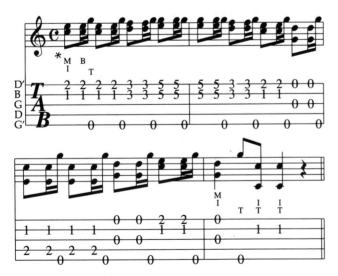

Music by Ludwig van Beethoven ("Ode to Joy", 1826) Banjo arrangement by Pete Seeger (1958) © 1993 by Sanga Music Inc.

* My middle fingernail is weak, so I usually pick up with my index finger and my ringer.

That's from Beethoven's 9th Symphony. The next is the famous two-part melody in his 7th. I play it with a fast sustained tremolo on the second and third strings of my banjo (G tuning, capoed up to B, a few frets). Occasionally I even got a crowd to hum the two parts together. Just this year, working with some choruses, and thinking of how hard it's been for men and women to work together, black and white, Asian and western, Arab and Jew, etc. — I worked out these short lyrics. My guess is they can be improved upon.

A nice, steady tremolo can be made with the right index finger, brushing back and forth lightly over a string or two.

It's easier if the index finger doesn't cross the string perpendicularly, but on a slant (the same as that of the right forearm). This makes it less liable for the fingernail to catch on the string.

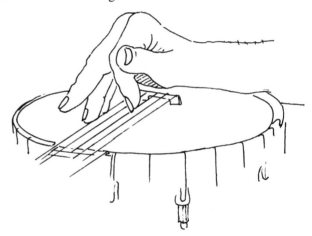

The finger is supposed to miss the 4th string, sound the 2nd and 3rd, and stop at the 1st.

It's easiest to make a tremolo on the 1st string (or the top two strings together); it's harder to make a tremolo on the other strings without sounding nearby strings by mistake. It can be done though. See the cross-sectional view sketched here. This technique I also use for a "drone" in "Abiyoyo," p. 60, also in "He Lies in the American Land," p. 118.

Visions of Children

We'll work to - geth - er,

though we work dif - frent.
e - ven though we work dif - frent - ly.

When we con - sid - er

all of the dan - gers
all the dan - gers sur - round - ing

Vi - sions of chil - dren

ask - ing us to save

them. All through the fu - ture,

Build - ing a - new.
Build - ing a - new.

Words by Pete Seeger (1993) Music by Ludwig von Beethoven (1812)
TRO - © 1993 Melody Trails, Inc., New York, NY.

I bet it would sound best with just maracas or shakere rhythm for accompaniment. Let that extraordinary two-part melody stand in the clear. How eloquent it is, though it moves slowly through a narrow range. I wonder if Beethoven ever heard two-part slavic melodies which also end one octave apart? No matter. This 7th Symphony will inspire human beings as long as there are human beings to be inspired.

PETE & LUDWIG AS JOINERS

Drawing by Eric Von Schmidt

Is it necessary that song lyrics rhyme? Sometimes yes, often no. Look at the great old spirituals which sing so well. They stick in your memory. "Steal Away." "Didn't My Lord Deliver Daniel." Look at some traditional lullabies.

As you work on song lyrics you'll become more conscious of why one word fits the tune better than another. Sometimes the rhythm is helped by a lot of sharp consonants: "Oh you can't scare me, I'm stickin' to the union." Sometimes you want the phrase to flow more smoothly. Listen to the words. Over years of songwriting you'll see why some words work in one way and others work in another way.

I went back and listened to the 7th Symphony again, because several people said I left out a fantastic bass part. It might be nice to add a bass when repeating the last 16 measures. I also found that I liked one note ("surrounding") a half-step higher than Ludwig did it.

If a chorus wanted to try it, I suggest they try out several different keys. When it's sung by women, or by men, or by women and men. Or when a bass or other parts are added. I sing it in B.

Here are new words to a South African wedding song. In Capetown Province, there was an old custom among the African people in which two choirs were formed: one by the friends of the bride, and the other by the friends of the groom. A traditional "competition" was held during the 24 hours or more of festivities in which certain traditional songs were always sung. This, including all the four-part harmony, was the original African music. I got the song out of the same book where I found the tune "Abiyoyo."

Here's To the Couple

Music: traditional (South African) transcribed by J.N.Maselwa & Rev. H.C.N.Williams   Original title: "Lo Mfan Unesongota"
English lyrics by Pete Seeger (1954)
© 1955 Lovedale Missionary Institution, South Africa. © 1956 (renewed) Stormking Music Inc.

1. Here's to the couple so valiantly wed,
       (BASSES: "…valiantly knotted untogether!")
    Here's to the years that for them lie ahead.
    We wish them good fortune and health of the best.
    We wish them good fortune and health of the best.
       (TENORS: "…and also have good neighbors")
    Strong children, good neighbors, and all the rest.
       (BASSES AND ALTOS: "Also good neighbors, and all
          the rest!")

2. Here's hoping that they never do part
       (BASSES: "…never have trouble with the baby")
    And all their quarrels be patched 'ere they start
    Let love be the teacher and make all the rules
    Let love be the teacher and make all the rules
       (TENORS: "Remember!")
    Let love be the doctor and cure the fools
       (BASSES & ALTOS: 'Love be the doctor and cure
          the fools')

3. They venture now out on life's stormy seas
       (BASSES: "…on the waves and the waters of
          the ocean")
    May they hold to their course, be it north, south
       or east.
    May they hold to their course though the tempests
       may blow
    And reach their goal, the goal of us all
       (TENORS: "Forever!")
    For them and their children, a world at peace
       (BASSES AND ALTOS: "And for their children, a world
          at peace")

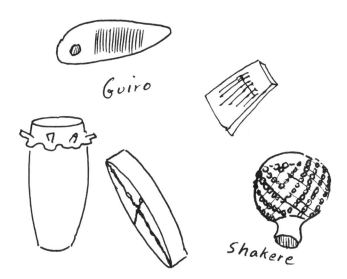

Guiro

Shakere

Somewhere in West Africa there was a songwriter who should have gotten royalties for the next song. It was never a top-40 hit; but the Weavers sang it, and I've sung it for audiences in all sorts of places.

I learned it in 1949 from Bryant French, who learned it from some West African students in Los Angeles. In those days, they said, the British controlled Nigeria and Ghana, and slapped weekday curfews on nighttime fun. It was a song of social commentary. All he learned was one verse in English and one verse in a Nigerian language, I think Yoruba.

I sang it for some children; they asked, "Is that all there is to the song?"

"I don't know any more," said I, "but this is a good song. Let's sing it in different languages." Soon there was

THE WEAVERS, 1950

a contest on between readers of *Sing Out!* magazine, in the early '50's, to see how many different languages we could sing it in. My only contribution to the situation was to realize that a really good tune doesn't need a lot of different verses, but maybe the same verse sung in different languages. You might consider this for other great melodies that you know.

Everybody Loves Saturday Night

West African song, adapted & arranged by Ronnie Gilbert, Lee Hays, Fred Hellerman & Pete Seeger (1948)
TRO - © 1953 (renewed) Folkways Music Publishers, Inc., New York, NY.

1. Ev'rybody loves Saturday night,
    Ev'rybody loves Saturday night,
    Ev'rybody, ev'rybody, ev'rybody, ev'rybody,
    Ev'rybody loves Saturday night.

2. Bobo waro faro Satodeh! (NIGERIAN—YORUBA)
    Bobo waro faro Satodeh!
    Bobo waro, bobo waro, bobo waro, bobo waro,
    Bobo waro faro Satodeh!

3. Tutti amano il Sabato sera, (ITALIAN)
    Tutti amano il Sabato sera,
    Tutti amano, tutti amano,
      tutti amano, tutti amano,
    Tutti amano il Sabato sera.

4. Yeder ener glacht Shabbas ba nacht, (YIDDISH)
    Yeder ener glacht Shabbas ba nacht,
    Yeder ener, yeder ener, yeder ener, yeder ener,
    Yeder ener glacht Shabbas ba nacht.

5. Tous le monde aime Samedi soir, (FRENCH)
    Tous le monde aime Samedi soir,
    Tous le monde , tous le monde ,
      tous le monde , tous le monde ,
    Tous le monde aime Samedi soir.

(COME BACK TO ENGLISH OCCASIONALLY)
Ev'rybody loves Saturday night,
Ev'rybody loves Saturday night,
Ev'rybody, ev'rybody, ev'rybody, ev'rybody,
Ev'rybody loves Saturday night.

6. El Sabado ama todo el mundo, (SPANISH)
    El Sabado ama todo el mundo…

7. Jeder mann liebt den Samstag abend… (GERMAN)

8. Alle elsker Lordag asften ..(DANISH)

9. Alle elsker Lordag kveld… (NORWEGIAN)

I'm sorry that we have no verses yet in Russian, Uzbek, Chinese, Japanese, Arabic, Hebrew, Finnish, Latvian, Swahili, Bengali, Urdu, Quechua, Portugese, Mongolian, etc., etc. You get 'em! Hey I leave the space below for you to write 'em in.

I didn't add a word or a note to this old German song. Why presume to include it? It's an example of a successful translation. "Dear Willie" sings better than "Lieber Heinrich." I also invented a way for one man to sing it. It works. I ham it up, look ridiculous, singing the man's verse only. Then I pick the banjo ever more briskly, just the melody, and ask women in the audience to sing the answer-back part.

There's a Hole in the Bucket

Traditional (U.S., originally German)

(Who translated this? When? Where? Pennsylvania maybe?
No matter. Great job.)

1. (MAN:) There's a hole in the bucket, dear Liza, dear Liza,
   There's a hole in the bucket, dear Liza, there's a hole.
   (I SPEAK:) *("All the women sing, 'Then fix it, dear Willie.'")*
   (WOMEN IN AUDIENCE:) Then fix it dear Willie, dear Willie,
      dear Willie,
   Then fix it dear Willie, dear Willie, then fix it

2. But how shall I fix it, dear Liza, dear Liza
   But how shall I fix it, dear Liza, but how?
   (SPOKEN BY THE SONGLEADER:) *("With straw, dear Willie.")*
   (WOMEN IN AUDIENCE:) With straw, dear Willie, dear Willie,
      dear Willie
   With straw, dear Willie, dear Willie, with straw

3. But how shall I cut it, dear Liza, dear Liza
   But how shall I cut it, dear Liza, but how?
      ("With a knife.")
   (WOMEN:) With a Kni-ife, dear Willie, etc.

4. But the knife needs sharpening, dear Liza, etc.
      ("Then sharpen it.")
   (WOMEN:) Then sharpen it, dear Willie, etc.

5. But how shall I sharpen it, dear Liza, etc.
      ("On a stone.")
   (WOMEN:) On a stone, dear Willie, etc.

6 But the stone needs water, dear Liza, etc.
      ("Then fetch it.")
   (WOMEN) Then fetch it, dear Willie, etc.

7. But how shall I fetch it, dear Liza, etc.
      ("In a bucket.")
   (WOMEN:) In a bucket, dear Willie, etc.

8. (AUDIENCE JOINS THE LEADER, FULL CHORDS, RITARD AT THE END:)
   There's a hole in the bucket, dear Liza, dear Liza,
   There's a hole in the bucket, dear Liza, there's a hole.

Often it's better not to try translating.

José Marti, born 1853, was one of the world's great writers. Seventy volumes of prose and poetry! Plays, novels, polemics. At age 17 he was banished from his home in Cuba because he was active in the movement for independence from Spain. For the next 25 years he made a living as a journalist, including 12 years in New York. In 1895 he went back to Cuba and was killed in an abortive uprising, age 42.

JOSÉ MARTI

In Havana 1949 a classical pianist and composer, Julian Orbon, found that the stanzas in Marti's last book, *Versos Sencillos* ("Simple Verses"), could be sung to a well-known melody. "Guantanamera" was first made up to satirize the women in Guantanamo who went out with American sailors. In '49 it was sung on the Havana radio every afternoon by "Joseito," who would open up the daily newspaper and improvise verses on the latest scandal of the day. "Joseito" was the professional name of José Fernandez Dias, who put together the original song back in the 1920's.

In 1961 a former student of Julian Orbon was in New York studying at the Manhattan School of Music. The student, Hector Angulo, had a summer job as a counselor in a children's camp in the Catskills, Camp Woodland. I visited to sing for the kids. The kids said, "Hey, we've got to teach you a great song we learned from our counselor." A shy, quiet young man was introduced to me.

I learned the song, taught it to the Weavers. A more commercial group, the Sandpipers, had a hit record of it. The song is known worldwide now —Marti's verses have ennobled the old melody. I urge people *not* to try translating it. Translations given here are not for singing.

Credit for the music should go to Joseito and to Orbon, who added an important note, the first note of the chorus

(B, formerly A, for the syllable "Guan"). But Angulo deserves credit, too, for thinking long and hard to select the right stanzas out of a possible two hundred to teach to the children — and to me. All I did was to find a less complicated accompaniment and way to teach it to Anglo audiences. It's one of two or three songs I most often perform. I've sung it in 40 countries; it rings true in every one.

Guantanamera

1. Yo soy un hombre sincero
    De donde crece la palma
    Yo soy un hombre sincero
    De donde crece la palma
    Y antes de morir me quiero
    Echar mis versos del alma

    (I am a truthful man,
    from the land of the palm.
    Before dying, I want to
    share these poems of my soul.)

CHORUS (AFTER EACH VERSE):
Guantanamera! Guajira!
Guantanamera!
Guantanamera, Guajira,
Guantanamera.

2. Mi verso es de un verde claro
    Y de un carmin encendido
    Mi verso es de un verde claro
    Y de un carmin encendido
    Mi verso es un ciervo herido
    Que busca en el monte amparo

    (My poems are light green,
    But they are also flaming red.
    My verses are like a wounded fawn.
    Seeking refuge in the mountain.)

3. Cultivo la Rosa blanca
    En junio, como en enero
    Cultivo la Rosa blanca
    En junio como en enero
    Para el amigo sincero
    Que me da su mano franca

    (I cultivate a white rose
    In June and in January
    For the sincere friend
    Who gives me his hand.)

4. Y para el cruel que me arranca
    El corazón con que vivo
    Y para el cruel que me arranca
    El corazón con que vivo
    Cardo ni ortigo cultivo
    Cultivo la rosa blanca

    (And for the cruel one who would tear out
    This heart with which I live.
    I cultivate neither thistles nor nettles.
    I cultivate a white rose.)

5. Con los pobres de la tierra
    Quiero yo mi suerte echar
    Con los pobres de la tierra
    Quiero yo mi suerte echar
    El arroyo de la sierra
    Me complace mas que el mar.

    (With the poor people of this earth,
    I want to share my lot.
    The little streams of the mountains
    Please me more than the sea.)

In Cuba, 1983, I learned two more of Marti's verses from a black man, head of a research farm.

6. Rojo, como en el desierto
    Salio el sol al horizonte
    Rojo, como en el desierto
    Salio el sol al horizonte
    Y alumbra un esclavo muerto
    Colgado a un seibo del monte

    (Red, as in the desert,
    Rose the sun on the horizon.
    It shone on a dead slave
    Hanging from a tree of the mountain.)

7. Un niño la vio, temblo
    De pasion por los que gimen
    Un niño la vio, temblo
    De pasion por los que gimen
    Y al pie del muerto juro
    Lavar con su sangre del crimen.

    (A child saw it, trembled,
    With passion for those that wept,
    And swore that with his blood
    He would wash away that crime.)

In Cuba it is traditional to improvise new verses to Guantanamera. "Fidel's beard is a broom to sweep the Yankees out of Latin America." In Hanoi in 1972, I accompanied a roomful of Cuban sailors for half an hour, improvising many verses, as they danced in a Conga line. We woke up the whole hotel.

My guitar accompaniment:

throughout the song, except for the first measure of the chorus:

Between Orbon and me, this song was, in a sense, Europeanized a bit. In Cuba, the tradition is to tear the melody to shreds. We regularized it. And my guitar accompaniment is a bit gringo, too. Perhaps it helped spread the song. Whether it improves the song is open to question.

And Orbon's one-note change also took it a step away from the Afro-Cuban tradition. Joseito's original refrain was:

but Orbon changed it (and Hector taught it to me as)

The former keeps the traditional chord changes. Orbon changed one note and the chord that went with it. If one bad note can ruin a song, one good note can make it.

Orbon lives in New York now and gets a small share of royalties. I've written the Cuban Author's Rights Association that I will not accept any of the royalties. Most of the money, a large sum, sits in a N.Y. bank because a federal law will not allow money to be sent to Cuba. When it's repealed (soon, I hope) money can be sent to Hector Angulo, and to the family of Joseito, and to the Marti Library in Havana, I guess. The song is a world "standard" now.

One thing you learn if you're a guest on TV is that you have to be brief and to the point. Time is money.

Of course, maybe in the long run TV will learn that there is a limit to how fast everything can be, and somebody will have a popular program which is also leisurely. I know some churches where they wouldn't think of singing a song if it didn't last for four or five or even 15 minutes.

Nevertheless, there's a time for short songs, and it so happened that I made up a short one about 20 years ago and, by gosh, I had a chance to use it on TV. Once I was a guest on the "Dick Cavett Show," but he was busy talking to James Brown, the "King of Soul," and then to Frank Borman, the astronaut. The show was almost over, and he still hadn't called on me. Suddenly he noticed the time and said to the audience, "Oh, I was going to have Pete Seeger sing a song. Pete, are you out there? Come on." I walked on the set. "Pete, do you have a very short song?" This is what I sang:

> *Here we are knee-deep in garbage,*
> *Firing rockets at the moon…*

The song took eight seconds. I sat down.

Cavett said, "Well, that *was* a short song. We have time for a question. What do *you* think of the space exploration program? Do you think it is worth the money that the taxpayers are putting into it?"

I replied, "It seems to me kind of silly to say that we can spend $60 billion going to the moon and then say we don't have enough money for schools or hospitals or job training and so on."

There was spontaneous applause from the audience. Poor Frank Borman didn't even have much time to say, "Well, that's very simplistic —."[1] The program was over. We were off the air. James Brown was sitting on the other side of Borman, but he reached right over to me in front of Borman and pumped my hand.

The tune for my song? One of the late Cole Porter's greatest hits, "You'd Be So Nice To Come Home To." I only used the first few bars.

Here We Are Knee-Deep in Garbage

Words & music adaptation by Pete Seeger (1974)
Adapted from the song "You'd Be So Nice to Come Home To" by Cole Porter

[1] Well, in a sense, most great songs are a triumph of oversimplification. Remember the saying of Alfred North Whitehead: "Strive for simplicity; learn to mistrust it."

O Canada
At last I breathe again
All thanks to you
Also your great north wind.
No customs tax, no border guards
Could keep your clean air out
So down here in the Polluted States
We all stand up and shout.
O Canada! O Canada!
O Canada—
The words stop in my mouth,
What happens to you when the wind blows
From the south?

We need more humor. Anger is good at times, but humor is too. Cruel as it may be. You know Charlie Chaplin's definition of humor? A newspaper reporter asked him, "Mr. Chaplin, what is your definition of humor?"

Pencil poised.

Charlie thought a second, reached into his pocket, pulled out a pocket knife. He reached across the table, cut the reporter's tie off.

"Hey, I didn't think that was funny!"

"I did," said Charlie.

There's probably not a joke one could tell anywhere that someone somewhere would not say seriously, "Hey, that's not funny."

But if another says, "You're too sensitive," tell this other: suppose your shoulder was rubbed raw and later I come along and just touch it. You wince with pain. It's not for me to say, "You're too sensitive."

Since this is a sort of musical autobiography, for historical honesty I've included many items of only passing interest. But is a song that lasts only a short time necessarily a bad song? Is a soufflé that lasts only five minutes any less a work of art? I'd like to see people through the world making up new songs for each other all the time, as well as remembering other songs that may be centuries old. A birthday, a wedding, a newspaper headline, is worth a song.

In 1951 I could see the Catskills, 45 miles away, when standing in Toshi's vegetable garden. Now only when the northwest wind blows can I see it. The next day smog has filled up the valley.

Thus, these new words to the national anthem of Canada. The music was written in 1880 by Calixa Lavallee, French-Canadian composer. A story of his life can be found in a back issue of *Sing Out!* magazine, Vol. V, #2 (1955).

O Canada

French lyrics by Hon. A.B. Routhier (1880) English lyrics by R. Stanley Weir (1908)
Music by Calixa Lavallee (1880) New verse by Pete Seeger (1965)

One of the best songwriters I know is Lorre Wyatt. He wrote "Somos El Barco," "Sailing Up/Sailing Down," and dozens more. Lorre started this song off. Had a good tune but too many verses. We made an appointment, set ourselves the task. It took us a day and a half. We boiled 'em down to this:

Huddie Ledbetter
Was a Helluva Man

Words by Lorre Wyatt with additional lines by Pete Seeger
Music by Lorre Wyatt

HUDDIE LEDBETTER ("LEADBELLY")

* Leadbelly's wife Martha pronounced his name "Hew-dy" and most of us who knew him in the 1940's picked up this pronunciation.
**European music notation can't show how Leadbelly's voice would swoop and glide, rather than proceed in neat steps. I think of his voice rising through this measure in one steady motion.

1. Huddie* Ledbetter was a helluva man,
   Huddie got his music from the heart of the land,
   In his voice you could hear John Henry's hammer ring
   While his hands would "buck and wing" upon the big
      twelve string;
   Sometimes a lion, sometimes a lamb,
   Huddie Ledbetter was a helluva man.

CHORUS (AFTER EACH VERSE):
He's a long time gone (He's a long time gone)
But his songs live on (But his songs live on)
He's a long time gone (He's a long time gone)
But his songs live on (But his songs live on)

2. Down in Lou'siana, eighteen eighty-eight
    There was a black baby born into a
        white man's state;
    He saw the cane and the cotton stretch for
        miles around,
    He heard his mama's voice a-singing when the sun
        went down;
    Into a <u>world</u> where having dark <u>skin</u> was a crime,
    Huddie was born—and started serving his time.

3. Teenage Huddie went to Shreveport town
    There he got in trouble, he was jailhouse bound
    The odds were slim that he would get out alive
    But somehow Huddie and his music survived
    He escaped just once and was put back again
    He was called Leadbelly by the rest of the men.

4. A collector, name a' Lomax, brought a
        record machine,
    Huddie sang 'em sweet and high, he sang 'em low
        and mean;
    And for years to come, they would tell the tale
    Of how Huddie Ledbetter sang his way out-a jail,
    Sayin', "If I had you, Governor, like-a you got me
    I would wake up in the morning and I'd set you free."

5. He got his farewell ticket back in '49
    He caught the Midnight Special on the
        Rock Island Line;
    And I'll bet you when he wakened from his
        earthly dream
    He was wakened with a kiss from a gal named Irene.
    Now millions of people the world around
    Are taking Huddie's hammer up and swinging it down!

REPEAT FIRST VERSE AND CHORUS

Leadbelly, "The King of the 12-string guitar," had a wonderful way with bass runs and melodies which his powerful right thumb picked out. In memory or him I made up this break for the guitar, tuned DADGBE, of course.

LORRE WYATT

And as long as we're singing about Leadbelly, here's a verse to add to one of America's greatest songs, the Texas prison blues "Midnight Special," which he taught us all. (For tune, see p. 227)

Old Huddie Ledbetter
He was a mighty fine man
He taught us this song
And to the whole wide land
But now he's done with all his grieving
His whoopin', hollerin' and a-crying
Now he's done with all his studyin'
About his great long time.

Can't remember when I put the above verse together — in the '50's or '60's. Leadbelly had a verse ending with the last four lines. I tacked my four lines in front of them.

Now we come to a section of this book with some truly great songs in it — none of them written by me. All I did was add a verse. I got the idea from Woody Guthrie. His extra verse to the old gospel song, "You Got To Walk That Lonesome Valley" just makes that song for me.

I'm just trying to carry on an old tradition. It's been done for ages, I'm sure.

Lonesome Valley
(Woody Guthrie's extra verse)

Now, though the road___
(though the road)___ be rough and rock-y
(rough and rock-y), and the hills
(and the hills)___ be steep and high___ (steep and
high), We can sing (we can sing)___ as we go
march-ing (we go march-ing) and we'll win that
One Big Un-ion bye and bye (bye and bye).

New words & music adaptation by Woody Guthrie
TRO - © 1963 (renewed) & 1977 Ludlow Music, Inc., New York, NY.

Incidentally, why is it that human beings can get a warm comfortable feeling as they all sing together about someone ready to kill themselves with despair? I don't know about Asia and Africa, but it's true with love songs in the Americas, and in Europe east and west.

Well, I get people harmonizing on it now. With a microphone I can call out the words to them, one phrase at a time, even though my voice is barely above a whisper. I added a sixth verse. The words and music can be found in *American Favorite Ballads, Tunes and Songs, as Sung by Pete Seeger*, Oak Publications, 121 West 47th Street, New York, NY. It wascollected by Cecil Sharp in 1904.

The Water is Wide

1. The water is wide, I cannot cross over,
   And neither have I wings to fly,
   Give me a boat that can carry two,
   And both shall row—my love and I.

2. A ship there was, and she sails the sea,
   She's loaded deep, as deep can be,
   But not so deep as the love I'm in
   And I know not how, I sink or swim.

3. I leaned my back against some young oak
   Thinking he was a trusty tree,
   But first he bended and then he broke
   And thus did my false love to me.

4. I put my hand into some soft bush
   Thinking the sweetest flower to find
   I pricked my finger to the bone
   And left the sweetest flower alone.

5. Oh, love is handsome, love is fine,
   Gay as a jewel, when first it is new,
   But love grows old, and waxes cold,
   And fades away, like summer dew.

6. The seagulls wheel, they turn and dive,
   The mountain stands beside the sea.
   This world we know turns round and round
   And all for them—and you and me.

REPEAT FIRST VERSE

"The Water is Wide" has long been one of the most widely known love laments in Britain. In both England and Scotland it has been in folk song collections for over a century or two, and known by a half-dozen or more names. This version I learned from my sister Peggy, thirty-five years ago. I made a singalong out of it, putting it in 4/4 time, with the sonority of the 12-stringer in Dropped D. Now it's well known throughout this country too.

I often sing this song right after a gang has raised the roof on "If I Had a Hammer," saying, "All our militance, enthusiasm, bravery will count for nothing if we can't cross the oceans of misunderstanding between the peoples of this world…"

6. The sea-gulls wheel,_____ they turn and

dive._____ The moun-tain stands_____

_____ be-side the_____ sea._____ This world we

know_____ turns_____ 'round and 'round,

and all for them, and_____ you and me._____

Traditional New last verse by Pete Seeger (1982)
Guitar arrangement by Pete Seeger
© 1993 by Sanga Music Inc.

As I write down these notes, I realize I never sang it twice the same. The guitar keeps fast "arpeggios" going like this. But the measures may have three or five or six beats. The chords look tricky but aren't. Arrows point to the string the thumb plucks.

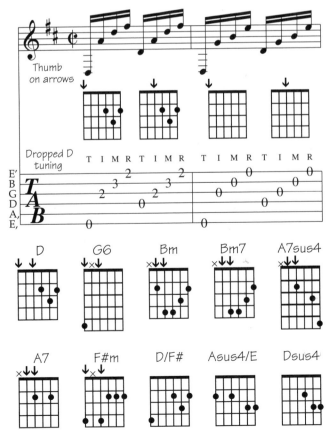

If you want to just strum, instead of playing jillions of fast little notes, it could turn out like this.

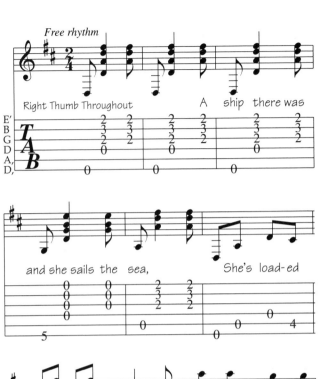

Right Thumb Throughout   A ship there was

and she sails the sea,   She's load-ed

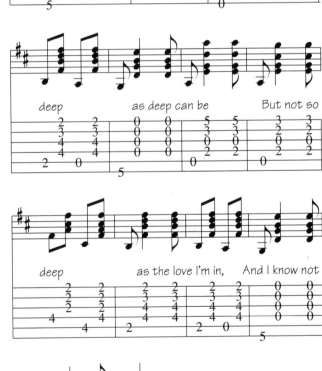

deep   as deep can be   But not so

deep   as the love I'm in,   And I know not

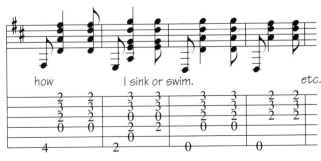

how   I sink or swim.   etc.

How do I get audiences to harmonize on it? Get the melody set firmly in people's minds, first.

I first play the great melody quite slowly, on a wooden recorder, or I whistle it along with the guitar. Then I tell folks how I can't sing it anymore, because my voice wobbles too much, but they can, because I'll give them the words.

"The water is wide, I cannot cross over..."

And then, very slowly, with the guitar leading, we start. Often, when it comes to the third or fourth line of a verse, I only give half a line at a time.

"But not so deep..." And while they are singing that wonderful word "deep" I'll give them the next five words, "...as the love I'm in..."

After they can sing the tune, for two or three verses, I encourage more harmony: "some people are singing a nice high part."

"We can use more of this. There's no such thing as a wrong note if you are singing."

If I have a good microphone I don't need to speak loudly to be heard above thousands of people. By the time we get to my new last verse, my voice is hardly above a whisper.

"This world we know..."

"And all for them..."

"And — you — and me..."

"The — water — is — wide!"

By this time they are learning *from each other*. I don't need to give the words again. As an accompanist, and a 'conductor of the chorus' my main job is to keep the song from speeding up, to get them to hold out the last notes of phrases, to encourage them to improvise harmony.

For several decades a group of science fiction fans who like to write satirical verses to well known tunes have exchanged mimeographed (now photocopied) song-sheets which they call "filksongs." Who exactly started this one off, no one knows, but it has so far accumulated over 500 verses. (Send $ to John Boardman, 234 East 19th Street, Brooklyn, NY 11226. He may be able to send you some photocopies.) Judy Gorman taught it to me. I selected my own favorites and then added a last verse of my own. Keep it brisk.

The "Filksong" Ole Time Religion

Gim-me that old time re-li-gion, gim-me that old time re-li-gion, gim-me that old time re-li-gion, (and) it's good e-nough for me.——*

Words: Anonymous, 6th verse by Pete Seeger (1982)
Music: traditional (gospel hymn), adapted by Pete Seeger (& others)
© 1993 by Sanga Music Inc.

CHORUS:
Gimme that Old Time Religion (3x)
It's good enough for me.

1. We will pray with Aphrodite
    We will pray with Aphrodite
    She wears that see-through nightie
    And that's good enough for me

2. We will pray with those Egyptians
    Build pyramids to put our crypts in
    Cover subways with inscriptions
    And it's good enough for me

3. We will pray with Zarathustra
    Pray just like we used ta
    I'm a Zarathustra booster
    And it's good enough for me

4. We will pray with those old Druids
    They drink fermented fluids
    Waltzing naked through the woo-ids
    And it's good enough for me

5. Hari Krishna he must laugh on
    With my robes all trimmed in saffron
    And my hair that's only half on
    But it's good enough for me

(TIME FOR AN INSTRUMENTAL BREAK.
AND I ADD MY OWN VERSE)

6. I'll arise at early morning
    When my Lord gives me the warning
    That the solar age is dawning
    And that's good enough for me.*

(END WITH A ROUSING LAST CHORUS)

* The last two measures of this song are often sung differently. I find it refreshing to syncopate the last lines of the verses while keeping the chorus more "straight," so everyone will join in. You make up your mind how you want to sing it.

This   or this   or this

I was only aged 33 when I put together an extra verse to the great blues written by Leroy Carr in the 1920's. I had no right to be so lugubrious. Then.

In the Evening

1. In the evening, in the evening, m-m- baby,
       when the sun goes down (2x)
    Ain't it lonesome, ain't it lonesome, ain't it lonesome
       when you're not around,
    When the sun goes down.

2. Well the sun rises in the east,
       sets down in the west (2x)
    Ain't it hard to tell, hard to tell, hard to tell,
       which one will love you the best,
    When the sun goes down.

3. Well, goodbye, my old sweethearts and pals,
       I'm going away
    I'll be back to see you all again, some old rainy day
    In the evening, in the evening, in the evening
       when the sun goes down,
    When the sun goes down.

Oh, what a song. I usually insert my verse next to the last.

When the fun, the fun is all o-ver, and the lik-ker's all gone dry, Oh, ba - by, you get to think-ing a man is bound to die. In the eve-ning, in the eve-ning, in the eve - ning when the sun go down, when the sun go down.

Words & music by Leroy Carr, new verse by Pete Seeger (1957)

SONNY TERRY, MEMPHIS SLIM, BROWNIE MCGHEE

Here's one of the great songs of the 20th century.

I made up an extra last verse when singing it at gatherings of the Hudson River Sloop *Clearwater* (no direct connection with the band Creedence Clearwater Revival).

Proud Mary
(Rolling on the River)

Words & music by John Fogerty, 4th verse by Pete Seeger (1980)
© 1969 Jondora Music. All rights reserved. Used by permission.

1. Left a good job in the city
   Workin' for the man every night and day
   But I never lost a minute a' sleepin'
   Worrying about the things that might have been

CHORUS (AFTER EACH VERSE):
Big wheel keep on turnin',
Proud Mary keep on burnin',
Rollin', rollin', rollin' on the river.
Rollin', rollin', rollin' on the river.

2. Pumped a lotta gas in Memphis
   Cleaned a lotta plates down in New Orleans
   But I never saw the good side of a city,
   Until I hitched a ride on a river boat queen.

3. If you go down to the river,
   Bet you gonna find some people who live
   You don't need to worry if you ain't got no money
   'Cause the people on the river are happy to give.

4. You get a job on the Clearwater
   Better not <u>mind</u> about the <u>kind</u> of pay that you get
   It may sound funny, you make hardly any money
   But you'll be richer by far than you ever been yet.

I told John Fogerty that for me the big wheel is the earth and Proud Mary the sun. He replied, "For me it's the whole universe." What a truly great song!

Of course no two singers sing the melody exactly the same. Here's how I first learned it. It's a favorite up and down the Hudson.

JONI MITCHELL

Here's another of my favorites from the '60's. Joni Mitchell has written a string of extraordinary melodies.

The version below is from Judy Collins' singing on *Wildflowers*. Dave Van Ronk sings "Clouds" in his gentle "big bear" way on *Dave Van Ronk and the Hudson Dusters* (see Discography).

Both Sides Now

1. Rows and floes of angel hair,
   And ice-cream castles in the air,
   And feather canyons ev'rywhere,
   I've looked at clouds that way,
       But now they only block the sun,
       They rain and snow on ev'ryone,
       So many things I would have done,
       But clouds got in my way.
   I've looked at clouds from both sides now,
   From up and down, and still somehow
   It's clouds illusions I recall;
   I really don't know clouds at all.

2. Moons and Junes and ferris wheels,
   The dizzy dancing way you feel,
   As ev'ry fairy tale comes real,
   I've looked at love that way.
       But now it's just another show,
       You leave 'em laughin' when you go.
       And if you care, don't let them know,
       Don't give yourself away.
   I've looked at love from both sides now,
   From give and take, and still somehow
   It's love's illusions I recall;
   I really don't know love at all.

3. Tears and fears and feeling proud,
   To say "I love you" right out loud,
   Dreams and schemes and circus crowds,
   I've looked at life that way.
       But now old friends are acting strange,
       They shake their heads, they say I've changed.
       But something's lost but something's gained
       In living ev'ry day.
   I've looked at life from both sides now,
   From win and lose and still somehow
   It's life's illusions I recall;
   I really don't know life at all.

(NEW VERSE FOR AN OLDER PERSON TO SING:)
4. Daughter, Daughter, don't you know
   You're not the first to feel just so,
   But let me say before I go,
   It's worth it anyway.
       Some day we may all be surprised,
       We'll wake and open up our eyes,
       And then we all will realize
       The whole world feels this way.
   We've all been living upside down,
   And turned around with love unfound,
   Until we turn and face the sun;
   Yes, all of us, everyone.

I first heard Joni's song on a car radio, added a fourth verse suitable for my age, and got a nice letter from Joni permitting me to sing it.

Garbage

I'm only one of many people who have made up extra verses to this now famous song. Some people like to shout out the word at random. I like to get a gang to mutter it throughout (for our mutter country).

I find the A# diminished chord a very useful one in this song. Just one extra finger is needed to make the change. The third verse repeats this measure seven times, with slight variations, and the fourth verse nine times. See next column.

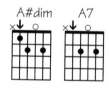

1. Mister Thompson calls the waiter, orders steak and
    baked potater
  But he leaves the bone and gristle and he never eats
    the skins;
  The bus boy comes and takes it, with a cough
    contaminates it
  And puts it in a can with coffee grounds and
    sardine tins;
        The truck comes by on Friday
          and carts it all away;
        And a thousand trucks just like it are
          converging on the bay, oh,

  Garbage! (garbage, garbage, garbage) Garbage!
  We're filling up the sea with garbage (garbage...)
  What will we do
  When there's no place left to put all the
  Garbage? (garbage, garbage, garbage...)

2. Mister Thompson starts his Cadillac and winds it
        down the freeway track
    Leaving friends and neighbors in a hydro-carbon
        haze;
    He's joined by lots of smaller cars all sending
        gases to the stars.
    There they form a seething cloud that hangs for
        thirty days.
            And the sun licks down into it with an ultra-
                violet tongue.
            Turns it into smog and then it settles in our
                lungs, oh,

    Garbage! (garbage, garbage, garbage) Garbage!
    We're filling up the sky with garbage (garbage...)
    What will we do
    When there's nothing left to breathe but
    Garbage (garbage, garbage...)

3. Getting home and taking off his shoes he settles
        with the evening news,
    While the kids do homework with the TV in one ear
        (Garbage, garbage)
    While Superman for the thousandth time sells
        talking dolls and conquers crime,
    Dutifully they learn the date-of-birth of Paul Revere.
            In the papers there's a piece about the Mayor's
                middle name,
            He gets it read in time to watch the all-star
                bingo game, oh,

    Garbage, (garbage, garbage, garbage)
        Garbage! (garbage, garbage, garbage)
    We're fillin' up our minds with garbage
        (garbage, garbage, garbage)
    What will we do when there's nothing left to read*
    And there's nothing left to need,
    Nothing left to watch,
    And nothing left to touch,
    There's nothing left to walk upon
    And nothing left to talk upon
    Nothing left to see
    And there's nothing left to be but
    Garbage? (garbage, garbage)

4. In Mister Thompson's fac-to-ry
        they're making plastic Christmas trees
    Complete with silver tinsel and a geodesic stand
    The plastic's mixed in giant vats
        from some con-glom-er-ation that's
    Been piped from deep within the earth
        or strip mined from the land.
            And if you question anything they say,
                "Why, don't you see
            It's ab-so-lute-ly needed for the
                e-co-no-my," oh

Garbage (garbage, garbage)
    Garbage! (garbage, garbage)
Their stocks and their bonds all garbage
What will they do
When their system goes to smash**
There's no value to their cash
There's no money to be made
But there's a world to be repaid
Their kids will read in history books
About financiers and other crooks
And feudalism, and slavery
And Nukes and all their knavery
To history's dustbin they're consigned
Along with lots of other kinds of
Garbage (garbage, garbage, garbage...)

* Sing next seven lines to essentially the same line of music.
**Sing the next nine lines also to this same line of music.

Sample variations.

Mike Agranoff of New Jersey made up the first seven lines of verse 4, disagreed with me about the rest, but allowed me to sing his lines anyway. Thanks, Mike; your complete verse is below. And, thanks Bill Steele. Bill tells me that dozens of people have added verses to his song, an underground classic.

In Mister Thompson's factory
    they're making plastic Christmas trees
Complete with silver tinsel and a geodesic stand.
The plastic's mixed in giant vats
    from some conglomeration that's
Been piped from deep within the ground
    or strip mined from the land.
        The residue gets flushed away
            through pipes beneath the ground,
        Gets dumped into the river
            and fills up Long Island Sound.

Garbage, (garbage, garbage, garbage)
    Garbage, (garbage, garbage, garbage)
We're killing off the fish with garbage,
    (garbage, garbage, garbage)
What will we do when there's no fish left to catch
And nothing left to swim in
And nothing left to drink but garbage!

God Blessed America
~~This Land Was made For You~~ + me   178
                                                                        W

This land is your land, this land is my land
From ~~the~~ California to the ~~New York~~ Island,
From the Redwood Forest, to the Gulf stream waters,
    God blessed America for me.

As I went walking that ribbon of highway
And saw above me that endless skyway,
And saw below me the golden valley, I said:
    God blessed America for me.

I roamed and rambled, and followed my footsteps
To the sparkling sands of her diamond deserts,
And all around me, a voice was sounding:
    God blessed America for me.

                         there
✓ Was a big high wall that tried to stop me
A sign was painted said: Private Property.
But on the back side it didn't say nothing —
    God blessed America for me.

When the sun come shining, then I was strolling
In wheat fields waving, and dust clouds rolling;
The voice was chanting as the fog was lifting:
    God blessed America for me.

One bright sunny morning in the shadow of the steeple
By the Relief office I saw my people —
As they stood hungry, I stood there wondering if
    God blessed America for me.

                    * all you can write is
                      what you see.

original copy
of this song   Woody G.
                                  N.Y., N.Y., N.Y.
                                  Feb. 23, 1940
                                  43rd st & 6th ave.,
                                  Hanover House

Above is the song "This Land Is Your Land" as Woody first wrote it down. Sometime between 1940 and 1949 he changed the last line and then recorded verses 1, 2, 3, and 5 for Folkways Records. A later handwritten version amended the words to one verse slightly to read:

Was a great high wall there that tried to stop me;
Was a great big sign there says "Private Prop'ty…"

Arlo sings this line as "A great big sign says "No Trespassing". And Woody later added a good new last verse:

Nobody living can ever stop me,
As I go walking my freedom highway.
Nobody living can make me turn back.
This land was made for you and me.

It was this last verse along with the 4th and 6th verses which Woody taught young Arlo in the early 1950's saying, "Arlo, they're singing my song in the schools, but they're not singing all the verses. You write 'em down now."

What comes next is an article I wrote about this song a few years back for The Village Voice.

This Land Is Your Land
(Portrait of a song as a bird in flight)

"A notation of folksong in a book is like a picture of a bird in a bird book. It was changing before the picture was taken, and changed afterward." (CLS)

"This Land Is Your Land," with its deceptively simple melody, was put together by Woody Guthrie in the 1940's. When he first got the idea for it, "God Bless America" was getting a big play on the radio. In his own handwriting in the 1940's, you see how he first wrote it. In the next 9 years he changed the last line, added a few verses. In the late 1940's he recorded it for Disc Records (now Folkways) in the 3-verse version printed below, now widely known. Around 1949 the Jewish Young People's Folksingers Chorus directed by Robert DeCormier in New York started singing it. They spread it. When Woody Guthrie went into the hospital in 1952 he signed over the rights to the then-little-known song to a publisher who now collects royalties for it and turns them over to Woody's family. Indirectly much of the royalties go to the Committee to Combat Huntington's Disease, which has been set up by Marjorie Mazia Guthrie.

By the mid-1950's a few school song books dared include it. By 1971 they all did. But only a chorus and three verses.

WOODY GUTHRIE & FAMILY, CONEY ISLAND, 1951

This land is your land, this land is
my land, From Cal-i-for-nia
to the New York Is-land, From the red-wood
for-est to the Gulf Stream wa-ter,
This land was made for you and me.

Words & music by Woody Guthrie (1940)
TRO - © 1956 (renewed), 1958 (renewed) & 1970 Ludlow Music, Inc., New York, NY.

(The three best-known verses were printed here. See page at left for all five of Woody's original verses, plus another one he taught Arlo).

The other three verses are not so generally known. When Arlo Guthrie was a child his father visited home from the hospital and had Arlo write down the verses which didn't get in the school songbooks.

I and others have started singing them. We feel that there is a danger of this song being misinterpreted without these new/old verses being added. The song could even be co-opted by the very selfish interests Woody was fighting all his life. Washington Bigwheel Clark Clifford in March 1950 addressed the wealthy businessmen at Chicago's Executive Club: "...The people have to feel that their small share of this country is as much theirs as it is yours and mine..." With only half of Woody's verses, "This Land Is Your Land" falls right into Mr. Clifford's trap. In other words, "Let people go ahead and sing the song. Meanwhile you and I know who really controls the country."

The song has now been used in movies and TV, and has been used to accompany television commercials. Today every American has heard the song at some time or another, even though it has never been at the "top of the charts." A few far rightists look upon the song as part of "the International Communist Plot," but the daughter of Ronald Reagan liked to include the song in her repertoire as a "folk singer" in the 1970's.

OK. Was Woody A Communist? Were Woody alive today I believe he would scorn to use the Bill of Rights to protect himself. "Sure I'm a communist" he once wrote in the mid-'40's in a personal letter. And at the time he wrote "This Land Is Your Land," he was writing a regular column "Woody Sez" for the *Daily Worker* and *People's World*, the two U.S. Communist newspapers. He once applied to be a member of the party but was turned down. He was always traveling, hated meetings and political discussions which used long words. Keep in mind that he considered Jesus was basically a Communist. In his own way Woody was very religious. When he went into a hospital in 1952, he said intently to us, "Only God can help me." When a nurse asked him what religion he was so she could fill out a form, he replied, "All." She asked him again and said he must give one or another; his reply was, "All or none."

Fred Hellerman went with Harold Leventhal (who set up the Woody Guthrie Trust Fund) to visit Woody at the first mental hospital he was sent to. "Is the food OK? Being treated all right?"

Woody said everything was fine. "Besides, I can get up here and shout 'I'm a Communist' and everybody'll shrug and say 'Aw, he's crazy' You try doing that on the outside and they'll arrest you. Why this is the last place in America that's really free."

Would Woody call himself a Communist today? Read his writings, prose and poetry. Decide for yourself.

Back to the song.

One young fellow wrote me that he was starting a campaign to make the song the national anthem. I wrote him, "Please stop! Can't you see U.S. Marines marching into another little country playing this song?" In any case, I for one would be sorry to see it made an official anthem. A song is not a speech. Like any work of art, it has many meanings for many people. It reflects new meanings as life shines new lights upon it. To make "This Land Is Your Land" an official song would be to rob it of its poetic career and doom it to a political straitjacket, no matter how well-fitting the jacket might seem to be at the time.

When I sing the song now, I still usually end up with the gloriously optimistic verse, "The sun came shining and I was strolling." But before this I do a lot of singing and talking and often throw in a couple new verses of my own.

Maybe you been working just as hard as you're able
And you just got crumbs from the rich man's table
Maybe you been wondering, is it truth or fable
This land was made for you and me.

My friend from Louisiana, Brother Frederick Douglas Kirkpatrick, sang "You just get crumbs from the white man's table."

Dozens of other verses have been written to the song within the last 10 years. Some of them simply change a few words to make the chorus apply to Canada or to England or Australia. There have been verses sung from New Mexico in Spanish. There have been anti-pollution verses. I always encourage anyone who loves any song not to be ashamed to try making up verses for it. Try some language other than English, if only to remind ourselves that this America of ours is a multi-national place. I'd like to hear verses in the Cherokee language, or Navaho, or Mohawk.

Consider the following verse made up a few years ago.

This land is your land, but it once was my land
Before we sold you Manhattan Island
You pushed my nation to the reservation,
This land was stole by you from me.

(BY CAPPY ISRAEL)

When I am on stage and sing the previous verse, it often gets applause, but still I find it hard to go right into the well-known chorus after that, so I tell them the story of how in May 1968 in Resurrection City, Washington, D.C., Jimmy Collier, a great young black singer from the midwest, was asked to lead this song. Henry Crowdog of the Sioux Indian delegation came up and punched his finger in Jimmy's chest. "Hey, you're both wrong. It belongs to me." Jimmy stopped and added seriously, "Should we not sing this song?" Then a big grin came over Henry Crowdog's face. "No, it's okay. Go ahead and sing it. *As long as we are all down here together to get something done.*" And then Jimmy sailed into the chorus and the crowd roared it along with him.

How can a disinherited people possess their future? Who are the disinherited? Certainly Native Americans are. Certainly African-Americans. I say the whole of industrialized, polluted humankind has, to a certain extent, sold our birthright for a mess of potage. If we are to survive, we must build a world in which the children of every human being on earth can share. Struggling, sure. But cooperating too, not threatening to kill each other. This song can help us in our search and our joyous struggle to possess our future:

Where poisons no longer fill our waters
Where peace and justice fill our borders
When hunger and hatred are past disgraces
This land was made for you and me.

As I was sailing that Hudson River
I saw around me the tow'ring timber
I saw beneath me all New York's litter
Still this land was made for you and me.

(BY JEAN WILCOX, ILLINOIS)

JIMMY COLLIER & PETE SEEGER

Many have written sarcastic verses.

As I was walking that ribbon of highway
I heard the buzzing of hundred chain saws
And the Redwoods falling, and the loggers calling
This land was made for you and me.

(BY COUNTRY JOE MACDONALD)

We've logged the forests, we've mined the mountains
We've damned the rivers, but we've built fountains!
We got tin and plastic, and crowded freeways,
This land was made for you and me.

(BY JERRY J. SMITH)

I've roamed and rambled, and followed the beer cans
From the toxic cities to the flooded canyons
And all around me were the billboards reading
"This land was made for you and me."

(BY ???)

On the other hand, they'd say to me, "Pete, you're
sentimental. Be realistic."

As I went walking the oil-filled coastline
Along the beaches fishes were choking
The smog kept rolling, the populations growing
This land was made for you and me.

(BY COUNTRY JOE MACDONALD)

Several people have made verses in Spanish.

Es vuestra tierra, es nuestra tierra
De la llanura a la sierra
De la mar Pacifica a la mar Atlantica
Fue hecha para ti, para mi.

(BY SALLY ROGERS 1990)

Esta Es Mi Tierra

Aqui llegaron mis antecesores.
Cruzaron aguas grandiosamente.
Montaron caballos hasta Sante Fe.
Mi bella tierra es para mi.

Esta es mi tierra, esta es su tierra
Tierra de hombres exploradores
Poblaron pueblos entre los Indios
Mi bella tierra es para mi.

Conquistador Hernando Cortez
Cabeza de Vaca y Coronado
Honorables hombres de nuestra Raza
Mi bella tierra es para mi.

Colonizador fue Juan de Onate
Diego de Vargas tambien lo fue
Hombre valiente fue Santa Anna
Fue gran ejemplo para mi

Esta es mi tierra, esta es su tierra
Desde California hasta el Rio Grande
Esas fronteras del Sudoeste
Mi bella tierra es para mi

Esta es mi tierra que hermosos valles
Sierras muy altas, montes muy verdes
Cielos muy claros, aires muy limpios
Mi bella tierra es para mi.

Esta es mi tierra, esta es su tierra
Sangre mexclada Indo-Hispano
Mi linda idioma es español
Mi bella tierra es para mi

(ALBERTO O. MARTINEZ, ESPANOLA, NM
PUBLISHED IN *EL GRITO DEL NORTE*, JUNE 1969.)

Some verses I made up when singing along the Hudson River, in the Clearwater campaign.

This river is your river, this river is my river
She'll return to us just as much as we all give her
She needs our love, more than gold or silver
This land was made for you and me.

I come a long way here, I got a long way to go yet
I got things to learn here, I got seeds to sow yet
So many sisters and brothers, we still don't know yet
This land was made for you and me.

Woodland and grassland and river shorelines
To everything living, bugs, snakes and microbes
Fin, fur, and feather, we're all here together
This land was made for you and me.

One final note: remember what I wrote on p.16. "Add, subtract. But beware of multiplying."

The publishers of this song, who have the difficult job of collecting royalties for its use and seeing that it is not misused, are probably wincing by now. I am certainly not making their job any easier. Let me say simply that all the verses printed in this article are copyrighted by the same company that copyrighted the original song. And I suggest that if you make more changes yourself, you send them in to the company so at least they'll have a complete list of all the good new verses. Here's their address: TRO, 11 West 19th St., New York, NY 10011-4298.

Footnote: The last three pages have been adapted from an article in a New York City weekly © Copyright 1971 by *The Village Voice*. Reprinted by Permission.

After this long discussion of one famous song, someone will say, "Why don't we just sing Woody's song like he wrote it? His verses are better than any that have been added."

Good point. It's true that sometimes a group of people get singing a good song and want to make it longer and longer. They add all the verses they know, and make up new ones. But maybe one of the more creative things a singer can do to a song is to forget.

Forget the verses which are forgettable.

Forget words, phrases. Substitute better ones.

Forget whole songs except for one unforgettable phrase which then gets incorporated into another song.

And finally the songs which a nation remembers are truly called folksongs, because so many folks have had a hand (or a throat) in shaping them.

Chapter VII   The Vietnam War

© Len Munnik, Amsterdam

"Any mule can kick a barn down. It takes skilled hands to build it up again."

Lyndon Johnson, 1967
(Give credit where credit is due)

There's nothing like a crisis to bring out the urge to write poetry. The 1960's were a productive period for me. I had been inspired by the Civil Rights movement. Every week I was singing at different colleges and was able to test out a new song on a live-wire audience. I knew I was doing O.K. when some person would loudly boo a line and then was promptly drowned out by thousands of cheers. The poor guy who booed probably looked around in astonishment, saying "What's happening to our country when traitorous words like that are applauded?" I hope I started him thinking.

I could remember that way back in 1954 when the French were being defeated in Vietnam, I read in the *Daily Worker*, "The U.S. establishment will move in now to try to control things there." President Eisenhower said, "The USA must have that tungsten."

But the first song I wrote about Vietnam, "King Henry," was 11 years later. It was inspired by a letter in a local newspaper. I took the words of the third, fourth, and fifth stanzas directly from it. The woman writing the letter was quoting her husband, who had been a U.S. "Adviser." I couldn't get her letter out of my head. I had taken my family skiing for two days. My conscience was getting to me. The words of the verses came to me on a ski slope. The tune is an ancient great one.

A couple years after I wrote it, this song got me in hot water. Toshi and I were on tour in Europe, east and west. In the Soviet Union I had sung songs of the Civil Rights Movement and the Labor Movement but purposely stayed away from the subject of Vietnam. In Moscow I was asked by one of the students at Moscow University if I'd give an extra concert for them. "None of us have been able to get tickets to your regular concert. It is sold out."

Peter Grose, the *New York Times* correspondent in Moscow, asked if he could accompany me to the concert. "They won't let me on the campus."

"Sure," said I, in all innocence, "come along. You can carry my guitar for me."

The short article he wrote was first printed in the Paris edition of the *New York Herald-Tribune*. He ignored all the positive songs I'd sung and mentioned only this one, which had actually been sung during the question-and-answer period, when one of the Moscow students asked, "What kinds of songs are being sung in American universities these days?" I told them about the songs of Phil Ochs and Bob Dylan and sang this.

Grose's article was picked up a couple days later by the *New York Times* and given the headline "Seeger Sings Anti-American Song in Moscow." The headline and the article were then picked up by my hometown paper in Beacon, New York, population 13,000, 60 miles north of the Big Apple. I called up the editor of the *Times*, and quoted the words of the song. He agreed they were not "anti-American," and said the headline had been changed in later editions. But the damage had been done.

King Henry

King Hen-ry marched forth,   a   sword   in his   hand,   Two thou-sand   horse-men   all   at   his   com-mand;   In   a   fort-night   the   riv-ers   ran   red   through   the   land,___   The   year   fif-teen   hun-dred   and   twen-ty.___

Words by Pete Seeger (1965) Music traditional (Scottish) "I Once Loved a Lass"
© 1965 (renewed), 1966 by Fall River Music, Inc.

1. King Henry marched forth, a sword in his hand,
   Two thousand horsemen all at his command;
   In a fortnight the rivers ran red through the land,
   The year fifteen hundred and twenty.

2. The year it is now nineteen sixty-five
   It's easier far to stay half alive.
   Just keep your mouth shut when the planes zoom
     and dive
   Ten thousand miles over the ocean.

3 Simon was drafted in '63,
   In '64, sent over the sea;
   Last month this letter he sent to me,
   He said, "You won't like what I'm saying."

4. He said, "We've no friends here, no hardly a one,
   We've got a few generals who just want our guns;
   But it'll take more than that if we're ever to win,
   Why, we'll have to flatten the country."

5. "It's my own troops I have to watch out for,"
     he said,
   "I sleep with a pistol right under my head";
   He wrote this last month; last week he was dead,
   And Simon came home in a casket.

6. I mind my own business, I watch my TV,
   Complain about taxes, but pay anyway;
   In a civilized manner my forefathers betray,
   Who long ago struggled for freedom.

7. But each day a new headline screams at my bluff,
   On TV some general says we must be tough;
   In my dreams I stare at this family I love,
   All gutted and spattered with napalm.

8. King Henry marched forth, a sword in his hand,
   Two thousand horsemen all at his command;
   In a fortnight the rivers ran red through the land,
   Ten thousand miles over the ocean.

I was due to sing at the local high school in two weeks. Some local "patriots"[1] started a petition campaign to stop the concert. They went up and down Main Street and got 700 signatures. Somebody started a forest fire at one end of our mountainside land one Sunday, and a week later another forest fire at the other end of our property. A liberal doctor in Beacon urged me, "You should cancel the concert. You know this is fascism. You're going to be run out of town."

Toshi and I decided it was worth making a stand, and sure enough, we were right. The Beacon High School students stuck up for me, and so did a few of the shopkeepers that we had traded with. I remember one elderly hardware store owner who was personally extremely conservative and had voted for Barry Goldwater in '64. He said, "Well, I don't know your politics, young man, but it's America. You got a right to your opinion."

The head of the school board, also an elderly man, said he could not legally refuse to allow the use of the high school. The New York State Supreme Court had only recently handed down a decision that if the schools rented to anybody, they had to rent to anybody regardless of their opinions. (The court's decision actually was related to the attempt of the John Birch Society to stop my concert in East Meadow, Long Island, a few years earlier.)

So it all turned out pretty well after all. With all this publicity, the high school auditorium was jam-packed, and the folks sang along well. Me, I learned an important lesson.

I realized belatedly that for 18 years I'd treated my home town like a hotel. I'd gone down to pick up my mail and groceries and gone back to our mountainside cabin. Most people in town didn't really know who the heck I was.

Well, the *Clearwater* campaign forced me to change my way of doing things. More of that later.

[1] Why do I use quotes? Because too often these types think they are the only patriots.

Bring 'Em Home

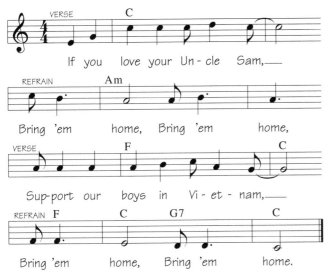

Words & music by Pete Seeger (1966)
© 1966 by Stormking Music Inc.

1. If you love your Uncle Sam,
   Bring 'em home, Bring 'em home.
   Support our boys in Vietnam,
   Bring 'em home, Bring 'em home.

2. It'll make our generals sad, I know,
   (REFRAIN: Bring 'em home..., etc.)
   They want to tangle with the foe.
   (REPEAT REFRAIN THROUGHOUT)

3. They want to test their weaponry,
   But here is their big fallacy:

4. Our foe is hunger and ignorance,
   You can't beat that with bombs and guns.

5. I may be right, I may be wrong,
   But I got a right to sing this song.

6. There's one thing I must confess,
   I'm not really a pacifist.

7. If an army invaded this land of mine,
   You'd find me out on the firing line,

8. Even if they brought their planes to bomb,
   Though they brought helicopters and napalm.

9. Show those generals their fallacy:
   They don't have the right weaponry.

10. For defense you need common sense,*
    They don't have the right armaments.

11. The world needs teachers, books and schools,
    And learning a few universal rules.

12. So if you love your Uncle Sam
    Support our boys in Vietnam.

* Have you heard the French definition of an expert? "Someone who avoids all the little mistakes on the way to the big fallacy."

(Many variant melodies)

Not one of my best, this. An editorial in rhyme. I always caution beginning songwriters, "Beware of editorials in rhyme. Better: Tell a story." Nevertheless it did its job, got thousands singing that short refrain. And some life-long passions got into the verses.

Next, a better song, written a year later.

This song took a couple weeks to write. I saw a newspaper photo of troops in the Mekong Delta and the last line came to me all at once — words, tune, rhythm. I wrote it down in my pocket notebook: then, as usual, I was unable to finish it. But it kept coming back to haunt me. Had to do something about it. In two weeks of tussling, I got it finished. I sang it everywhere I could. At colleges it got an explosive reaction. This was early in '67.

In the fall I got a phone call from two friends, Tommy and Dick Smothers, who had started in night clubs as comedians making fun of "folk singers," and now had a successful weekly national TV show. In early '67 their bosses at CBS, overjoyed at their high ratings, had asked what they could do to make their stars happier. "Let us have Seeger as a guest on our show," shot back Tommy.

"Well—hm—let's think about that."

In October CBS said O.K. I flew to L.A., sang a medley of soldier songs on the show, starting with "The Riflemen of Bennington" (1778), "John Brown's Body" (1863), "The D-Day-Dodgers" (1944) and ended with "Big Muddy." The videotape was flown to New York City for the CBS brass to check it before it went out over the network. When it was aired a couple days later, "Big Muddy" had been cut out of the tape. One moment I had a guitar in my hand; a second later I had a banjo in my hand — it was an obvious cut.

The Smothers Brothers took to the print media, "CBS is censoring our best jokes; they censored Seeger's best song." Finally in January CBS said, "O.K., O.K., you can have Seeger sing it." On 24 hours' notice, I again flew to L.A., taped the song. Seven million viewers saw it. Only a Detroit station deleted the song.

This was one time in my entire life I really wished I had been able to properly promote a song and get it heard by the whole country. It could have saved lives. John Hammond, then overseeing my recording at Columbia, agreed to release the song as a single. But neither he nor I had much influence with the sales department. In Denver a young man told me, "Pete, I was working in the office of the local distributor for Columbia Records when your single of 'Big Muddy' came in. My boss took one listen and exploded, 'Those guys in New York must be nuts to think I can sell a record like this.'

"Pete, your record never even left the shelves," said my friend.

However, a month after the TV program, LBJ threw in the sponge, said he would not run for re-election. Did this song help? Who knows?

Waist Deep In The Big Muddy

It was back in nine-teen for-ty-two,— I was a mem-ber of a good— pla-toon.— We were on ma-neu-vers in-a Loo-zi-an-na, one night by the light of the moon.— The cap-tain told us to ford a riv-er, That's how it all be-gun.— We were knee deep in the Big Mud-dy, but the big fool said to push on.—

(Also known as "The Big Muddy")
Words & music by Pete Seeger (1967)
TRO - © 1967 Melody Trails, Inc., New York, NY.

1. It was back in nineteen forty-two,
    I was a member of a good platoon.
    We were on maneuvers in-a Loozianna,
    One night by the light of the moon.
        The captain told us to ford a river,
        That's how it all begun.
        We were—knee deep in the Big Muddy,
        But the big fool said to push on.

2. The Sergeant said, "Sir, are you sure,
    This is the best way back to the base?"
    "Sergeant, go on! I forded this river
    'Bout a mile above this place.
        It'll be a little soggy but just keep slogging.
        We'll soon be on dry ground."
        We were—waist deep in the Big Muddy
        And the big fool said to push on.

3. The Sergeant said, "Sir, with all this equipment
    No man will be able to swim."
    "Sergeant, don't be a Nervous Nellie,"
    The Captain said to him.
        "All we need is a little determination;
        Men, follow me, I'll lead on."
        We were—neck deep in the Big Muddy
        And the big fool said to push on.

4. All at once, the moon clouded over,
    We heard a gurgling cry.
    A few seconds later, the captain's helmet
    Was all that floated by.
        The sergeant said, "Turn around men! *
        I'm in charge from now on."
        And we just made it out of the Big Muddy
        With the captain dead and gone.

5. We stripped and dived and found his body
    Stuck in the old quicksand
    I guess he didn't know that the water was deeper
    Than the place he'd once before been.
        Another stream had joined the Big Muddy
        'Bout a half mile from where we'd gone.
        We were lucky to escape from the Big Muddy
        When the big fool said to push on.

6. Well, I'm not going to point any moral;
    I'll leave that for yourself
    Maybe you're still walking, you're still talking
    You'd like to keep your health.
        But every time I read the papers **
        That old feeling comes on;
        We're—waist deep in the Big Muddy and the
        Big fool says to push on.

7. Waist deep in the Big Muddy
    And the big fool says to push on
    Waist deep in the Big Muddy
    And the big fool says to push on.
        Waist deep! Neck deep! Soon even a
        Tall man'll be over his head, we're ***
        Waist deep in the Big Muddy!
        And the big fool says to push on!

Variant melodies:

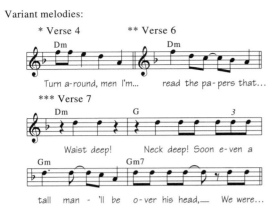

* Verse 4 ** Verse 6

Turn a-round, men I'm...   read the pa-pers that...

*** Verse 7

Waist deep!   Neck deep! Soon e-ven a

tall man - 'll be o-ver his head,— We were...

P.S. After singing in a midwest college, I stayed overnight at the home of a professor. At lunch he came in laughing, "At my first class I started briskly announcing that we had to get cracking the books; from the rear of the room I heard some student mutter, 'The big fool says to push on.'"

In April the civil rights coalition was falling apart. Dr. King was assassinated; Robert Kennedy soon after. The Democratic Party convention in Chicago ignored the anti-war protests. In the fall Nixon was elected. Soviet tanks rolled into Prague. I was 49 years old.

As in any blues, the melody changes from verse to verse, and every time you sing it. Incidentally, I usually do it down in G or A. The banjo gets better blue notes. You have heard it asked, "Can a white man sing the blues?" Rande Harris counters, "Can a blue man sing the whites?"

False From True

When my songs   turn to ash-es— on my
tongue,—   When I look   in the mir-ror and
see I'm no long-er young;—
Then I   got to start a-gain— the job of
sep - a - rat - ing false   from true,—

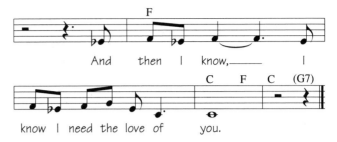

And   then   I know,——   I
know   I need the love of   you.

Words & music by Pete Seeger (1968)
© 1968 by Sanga Music Inc.

1. When my songs turn to ashes on my tongue,
   When I look in the mirror and see I'm no longer young,
   Then I got to start the job of separating
      false from true,
   And then I know, I know I need the love of you.

2. **When I found tarnish on some of my brightest
      dreams,
   When some folks I'd trusted turned out not quite
      what they seemed;
   Then I got to start the job of separating
      false from true,
   Then once more I know, I know I need the love of you.

3. No song I can sing will make Governor Wallace
      change his mind*,
   No song I can sing will take the gun from a
      hate-filled man;
   But I promise you, and you, brothers and sisters
      of every skin,
   I'll sing your story while I've breath within.

4. *** We got to keep on keeping on, even when the
      sun goes down,
   We got to live, live, live until another day
      comes 'round;
   Meanwhile, better start over, separating
      false from true,
   And more and more, I know I need the love of you.

* Hey, I wrote this 25 years ago. Maybe he *has* changed his mind.

** Verse 2

When   I   found   tar-nish...

*** Verse 7

We got to keep on keep-ing on,   e-ven when the...etc.

The next song was sparked by one line in a poem in a popular magazine: "In April they sent us the bill for the killing of the children." Now I've lost the poet's name. I sent her a copy of my song, thanked her, and got a nice letter in reply. In the 1990's the Short Sisters (Kim Wallach, Fay Baird and my niece, Kate Seeger) recorded it.

The Calendar

1. May, May, the flow-ers bloom;— a June wed-ding, an emp-ty room.— Ju-ly— was ver-y warm - O, Li - lo, lull- o, li - lo.—

2. Au - gust, we beat the heat, Fled the sub-urbs for the beach.— Sep-tem - ber, bought a car - O, Li - lo, lull- o, li - lo.—

3. Oc - to - ber, red and gold; No - vem - ber, turn-ing cold.— De - cem - ber, 'round the tree - O,

4. Jan - u - a - ry brought the snow, Next month, ski-ing all did go.— March, my God, how did the wind blow! Li - lo, lull- o, li - lo.—

5. A - pril, cru - el, sweet A - pril!— Now they pre-sent to us the bill.— For the burn-ing of the chil - dren, For the burn-ing of the chil - dren. Lie * low, Lie low, Lie low.

Words & music by Pete Seeger (1969)
© 1969 by Sanga Music Inc.

* Pronounce "Lie-low" at the end — La-ee-lo.

Postscript: Singers in many parts of the world like to give out sounds that have no strict meaning. Why? Why do we like music anyway? Some Native American songs are mostly "vocables." Irish songs and some English and Scottish songs are full of "nonsense words." "Hey diddle diddle, Too-ri-oo-ri-ay." I think it's a little like repeating the last line of a song (see p. 120). In a narrative song with compact words, they slow down the action so you can savor it.

African-American songs have a lot of it, too, but of a different type — more "Ohhs" and "Heys." Gospel songs will have a lot of repetition instead.

Sometimes, as in scat singing, the "nonsense" words end up meaning more than the listener thought, at first hearing. In this song, "The Calendar," it comes out in the last line of the last verse.

In 1969 I took a nap in a student dormitory before singing in a small southern college. At the foot of the bed was a huge American flag. At the head of the bed was a huge photo-enlargement of Leon Trotsky. I didn't know which was "camp." Couldn't sleep. Got up. Wrote verses. The first line is swiped from a poem by my uncle, Alan Seeger, who was the second American killed in World War I — he was a volunteer with the French Foreign Legion. My father, his older brother, had written him: "Alan, you're a damn fool. Don't you know the class of people that run France is the same class that runs Germany? You should have stayed out of it. I don't expect to see you again." And he didn't. But my uncle's poem was widely reprinted. I sometimes recite both together. (I tried putting a tune to mine — it didn't help it.) Here's Alan's original.

ALAN SEEGER (1888–1916)

I Have A Rendezvous With Death

I have a rendezvous with death
At some disputed barricade
When the spring comes back with rustling shade
And apple blossoms fill the air
I have a rendezvous with death
When spring brings back blue days and fair.
    It may be he shall take my hand
    And lead me into his dark land
    And close my eyes and quench my breath
    It may be I shall pass him still
I have a rendezvous with death
On some scarred slope of battered hill
When spring trips north again next year
And the first meadow flowers appear

    God knows, 'twere better to be deep
    Pillowed in silk and scented down
    Pulse nigh to pulse and breath to breath
    Where love throbs out in blissful sleep
    And hushed awakenings are dear.
But I've a rendezvous with death
At midnight in some flaming town
When spring comes 'round again next year
And I to my pledged word am true.
I shall not fail my rendezvous.

By Alan Seeger (1915)
From his *Collected Poems* published by Scriber & Sons in 1916.

So now after that great poem, I make so bold as to put my lesser poem. Tried and failed to get a worthwhile melody for it. It has been of use, though. I've been reciting it more the last few years, at the request of African-American friends.

The Torn Flag

At midnight in a flaming angry town
I saw my country's flag lying torn upon the ground.
I ran in and dodged among the crowd,
And scooped it up, and scampered out to safety.
    And then I took this striped old piece of cloth
    And tried my best to wash the garbage off.
    But I found it had been used for wrapping lies.
    It smelled and stank and attracted all the flies.
While I was feverishly at my task,
I heard a husky voice that seemed to ask;
"Do you think you could change me just a bit?
Betsy Ross* did her best, but she made a few mistakes.
    My blue is good, the color of the sky.
    The stars are good for ideals, oh, so high.
    Seven stripes of red are strong to meet all danger;
    But those white stripes: they, they need some
        changing.
I need also some stripes of deep, rich brown,
And some of tan and black, then all around
A border of God's gracious green would look good there.
Maybe you should slant the stripes, then I'd not be so
    square."
    I woke and said: "What a ridiculous story.
    Don't let anybody say I suggested tampering with
        Old Glory."
    But tonight it's near midnight, and in another
        flaming town
    Once again I hear my country's flag lies torn upon
        the ground.

By Pete Seeger (1969)
TRO - © 1970 Melody Trails, Inc., New York, NY.

* Research of Earl Williams, Jr., of Washington, D.C., has discovered that Francis Hopkinson actually proposed the design.

Some parts of the world (Japan is one) like songs in a minor mode. Some individuals also. Most of us now go back and forth easily — too easily? — from one mode to another. The next song, like the last two, is in a minor key.

The weakness of any allegory, here, or in the Bible or anywhere, is that it can be too pat. The "meaning" of a work of art should shift, change, expand. However, this allegory worked. I've had requests for it 20 years later. Today the "eggheads" are warning us about the oxone layer, global warming, overpopulation, etc.

All My Children of the Sun

Words & music by Pete Seeger (1969)
© 1969 by Sanga Music Inc.

1. The navigator said to the engineer,
   I think our radio's dead.
   I can hear but I can't send,
   And there's bad weather ahead.
       The pilot said to the co-pilot,
       Our right engine's gone.
       But if we can make it over these mountains,
       Perhaps I can set her down.
   All my children of the sun!

2. Five hundred miles from nowhere
   We bellylanded on a river.
   We bid a quick goodbye
   To that ship of silver.
       Twenty-five piled out the window,
       Twenty reached the shore.
       We turned to see our metal bird
       Sink to rise no more.
   All my children of the sun!

3. We found some floating logs,
   We found some sharp stones.
   We cut some vines and made a raft.
   It was our only hope.
       The navigator said he thought there was
       A town somewhere downstream.
       So now each tried to do his best
       To paddle as a team.
   (OMIT LAST LINE)

4. All except one young guy
   Who kept arguing with the navigator.
   He said he'd read about a waterfall
   We would come to sooner or later.
       At a river's bend he persuaded us
       To bring our craft to beach.
       But a search party found the river smooth
       As far as eye could reach.
   All my children of the sun.

5. Once again he persuaded us to stop.
   We cursed at the delay.
   Once again we found the river
   Flowing on the same old way.
       We said, shut up your arguing.
       You give us all a pain.
       Why don't you pitch in and do your part—
       Be constructive for a change?
   All my children of the sun.

6. Still egghead kept on talking
    In the same longwinded way.
    We said, if you won't paddle,
    Get the hell out of our way.
       We told him to go sit
       Far back at the stern.
       Then we strained to paddle harder,
       And then the river made a turn.
    All my children of the sun.

7. One paddler heard sound of tapping
    And what he saw, when he did turn,
    Was egghead with a sharp stone,
    Cutting the vines that bound the stern.

(THE FOLLOWING FOUR LINES USE SAME TUNE AS THE PREVIOUS FOUR)

    With a cry of rage the paddler
    Leaped up to his feet.
    He swung his long pole
    Knocked egghead into the deep.
       But now the logs were splaying out.
       The raft had come unbound.
       Like mad we paddled for the shore,
       Before all would drown.
    All my children of the sun.

8. A search party went out to find more vines
    To tie the raft up tight.
    In twenty minutes they returned,
    Their faces pale with fright.
       They said a quarter mile down river
       We _did_ find a waterfall.
       It's over a hundred feet in height.
       It would have killed us all.
    All my children of the sun.

9. And that is why on the banks
    Of a far off wilderness stream,
    Which none of us, none of us,
    Will ever see again,
       There stands a cross for someone,
       Hardly older than a boy.
       Who, we thought, was only
       Trying to destroy.
    All my children of the sun.

My accompaniment to this was some fast banjo picking, as on a Kentucky mountain ballad. Tuning was "Mountain minor" — EBEAB (I have a long-neck banjo) and so the Am6 and B7 chords are fretted as below. Without this exciting accompaniment, this is a boring melody.

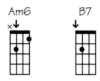

The fast banjo rhythm sets the tense feeling for this story. Below are the notes I play between the verses. You may want to work out something different.

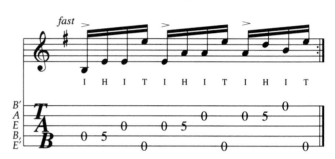

About the same time I made up a verse to sing to Bob Dylan's somg, "The Times, They Are A-Changin'."

    Yes, this is me,
    Old stick-in-the-mud
    Still shovelling away
    At a mountain of crud,
    Still hoping that songs
    Can stanch rivers of blood
    Though the evidence I may be evading
    But till this throat is choked
    And I'm drowned in the flood
    It will sing for the times ever changing.

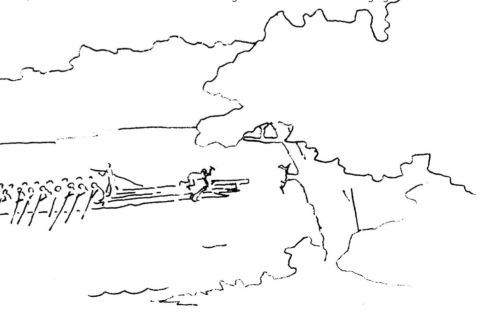

Two Against Three: A Rhythm Skill
(A Musical Interlude)

When people sing two-part harmony, they sing two notes at the same time. Can you also beat two different rhythms at the same time?

From Mexico down to Chile and Argentina it is common to see one guitar playing 3/4 time, like a waltz, and another guitarist nearby playing 6/8 time, that is, two beats per measure.

Technically, "two-against-three" is called "hemiola." It's not unknown in European music, but it's rare.

Here's a way to learn how to get the feel of it. Count off six rapid beats over and over, and pat with your left hand on your knee on the first and fourth beat only.

"ONE two three FOUR five six
ONE two three FOUR five six
ONE two three FOUR five six."

After about 20 seconds stop patting with your left hand but keep counting to six over and over. Now with your right hand tap your right knee on the first, third, and fifth beats:

"ONE two THREE four FIVE six
ONE two THREE four FIVE six
ONE two THREE four FIVE six."

Now here's the tricky part. Bring down *both* hands on the beat "ONE." When it comes to "three four five," do a "right-left-right." Keep counting to six over and over without changing speed. Eventually you can stop counting "two" and "six." Once you get it into your muscles (so your brain can forget counting), you've got it made.

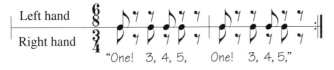

Chopin also once composed an A♭ piano "Etude" ("study") where the left hand played in 2/4 time and the right played two sets of triplets in each measure.

He also wrote "Marche Militaire." It's become a well known melody. But I remember it this way. This is the two-against-three pattern.

(One way to remember the above notes is to sing "Big bagashit, Big bagashit, Big bagashit now -" After a while you'll get the rhythm in your head and hands, which is where music should be.)

Back to the subject of this chapter.

In November 1969 in Washington, D.C., the "two-against-three" skill came in handy when I faced one of the largest crowds I've ever sung for. A half million people, all protesting the Vietnam War. Music, speeches alternated all afternoon. Suddenly it was my turn with Brother Fred Kirkpatrick, the great civil rights singer. We tried getting the crowd to join in on "Bring 'Em Home" (p. 149). No luck. By the time the beat got way out to that huge crowd, it came back a beat and a half late. Sound only travels 1,200 feet a second.

We tried Kirk's song, "Everybody's Got A Right To Live." Same problem. I looked over at Cora Weiss, holding a stopwatch on the proceedings. With a questioning look, I held up one index finger, meaning "OK, to sing one more song?"

She nodded.

I decided it was worth a gamble to try the short refrain by Yoko Ono and John Lennon, which I'd heard only three days before, and only sung once:

Give Peace a Chance

All we are say - ing,——— is

Give Peace a Chance.

Words & music by John Lennon & Paul McCartney

That's all there is to it. A song only seven seconds long. We sang it over and over. After 30 seconds a few thousand were singing it with us. After a minute tens of thousands. Peter, Paul and Mary suddenly joined us on our left. Half a minute later Mitch Miller (yes, "Sing along with Mitch") jumped up on our right and helped, waving his arms to keep everyone in rhythm. Two, three, four minutes went by as 500,000 sang it over and over.

Looking out at that sea of faces, it was like a huge ballet, flags, banners, signs, would move to the right for three beats (one measure) and then left for the next measure. Parents had children on their shoulders, swaying in rhythm.

I used the pauses to shout out short phrases. At first:

All we are say - ing, ("Sing it with us now!") is

Give Peace a Chance, ("Sing it o-ver, Sing it o-ver,")

Then:

All we are say - ing, ("Are you lis-ten-ing, Nix-on?") is

Give Peace a Chance, ("You bet-ter lis-ten, Ag-new.")

It went on for five or six minutes. A litany! Everyone got caught up in it. Finally we let it end softly as in a gospel church when a hymn has been sung till no one can add more.

How does all this relate to a "two-against-three rhythm"? Simply this: I accompanied it in 6/8 time, that is two strong beats against the 3/4-rhythm of the melody. I had a big 12-string guitar. Sonorous bass notes. My usual "dropped D" tuning, even though we were in the key of G. I got one rich low "D."

© Bettman Archives (Vietnam, 1969)

The hemiola gave it a rhythmic bite it would not have had otherwise. You try it, see if I'm not right.

Words & music by John Lennon & Paul McCartney
Adaptation and guitar arrangement by Pete Seeger
© 1969, 1993 Northern Songs. All rights controlled & administered by MCA Music Publishing, a division of MCA Inc., 1755 Broadway, New York, NY 10019 under license from Northern Songs. International copyright secured. All rights reserved.

Postscript: Dozens of television cameras recorded the afternoon's songs and speeches. A few days later I asked a friend at CBS if there was a chance to get a copy of the tape of that song. He said that one day after the demonstration orders came down from the top to destroy all the tapes.

TOSHI & PETE,
WASHINGTON MONUMENT, NOVEMBER 15, 1969

Lisa Kalvelage

Steady tempo

1. My name is Li-sa Kal-ve-lage, I was born in Nu-rem-berg, And when the trials were held there, nine-teen years a-go It seemed to me ri-dic-u-lous to hold a na-tion all to blame For the hor-rors that the world did un-der-go. A short while lat-er when I ap-plied to be a G. I. bride, An A-mer-i-can con-sul-ar of-fi-cial ques-tioned me. He re-fused my ex-it per-mit, said, my ans-wer did not show I'd learned my les-son a-bout res-pon-si-bil-i-ty.

Originally titled "My Name Is Lisa Kalvelage"
Words adapted & music by Pete Seeger (1972)
© 1966 by Sanga Music Inc.

1. My name is Lisa Kalvelage, I was born in Nuremberg
And when the trials were held there 19 years ago
It seemed to me ridiculous to hold a nation all
    to blame
For the horrors that the world did undergo
A short while later when I applied to be a G.I. bride
An American consular official questioned me
He refused my exit permit, said my answer did not
    show
I'd learned my lesson about responsibility

2. Thus suddenly I was forced to start thinking on
    this theme
And when later I was permitted to emigrate
I must have been asked a hundred times where I was
    and what I did
In those years when Hitler ruled our state
I said I was a child or at most a teen-ager
But that only extended the questioning
They'd ask, where were my parents my father,
    my mother
And to this I could answer not a thing

3. The seed planted there at Nuremberg in 1947
Started to sprout and to grow
Gradually I understood what that verdict meant
    to me
When there are crimes that I can see and I can know
And now I also know what it is to be charged with
    mass guilt
Once in a lifetime is enough for me
No, I could not take it for a second time
And that is why I am here today.

4. The events of May 25th, the day of our protest,
Put a small balance weight on the other side
Hopefully, someday my contribution to peace
Will help just a bit to turn the tide
And perhaps I can tell my children six
And later on their own children
That at least in the future they need not be silent
When they are asked, "Where was your mother,
    when?"

This story was in a newspaper clipping sent me from San Jose, California. Lisa Kalvelage and two other women, dressed in their Sunday best, stopped a shipment of napalm by standing on a loading platform and refusing to budge. Arrested, and in court she told this story to a newspaper reporter. She is still active in the peace movement there. I've done a few benefit concerts for them.

Words & music by Pete Seeger (1970)
© 1970 by Sanga Music Inc.

LISA KALVELAGE WITH FAMILY

I sing the song with a steady tempo, as Woody might have. I heard Rutthy Taubb in a street demonstration (she had a mike) do it unaccompanied, with a more free rhythm. It was beautiful to hear her voice floating above the street noise.

No two people would sing it exactly the same, and as you see here, the details of rhythm and pitch changed from verse to verse. This is standard practice, I suspect, when singing narrative ballads in various countries, in various traditions.

Seymour Hersh broke the story on the My Lai massacre. Later there was a trial and the two officers most immediately responsible got light sentences. I sang the song during the '70's. The American media ignored it, but the song got on Swedish TV. Nuremberg refers to the 1947 war-crimes trials of some of Hitler's accomplices.

Last Train to Nuremberg

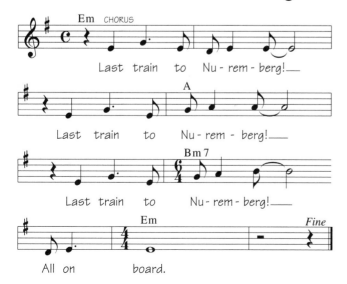

CHORUS (AND AFTER EACH VERSE):
Last train to Nuremberg!
Last train to Nuremberg!
Last train to Nuremberg! All on board!

1. Do I see Lieutenant Calley?
   Do I see Captain Medina?
   Do I see Gen'ral Koster and all his crew?
   Do I see President Nixon?
   Do I see both houses of Congress?
   Do I see the voters, me and you?

2. Who held the rifle? Who gave the orders?
   Who planned the campaign to lay waste the land?
   Who manufactured the bullet? Who paid the taxes?
   Tell me, is that blood upon my hands?

3. Go tell all the young people, tell all the little children
   Don't, don't you get aboard this train!
   See where it's come from, see where it's going.
   Don't, don't you ride it ever again.

4. If five hundred thousand mothers went to Washington
   And said, "Bring all of our sons home without delay!"
   Would the man they came to see,
   say he was too bizzee?
   Would he say he had to watch a football game?

Ho Chi Minh, who died in 1969, is one of my all-time heroes. Could he have humanized bureaucracy? I think so. A poet, a storyteller with a great sense of humor. The son of a small town school teacher, he got a job on a ship, made his way to France to study this thing called social-ism, while working in a restaurant. Attending socialist conferences after WWI he chided the French proletariat for not pushing to give French colonies their freedom. Toshi and I learned about him when we visited Hanoi in '72. Here's one of the many stories circulating about "Uncle Ho."

He's visiting an army camp, sees all the officers seated in the front row, the non-coms behind them, and the privates in back of them. He immediately goes to the rear of the hall, shouts "about face" and gives a short speech to the effect that the rank-and-file are the most important part of the army, the country, the world. And by his example he showed his generals that the best leaders are those that can inspire the rank-and-file to do their best.

HO CHI MINH

Teacher Uncle Ho

He ed-u-cat-ed all the peo-ple.

He dem-on-strat-ed to the world: If a

man will stand for his own land___ he's got the strength of ten. (Bass acc.)

And if we'd on-ly learn the les-son,

It could e-ven be a bless-in'.

He and me might dis-ag-ree___ but we need-n't go to shoot-ing a-gain.___ And if

sol-dier boys___ in ev-'ry land___ said:

Hell no, we won't go ("what did you say?")

Hell no, we won't go ("say it a-gain")

HELL NO, WE WON'T GO. I'll have to say___ in

my own way,___ the on-ly way___ that I

know, that we learned pow-er to the peo-ple and the

po-wer to know___ from Teach-er, Un-cle Ho!

Words & music by Pete Seeger (1970)
© 1970, 1993 by Stormking Music Inc.

He educated all the people.
He demonstrated to the world:
If a man will stand for his own land,
He's got the strength of ten.

And if we'd only learn the lesson,
It could even be a blessin',
He and me might disagree,
But we needn't go to shooting again.

And if soldier boys in every land say,
"Hell no, we won't go," ("what did you say")
"Hell no, we won't go," ("say it again!")
"HELL NO, WE WON'T GO!"

I'll have to say in my own way,
The only way I know,
That we learned power to the people and the power
  to know
From Teacher Uncle Ho!

Incidentally, this tune is one of my best. It's basically a steel drum melody, although it could be played by a mandolin, or nowadays a keyboard. I composed it years before I found words for it.

I used to get a college audience shouting, "Hell no, we won't go." The whistling interlude was a fun part. Then I'd sing the whole verse again. But it was a difficult song to perform. No one but me ever tried it, to my knowledge. The main difficulty, besides spitting the words out clearly, is to find the proper key. If it's comfortable to sing it, it's difficult to whistle. Perhaps the solution is to play the "Whistling Interlude" on some instrument, and just pitch it where you can sing it.

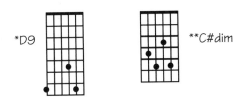

Here's a couple of unusual chord positions which are fun to try if you used Dropped D tuning (see asterisks).

The song is fun to play on an instrument, but has a bigger range than the "Star Spangled Banner."

Well, at the moment the song is mainly of historical interest. Maybe someone will find another use for the tune someday.

And this next song was inspired by a line in a student newspaper.

Our Generation

1. Our gen-er-a-tion ____ has san-dals like Vi-et-nam-ese. ____ Our gen-er-a-tion ____ wears long hair ____ with our clob-bered minds. ____ We still wink an eye to say, ____ Meet me, meet me ____ at the bot-tom of the stairs. ____

Words & music by Pete Seeger (1970)
© 1970, 1993 by Sanga Music Inc. All rights reserved

1. Our generation has sandals like Vietnamese.
    Our generation wears long hair.
    With our clobbered minds, we still wink an eye to say
    Meet me, meet me at the bottom of the stairs.

2. Our generation whistles in the dark,
    Has faith in faithlessness and in blue sky.
    Our heroes now are either none, or ev'ryone.
    Our saints also are only you and I.

3. Our generation won't remake this ravished world.
    Our generation can only try
    To wink an eye at ev'ryone, yes, ev'ryone.
    Saying meet me at the beginning of the sky!

Artist Unknown

In 1970 I knew students, black and white, who were convinced that a bloody uprising was soon coming. But students are often over-enthusiastic about revolution. In '71 in Spain I was forbidden by the Franco government to sing for the students at Barcelona University. Later a student asked me what I thought of Spain. I replied, "I think it is like a steam engine when someone has tied down the emergency release valve and the pressure is building up so there is danger of the boiler exploding."

"Oh, I hope it comes soon," said the student enthusiastically. An older man and woman standing near him didn't look so enthusiastic. They'd lived through three years of bloody civil war.

Hence the song below.

If A Revolution Comes To My Country
(Hear The Thunder! Hear The Thunder!)

If a rev-o-lu-tion comes to my coun-try, let me re-mem-ber now. ____ I mean, if blood-y con-flict rag-es, I bet-ter learn right now. ____ How to catch and skin and cook a rat, ____

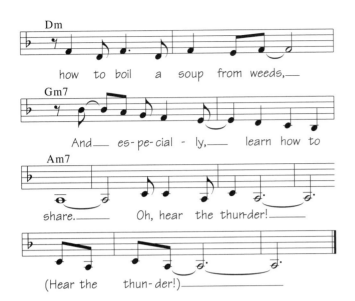

Words & music by Pete Seeger (1971)
TRO - © 1976 Melody Trails, Inc., New York, NY.

1. If a revolution comes to my country
    Let me remember now
    I mean if bloody conflict rages
    I better learn right now
    How to catch and skin and cook a rat
    How to boil a soup from weeds
    And especially learn how to share
    Oh, hear the thunder…

2. If a revolution comes to my country
    Let me remember now.
    I mean if civil war breaks down everything
    I better learn right now
    How to sleep ten in one room
    How to keep dry outside when it rains
    And especially learn how to share
    Oh, hear the thunder…

3. If a revolution comes to my country
    Let me remember now
    There'll be sickness, epidemic
    I better learn right now
    How long to boil water safe to drink
    How to recognize gangrene
    And especially learn how to share
    Oh, hear the thunder…

4. If a revolution comes to my country
    Let me remember now
    Old dollar bill, you won't mean much
    I better learn right now
    What in life has true value
    And, oh, if we'd only learn to share
    Then, oh, then would be the revolution
    Oh, hear the thunder…

5. If a revolution comes to my country
    Let me remember now.

JOAN BAEZ & PETE SEEGER, U.S. CAPITOL

At the same time the previous songs were being sung, the *Clearwater* project was starting up, and I was starting to do more work with young folks in my own home town. I realized that the tragedy of small towns is that often the best people of each generation leave town for better opportunities elsewhere. I wrote this for high school students, black and white, that I saw leave Beacon, New York.

Snow, Snow

Capo up—use Am chords, they sound Cm

Words & music by Pete Seeger (1964)
TRO - © 1965 (renewed) Melody Trails, Inc., NY, NY.

CHORUS (AND AFTER EACH VERSE):
Snow, snow, falling down;
Covering up my dirty old town.

1. Covers the garbage dump, covers the holes,
   Covers the rich homes, and the poor souls,
   Covers the station, covers the tracks,
   Covers the footsteps of those who'll not be back.

2. Under the street lamp, there stands a girl,
   Looks like she's not got a friend in this world.
   Look at the big flakes come drifting down,
   Twisting and turning, round and round.

3. Covers the mailbox, the farm and the plow.
   Even barbed wire seems—beautiful now.
   Covers the station, covers the tracks.
   Covers the footsteps of those who'll not be back.

When the Soviet magazine *Krugozor* (Horizon) printed one of my songs, this is the one they chose. The guitar part is also one of the better pieces I ever put together. You play the melody with the index finger on the top strings, while the thumb keeps a steady rhythm with the bass and middle strings. On the next page I give chord diagrams for left hand of the guitar, arrows point to the melody string for the index finger. Thumb keeps bass-chord pattern going. Single strings sound best.

Intro. & Between verses

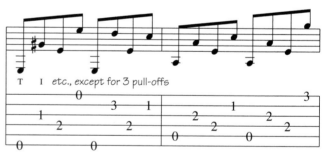

If, like me, you find it easier to read chord diagrams than tablature, try deciphering this. Here the arrows point to the melody notes.

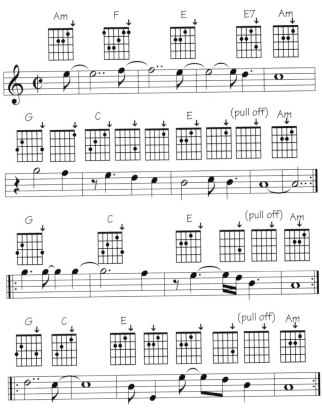

Postscript: I've rarely refused copyright permission for someone to change one of my songs. After all, I've changed so many other people's songs, what right have I to be picky about my own?

But when someone wanted to record this as "my little old town," I said, "No." The whole point of the song is the contrast between the clean snow and the dirty town.

Is that unfair to towns that really try to keep clean? No. The folks trying to clean 'em know that try as we might, we've only half succeeded.

Keep in mind that I'd only sing one or two or at most three of these songs during a concert, even at the height (depth!) of the Vietnam War. I'd try to touch base with a variety of people in the audience, as always singing "something old, something new, something borrowed and something blue."

And not forgetting something funny. What a stupid race we are. The gods must be laughing. We have the know-how to provide education and other necessities for every soul on earth. Instead we waste most of it fighting.

Few people but me recorded any of the songs in this chapter. Country Joe MacDonald's song, "Fixing To Die Rag" (One-two-three-what are we fighting for?) was the best known song against the war; it got in the movie *Woodstock*. If my country was as free as it claims to be, his song would have been "at the top of the charts" in 1971.

But one song of mine, written back in '55, spread from soldier to soldier. When General Vann was buried with military honors in Arlington Cemetery, his widow had the band play it.

October 1955, I was sitting in a plane bound for Ohio to sing for the students at Oberlin College. Half dozing. Found in my pocket three lines copied a year before when reading (in translation) *And Quiet Flows the Don*, the Soviet novel by Mikhail Sholokhov. He describes the Cossack soldiers singing as they galloped off to join the Tsar's army.

> Where are the flowers? The girls have plucked them.
> Where are the girls? They've taken husbands.
> Where are the men? They're all in the army.

Something clicked in my subconscious. I remembered the phrase I'd thought of a couple years earlier, "Long time passing." A singable three words. Then I added the handwringer's perennial complaint, "When will they ever learn?" Twenty minutes later it was completed; that evening I taped it to a mike and tried it out. Three verses.

I originally wrote it a little shorter and differently than most people know it now.

Where Have All the Flowers Gone
(Original Version)

1. Where have all the flowers gone?
    Long time passing
    Where have all the flowers gone?
    Long time ago —
    Where have all the flowers gone?
    Girls have picked them ev'ry one
    Oh, when will you ever learn?
    Oh, when will you ever learn?

2. Where have all the young girls gone?
    Long time passing
    Where have all the young girls gone?
    Long time ago —
    Where have all the young girls gone?
    They've taken husbands every one.
    When will they ever learn?
    When will they ever learn?

3. Where have all the young men gone?
    Long time passing
    Where have all the young men gone?
    Long time ago —
    Where have all the young men gone?
    They're all in uniform.
    Oh, when will <u>we</u> ever learn?
    Oh, when will <u>we</u> ever learn?

Slightly different melody, last 3 lines:

Recorded it this way for Folkways in '56 with several other short songs. A year later stopped singing it, thinking it one more not-too-successful attempt. But Joe Hickerson, leader of the Oberlin College Folksong Club, picked it up, added two verses. Next summer Joe was the music counselor at Camp Woodland in the Catskills. The kids liked it.

He gave the song some rhythm. He tried out all sorts of verses such as, "Where have all the counselors gone? Broken curfew every one…"

In Greenwich Village, New York City, Joe's rhythmic version got to Peter, Paul and Mary, who started singing it at the beginning of their career. The Kingston Trio picked it up from them, recorded it a year later. My manager, Harold Leventhal, asked me, "Pete, didn't you write a song called 'Where Have All the Flowers Gone?'"

"Yeah, a couple years ago."

"Did you ever copyright it?"

"No, I guess I didn't."

"Well, the Kingston Trio have just recorded it."

I got on the phone to Dave Guard.

"Oh, Pete, we didn't know you wrote it. We thought it was an old song. We'll take our name off of it."

It was really nice of them, Technically, legally, I had "abandoned the copyright." But I knew Dave well. About four years before, I had got $1.59 from him and sent him a copy of my self-mimeographed book, *How to Play the 5-String Banjo*. A year later I got another letter from Dave: "Dear Pete, I've been putting that book to hard use. I and two other students here at Stanford have a group we call the Kingston Trio."

The song is usually sung now with Joe's extra two verses and rhythm, and with Peter, Paul and Mary's tune changes.

Where Have All the Flowers Gone
(Adapted Version)

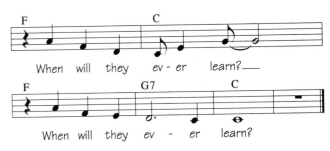

Words & music by Pete Seeger (1955) with new 4th & 5th verses by Joe Hickerson
© 1961 (renewed) by Sanga Music Inc.

1. Where have all the flowers gone,
   Long time passing.
   Where have all the flowers gone,
   Long time ago.
   Where have all the flowers gone?
   The girls have picked them every one,
       When will they ever learn?
       When will they ever learn?

2. Where have all the young girls gone,
   Long time passing.
   Where have all the young girls gone,
   Long time ago.
   Where have all the young girls gone?
   They've taken husbands every one.
       When will they ever learn?
       When will they ever learn?

3. Where have all the young men gone,
   Long time passing.
   Where have all the young men gone,
   Long time ago.
   Where have all the young men gone?
   Gone for soldiers, every one.
       When will they ever learn?
       When will they ever learn?

4. Where have all the soldiers gone,
   Long time passing.
   Where have all the soldiers gone,
   Long time ago.
   Where have all the soldiers gone?
   Gone to graveyards, every one.
       When will they ever learn?
       When will they ever learn?

5. Where have all the graveyards gone,
   Long time passing.
   Where have all the graveyards gone,
   Long time ago.
   Where have all the graveyards gone?
   Covered with flowers every one.
       When will <u>we</u> ever learn?
       When will <u>we</u> ever learn?

JOE HICKERSON AND SON, 1970

My phrase, "Where has all the (something) gone?" seems to have entered the English language. Toshi and I spot it at least once a month, in a headline or an ad. The way I usually sing the song now is to start the first line quite slowly with no accompaniment and no rhythm, more as I originally sang it.

But soon the rhythm starts, and from here on the audience sings the song for me.

On the last verse, whether I sing five verses or the original three-verse way (pithier), I get them to slow down at the end as I originally sang it.

Yes, when will we ever learn — to once again combine work with fun, to make a dance out of sweeping floors, making beds. We have songs for putting a baby to sleep. Why not songs for other jobs? We have songs for singing at church, at a rally, a meeting, a party. Why not songs to sing while waiting for a bus, while waiting for a game to start, when pushing a car out of a mudhole, for picking up litter, for calling a meeting together? (See pp. 219–220.)

Incidentally, *Sing Out!* magazine[2] offered a prize for anyone who could locate the original Russian song. A. L. Lloyd in England won the prize, sending in this.

Koloda Duda

Traditional Russian folksong

1. Koloda Duda,   (Koloda Duda*
   Ee-dye-zh tih bihla?   *Where have you been?*
   Konei steregla.   *Minding the horses.*)

2. Chevo vysteregla?   (*Which were you minding?*
   Konya s sedlom,   *The horse with the saddle*
   s zolotym makhrom.   *With the golden fringe.*)

3. A ee-dye-zh tvoi kon? (*But where is your horse?*
   Za vorotami stoit.   *Standing by the gate.*)

4. A ee-dye-zh vorota?   (*And where is the gate?*
   Voda unesla.   *Carried away by the water.*)

5. A ee-dye-zh gusi?   (*And where are the geese?*
   V kamyh ushli.   *They've gone to the reeds.*)

6. A ee-dye-zh kamysh? (*And where are the reeds?*
   Devki vyzhali.   *The girls have gathered them.*)

7. A ee-dye-zh devki?   (*And where are the girls?*
   Devki zamuzh ushli.   *The girls have gotten married
                       and gone away.*)

8. A ee-dye-zh kazaki?   (*And where are the Cossacks?*
   Na voinu poshli.   *They've gone to war.*)

* a woman's name

2 In 1993, Box 5253, Bethlehem, PA 18015. Quarterly, $18 a year. Worth it many times over.

I originally thought that I wrote the tune all by myself. Around 1960 Ernie Marrs of Atlanta pointed out that I got the first two lines from an Irish-American lumberjack song collected by Marjorie Porter.

John - son says he'll load more hay,

Says he'll load ten times a day——

More than any song I ever put together, the song has crossed borders, been translated. I'm a lucky songmaker.

MARLENE DIETRICH

Here's the German translation of "Where Have All the Flowers Gone." It sings better in some ways than the English original. Marlene Dietrich helped Max Colpet do it. When she returned to Germany on a tour in 1959 the old Nazis were out to put her down. ("She sang for the American troops fighting us!")

But her recording of this song became a #1 hit on German radio. She didn't need to say a thing. The song said it for her: "It's not me who is out of step with the German people." She had a triumphal tour. Now the Berlin musical show about her life uses this as its title.

Sag Mir Wo Die Blumen Sind

1. Sag mir, wo die Blumen sind? *
   Wo sind sie geblieben?
   Sag mir, wo die Blumen sind?
   Was ist geschehn?
   Sag mir, wo die Blumen sind,
   Mädchen pflückten sie geschwind.
   Wann wird man je verstehn?
   Wann wird man je verstehn!

2. Sag mir, wo die Mädchen sind?
   Wo sind sie geblieben?
   Sag mir, wo die Mädchen sind?
   Was ist geschehn?
   Sag mir, wo die Mädchen sind,
   Männer nahmen sie geschwind.
   Wann wird man je verstehn?
   Wann wird man je verstehn!

3. Sag mir, wo die Männer sind?
   Wo sind sie geblieben?
   Sag mir, wo die Männer sind?
   Was ist geschehn?
   Sag mir, wo die Männer sind,
   Zogen fort, der Krieg beginnt.
   Wann wird man je verstehn?
   Wann wird man je verstehn!

4. Sag, wo die Soldaten sind?
   Wo sind sie geblieben?
   Sag, wo die Soldaten sind?
   Was ist geschehn?
   Sag, wo die Soldaten sind,
   Uber Gräber weht der Wind.
   Wann wird man je verstehn?
   Wann wird man je verstehn!

5. Sag mir, wo die Gräber sind?
   Wo sind sie geblieben?
   Sag mir, wo die Gräber sind?
   Was ist geschehn?
   Sag mir, wo die Gräber sind?
   Blumen bluhn im Sommerwind.
   Wann wird man je verstehn?
   Ach, wird man je verstehn!

German translation by Max Colpet (1958)
© 1961, 1962 (renewed) by Sanga Music Inc.

* This line is unbeatable. Pronounce it "zahg meer vo dee bloomen zint"

In most nations, in most ages, the local or national establishment tries to warp almost any good idea to its own ends. Music, art, science, humor. Religion, too.

What are its own ends? Roughly, "We are the best qualified ones to be in charge here. It only complicates matters to have others arguing and confusing the issues, and trying to go 50 different directions at once."

And the funny thing is, quite often they are right — in the short run. Are all people created equal? Nonsense. We are different heights, widths, shapes. We are more or less talented and untalented in sports, arts, patience, energy, honesty, mathematics, perseverance, health, languages and a hundred other things.

But in the long run, ever since our tribal days, technology has enabled a few talented individuals to bequeath their power to their less talented offspring. In a little while the establishment is being run by the untalented. Considering that the original talent was often a talent for piracy, the end result is pretty bad. There never was much talent for honesty, farsightedness, generosity. Now there is next to none.

Not that the establishment doesn't try from time to time to co-opt talent. It tries very hard. The talented poor youth is often encouraged to rise — not "to the top" — but rise pretty damn high — *if* he or she is willing to accept the establishment. But to outspokenly speak truth to power is usually judged a crime, or at least cannot be permitted.

Our job now is to learn *how* to speak truth to power — without being thrown in jail too often. Don't say it can't be done. We can do it in a thousand ways. I've tried it with banjos and boats. Others are doing it with cooking and clothing, quiltmaking, paint and paper, games and gardens, swimming and science. We just have to be aware that it is a struggle, all the way, to keep from being co-opted. And that brings us back to where we started, 340 words ago.

— written in 1974

The Long March

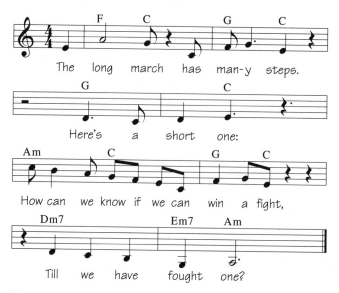

Words & music by Pete Seeger (1974)
TRO - © 1993 Melody Trails, Inc., New York, NY.

I find it easier to think of a refrain than to put together the verses to precede it. These few lines keep returning to me, though. Maybe someone will be able to use them.

In the '70's the women's movement started up again in a new kind of way. I, like a lot of other men, started learning things I should have learned long before. So here's another chorus needing a song.

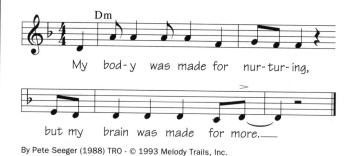

By Pete Seeger (1988) TRO - © 1993 Melody Trails, Inc.

Which leads us into another song and another chapter.

Chapter VIII

From The Great Old Book

This song, inspired by Genesis, in the Bible, was originally meant to be a dialogue between a pacifist and a freedom fighter. Then it got changed to be more a song for women everywhere.

Letter to Eve

1. Oh Eve,____ where is Ad-am,

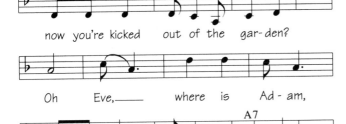

now you're kicked out of the gar-den?

Oh Eve,____ where is Ad-am,

now you're kicked out of the gar-den?

Been wand-'ring from shore to shore,____

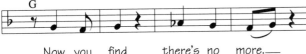

Now you find there's no more.____

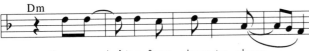

Oh,____ Pa-cem in Ter-ris, Mir,

Shan-ti, Sa-laam,____ Hey Wa!____

Words & music by Pete Seeger (1967)
© 1967 by Sanga Music Inc.

1. Oh, Eve, where is Adam, now you're kicked out
   of the garden? (2x)
   Been wandering from shore to shore,
   Now you find there's no more
   Ohh, Pacem in Terris, Mir, Shanti, Salaam, Hey Wa.

2. Don't you wish love, love alone, could save this
   world from disaster? (2x) *
   If only love could end the confusion—
   Or is it just one more illusion? Ohhh, ...etc.

3. Well if...you want to have great love, you got to
   have great anger (2x)
   When I see innocent folk shot down,
   Should I just shake my head and frown? Ohhh, ...etc.

4. Well if...you want to hit the target square, you
   better not have blind anger (2x)
   Or else it'll be just one more time
   The correction creates another crime. Ohhh, ...etc.

5. Oh Eve, you tell Adam, next time he asks you (2x)
   He'll say, "Baby it's cold outside;
   What's the password to come inside?"
   You say, Ohhh, Pacem...etc.

6. Oh, Eve, go tell Adam, we got to build a new
   garden (2x)
   We got to get workin' on the building
   Of a decent home for all o' God's children. Ohh, ...

7. If music...could only bring peace, I'd only be a
   musician (2x)
   If songs could do more than dull the pain,
   If melodies could only break these chains
   Ohh, Pacem...etc. (SPOKEN:) ("Keep on singing")

8. Ohh, pacem in terris, mir, shanti, salaam,
   hey wa! (2x)
   Four thousand languages in this world,
   Means the same thing to every boy and girl
   Ohh, Pacem...etc. (CHANTED:) ("Sing it over") **

If you want to get erudite, here's the way to write

PACEM IN TERRIS

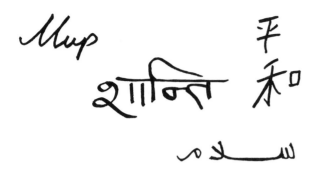

If you are leading this song with folks who don't know it, well, take time to teach 'em the last line:

"Those strange words are really the same word spoken in five of the world's many languages. The first is the Italian way of pronouncing Latin. Patchem In Terris...repeat...PATCHEM IN TERRIS. Next, Meer...MEER. That's Russian for 'Peace.' Shahntee...SHAHNTEE. Eight hundred million people in India would understand that. Salaam...SALAAM. That's known not only in the mid-East; most of Africa knows it too, Indonesia, Pakistan, etc. as well. 'Hey Wa' is the Japanese way of pronouncing two Chinese characters that mean the same thing: peace in the world."

If you find yourself wanting to make the song even longer, here's a possible verse.

9. Oh, when it's stormy weather good people got to gather together ***
    Oh, when it's stormy weather, good people got to gather together
    We know there's no place to hide,
    Still in friends one can confide
    Ohh, Pacem in Terris, Mir, Shanti, Salaam, Hey Wa.

Sample variations in the melody:

If human civilization (and the biosphere) survives, I think it will be partly because the feminine tradition of nurturing takes precedence over the male tradition of adventure, achievement, of power and glory. The '70's and '80's were a big education for me. And as a songwriter I was — and am — fascinated by the wealth of great songs being made up by women — by wives and mothers — by independent types and lesbians. I've told you about Malvina Reynolds. In my own family I've seen examples of strong, independent-thinking women in several generations. Through *Sing Out!* magazine, through the People's Music Network, and Clearwater folks, I learned the songs of Holly Near, Bernice Reagon, Cris Williamson, Pat Humphries, Joni Mitchell, Ysaye Barnwell, Ruth Pelham, Sis Cunningham, Gretchen Reed, Luci Murphy, and many others. Not just writing new songs, but rewriting old ones. I've sung their songs, and occasionally tried adding my words, as you know.

THE BYRDS

Funny story how the next song came to be put together. About 1959 I got a letter from my publisher complaining, "Pete, can't you write another song like 'Goodnight Irene'? I can't sell or promote these protest songs."

I angrily tore off a note to him, "You better find another songwriter. This is the only kind of song I know how to write." I leafed through my pocket notebook to some verses I'd copied down a year before, verses by a bearded fellow with sandals, a tough minded fellow called Ecclesiastes who lived in Judea, like 3,000 years ago. I added one line ("a time of peace, I swear it's not too late"), omitted a few lines, and repeated the first two lines as a chorus, plus one new word repeated three times. Taped it. Mailed it next morning.

Got a letter from the publisher two days later, "Wonderful; just what I hoped for." Myself, I was delighted by the version of the Byrds: all those electric guitars. Like clanging bells. And maybe this is a good place to say clearly that when Bob Dylan switched to an electric guitar at Newport in 1969 I was not upset with him. I *was* furious at the sound system. I wanted to cut the cable. Bob was singing "Maggie's Farm," one of his best songs, but you couldn't understand a word, because of the distortion.

I wonder what Ecclesiastes looked like. I bet he was short, wiry, irascible. I thought no one knew his/her real name — last year I read it was "Koholeth."

Turn! Turn! Turn!
(To Everything There Is A Season)

To ev'-ry- thing (Turn, Turn, Turn,) There is a
sea - son (Turn, Turn, Turn,) and a
time for ev'- ry pur-pose un - der heav-en.

VERSE
1. A time to be born, a time to die; A time to
plant, a time to reap, A time to kill, a time to
heal, A time to laugh, a time to weep.____

Words from the Book of Ecclesiastes
Music & additional words by Pete Seeger (1954)
TRO - © 1962 (renewed) Melody Trails, Inc., New York, NY.

CHORUS:
    To everything (Turn, Turn, Turn)
    There is a season (Turn, Turn, Turn)
    And a time for every purpose under heaven.

1. A time to be born, a time to die
    A time to plant, a time to reap
    A time to kill, a time to heal
    A time to laugh, a time to weep.

2. A time to build up, a time to break down
    A time to dance, a time to mourn
    A time to cast away stones
    A time to gather stones together

3. A time of war, a time of peace
    A time of love, a time of hate
    A time you may embrace
    A time to refrain...from embracing

4. A time to gain, a time to lose
    A time to rend, a time to sew
    A time of love, a time of hate
    A time of peace...I swear, it's not too late.

Here's some verses to sing for children, Toshi suggested.

    A time for work, a time for play
    A time for night, a time for day
    A time to sleep, a time to wake
    A time for candles on the cake.

    A time to dress, a time to eat
    A time to sit and rest your feet
    A time to teach, a time to learn
    A time for all to take their turn.

    A time to cry and make a fuss
    A time to leave and catch the bus
    A time for quiet, a time for talk
    A time to run, a time to walk.

    A time to get, a time to give
    A time to remember, a time to forgive
    A time to hug, a time to kiss
    A time to close your eyes and wish.

    A time for dirt, a time for soap
    A time for tears, a time for hope
    A time for fall, a time for spring
    A time to hear the robins sing.

A day or so after writing the melody for the last song, I worried that I was getting into a rut with my melodies — it was so similar to the melody I'd found for "Bells of Rhymney" (p. 98), which I'd worked out less than a year before. And a couple others.

And on closer examination I realized that both tunes owed more than a little to that ancient mother-of-tunes, "Twinkle, Twinkle, Little Star," starting on the first note of the scale, going up to the fifth note and working their way back down to the first note again.

About the same year I'd heard a Welsh music hall ditty, a comic song, similar to them both.

Cosh - er Bai - ley ran an en- gine...

Both the melodies "Rhymney" and "Turn, Turn" are fairly conventional, one might even say "cautious," except that they are more rhythmically adventurous. Some singers have tried to even out the irregularities.

I've urged them not to.

My father called it "the lingocentric predicament" — similar to the word used by ethnologists — "the ethnocentric predicament" meaning that a person raised in one culture can probably never completely understand another culture. Try as they might, they are always looking through their own colored glasses so to speak.

Similarly, said my father, people using words tend to forget that others hearing those same words have different meanings for them.

Religious leaders, philosophers, politicos, write whole books trying to define one word.

Or, they pick on one disputed word and tell us "don't ever say it."

My solution here is the comedian's — smile at our different definitions. Learn to take all words with a grain of salt.

Words, Words, Words

Words & music by Pete Seeger (1967)
© 1967 by Sanga Music Inc.

1. Words, words, words
   In my old Bible
   How much of truth* remains?
   If I only understood them,
   While my lips pronounced them,
   Would not my life be changed?

2. Words, words, words
   In Tom's old Declaration **
   How much of truth remains?
   If I only understood them,
   While my lips pronounced them,
   Would not my life be change?

3. Words, words, words
   In old songs and stories
   How much of truth remains?
   If I only understood them,
   While my lips pronounced them,
   Would not my life be changed?

4. Words, words, words
   On cracked old pages
   How much of truth remains?
   If my mind could understand them,
   And if my life pronounced them,
   Would not this world be changed?

* Truth? See p. 12.

**Variant melody

In Tom's old Dec-la-ra-tion, How much of

When Thoreau at age 44 was about to die from tuberculosis, his aunt said, "Henry, have you made your peace with God?" He replied, "(cough) I didn't know we had ever quarreled."

Well I, at age 74, finally decided I have made my peace with at least the word "God." Most of my youth, thinking religion was the opiate of the people, I disliked using the word. But I found, like many other European-Americans, that I truly loved the religious songs of African-Americans. It was as though I rediscovered my own humanity through them. I knew Mahalia Jackson. She sang, "I've seen God; I've seen the sun rise." I'm with you, Mahalia. I feel my heart lift every time I see the sun rise. Or the moon. Really, every time I see anything I feel I see God. Now this will no doubt offend some. They'd say, "You see the *handiwork* of God." But I think if I looked on the screen of an electron microscope and saw some molecule only one millionth of an inch in size, I see God. And I believe God is infinite, so compared to something infinitely small, that molecule is infinitely large. (see pp. 197–198). And if I looked at the screens of one of the big radar telescopes that my older brother, Charles, helped design, and saw a galaxy of stars five billion light years distant, I believe I'd be seeing God. And compared to something infinitely large, those five billion light years are an infinitely short distance. How lucky we are to be so spaced out.

In the book *Number, the Language of Science* by Damansky, I read that a "googol" is the number one followed by 100 zeroes. A googol is more than all the molecules in the known universe.

But imagine a "ga-gahll" — the numeral one followed by a line of zeroes stretched five billion light years away. And realize that, compared to Old Infinity Herself, this number is infinitely small.

No. In a sense all of us have some kind of faith. Some are very dangerous faiths. Many scientists have faith that an infinite and uncontrolled increase in empirical knowledge is a good thing. But if the world were destroyed by misuse of this knowledge, would one say it was a good thing to be a scientist? Is it a good thing to be a musician? Sometimes. Sometimes not. (When you're trying not to wake the baby. When there are important other jobs that can't wait.) There are limits to everything.

My mother's father was a doctor, a gentle, conservative man. His favorite motto was "Everything in Moderation." Today I'd argue with him. Even moderation in moderation. There are limits to everything.

Limits to earning money, or stealing it. Tell that to Ivan Boesky and Donald Trump.

Limits to freedom of speech — we don't shout "Fire" in a crowded theater. We learn not to use words that insult some race or ethnic group — and we learn why.

Limits to freedom of press: If some clever chemist discovered a new, super powerful plastic explosive which could be made by mixing three new but commonly available products, would we want the recipe published in the *National Enquirer*?

Few of us like to be disciplined. But if we are lucky enough to live long lives, we realize that sometimes discipline has been good for us. When we get angry, don't reach for a weapon. We hold our tongues at times.

But one can have too much discipline. Here, too, moderation. Art is long, life is short.

Malvina Reynolds once wrote a 10-page booklet, *The Soul Book*, which she mailed to friends as a New Year's greeting. Here it is:

You have been directed to look inside yourself for
   the meaning of life, for your soul.
You may find nothing there.
Because the soul is not inherent. The soul is
   something we accumulate in the course of living.

Living means love.
Living includes work and conflict.
How can you love if you do not face and resist the
   forces of destruction?
Such a course requires courage, and courage is a
   true value.

How can you live if you do not create, in return for the
sustenance you need?
This requires effort, and effort is a true thing.
It is the source of food and beauty, and, in its use, of a
   resilient mind and body.

The valid community is mutually supporting.
You are not alone. You are nothing alone.
Living together, working, communicating, has made us
   what we are — a meaning.
In the monster cities of our time, communities
   disappear. People are alien to one another. The
   system of values of now prevents them from helping
   one another.

I believe that a new community is happening. It is
   smothered many times by the establishment, but it is
   bound to grow again.

Conversation is thinking in its natural state.
Thinking is the conversation within us.

Words distinguish us from the blessed beasts.
Words began in human beings in the process of
   transforming gregariousness into cooperation.
But words corrupted to manipulate others for selfish
   purposes are as poisonous as polluted water.

Being is the process of becoming.
Now is all that went before and the direction in which it
   is going.

The soul is not an inner pearl.
It is a patina created as an individual functions in
   a community.
Not knowing, people called it God, for it was not in the
   unique self nor in the world, so they could not explain it.
The soul is a function of communal being.

Malvina also wrote another poem I memorized:

If this world survives
And every other day I think it might
In good part it will be
Because of the great souls
In our community.

There are a lot of them
I've seen them walk
In lonely thousands down a city's streets
Or hand out leaflets in the rain
Or turn the handle of a print machine
Or empty their pockets as the plate comes by
Or gaze into the camera's eye.

And answer the question:
"Will the world survive?"
And they have said
"We'll try. We'll try."

There's an honorable and long Christian tradition of songs that don't mention the name of God or Jesus, of heaven or hell. "Dona Nobis Pacem." "Amazing Grace." Likewise, many 19th century hymns, still sung by people who use the "shape note" hymnbooks — so-called because they used square and triangular shapes for the music notes, as well as the oval shape.

> The day…is past and gone;
> The evening shades draw nigh.
> O may we all (O may we all)
> O may we all remember now
> The night of death is near.

Here's another, collected in 1927 by Vance Randolph from Mrs. Francis Hall in the Ozark mountains. The song as Randolph collected it was printed in *Sing Out!* magazine, Spring 1992. I've changed it only slightly.

Only Remembered

Freely—No accompaniment needed

1. Up and a-way like the dew of the morn-in',—

Up and a-way, born a-loft by the sun,

So we take leave of earth's treas-ures and toil-ing,

On-ly re-mem-bered for what we have done.

CHORUS*

On-ly re-mem-bered,— On-ly re-mem-bered,—

On-ly re-mem-bered— for what we have done.

On-ly re-mem-bered,— On-ly re-mem-bered,—

On-ly re-mem-bered— for what we have done.

Traditional (Ozarks)

1. Up and away like the dew of the morning.
   Up and away, born aloft by the sun
   So we take leave of earth's treasures and toiling,
   Only remembered for what we have done.

CHORUS: *
Only remembered, only remembered,
Only remembered, for what we have done.
Only remembered, only remembered,
Only remembered for what we have done.

2. Shall we be missed when others succeed us?
   Reaping the field that in springtime we've sown
   No, for the sowers can rest from their labors
   Only remembered for what they have done.

3. Only the truth that in life we have spoken
   Only the seeds that on earth we have sown
   These shall live on and live on forever
   And we'll be remembered by what we have done.

* The chorus could be written in 4/4 time. The original song had "I" for the first verse, "they" for the second, "we" for the third. I decided I liked "we" throughout and changed a dozen words.

JOHN SWENEY, 1878

As this book goes to press I hear from my friend Joe Hickerson, who wrote the extra verses to "Where Have All the Flowers Gone." He is now in charge of the Archive of Folk Culture in the Library of Congress. He sent me this copy of the "original" song, printed in Philadelphia in 1886. Reverend Bonar wrote the original words, except for Mrs. Halls' third verse. Several people put the words to music, but this setting by John R. Sweney appears to be the ancestor. Sweney was a famous Methodist songleader and songwriter. He led choruses of hundreds, with singalong audiences of thousands. And his grand-daughter was Joe Hickerson's mother!

We are born in simplicity and die of complications. The next song was an attempt to wrestle with the contradictions of the last verse of "All Mixed Up" (p. 14). I've sung it only a few times in my life, but it keeps coming back to me.

Once upon a time when we lived in small villages and tribes, there were only a few levels on which people lived: infancy, childhood, the men's hunting party, the women's work party.

Now there are hundreds (thousands?) of "vertical and horizontal" divisions in modern society.

Different rooms.

My wife's Virginia grandmother, a genteel daughter of the Old South, once when asked where she'd been, (she'd been sitting on the toilet) replied, "I've been talking to God."

And lovers usually close the door of the room — or the car.

Now we recognize dozens of kinds of rooms, in order to try and make sense of our complicated 20th century life.

The first line is from John 14:2.

Such sonorities. Such rhythms. Such certainties.

George Bernard Shaw pointed out that the custom of reading the Bible is not so common in various countries as it is in English-speaking countries, because few other languages have such great translations. The committee put together at the request of King James in the early 17th century was humble: "We aim only to make an earlier translation better." they decided to be anonymous. Only scholars know their names.

They took several years for the job. Individuals took responsibilities for different sections, then brought their efforts to a subcommittee for improvements, and the larger committee for final approval. I wonder: they were all men. Did they check anything with wives, daughters, mothers? With local congregations, students? I still shake my head in wonderment. Such sonorities. Such rhythms. Such certainties. I stayed away from churches much of my life, but at various times dip into the Great Old Book.

My Father's Mansion

Freely (suggest singing in unison with no accompaniment)

1. My fa-ther's man-sion has man-y rooms, With room for all of his chil - dren, As long as we do share His love,_____ And see that all are free._____

2. And see that all are free to grow, And

see that all are free to— know, And

free to o-pen or to close____ The

door of their own room.____

Words & music by Pete Seeger (1966)
© 1966 by Stormking Music Inc.

Rev. Maurice McCrackin, pacifist preacher of Cincinnati, told me of a young minister being hired after a long session with a board of elderly deacons. One of them warns him: "Young man, you can glorify. You can edify. You can testify. But don't you specify."

1. My father's mansion has many rooms
    With room for all of his children
    As long as we do share His love
    And see that all are free

2. And see that all are free to grow
    And see that all are free to know
    And free to open or to close
    The door of their own room.

    (ALL THE REST OF THE VERSES ARE SUNG TO THE MELODY FOR VERSE 2.)

3. What is a room without a door
    Which sometimes locks or stands ajar?
    What is a room without a wall
    To keep out sight and sound from all?

4. And dwellers in each room should have
    The right to choose their own design
    And color schemes to suit their own
    Though differing from mine.

5. Yes, and each room has its own design
    To suit the owner's state of mind
    And those who'd want them all the same
    Don't understand—the human game.

6. My family's mansion's many rooms
    Have room for all of His children
    If we do but share in His love
    And see that all are free.

7. The choice is ours to share this earth
    With all its many joys abound
    Or to continue as we have
    And burn God's mansion down.

Footnote: Some have urged me to change the title. They can if they wish.

In the 1980's I fell in love with a West African song performed by the Paul Winter Consort. Paul learned the song from the Ballets Africaines when they toured USA in 1967. The original words are roughly:

Minuit — s'amuse — minuit
TRANSLATION:
At midnight the baby seeks its mother's breast
Midnight pleases itself, midnight
At midnight the lover pleads with the beloved
Midnight pleases itself, midnight
At midnight the witch doctor pleads with the gods
Midnight pleases itself, midnight

The original words by Keita Fodeba are all in French as spoken in the Republic of Guinea, West Africa; Winter's group only sings one line and the refrain, over and over, asking the audience to sing a short phrase suggested by Andrew Tracey, the South African folklorist. The audience repeats it throughout the entire song.

I ended up making up new words based on the old parable of the sower (in all Gospels except John). But I confidently expect that before another century is out, there will be many sets of words in many languages to this extraordinary piece of music. You can hear it best on the tape or disc *Common Ground* by the Paul Winter Consort, Box 72, Litchfield, CT 06759.

I give it here with my words, and the music as a chorus might do it. A single skilled songleader might be able to get a group to join in. Or two or three individuals to sing it together.

Two words of caution: 1) If any money is made from the song, be sure to contact Winter, who has arranged for royalties to go to the widow of Keita Fodeba, the composer. 2) Watch the rhythm.

The Sower of Seeds
(Minuit)

This is a song in several parts, which all blend. You'll find the rhythmic subtleties difficult to learn. Each phrase starts *before* the downbeat with its change of chords. Only "AH!" is *on* the beat. And in the first verse, the last word, "ground."

Rhythmic accompaniment begins

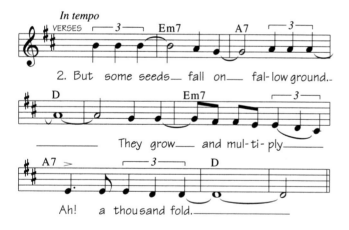

Now more voices are needed.

More voices can also join in when the verses are repeated.

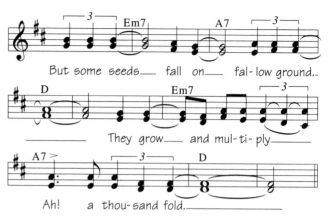

Now the entire audience should be brought in to help. They repeat the next four bars throughout the entire song.

Between the 3rd and 4th verses the audience hears itself clearly for 8 measures singing:
"La la la la la"

Alto countermelody—after 4th verse

A lovely improvisation by Susan Osborn and John Guth for higher voices of women:

Mid-night has come,— I hear mu-sic,——
mu - sic, oh, oh, oh, oh, mu - sic.
(5. We are seeds...)

Music & Guinean lyrics by Keita Fodeba
English lyrics by John Guth & Susan Osborn
Arrangement & adaptation by Paul Winter (1972)
Verses by Pete Seeger (1982)
© 1989 & 1993 Umpawaug Music (ASCAP). All rights reserved.
Courtesy of Living Music.

SHORT INTRODUCTORY VERSE—NO RHYTHM:
1. Behold the sower in the field,
   With her arm she scatters—ah! the seeds.
   Some seeds are trodden in the pathway;
   Some seeds fall on sto-ny ground.

(RHYTHMIC ACCOMPANIMENT BEGINS)
2. But some seeds fall on fallow ground
   They grow and multiply—ah! a thousand fold.
     Oyey, oyey, oyey, oh—oo
     Oyey, oyey oyey, oyey
   Some seeds fall on fallow ground,
   They grow and multiply—ah! a thousand fold.

(AUDIENCE IS TAUGHT A SHORT PHRASE WHICH THEY CONTINUE SINGING
THROUGH THE ENTIRE SONG:)
   La la la la la, La la la la la,
   La la la la la, La la la la la,

3. Tomorrow we scatter like seeds,
   Tomorrow—ah! we are seeds.
     Oyey, oyey, oyey, oh—oo
     Oyey, oyey oyey, oyey
   Tomorrow we scatter like seeds,
   Tomorrow—ah! we are seeds.

4. Lookaway, lookaway, don't you see?
   One and one don't make two—ah they make three.
     Oyey, oyey, oyey, oh—oo
     Oyey, oyey oyey, oyey
   Lookaway, lookaway, don't you see?
   One and one don't make two—ah! they make three.

(ALTOS SING THE NEXT SHORT MELODY FOUR TIMES:)
   Midnight has come, I hear music
   And I'll keep on singing (REPEAT 4 TIMES)

(ALL VOICES:)
5. We are seeds, we are seeds, we are seeds,
   We will grow, we will grow—ah! we will grow.
     Oyey, oyey, oyey, oh—oo
     Oyey, oyey oyey, oyey
   We are seeds, we are seeds, we are seeds,
   We will grow, we will grow—ah! we will grow.

(ALTOS, ACCOMPANIED BY THE AUDIENCE AND THE REST OF THE GROUP ON "LA
LA LA," REPEAT THEIR MELODY EIGHT OR MORE TIMES, GETTING SOFTER AND
SOFTER, TO THE END)
   Midnight has come, I hear music...

The end of the song has at least two parts equally important, sung simultaneously: the audience "La, la, la, etc." and the altos "Midnight, etc." If some singers want to overlay the "Oyey, Oyey" that is possible too — but not too loud. It all harmonizes. I sometimes whistle the melody of the verse. I once heard Jim Scott stretch out the ending for another five minutes, as the audience realized everything blended, and some improvised new parts. But the audience's "La la la la la" should not stop till the end.

The whole song should get more and more quiet till a roll of maracas or shakers can end it. Tempo is maintained; no ritard. The sustained rattle of seeds in the maracas brings the song to the end.

Stick with me, now. This is African music.

It is theoretically possible for one person to lead this song, but two or three people, or even a chorus, could do it much more easily. The charm of it is when several different rhythms are going on at once. The contrasting simple melodies and harmonies make a beautiful pattern.

If you have good tenors or sopranos, of course do it in a higher key. Jim Scott sings it in F.

What if the crowd wants to keep on singing? I urge any lover of music, harmony, rhythm, to consider making up new words to this song in any language convenient. It will not be easy. The English language is not as good as the Latin languages, which end more words on a vowel. You can use lots of "oo" and "ee" sounds. In one place an "AH!" is important. Consonants like L,M,N,V,Z, are better than D,B,K,T, which end a syllable so abruptly. The original French by Keita Fodeba is unbeatable.

	Em7	A7	D	D

"Mee-noo-wee sah-moo-zay mee-noo-wee-

		Em7	A7	D	D

"Mee-noo-wee...sah-moo-zay-Ah! mee-noo-wee-

BEWARE. TRICKY RHYTHM.

Each verse, as you see, has two lines. Each line has three groups of three syllables each. The "downbeat" of each measure comes *after* the words are sung. The syllable "Ah!" is the exception. Likewise in the refrain, only one measure in each line has a word starting on the down beat (underlined). The downbeat comes where chords are given in parentheses.

Oy-yey (Em7) Oy-yey, (A7) Oy-yey, Oh—oo (D)… (D)…
Oy-yey (Em7) Oy-yey, (A7) Oy-yey, (D) Oy-yey… (D)…

Want to try improvising new verses?

Here's some ideas. If there is a small child or baby present, sing them this verse:

> I look at you and wonder, what will you see?
> When you're as old — ah! — as me.

Improvised verses don't have to be deathless. At a Clearwater meeting we've tried (see p. 220):

> Take a seat, everybody, sit down…

A pop songwriter might try:

> Louise! Why won't you sleep with me?

But these days we can foresee the response:

> The reason I won't sleep with you
> Is that sleeping's not what you want me to do.

My friend Lorre Wyatt tried developing the "Midnight" theme:

> Here we are in the dark of the night
> Which way will lead — ah! — to the light?

Then to the melody of the refrain he wrote"

> One way leads us deeper into darkness,
> One way will lead to the light.

Poet Robert Bly sent Paul Winter some beautiful lines, which someday someone may find a way to use:

> Silver wolf, come to me, running free.
> Ocean child, come to me, singing free.
> Eagle Bird, come to me, soaring free.
> Mother whale, sing to me, mother whale.

As I've pointed out elsewhere in this book, many African-American songs need more than one person to sing them. It's like playing tennis.

Is one person with a tennis racket and ball playing tennis? No, it takes two or four, bouncing the ball back and forth. Similarly, in some African traditions a song is not *a* melody and words sung by one person, but rather for several singers, a solo or group, bouncing musical phrases back and forth.

Future historians will record that in these troubled times the riches of African music helped the people of the world to get together.

The foregoing pages were put down in 1989.

It's now 1993. I've sung this song dozens of times, at small gatherings and at huge ones. I usually ask others to help me. Like my grandson Tao, or Arlo Guthrie at the piano. I've decided it's a usable song, though I admit it's not been picked up by many others. But that was true of other songs I've put together.

Because my voice now wobbles so badly on long high notes, I don't sing the introductory verse. I shake a pair of maracas, and speak somewhat as follows:

"These maracas are more difficult to play than I used

to think…Also, consider: only one of the seeds inside is right on-the-beat! The rest are before the beat or after the beat…Ah well, in this world nobody's perfect but if everybody's trying, the job gets done. Right? Here's a story about seeds: Two thousand years ago a young man saw that his friends were very discouraged. He told them: 'Think of the sower, sowing seeds in the field. It's true, some seeds fall in the pathway; they are stepped on and never grow. Some seeds fall on bare stones. They never even sprout.'" The guitar and maracas start a rhythm.

And I start singing the rhythmic second verse:

> But some seeds fall on fallow ground…etc.

Many other rhythm instruments can be added *if* they are handled well — but beware of them in unsure hands. Maracas are a pleasure, alternating, eight-to-the-bar.

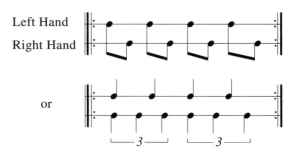

I like a circular motion with the right-hand maracas. If the crowd wants to clap, discourage them: "Hey, don't think you can get away without singing!"

Someone with a good sense of rhythm may be needed to keep the crowd singing the triplets throughout. They should be heard clearly in the breaks between all verses for at least eight measures. (A most important part of the song.)

This:

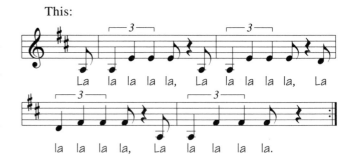

Not this!   Not this!   Not this!

Jim Scott gets audiences singing with him using only a nylon-string guitar as accompaniment. I use a 12-string guitar with heavy steel strings. In any case, stay away from full chords, four-to-the-bar. Single strings, eight-to-the-bar is better. Once accompanying Jim on the banjo, I found these notes:

Here are the guitar chords I use (Tuning: DADGBE)

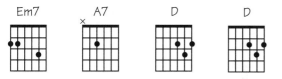

But in standard tuning, try using a capo and play in the A position. Five frets up makes it sound D major.

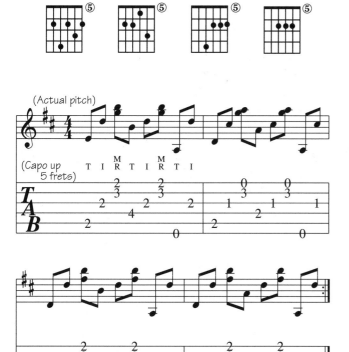

Is there a piano player around? Tell them the left hand below has the same notes the African musicians were playing on the Kora (big West African banjo harp with 21 strings).

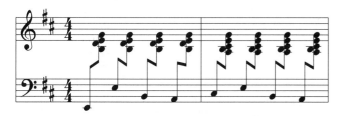

Paul Winter adds these notes played by a guitar:

I've gone into such detail with this song, because I believe that 50 years from now it will be known around the world, with words in many different languages.

In 1949, when Guinea was still a French colony, Keita Fodeba was a young African student in Paris. He put together a program of African dances with some fellow African students. It was so well received that they did a program in Brussels, too. Ten years later Guinea was an independent republic, and the government funded him to put together a large troupe including women as well as men. Ballets Africaines successfully toured Europe and America in the '60's.

But governments change. In 1969, Fodeba was arrested, charged with conspiracy, and executed. His wife fled with their children to neighboring Mali. Now his grown son, an engineer, is back in Conakry, the capital city of Guinea. Mrs. Fodeba is now in touch with Paul Winter, and receiving copyright royalties on this song.

Bless your memory, Keita Fodeba, executed unjustly in 1969.

KEITA FODEBA

I was about 10 or 11 years old when I read that H.G. Wells said, it's a race between education and disaster. A great many members of my family have been teachers, and so am I, after a fashion. This chapter might be a good place for another quote from that English mathematician and philosopher, Alfred North Whitehead.

> When one considers in its length and in its breadth the importance of this question of the education of a nation's young, the broken lives, the defeated hopes, the national failures, which result from the frivolous inertia with which it is treated, it is difficult to restrain within oneself a savage rage. In the conditions of modern life the rule is absolute, the race which does not value trained intelligence is doomed. Not all your heroism, not all your social charm, not all your wit, not all your victories on land and sea, can move back the finger of fate. Today we maintain ourselves. Tomorrow science will have moved forward yet one more step, and there will be no appeal from the judgment which will then be pronounced on the uneducated.
>
> We can be content with no less than the old summary of an educational ideal which has been current at any time from the dawn of our civilization. The essence of education is that it be religious.
>
> …A religious education is an education which inculcates duty and reverence. Duty arises from our potential control over the course of events. Where attainable knowledge could have changed the issue, ignorance has the guilt of vice. And the foundation of reverence is this perception, that the present holds within itself the complete sum of existence, backwards and forward, that whole amplitude of time, which is eternity.
>
> Alfred N. Whitehead, *The Aims of Education.*

So I give you now the chorus of an old spiritual Alan Lomax taught me in 1959. I found that I could use it as a refrain to a series of four or five short stories. You could use it for a different set of parables.

Seek and You Shall Find

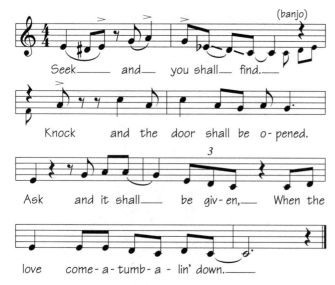

Traditional (African American hymn) Adapted & arranged by Pete Seeger
TRO - © 1993 Melody Trails, Inc., New York, NY.

I usually first get the crowd to learn this chorus well, with a little harmony, repeating the last line. On the word "knock," I often point right at them. It's not hard to teach a little high harmony.

Once there was a king who had three sons, and he wanted to give them a good education. He called in his wise men. He said, "I want you to boil down all the world's wisdom into one book; I'll give it to my sons and have them memorize it." It took them a year; they came back with a volume bound in leather, trimmed in gold. The king leafed through it. "Hm, very good." He turns to his sons. "Learn it!" Now he turned to the wise men. He said, "You did such a good job with that, see if you can boil down all the world's wisdom into one sentence."

It took them five years. They came back and bowed low. "Your majesty, the sentence is 'This too shall pass.'" The king didn't like that so well. He said, "See if you can boil down all the world's wisdom into one word." It took them ten years. When they came back, their beards were draping on the ground.

They bowed low. "Your majesty!
The word is, (PAUSE) *'Maybe.'"*

> Seek and you shall find
> Knock, and the door shall be opened
> Ask and it shall be given
> When the love come a-tumblin' down

(Here are some more stories — you'll have to pick the ones you want to tell. There are others scattered through this book.)

There was another king in another country sitting in his palace. A messenger comes, out of breath. He said, "Your majesty, your majesty, a sea captain has landed his vessel on your coastline, and in the hold of the ship is a strange animal called an elephant." The king was busy enjoying himself; so he called his wise men. He said, "Go down. Bring back a report on this beast." The wise men got into the carriages. Clip clop, clip clop, they went down to the seacoast, and they were taken out to the ship. You know, they had been reading books so long, they were all blind as bats. And one felt the side of the elephant. "Hm," says he. The next felt the ear of the elephant. "Hm." And the next felt the tusk; the next felt the trunk; and the last one pulled on the tail. Then they all got back in the carriage, clip clop, clip clop, and went back to the palace. "Your majesty," says the first, "this elephant is very like unto the side of a building." "Oh, you're quite wrong," says the next. "I felt it myself. It's like the trunk of a small tree." The third one was shouting, "No, you're both wrong. I felt it myself. It's like a large leaf of a large plant." Now they are all shouting. The next says, "Your majesty, it's like a smooth spear." "No, no, your majesty, it's like a big snake." And the last one says, "Your majesty, it's like a rope hanging down from heaven. You pull on it, and the heavens open up with waste."

> Seek and you shall find
> Knock, and the door shall be opened
> Ask and it shall be given
> When the love come a-tumblin' down

There were once two little maggots, two little worms. They were sitting on the handle of a shovel, and the shovel was in a workshop. Early in the morning a workman came, put the shovel on his shoulder, and started down the street to work. The two little maggots held on as long as they could, but finally they jiggled off. One fell into a crack on the sidewalk, and the next one fell onto the curb. And from the curb he fell into a cat, a very dead cat. Well, the second maggot just started in eating. And he ate and ate and ate for three days until he could eat no more. Finally he straightened up, said, "Huhh, I guess I'll go hunt up my sister." And the second maggot humped himself up over the curb and along the sidewalk until he came to the crack.

"Hello, you down there, sister?"

"Yes, I've been here three days without a bite to eat or a drop to drink. I'm nearly starved to death. But you, you are so sleek and fat. To what do you attribute your success?"

"Brains and personality, sister. Brains and personality."

> Seek and you shall find
> Knock, and the door shall be opened
> Ask and it shall be given
> When the love come a-tumblin' down

Early one morning a man got up and went out for a walk. He saw a lion. The lion saw him. The man started running. The lion started running. Faster. The man came to a cliff. There was no place to go but down. He saw a branch sticking out from the cliff a few feet down, and he climbed down and hung onto that branch. Looking up, he saw the lion snarling at the brink of the cliff. Looking

down, he saw another lion at the bottom of the cliff. Out at the end of the branch he saw a beautiful red strawberry. He reached out and plucked it. You know, it was the sweetest thing he'd ever tasted in all his life.

> Seek and you shall find
> Knock, and the door shall be opened
> Ask and it shall be given
> When the love come a-tumblin' down

With scientific surety the math professor detailed the processes of working with negative and positive numbers, and ended "…thus you see, it is impossible in any way for two positives to make a negative."

From the back of the room could be heard a derisive mutter.

Yeah,   yeah.

> Seek and you shall find
> Knock, and the door shall be opened
> Ask and it shall be given
> When the love come a-tumblin' down

This story was originally in Yiddish. A hundred years ago, in a small city in Russia, a traveling salesman got measured by a tailor, to make a pair of trousers. "I'll pick them up next month when I'm back here again," said the salesman.

But next month the trousers were not ready. "No matter," said the salesman. "I'll pick them up next month."

But next month they were still not ready — nor the next, nor the next. Nor the next! "See here," said the salesman, "either finish these trousers or give me my money back." The tailor knew the heat was on. Next month the trousers were finished when the salesman knocked.

He tried them on. They fit _perfectly_. "Tell me, though," asked the salesman, "Don't you think seven months is a little long to make a pair of trousers? After all, the Lord made the world in seven _days_."

Said the tailor, "That's true … but look at the world … and look at my trousers!"

> Seek and you shall find
> Knock, and the door shall be opened
> Ask and it shall be given
> When the love come a-tumblin' down

A woman driving down a narrow country dirt road saw a car come around a curve ahead. To be polite she pulled off, two wheels in the ditch. As the other car passed her, a man stuck out his head and hollered "Pig!"

Outraged, she put her foot on the gas, zoomed out of the ditch, down the road, around the curve. And ran into a pig.

> *Seek and you shall find*
> *Knock, and the door shall be opened*
> *Ask and it shall be given*
> *When the love come a-tumblin' down*

Who should I give credit to for the stories in this book? I've forgot where I heard them. Except the next: my father told it to my sister decades ago.

> *Jesus and the Devil were walking down Fifth Avenue. Jesus looked down, and saw Truth written on a stone. He reached down and picked it up. Looked at it. Held it to his bosom.*
> *"With this stone I shall found my church," said Jesus.*
> *"I'll help you," said the Devil.*

> *Seek and you shall find*
> *Knock, and the door shall be opened*
> *Ask and it shall be given*
> *When the love come a-tumblin' down*

You can find other such stories scattered elsewhere in the book.

A musical note:

The tempo (speed) of this song should be about ♩ = 88. That means take about 22 seconds to sing this 16-bar chorus (without any repeat of the last line).

Standard military marches are ♩ = 120, meaning two steps per second. Square dancers usually like ♩ = 125, ♩ = 130 or faster. Most people's hearts beat about 72 times a minute (♩ = 72).

Now, as to the complicated notation on p. 184.

Once upon a time I would have written these notes much more simply.

Or, slightly more accurately,

But for the sake of those who just have these pages in hand — no tape recording to help, I really wanted to get it right. As in so much African-American music, you should feel the pulse under a long-held note, like "seek." Without this pulse the note could droop at the end, if you can imagine an arrow falling.

Not good, it should be more like:

If I was a choral director, I'd be waving my hands:

On the very last chorus, the last line can have a ritard, which could be written

but would sound more like

I guess I should just urge you to tap your foot, sway your body, snap your fingers as you sing — and realize that your body could move in several different ways, and there could be many ways of singing the word "seek."

The vowel "ee" can be made in several different ways, depending on how you shape your lips, or how far back in your mouth you shape your tongue. Try pushing out your lips, as when saying "Sh-h" and put the "ee" in the forward part of your mouth.

Enough of all this technical talk. Too confusing. Sing it like you feel it. And maybe someday a wordsmith will make verses worthy of this great refrain.

I even have a melody for the verses you might try. The problem is, it would probably deeply offend the ears of any lover of Celtic music, because the last 4½ measures are a direct steal from a famous melody by O'Carolan, great 18th Century Irish harper and composer.

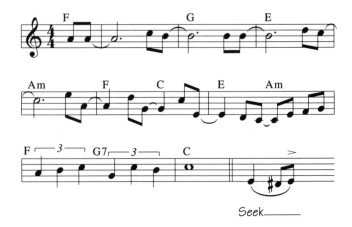

New England Puritans disapproved of carol singing. It probably originated as a European pagan custom. A carol was a dance.

In mid-19th century England, people were moving to cities and forgetting their country ways. Some young preachers in London decided to revive carol singing. They translated "The First Noël" from French. They found a Swedish Easter carol melody and made up words to it about a Bohemian king named Wenceslas. And they translated this Welsh New Year's carol into English. One of my favorites for 70 years. Thinking that other guitar pickers might like to try deciphering the tablature, here 'tis.

Deck the Halls

Dropped D tuning

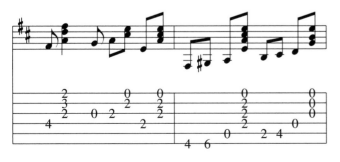

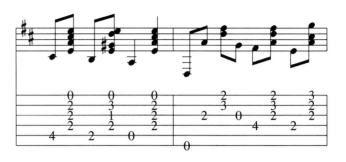

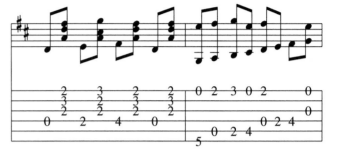

Music: Welsh New Years carol
Guitar arrangement by Pete Seeger (1956)
© 1993 by Sanga Music Inc.

My mother's grandmother was a good pianist at age 17. A local church committee asked her parents if they might rent a hall and sell tickets for a concert.

"Absolutely *not*!" said her parents. "A lady does not appear on stage." (Her father was a Philadelphia banker.)

"But we want to raise money for the church, and no one's home is big enough for all the people that want to hear her play."

A compromise was finally reached. She would be allowed to give the concert on the stage, but a screen had to be put between her and the audience. This was about the year 1850.

She lived to a ripe old age, raised six children. My father and mother remembered her in her eighties, with hands rippling up and down the piano keys.

© Len Munnik, Amsterdam

This North American version of an old English Christmas carol has long been a favorite of mine. I think I heard John Jacob Niles sing it first. The Weavers liked it too, and they asked me to play the recorder along behind it.

Surely many artists must feel as perplexed as I am when I am asked, "How do you write a good melody?" Melodies seem to spring out of the subconscious. God had something to do with it, perhaps. All I know is that one of the best melodies I ever invented was a little piece for the recorder as an introduction to this song.

If you want the ancient words, look them up under the title, "The Coventry Carol." If you want the verses Lee Hays made up for the Weavers to sing, write our music publisher (TRO, 11 West 19th Street, New York, NY 10011-4298). I purposely leave them both out here, hoping that in the next few decades some woman or man will find words for a new soul arriving in a world trembling on the brink of extinction.

Dm   Dm7   C   Am

1. Lul - loo,___ lul - lay,___ my ti - ny child,___

Dm   Gm   Am

Bye, bye,___ lul - loo,___ lul - lay.

Gm   Dm   Am

Lul - lay,___ my ti - ny lit - tle child,___

Bb   C   Dm

Bye, bye,___ lul - loo,___ lul - lay.

Traditional English Christmas carol

Lulloo, Lullay

Part for soprano or tenor recorder, in C.
Or a harmonica. Or whistle it.

When do you breathe in this song? Whenever you feel like it. If several people sing it together, they can breathe at different times, so the melody seems to flow endlessly.

My older brother John taught me this old English carol back in the 1940's. I still like the last line as given here better than the way most books print it.

We Wish You a Merry Christmas

1. We wish you a Mer-ry Christ-mas, We
wish you a Mer-ry Christ-mas, We wish you a Mer-ry
Christ-mas, and a Hap-py New Year.

When singing it with the Weavers, I got the idea for an introduction and an ending to give it a "performance framework." I'm proud that it has caught on and others now sing these extra parts. The old English carol was just three short choruses, far too short for a good song.

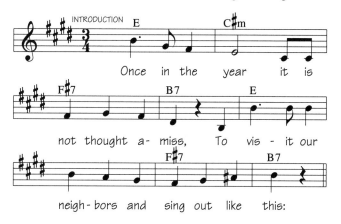

INTRODUCTION
Once in the year it is
not thought a-miss, To vis-it our
neigh-bors and sing out like this:

1. We wish you a merry Christmas,
   We wish you a merry Christmas,
   We wish you a merry Christmas
   And a happy New Year.

2. We want some figgy pudding (3x)
   And a cup of good cheer.

3. We won't go until we get some (3x)
   So bring it out here.

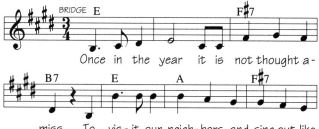

BRIDGE
Once in the year it is not thought a-
miss, To vis-it our neigh-bors and sing out like

this, Of friend-ship and love, good neigh-bors a-
bound, And peace and good-will,— the whole year a-
round. Pa-ce!* Po-koy! Frie-den, Mir, Sha-
lom! The words mean the same, what-
ev-er your home. Why can't we have
Christ-mas the whole year a-round?— Why
can't we have Christ-mas the whole year a-round?

REPEAT VERSE 1

* Latin, then Polish, German, Russian, Hebrew. (1950 Eurocentrism)

With a ritard at the end, the whole crowd should sing it with you.

> We wish you a merry Christmas,
> We wish you a merry Christmas,
> We wish you a merry Christmas
> And a happy New Year.

It's almost sacrilegious to draw into this profane volume one of the greatest musicians of all time, Johann Sebastian Bach. He, the heavenstormer, born over 300 years ago in Germany. But he loved rhythm. I believe he would have delighted in the needle-like tones of the banjo. This particular arrangement (of the organ obligato to one of his chorales) sounds best when played rather softly, and not too fast.

Bach wrote it in the key of G. With my rusty voice I usually capo up and sing it way down in B flat. But read on.

Jesu, Joy of Man's Desiring

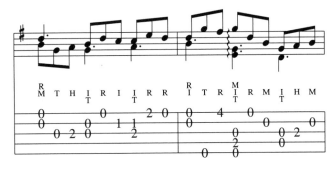
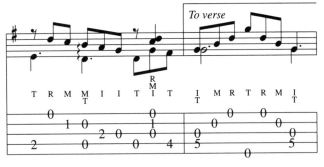

Music by Johann Sebastian Bach (1716)
Arranged with English words by Pete Seeger (1989)
© 1993 by Stormking Music Inc.

1. Jesus bleibet meine Freude,
    Er ist eines Herzens Trost und Saft.
      (Jesus remains my joy,
        He is my heart's consolation and life blood.)
PRONOUNCE:
    "Yayzoos bly-bet my-neh Froydeh
    "Air ist my-ness Hair-tzenz Trohst und Sahft."

In 1989 I thought of some verses in English to try with Clearwater's Walkabout Chorus.

2. We will love or we will perish.
    We will learn the rainbow to cherish.

3. Dare to struggle, dare to danger,
    Dare to touch the hand of a stranger.

4. Dare to struggle, dare to danger.
    Dare to touch the soul of a stranger.

REPEAT VERSE 2

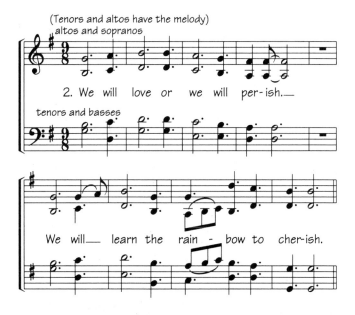

Play it through again. Of course, if you have a good organist or pianist, Bach modulated it beautifully.

Did you know that in the year 1717, at the age of 32, Bach was thrown into prison by Wilhem Augustus, the new Duke of Saxe-Weimar. Bach threatened to quit the Duke's service to accept an offer as the chief organist and composer at the court of Bach's more appreciative friend, Prince Leopold of Anhalt-Cothen. Despite his growing fame and talent, Bach was dissatisfied with his lot at Saxe-Weimar and wanted to leave. The Duke had him locked up for nearly nine months — from April 6 to December 2, 1717 — but when Bach persisted in quitting, the Duke was finally forced to let him go.

The above information is from an article by Dave Platt in the magazine, *Jewish Currents* — New York City.

Which leads us to the next song. Platt quotes a poem by the late Yuri Suhl, with Suhl's introduction. Treblinka was one of the Nazi death camps. An orchestra of prisoner musicians was compelled to play each morning when prisoners marched off to their slave labor details.

Ode to a Composer

You're one of us now
Johann Sebastian Bach
your statues stand
but you
chained in your own score
were dragged to Treblinka
where murder and music
go hand-in-hand.

Bach at Treblinka

Poem ("Ode to a Composer") by Yuri Suhl (1973)   Music by Pete Seeger (1983)
TRO - © 1973 & 1993 Yuri Suhl & Melody Trails, Inc., New York, NY.

The Weavers used to sing another Bach chorale, "O Sacred Head Now Wounded," with English lyrics by Tom Glazer (degenderized by Tom in 1987).

The Whole Wide World Around

Because all men are brothers, wherever men may be,
And women all are sisters, forever proud & free,
No tyrant shall defeat us, no nation strike us down,
And all who toil shall greet us the whole wide world
    around.

My brothers & my sisters, forever hand in hand,
Where chimes the bell of freedom, there is my native land.
My brothers' fears are my fears, yellow, white or brown,
My sisters' tears are my tears the whole wide world
    around.

Let every voice be thunder, let every heart by strong,
Until all tyrants perish, our work will not be done.
Let every pain be token, the lost years shall be found.
Let slavery's chains be broken the whole wide world
    around!

Words by Tom Glazer   Music by J.S. Bach ("St. Matthew Passion")
© 1948 Tom Glazer. Copyright assigned Songs Music, Inc., Scarborough, NY 10510.
Renewed 1975. Lyrics reprinted herein by permission.

Next are additional words by me.

O Sacred World Now Wounded

O sac-red world now wound-ed, we pledge to make you free Of hate, of war, of hun-ger, and self-ish cru-el-ty. And here in our small cor-ner we plant a ti-ny seed, And it will grow to beau-ty to shame the face of greed.

Words by Pete Seeger (1988)
Music by Hans Leo Hassler (1601)   Harmonized by J.S. Bach (1719)
TRO - © 1993 Melody Trails, Inc., New York, NY.

In the early '70's, on the cobblestone streets of an old English town, I thought of this next tune, wrote it down. Worked out a spare way of playing it on the guitar. It is intended to be soft, with open notes on high strings as well as low strings, ringing out as long as possible. I wiggle my left hand as violinists do, to get a bit of vibrato.

The Emperor Is Naked Today-O!

A few years later I was able to fashion the lyrics. I was glad to hear Barbara Dane sing it in a jazz tempo. The test of a usable song is its ability to be sung several different ways. I usually alternate playing the tune, then singing it, then end by playing it again.

1. As the sun
rose on the rim of
And this one
world that we love was
east-ern sky,
try-ing to die.
We said: Stand and sing out for a great hoo-
ray-O!_____ Your child may be the

one to ex-claim: The emp-r'or is na-ked to-day- O!

Originally titled "As the Sun"   Words & music by Pete Seeger (1970)
© 1977, 1979 by Fall River Music Inc.

© Len Munnik, Amsterdam

1. As the sun
    Rose on the rim of eastern sky
    And this one
    World that we love was trying to die
        We said stand!
        And sing out for a great hooray-o!
        Your child may be the one to exclaim
        The emperor is naked today-o!

2. Four winds that blow
    Four thousand tongues, with the word: survive
    Four billion souls *
    Striving today to stay alive
        We say stand!
        And sing out for a great hooray-o!
        Why don't we be the ones to exclaim
        The emperor is naked today-o?

3. Men — have failed
    Power has failed, with papered gold.
    Shalom-salaam
    Will yet be a word where slaves were sold **
        We say stand!
        And sing out for a great hooray-o!
        We yet may find the way to exclaim
        The system is naked today-o!

* In 1993 almost 6 billion.
**Jerusalem, which is why I put the song in this chapter.

I was about age nine when my father mentioned to me that one of the world's great melodies was nicknamed "Old Hundred." Years later I learned more about it.

In the 16th century, the hymn got its start in Switzerland. Louis Bourgeois was songleader for the Protestant leader, John Calvin. And I'll bet he got the idea for the tune from some old French dance tune, and just slowed it down. He probably thought as John Wesley did: "Why should the Devil have all the good tunes?"

In the 17th century it got English words, several sets of them. One was nicknamed "Old Hundredth" because the words were based on the 100th Psalm. Here the melody is given on the middle staff. Altos can sing the bass part or go even lower to sing the tenor part, one octave below the soprano. Sopranos and tenors should try to reach the high notes printed on the top staff. Or make up new parts.

My first line is part of the old hymn. The rest of the words I made up in 1984.

Old Hundred

Words & music arrangement by Pete Seeger (1984)
From the original hymn by Louis Bourgeois (ca. 1510–1561)
© 1985 by Sanga Music Inc.

1. All people that on earth do dwell,
    Sing out for peace 'tween heav'n and hell.
    'Tween East and West and low and high,
    Sing! peace on earth and sea and sky.

2. Old Hundred, you've served many years
    To sing one people's hopes and fear,
    But we've new verses for you now.
    Sing peace between the earth and plow.

3. Sing peace between the grass and trees,
    Between the continents and seas,
    Between the lion and the lamb.
    Between young Ivan and young Sam.

4. Between the white, black, red and brown,
    Between the wilderness and town,
    Sing peace between the near and far,
    'Tween Allah and six-pointed star.

5. The fish that swim, the birds that fly,
    The deepest seas, the stars on high,
    Bear witness now that you and I
    Sing peace on earth and sea and sky.

REPEAT FIRST VERSE

If the song is going well I'll add another verse and get a crowd to sing the first verse still one more time.

6. Old Hundred, please don't think us wrong
    For adding verses to your song.
    Sing peace between the old and young,
    'Tween every faith and every tongue.

REPEAT FIRST VERSE
    (Ah…women and men…and children!) *

* See below, p. 196.

The idea for this "unorthodoxology" actually came to me when listening to Grupo Moncotal. The Nicaraguan band played at a huge "Festival de la Nueva Canción" (Festival of New Song) in Ecuador, 1984. With that tremendous pulsing rhythm going on stage I wondered what it would be like to superimpose, right on top of it, some north-European long slow melody like this one. Here might be the rhythm:

When all is cooking — drum, guiro, maracas, claves, etc. then start the hymn in full harmony. But *not* in regular meter. It should float, as a Kentucky ballad does, above the driving rhythm of a banjo. I'll try to write it below — first word slow, next three or four syllables fast, then slower, so the last syllable of each line is held out, thus:

After having described it to you, I confess —I've never heard it done. When I perform the song I usually first play the melody on the guitar, in a lower key — D or E flat. I don't want to discourage anyone from singing because it seems too high.

That last line is fun to play. Here's the chord diagrams for:

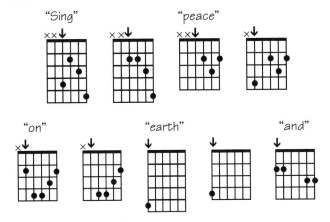

After I've played the tune on the guitar, I call out, "A lot of you know this melody. I'll give you some new words for it. All people that on earth do dwell!" Then I sing it, hoping a few will join in.

A small percentage do sing the first line with me.
"Sing out for peace 'tween Heaven and Hell."
A few more join in, sing the second line with me,
"'Tween east and west and low and high"
Now more are singing. I'm shouting now.
"Sing peace on earth! And sea! And sky!"

After they sing this line I say, "There must be some people here who like to sing tenor or soprano. It's not hard; just three notes above the melody."

And although only a few may attempt it, I go through the whole four lines again, singing them, each line twice in the tenor-soprano part, so they can sing them back to me.

"Very good! Now, altos and basses! You have the best part of all."

I sing the first line of the bass part, but, of course, in the key of D it's much too low. Only a few basso profundos can make the last low note.

"Uh oh. I guess we better come up out of the cellar." I change the capo on the guitar if necessary, so we can sing it in F or G. "Let's try that again."

Now basses and altos learn the four lines, as I sing them out, one line at a time.

"Now let's put it all together."

"If you know your part well, sing out strong, so those who are not so certain will take courage from your efforts. That's how it is in this world. Them as knows must lead. If you can only decide who knows."

"If you hear too many people singing high, you sing low, and vice-virtue and here we go. Some start up here. All —" (I sing a B note). "The rest start here. All —" (I sing a G note).

Now we sing Verse 1 in three parts, with me feeding them the words one line at a time. Sometimes I have to encourage the high voices after the word "dwell."

...do dwell ("Where's the ten - ors?")

Or I encourage the basses.

...and_____ hell ("Where's the Bass-es?")

We get a fine ending on "sky." Then I sing the second verse briskly by myself.

2. Old Hun-dred, you've served man-y years___
To sing one peo-ple's hopes and fears,___
But we've new vers-es for you now.___
Sing___ peace bet-ween the earth and plow.

— and the third, fourth and fifth verses also briskly, before calling out the line that brings them all back for a repeat of the first verse.

5. The fish that swim, the birds that fly,
The deep-est seas, the stars on high,___
Bear wit-ness now that you and I___
Sing peace on earth and sea and
sky.   6. All...

SONGLEADER   5

"All peo-ple that on earth do dwell!" 6. All...

After some grand harmony, if all is going well, I'll sing verse 6 by myself, and bring them back for another repeat of verse 1 and finally end, with a pun on the word "Amen." If children are in your chorus, they can give it a final tag.

Ahh,___ wom-en and men! And chil-dren!___

In a hall with a lot of echo, people are often surprised how good it sounds. "You didn't know you were such a good chorus, did you? Well, it's like the whole world doesn't know what a great world we can make it if we start trying to work together."

In this book I go into some detail to show you how I teach the songs to audiences, not because I think others should slavishly try to copy my songleader techniques. I think there could be dozens of different ways to sing the songs. Slow. Fast. High. Low. Long. Short. With a bagpipe drone. Modulating to different keys. Using different accompaniments. Or none.

In 1984, when writing new verses for this I let imagination run amok. Then I found myself unable to make a proper selection. It was Arlo Guthrie who glanced over the lot, and unerringly checked off the six verses I sing now. "Sing these; forget the rest." He was right, as you can see. Here's the discards.

> Between the cats and rats and mice
> Between the fire and the ice
> Between what we've seen and what we've heard
> Between the rhythm and the word
>   'Tween rank and file and the elite
>   Between the tofu and the meat
>   'Tween short and tall and fat and thin
>   Between the solar and the sin
> 'Tween fast and slow and in and out
> Between the whisper and the shout
> 'Tween Yankee North and Latin South
> Between the stomach and the mouth
>   'Tween what we squelch and what we say
>   Between the wide and narrow way
>   Sing peace before we're laid away
>   Between tomorrow and today
> Old hundred please don't think us wrong
> For adding verses to your song
> We all need shadows and the light
> Before we bid you all good-night
>   All people that on earth do dwell
>   Sing out for peace 'tween heaven and hell
>   Not bombs nor guns nor ancient pride
>   Let honest discourse now decide
> We see the world we see the shame
> Of cruel deeds in freedom's name
> Sing peace 'tween Luther and the Pope
> Sing peace between despair and hope
>   For snakes and snails and stars on high
>   Sing peace on earth and sea and sky
>   Let laser beams and poison gas
>   Join spears and arrows of the past
> All people now, both old and young
> Sing peace 'tween every skin and tongue
> An end to bombs and poison schemes
> We'll build the world which poets dreamed
>   Between our hands and our machines
>   'Tween what we've felt and what we've seen
>   'Tween what is read and what is heard
>   Between the rhythm and the word
> When every soul can sing as one
> I'll know my work on earth is done
> Though mortal shell is dead and gone
> My spirit shall go singing on
>   The struggle now in every breast
>   Will give each living soul no rest
>   Till bombs and guns are put aside
>   And reasoned discourse now decide
> All people that on earth do dwell
> Sing peace between old heaven and hell
> For snakes and snails and stars on high
> Sing peace on earth and sea and sky.

> (A verse for Clearwater)
>   By peace we mean one simple thing
>   An end to bombs and all such things
>   Like sharpened knives between the ribs
>   And now let's raise mainsail and jib.

> So here's to motion slow or swift
> Here's to continents that drift
> Let Marx and Pope now sing the worth
> Of peace 'tween continence and birth
>   Between the water and the rock
>   Between the shepherd and the flock
>   Sing peace between the hand and wheel
>   Between the willow and the steel
> The struggle now in every breast
> Will give each living soul no rest
> Till poison hate is put aside
> And reasoned discourse now decide.
>   I find I still have one more rhyme
>   Praise be to women of all time
>   May women lead as now we build
>   A world where hopes can be fulfilled

At the end of this chapter I have a question for Christians. Why did you leave Rabbi Hillel out of your Bible? He lived in Jerusalem a little before the time of Jesus. He put together three of the world's greatest questions,

> If I am not for myself, who will be ?
> If I am only for myself, what am I?
> If not now, when?

Above is how it was taught to me by Jo Schwartz. Vlad Pozner points out that the Oxford Dictionary of Quotations has it differently:
"If I am not for myself, who is for me, and being for my own self, who am I? If not now, when?"

> "What is peace? Respect for the rights of others."
>   Benito Juarez (1806-1872),
>   the greatest President of Mexico.

In any case, I'm no longer so shy of the word "God."

> I will not be dismayed
> Through all the sun and shade
> We're finding our human soul
> As we struggle on.

God, in my opinion, is infinitely small as well as infinitely large. Hence the science fiction fantasy following.

The Beethoven Phenomenon

It's the 100th birthday party of a nuclear scientist. The large room is filled with other scientists, men and women from four continents. After the speeches, toasts, the old guy rises shakily to his feet, peers over his glasses, clears his throat, raises a glass, speaks slowly.

"Friends...all! I toast <u>you</u> with this glass of the world's most precious liquid; you know what it is. And I have a present for you. Yes, I see the red light of the United Nations TV camera on me. Hello out there! This present is for all of you, too. I've avoided TV most of my life, because of a well-known rule that fame reduces one's ability to think logically. But these days I don't think logically anyway. Only romantically. My close partner of seventy years died ten years ago, but she is here in spirit. Like Joe Hill, she is at my side. She was the one who, using the World Women's Network, made the breakthrough in the invention of the Super High Speed recording machine. And it is this Super High Speed recording machine that has enabled me — us! — to give this present to you tonight.

"For the benefit of those out there looking at me on an electronic screen, I remind you that in this mid-Twenty-First Century, the Big Bang has been verified by thousands of observations. All of our hundreds of billions of galaxies, some as distant as 10 billion light years away, started our journey at one instant about 20.9 billion years ago. Also verified has been the Beethoven Phenomenon — the fact that before the Big Bang there were three large crunches, as in the 5th Symphony of the German composer Beethoven: Ba...ba...ba...BOOM!

Ba - ba - ba   BOOM!

'But I always liked to call it the Great Sneeze, as in 'ah...ah...ah...CHOO!' I agreed with Bertolt Brecht, Beethoven symphonies reminded him of paintings of battles, and he didn't like battles. Nor do I. But I'm wandering. Centenarians are garrulous.

"As most of you know, I've spent my life's work not with radar telescopes, but rather at the small end of the space-time scale, with the electron microscope and now with the quarkscope.

"Until now, we were certain that there are no particles smaller than a subquark, of which there are over a hundred to each hydrogen atom. They seem to appear and disappear about ten thousand times a second. What I am able to give you tonight is the <u>sound</u> of a <u>subquark</u> just as it starts its brief period of expansion and contraction. I have in my hand the button which will activate the Super High Speed recording machine. What you are about to hear has been slowed down by a factor of 20 billion, so our ears can hear it."

The old scientist presses a button. He points at the TV camera, cupping his ear with the other hand, as though urging TV viewers to listen. The room is silent.

Suddenly is heard clearly, as if in a child's voice: "Ah...Ah...Ah...CHOO!"

My best songwriting in the year of '73 was to find three words which could be used for a new last line to this old African-American "spiritual." It took me 20 years to find 'em.

The old last line, "Soldiers of the cross," is good, but I wanted to sing the song for many different kinds of people, reminding them that heaven (and revolutions) are achieved neither in one big bang, nor by throwing open of gates.

My voice prefers the song in the key of C, as here, though a group of women might prefer it a shade lower. And for a crowd that is really warmed up I'd do it in D, urging the crowd to harmonize.

Harmonize! This is what musicians can teach the politicians: not everyone has to sing the melody.

I know most songbooks give the song in 3/4 time, but 4/4 gives a songleader a few extra seconds to call out the new words and verses, and exhort basses, altos, etc. to do their best. Arlo Guthrie and I often close a concert with it. Note the harmony on the last two measures. Of course no two verses will have exactly the same melody, and verses may be added or subtracted. This is traditional. It's also traditional for tempo to stay rock steady. Sometimes I sing four verses, sometimes eight, and repeat the first verse at the end.

Since I have a long-necked 12-string guitar tuned low, I can use a D tuning (see Appendix) but it sounds in C, and I start a rhythm on just the lowest pair of strings. In parentheses I give words such as I use to get a crowd singing, but you use what words you think best.

Jacob's Ladder

1. We are climb-ing Ja-cob's lad-der. We are climb-ing Ja-cob's lad-der. We are climb-ing Ja-cob's lad-der,

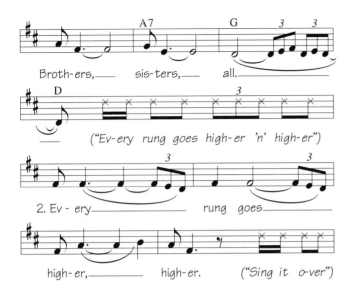

Broth-ers,—— sis-ters,—— all.

("Ev-ery rung goes high-er 'n' high-er")

2. Ev - ery——— rung goes———

high-er,——— high-er. ("Sing it o-ver")

Music: traditional (African American spiritual)
Additional words by Pete Seeger (1973)
© 1993 by Sanga Music Inc.
Verses 4 and 5 from women in Milwaukee,
verses 9 and 10 by Bill Goodman in Chicago.

1. We are climbing Jacob's Ladder (3x)
   Brothers, sisters, all.

2. Every rung goes higher, higher (3x)
   Brothers, sisters, all.

3. Every new one makes us stronger (3x)
   Brothers, sisters, all.

4. We are dancing Sarah's circle...*
   Sisters, brothers, all.

5. Every round a generation...*
   Sisters, brothers, all.

6. Struggle's long but hope is longer...
   Sisters, brothers, all.

7. People all need jobs and justice...
   Sisters, brothers, all.

8. We are climbing Jacob's ladder...
   Brothers, sisters, all.

9. Peace and love can conquer anger...
   Brothers, sisters, all.

10. Peace and justice will bring freedom...
    Brothers, sisters, all.

* A priest liked these marked verses so much he wrote a whole long
  sermon on the value of going in circles.

As you see, I'm hoping that a crowd will feel the spirit so strongly that they can sing harmony, even if they never did it before. Of course, you don't have to sing all the verses. No two songleaders will do it the same.

If I'm with any group that knows how to harmonize I'll hold up four fingers, on the word "all," indicating to switch to the F chord ("subdominant") at the end. Then one finger pointed high indicates back to C ("tonic").

Singing in Chile and Argentina in 1988 I got help and we found Spanish words for this song.

1. Ya su-bimos... Todos... juntos (3x)
   Todos... juntos... ya.

2. Es muy... largo... la esca-lera (3x)
   Todos... juntos... ya.

3. Los pel-daños... suben... suben (3x)
   Todos... juntos... ya.

4. Pan jus-ticia... nuestro... meto (3x)
   Todos... juntos... ya.

5. Larga... lucha... hemos... vivido (3x)
   Todos... juntos... ya.

6. No más... largo... la esper-anza (3x)
   Todos... juntos... ya.

"We are all bastards, but God loves us anyway."
—Rev. Will Campbell, Mount Juliet, Tennessee

Overleaf: This highly simplified slant view of a spiral galaxy reminds us of our position in the universe. Earth and our sister planets, asteroids, and comets all revolve around the sun, a common type of star. Our Solar System revolves around the center of our spiral galaxy, "the Milky Way," once every 200,000,000 years or so. At approximately 27,000 light years from the center, the Sun is about halfway from the galactic center to the outermost observed members of the galaxy.

The spiral arms in our galaxy are clumpier than shown. Our galaxy is a fairly large one, as galaxies run, but noticeably smaller than the largest. Spiral galaxies seem to outnumber the non-spiral ones.

Because of interstellar dust clouds we cannot see much of our galaxy, including the center, but it is estimated that between 100 billion and 400 billion stars rotate. As the sensitivity of our telescopes increases, the number of galaxies observed in the universe increases. Current estimates are that there are at least as many galaxies in the universe as there are stars in our galaxy.

YOU ARE HERE

Chapter IX   Think Globally, Sing Locally

POLLUTION

Drawing by Paul Loring

In the "Frightened '50's" I sang a variety of songs out of American history, going from college to college, summer camp to summer camp. I relayed songs of Woody and Leadbelly to a batch of younger folks. It was probably the most important job of music I'll ever do. I could have kicked the bucket in the early '60's — my job was done. A lot of talented new songwriters came along to pick up where Woody and Leadbelly left off.

In 1963, Rachel Carson's book *Silent Spring* made a turning point in my life. As a kid I'd been a nature nut. Age 15 and 16, I put all that behind me, figuring the main job to do was to help the meek inherit the earth, assuming that when they did the foolishness of the private profit system would be put to an end.

But in the early '60's I realized that the world was being turned into a poisonous garbage dump. By the time the meek inherited it, it might not be worth inheriting. I became an econik; started reading books by Barry Commoner and Paul Ehrlich.

About this time I also fell in love with sailing. I'd started earning money and got a little plastic bathtub of a boat. Such poetry! The wind can be from the north, but depending how you slant your sails, you can go east or west. (Don't let anyone tell you, "I had to do it." The same pressures will make one person do the right thing, another a stupid thing.)

Also, 500 years ago African sailors showed European sailors that if you used triangular sails instead of square sails, you could actually use the power of a north wind to sail towards the north, first northeast, then northwest. You can zigzag into the very teeth of the gale that's trying to force you back. That's good politics, too. Martin Luther King used the forces against him to zigzag ahead.

But sailing on the Hudson, I saw lumps of toilet waste floating past me. The ironies of "private affluence and public squalor" (thankss, J.K. Galbraith) got to me. I wrote the next two songs, then a string of others.

Sailing Up My Dirty Stream

1. Sail-ing up my dir-ty stream,— Still I love it and I'll keep the dream That some day, though may-be not this year,— My Hud-son Riv-er— will once a-gain— run clear. She starts high in the moun-tains of the north,— Crys-tal clear and i-cy, trick-les forth, With just a few float-ing wrap-pers of chew-ing gum,— Dropped by some hik-ers, to warn of things to come.——

Also known as "My Dirty Stream" or "The Hudson River Song"
Words & music by Pete Seeger (1961)   © 1964 (renewed) by Fall River Music Inc.

1. Sailing up my dirty stream
    Still I love it and I'll keep the dream
    That some day, though maybe not this year
    My Hudson River will once again run clear.
    She starts high in the mountains of the north
    Crystal clear and icy trickles forth
    With just a few floating wrappers of chewing gum
    Dropped by some hikers to warn of things to come.

2. At Glens Falls five thousand honest hands
    Work at the Consolidated Paper Plant
    Five million gallons of waste a day,
    Why should we do it any other way?
    Down the valley one million toilet chains
    Find my Hudson so convenient a place to drain.
    And each little city says, "Who, me?
    Do you think that sewage plants come free?"

3. Out in the ocean they say the water's clear
    But I... live right at Beacon here*
    Halfway between the mountains and the sea,
    Tacking to and fro, this thought returns to me:
    Sailing up my dirty stream
    Still... I love it and I'll dream
    That some day, though maybe not this year,
    My Hudson River and my country will run clear.

* OR: "But we... live on the river here."

I was learning to sail, and spent my first night alone on the river, seeing the evening light go from golden to rose, to purple, to night. Made up a tune as I went along, and only realized a month later that I'd swiped the first part of the melody from one of my favorite Christmas carols, "Deck the Halls." (See p. 187.)

Sailing Down My Golden River

1. Sail-ing down my gold-en riv-er, Sun and wa-ter all my own,— Yet I was nev-er— a-lone.— Sun and wa-ter, old life-giv-ers, I'll have them where-e'er I roam,— And I was not far from home.——

Originally titled: "Sailing Down This Golden River"
Words & music by Pete Seeger (1962)
TRO - © 1971 Melody Trails, Inc., New York, NY.

1. Sailing down my golden river
   Sun and water all my own
      Yet I was never alone.
   Sun and water, old life-givers
   I'll have them where'er I roam
      And I was not far from home.

2. Sunlight glancing on the water
   Life and death are all my own
      And I was never alone.
   Life to raise my sons and daughters
   Golden sparkles in the foam
      And I was not far from home.

3. Sailing down this winding highway
   Travellers from near and far
      Yet I was never alone.
   Exploring all the little by-ways
   Sighting all the distant stars
      Yet I was not far from home.

REPEAT FIRST VERSE.

1. Sail - ing down my gold-en riv - er,—
sun and— wa-ter all my own,—

Arlo Guthrie used to sing it rhythmically with his pounding electric band, Shenandoah.

This song has been sung many different ways. As I put it down above, it might be taught to a group of people who never heard it, but are willing to try learning it out of a book.

When I first made it up, I sang it very freely; I opened with the guitar.

Dropped D tuning

I guess if I had a voice and was able to sing it now, I'd like to put in more triplets.

2. Sun-light glan-cing on the wa-ter,
life and death are all my own,—
Yet I was nev-er— a-lone.—
Life to raise my sons and daugh-ters... etc.

You who read this, decide for yourself what's the best way.

Ernie Marrs, one of the best wordsmiths I know, sent me these lyrics and I put a tune to 'em.

The People Are Scratching

1. Come fill up your glass-es and set your-selves down,

I'll tell you a stor-y of some-bod-y's town.___

It is-n't too near___ and it's not far a-way,___

And___ it's not a place where I'd want to stay,___ be-cause

CHORUS

The peo-ple are scratch-ing all o-ver the street,

___ Be-cause the rab-bits had noth-ing to eat.

Words by Ernie Marrs & Harold Martin   Music by Pete Seeger (1962)
© 1963 (renewed) Fall River Music Inc.

ERNIE MARRS

1. Come fill up your glasses and set yourselves down,
    I'll tell you a story of somebody's town.
    It isn't too near and it's not far away
    And it's not a place where I'd want to stay, because

CHORUS (AFTER EACH VERSE):
The people are scratching all over the street
Because the rabbits had nothing to eat.

2. The winter came in with a cold icy blast.
    It killed off the flowers, and killed off the grass.
    The rabbits were starving because of the freeze
    And they started eating the bark off the trees, now

3. The farmers said, "This sort of thing won't do,
    Our trees will be dead when the rabbits get through;
    We'll have to poison the rabbits, it's clear,
    Or we'll have no crops to harvest next year," now

4. So they bought the poison and spread it around
    And soon dead rabbits began to be found.
    Dogs ate the rabbits, and the farmers just said,
    "We'll poison those rabbits 'til the last dog is dead,"
    now

5. Up in the sky there were meat-eating fowls
    The dead rabbits poisoned the hawks and the owls,
    Thousands of field mice the hawks used to chase
    Were multiplying all over the place, and

6. The fields and the meadows were barren and brown,
    The mice got hungry and moved into town.
    The city folks took the farmers' advice,
    And all of them started to poison the mice, and

7. There were dead mice in all the apartments and flats,
    The cats ate the mice, and the mice killed the cats.
    The smell was awful, and I'm glad to say
    I wasn't the man hired to haul them away, and

8. All through the country and all through the town
    There wasn't a dog or a cat to be found,
    The fleas asked each other, "Now where can we stay?"
    They've been on the people from then till this day,
    yes

9. All you small creatures that live in this land,
    Stay clear of the man with the poisonous hand!
    A few bales of hay might keep you alive,
    But he'll pay more to kill you than to let you survive,
    oh

In 1964 I took my youngest daughter, then age nine, canoeing on a beautiful lake in Maine. We camped on a little island, and were dismayed to see the beach littered with bottles and cans. We picked 'em all up. I had a magic marker with me and wrote this graffiti on a flat stone. Yes, graffiti.

Cursed Be The Nation

Cursed be the Nation of any size or shape
Whose citizens behave like naked apes
And drop their litter where they please
Just like we did when we swung through trees.

But blessed be the nation, and blessed be the prize
When citizens of any shape or size
Can speak their mind for whatever reason
Without being jailed or accused of treason.

By Pete Seeger (1967)
© 1993 by Fall River Music Inc.

(No, I never made up a tune for it. Someone else can try. Remember, you can change words, add words.)

Drowned In Paper

Words & music by Pete Seeger (1962)
© 1963 (renewed) by Fall River Music Inc.

CHORUS:
Drowned in paper and strangled in wire
Our civilization is bound to go down.
And the birds and the bees and the bugs will take over
And the old green world go spinning around.

1. Some say the world will be ended in fire
   Some say it'll be frozen in ice to the heart.
   But I think I know how our race will expire
   It'll be our own doing from being so smart.

(I made up some forgettable verses for this, but the chorus comes back to haunt me. You try.)

In '63 an artist friend, Vic Schwarz, told me they used to have sloops on the river with a boom 70 feet long.

"Oh, don't give me that," says I, unbelieving. "There never was a sloop that big, except an America's Cup racer."

"No, I've got a book all about them; I'll lend it to you," says Vic. Soon after he sends a dog-eared volume, *Sloops of the Hudson*, written in 1908 by two middle-aged gents, William Verplanck and Moses Collyer. "Before we die we want to put down what we can remember of these sloops, because they were the most beautiful boats we ever knew, and they will never be seen again."

I read it through twice. Wrote a long "poem" about sloops (next page). Finally after a couple years couldn't stand the temptation. Stayed up till 2 a.m. typing a seven-page letter to Vic. "Why don't we get a gang of people together and build a life-size replica of a Hudson River sloop? It would probably cost $100,000, but if we got enough people together we could raise it."

Then I forgot about the letter. Four months later I happen to meet Vic on a railroad station platform. "When are we going to get started on that boat?" says he.

"What boat?" says I.

"You wrote me a letter!"

"Oh, that's as foolish as saying let's build a canoe and paddle to Tahiti."

"Well, I've passed your letter up and down the commuter train; we've got a dozen people who don't think it's foolish."

"Hm. Maybe if there are enough nuts, we just might do it."

This isn't the place to go into more detail, except to say that three years later the sloop *Clearwater* was launched. It's owned by a democratic non-profit organization of 15,000 members (in '93). Over 24 years it has taken hundreds of thousands of people out on educational sails, 50 at a time. The Hudson is noticeably cleaner, and *Clearwater* is one of the reasons why.

My violinist mother once said, "The three B's are Bach, Beethoven and Brahms." I retorted, "For me they are ballads, blues, and breakdowns." But now I guess it's boats, banjos, and biscuits. Because one of *Clearwater*'s main education devices has been riverside festivals, with lots of good food and music. Along the line, people get some ideas about getting together to clean up a beautiful river.

Hudson River Sloops

"I can see them now," said old Verplanck in 1908,
65 to 75 feet long, 20 to 25 feet wide.
Draught 7 or 8 (13 with centerboards down),
Mast 90 to 100 feet, topmast another 30 to 50,
Boom 70 to 90 feet, bowsprit 25
Capacity 50 to 200 tons of cargo
Crew of six, including captain, cabin boy, and cook."

Four hundred plied the river in 1860
Often built in small yards, in towns like
Cornwall, Marlborough, New Hamburg.

"When the wind was fair we could compete with
steam — and even beat her!"
But with no wind,
It could be five days drifting up to Newburgh
And longer, back to New York.
Or, five hours, with the right wind and tide.

Cargo? Grain, pickles, salt meat in barrels, livestock,
hay for New York's horses, bricks, plaster, slate for
sidewalks. In early times panelled staterooms for the
rich. (Poor folk walked to Albany.)

The Highlands were beautiful but tricky. If the wind
was from the west, as many as 50 sloops might be
waiting near Peekskill, unable to breast the narrows
with wind and tide against them. When the tide
changed, off they'd race. By Newburgh, they'd be
stretched out a mile or more.

Most treacherous was the "Worragut"
Four miles from West Point to Pollopel Island
(Bannerman's)
Here the *Neptune* overturned in 1824 on a gusty day
And 35 of its 50 passengers drowned.

The railroad took passenger and mail service after 1847.

"The river teemed with sturgeon in those days—big
fellows weighing 250 pounds would be seen leaping
several feet in the air. Now and then one would fall
on the deck of a small boat. Catching and packing
these fish was an important industry. Sturgeon was
known as 'Albany Beef.'"

By the early 20th century, sloops finally abandoned the
river.

"They were the most beautiful boats we ever knew.
And they will never be seen again."

By Pete Seeger (1964)
© 1993 by Fall River Music, Inc.

Don McLean, who was on the first crew of the
Clearwater, sang an old hymn which gave me the idea for
a tune to use for a short piece of poetry quoted by Robert
Boyle in his book, *The Hudson, A Natural and Unnatural
History*. The original was in Dutch, about the year 1640
— Bob got the translation from the book *Portrait of New
Netherland* by Ellis L. Raesly, © 1945 in New York City.

This Is A Land

Original Dutch words by Jacob Steendam (1635)
English translator unknown   New music adaptation by Pete Seeger (1971)
TRO - © 1975 Melody Trails, Inc., New York, NY.

This is a land
Of milk and honey flowing
With healing herbs
Like thistles, freely growing
Where buds of Aaron's Rods are blowing
O! This is Eden!

When I'm singing on stage, I'll follow this song immediately with "Little Boxes."

The Old Ark's A-Moverin'

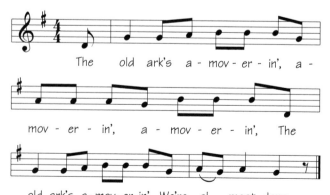

Traditional (African American spiritual)

That old spiritual was collected and printed over a hundred years ago. I haven't the faintest idea when it was put together — probably sometime in the mid-19th century by slaves or recently freed slaves. My new words for it below were put together about 1970 after I read in the book *The Population Bomb*, by biologist Paul Ehrlich, that the human race was doubling every 32 years. I think Karl Marx would have liked the song. He is the one who pointed out the Capitalist economic system was in trouble any time it could not expand; so sooner or later it would be in big trouble. Now I read that if an investor can't double his money in 10 years, he thinks he's doing something wrong. Growthmania needs a better song than this, but it's all I have right now.

We'll All Be A-Doubling

Words by Pete Seeger (1965)
Music: traditional ("The Old Ark's A-Movering")
TRO - © 1970 Melody Trails, Inc., New York, NY.

CHORUS (AND AFTER EACH VERSE):
We'll all be a-doubling, a-doubling, a-doubling,
We'll all be a-doubling in thirty-two years.

1. Two times two is four.
    Two times four is eight.
    Two times eight is sixteen,
    And the hour is getting late.

2. Twice sixteen is thirty-two
    Next comes sixty four
    Next a hundred and twenty-eight
    Do we need to hear more?

3. Next is two hundred fifty-six
    Next five hundred and twelve
    Next one thousand and twenty-four
    So figure it out yourself.

4. Keep doubling ten generations
    You can have children over a million
    Keep going another twenty
    Your children would be over a trillion.

5. Give it another three hundred years,
    Your children number a billion;
    Keep doubling another millennium,
    You can have another quadrillion.

6. Either people gonna have to get smaller
    Or the world's going to have to get bigger;
    Or there's a couple other possibilities,
    I'll leave it to you to figger.

Along the Hudson River new verses should be written. The *Clearwater* (see below), having helped to partially clean up the waters, is now having to fight to save the shores. If we don't watch out, it will be an unbroken chain of high rises from Albany to the sea, walling off the river from the less affluent behind them. One of my local Democratic politicians (a really nice guy) says to me, "Pete, what can you do? If you don't grow, you die." Only late at night I realized the answer. "Yes, I suppose that's true. Doesn't it then follow that the quicker you grow, the sooner you die?"

One of the more stupid things that Mao Tse-tung did 40 years ago was not alerting his countrymen to the need to keep the population down. Now it has reached panic proportions and has led to terrible things like infanticide.

In the "good old days" each tribe kept the other tribe's population down.

An Arab story. Arabs are proud that the whole world uses their system of numbers.

If you have your health, put down the number one. If you have a family, put a zero next to it. Ten! How lucky you are. If you have land, put another zero down. One hundred! Who could want more? Well, if you have a good reputation, put down another zero. You have health, family, land, a good reputation! But take away the "one," and what have you left?

Bud Foote, professor of English at Georgia Tech., is a first-rate songmaker. He was visited in late '69 by a friend, Jonathan Eberhart, who was on the first crew of the *Clearwater*. Jon is a good journalist and storyteller and did half the job of condensing the story of the sloop's first summer.

Bud wrote the ballad soon after and set it to what I call "The Great American Folk Melody." It's an old Irish tune, but has been used in the USA for hundreds of different songs. "My Little Old Sod Shanty," "He's the Lily of the Valley," "Little Joe the Wrangler," "Ballad of Harry Bridges," and others.

My only contribution was to give it a more upbeat last verse, and to repeat each last line, so the audience can sing along.

Ballad of the Sloop Clearwater

Words by Bud Foote, 7th verse by Pete Seeger (1969)
Music: traditional ("The Great American Folk Melody")
© 1971 by Fall River Music.

1. I was sitting on my front porch as I watched this river rot,
    Thinking about the sturgeon that are gone but not forgot,
    And the buffalo all restless underneath the prairie sod,
    And the smoke stacked up to heaven so's it hid the face of God.

    There were soldiers marching past my door and a tap upon my phone,
    A freeway inching tow'rd me that would someday take my home.
    And the smokestacks hid a sunset that would never come again
    When they brought the sloop Clearwater sailing 'round the bend.
        ("Sing it over.")
    When they brought the sloop Clearwater sailing 'round the bend.

2. The Captain had a moustache that was nineteen inches long.
    The shanty master paced the deck, roaring out a song.
    The man who held the tiller wore his hair down to his knees,
    And a hundred tons of canvas billowed out into the breeze.

But the redwood trees are crashing down out on
the western coast,
An angry shadowy army follows Crazy Horse's ghost.
The eagle's nest is barren as the mountain lion's den.
As they brought the sloop Clearwater
sailing 'round the bend. (2x)

3.   The Sloop cut through the sewage lying on the
river's face.
They docked her mid the garbage that was all
around the place.
The crew struck up a hornpipe, and the boots
rang on the wood,
It echoed on the river, and the river found it good.

But there's lightning in the Asian skies and thunder
in the slums.
You can hear the Indians tuning up their
long-forgotten drums.
Children clap their hands and laugh while men
are killing men,
As they brought the sloop Clearwater
sailing 'round the bend. (2x)

4.   I said, "You people must be fools to dance and sing
and shout
When your ship's so deep in liquid shit, it never
can get out.
Right now children cry from hunger, grown men
get mean with shame.
A war rages in every heart; the very ground's in
flame.

"You sail your dirty river; you sing your little songs.
You dance your pretty dances and recite your
petty wrongs.
Don't you know that Abiyoyo's making footprints
in the fen?
While you bring your Sloop Clearwater
sailing 'round the bend." (2x)

5.   The crew just laughed and danced some more, and
beads began to ping.
Beards were lifted to the skies as the crew began
to sing,
A black man rose upon the deck and preached a
sermon there,
And a crewman capered on the mast like a
dancing grizzly bear.

I said, "You people all are fools, but I guess I am one too."
Suddenly the guns went quiet. The river all was new.
The smoke clouds cleared. I almost wept to see
the sky again.
When they brought the sloop Clearwater
a-sailing 'round the bend. (2x)

6.   Well, the mountains rang, the children laughed,
the women sang a song.
The bison thundered down the plain a hundred
thousand strong.
The ghost dance tent was raised again
The lion wandered free.
The river ran like silver from the mountains to
the sea.

There was love and joy and brotherhood, and peace
the whole world round
Life and paint and energy, and trees and taste
and sound
And Abiyoyo danced a solemn waltz out in the fen
When they brought the sloop Clearwater
a-sailing 'round the bend. (2x)

7.   Now, the Sloop is gone, once again I'm ready
to watch that river rot
While others feel the skyfire, and others hug
the shot.
But some folks in town are up and around
asking, "What—how—why—and—when!"
Ever since that Sloop Clearwater
came sailing 'round the bend.
Ever since that Sloop Clearwater
came sailing 'round the bend.

The 1899 Rivers and Harbors Act said that nothing can be dumped in the waters without permission of the Corps of Engineers. The law was rediscovered in 1967 by Fred Danback of Yonkers when cleaning out the files of the Yonkers Lifesaving Corps with a friend. "Hey, Gus, listen to this. Wouldn't it be great if we had a law like this nowadays? It says the person who turns in the polluter gets half the fine!"

Gus said, "How do you know it's not still a law?" Fred wrote to the government printing office, and two weeks later got a letter to the effect: "Dear Mr. Danback, so far as we can discover that law is still on the books and has not been repealed."

Fred went now to see his Congressman, Richard Ottinger. "Hey, when I come to a red light, I got to stop. How come these guys are not stopping?"

Within a few years there were 500 cases in the U.S. courts. Bounty hunters were canoeing up waterways, taking test tube samples from every pipe. Manufacturers descended on Congress. "Do something! Repeal that law! We didn't know anything about it. We're all sitting ducks!"

Congress says, well, we can't repeal it now while everybody's talking about pollution. But we'll do something." So in 1972 they passed the Water Pollution Amendments to the Clean Water Act. It just incidentally superseded "old 1899."

The new law wasn't all bad though, and slowly citizen pressure started cleaning up the waters. As of this writing (1993) the Hudson is safe to swim in again from Yonkers to Catskill, and within another 10 years should be swimmable near New York City. I call it a 50 percent cleanup with a five percent effort. The next century will see a long, slow struggle to rid the river of toxic chemicals from industry, agriculture, and surface run-off as well. I think it's a sure thing that the river will be clean as a whistle 100 years from now. But it can happen in one of two ways. The human race will get rid of wars, injustice, and pollution. Or it won't, and there will be no more people around to pollute it. We don't have another 2,000 years to learn the Sermon on the Mount.

This song has far more verses than it needs. I've a habit of "over-writing," then paring things down to a usable size. For purposes of this book, though, I decided to print all verses, and put parentheses in front of the verses I ended not singing. In a distant city, 15 years after writing the song, I found a total stranger singing it.

In '74 I'd borrowed a shad net, thinking to learn something about fishing. In '75 I thought of the opening line of this song when I saw it hanging unused in my garage.

Throw Away That Shad Net
(How Are We Gonna Save Tomorrow?)

Also known as: "The PCB Song"
Words & music by Pete Seeger (1975)
TRO - © 1976 Melody Trails, Inc., New York, NY.

1. Throw away that shad net, get rid of hook and line.
   There's no more Hudson fishing, not for a long
      long time.
   The poison's in the riverbed, no matter whose
      the crime.
   But how are we gonna save tomorrow?

2. One thousand honest workers need that paycheck
      every week
   Way up in Fort Edward where the PCB's did leak
   And the GE Corporation knows the profits it must
      seek
   But how are we gonna save tomorrow?

3. The river was looking cleaner, it was starting to
      get clear
   We looked forward to the fishing getting better
      every year
   Now the scientists tell us, things are not what they
      appear
   But how are we gonna save tomorrow?

(4.) PCB was a clever thing, 'way back in twenty-nine
   Transformers and capacitors got turned out
      on the line
   Nobody suspected what they'd do to us in time
   And now we got to worry 'bout tomorrow

(5.) Well, the purpose of technology is gonna take a
     different turn
We'll test each new thing carefully, that's one thing
we have learned
We need a clean world for all to share, and all
     to work and earn
Then maybe we can save tomorrow.

6. Well, the experts knew about it, so why not you
     and me
Who controls the information in this land of
     the free?
The laws didn't seem to help in stopping PCB
So how are we gonna save tomorrow?

(7.) The longest journey taken needs a first step to begin
This cleanup's gonna take a while, but now we
     must begin
Clearwater says to lend a hand, a claw, a paw, a fin
'Cause now we got to work to save tomorrow.

SPOKEN: *"This song's too sad."*

8. Here's to the lowly blue crab, because he has no fat
And so he's got no PCB (hardly) we say, hooray
     for that
So I'll not quit my crabbing, you can stick that
     in your hat
Some how, we're gonna save tomorrow.

SPOKEN: *"In the old days, coal miners took a canary down
to test the air."*

9. Here's to the canary we took down in the mine
Here's to the Hudson stripers, may their warning
     be in time
Here's to all the young folks singing, "This land
     is yours and mine"
That's how we're gonna save tomorrow.

(10.) Oh, the glory's on the river, and the struggle's
     on the shore
Next year is 1976; let's start a little war
Anyone who thinks we're quitting better take just
     one think more
And that's how we're gonna save tomorrow.

11. So don't throw away that shad net, don't junk that
     hook and line
We're gonna make some changes, we're gonna start
     in time
Clearwater sings to all of us, this land is yours
     and mine
And that's how we're gonna save tomorrow.

1975 news item: "Environmental Commissioner Ogden Reid declared in August that polychlorinated biphenyls (PCB's) in Hudson striped bass made them now unfit to eat. John Cronin, working then for the Clearwater, discovered that EPA investigators knew about the industrial discharge of PCB's and did not stop them. The Clearwater initiates a campaign to phase out use of PCB's nationally and internationally."

In 1985 Clearwater clubs started up shoreside shad festivals again, because PCB levels in shad had sunk to 2 parts per million (ppm). In '93 arguments have started up again, because it's been found that PCB is more liable to cause birth defects than they once thought. The Beacon shadfest was cancelled.

Striped bass from the Hudson have 30 ppm. And eels, 200 ppm. And Hudson snapping turtles, 2,000 ppm! They're higher on the food chain. We are, too.

A STURGEON GOT CAUGHT IN THE SHAD NET!

Engraving: *Frank Leslie's Illustrated Newspaper,* 1878

We have some good jazz musicians among the Hudson River sloop singers. A young woman who is a good dancer would tap dance between the second and third verses.

It's a true story. I drove my daughter past the little station and saw it being renovated. "Hooray, we turned the clock back," I exclaimed first. And second, "Hey, I got a song."

The New Hamburg Clockback

Words & music by Pete Seeger (1981)
© 1993 by Fall River Music Inc.

1. There's a railroad station here at New Hamburg,
   That closed ten years ago
   The railroad bosses said, "Uneconomic!
   It's adding to the railroad's woes."
   But some folks in town, they didn't give up.
   They passed a petition around.
   And what do you know! It's open again.
   And we can take a train to town.

CHORUS (AFTER EACH VERSE):
   Hooray, (Hooray!) We turned the clock back,
   In one more little way
   Hooray, (Hooray!) We turned the clock back,
   That's progress for today
   Hooray, (Hooray!) We turned the clock back,
   There's a little more hope now, that's a fact
   And when the nuclear maniacs get the sack
   That'll be the clockback day, Hooray!
   That'll be the progress day.

2. New Hamburg's just about two hundred souls,
   On the river near Wappinger Falls
   Thank God, they didn't believe that lie,
   "You can't fight City Hall"
   Here's to the folks that didn't give up,
   And passed that petition around.
   Who knows, who knows, with spirit like that,
   We could have progress the world around.

3.   Look out the window, there's old mama Hudson
     Rolling on down to the sea
     And no matter what shape—size—color you are,
     She's got a message for you and me
     We oughta quit being petroleum junkies
     And get on the track again
     The locomotive of history is the people
     When we sing out loud and plain.

Again, no two singers will sing the exact same notes. Here are some of the variant melodies I use.

Verse 2 — Thank God they did-n't be-lieve___ that lie

Verse 2 — Who knows,_ who knows,_ with spir-it like that,_ We can have prog-ress the world a-round!___

Verse 3 — Look out the win-dow, There's old Ma-ma Hud-son roll-ing on down to the sea.

Verse 3 — And no mat-ter what shape, size, col-or you are_

Last Chorus–6th line — There's a lit-tle more hope and that's a fact,___ And when the nu-cle-ar ma-ni-acs get the sack_ etc.

© Len Munnik, Amsterdam

The best of the *Clearwater* songs are not in this book. Such as the new words Lorre Wyatt put to one of Jimmy Reed's rocking blues:
     Sailing Up (Sailing Up)
     Sailing Down (Sailing Down)
     Up! (down!) Down! (up!)
     Up and down the river
     Sailing on (sailing up, up, sailing up)
     Stopping all along the way
     The river may be dirty now
     But it's getting cleaner every day.

—also Rick Nestler's "River That Flows Both Ways"
     "I could be happy spending my days
     On the river that flows both way-y-ys."

Bob Killian's "Wind On the Water"

Wind on the wa-ter, blow-in' a-cross the bay!_

— and Bob's "There'll Come A Day"

There'll come a day___ the riv-ers will run a-gain

A favorite with every crew is the song by Bill Staines

All God's crit-ters got a place in the choir

— and Lorre Wyatt's

So-mos el bar-co, so-mos el mar

— also Pat Humphries' "Swimming to the Other Side," Bob Reid's "Animals Need Water," Dan Einbender's "It Really Isn't Garbage." And many, many others. Some old ones are still favorites: "Drunken Sailor," "Shenandoah," "Bound for South Australia," "Roll the Old Chariot Along."
     For these and hundreds of other Clearwater songs, get *For the Beauty of the Earth: An Environmental Songbook to Benefit the Hudson River Sloop Clearwater*, edited by Liza DiSavino, $16.05 postpaid from Clearwater, 112 Market Street, Poughkeepsie, NY 12601.

I saw a movie made by an anthropologist in the western Pacific, showing islanders strumming and a small crowd singing a friendly-sounding song. Said to myself, why couldn't we have a friendly-sounding song like that along the Hudson? Doesn't need a fancy melody. Just leave some ways a gang can join in without having to memorize a lot of words.

Broad Old River

Friendly rhythm. Lots of harmony needed.

Come a-long with me— (come a-long with me) — Up-on this broad old riv-er. Come a-long with me (come a-long with me)— Up- on this broad old riv-er. We will see (we will see) What we can do (what we can do) For when we work to-geth-er, in all kinds of weath-er, There's no tell-ing what the pow-er of the peo-ple And the riv-er can do (and the riv-er can do).

Music by Pete Seeger   Words by Pete Seeger and others
TRO - © 1993 Melody Trails, Inc., New York, NY.

1. Come along with me (come along with me)
   Upon this broad old river.
   Come along with me (come along with me)
   Upon this broad old river.
   And we will see (we will see)
   What we can do (what we can do)
   For when we work together, in all kinds of weather,
   There's no telling what the power of the people
   And the river can do (and the river can do).

2. Don't you be scared (don't you be scared)
   Upon this broad old river.
   Don't you be scared (don't you be scared)
   Upon this broad old river.
   Rockin' and rollin' (rockin' and rollin')
   On all those waves (on all those waves)
   For when we work together, in all kinds of weather,
   No matter how the wind's gonna blow
   We can be saved (we can be saved).

"We have an acronym, W.I.F.T.I., W.A.F.T.I.—Wind Is Fickle, Tide Implacable, Winds Are Fickle, Tides Implacable."

3. It's wifty wafty (it's wifty wafty)
   Out on this broad old river
   It's wifty wafty (it's wifty wafty)
   Out on this broad old river
   You can't half tell (you can't half tell)
   What the future brings (what the future brings)
   But if we work together, in all kinds of weather
   When the fickle winds fail we still
   Got songs to sing (got songs to sing).

4. Lotsa songs to sing (Lotsa songs to sing)
   Upon this broad old river
   Lotsa songs to sing (Lotsa songs to sing)
   Upon this broad old river.
   And we can sing (And we can sing)
   When the old wind fails (When the old wind fails)
   For when we sing together, in all kinds of weather
   With the power of the people and the voices
   We can fill the sails (We can fill the sails).
   (VERSE BY DAN EINBENDER)

5. Don'tcha give up hope (don'tcha give up hope)
   Upon this broad old river.
   Don'tcha give up hope (don'tcha give up hope)
   Upon this broad old river
   Sooner or later (sooner or later)
   The tide will turn (the tide will turn)
   And when we work together, in all kinds of weather,
   The teachers and the students
   They both will learn (they both will learn).
   (VERSE BY ???)

6. Come for a swim (come for a swim)
   Into this broad old river.
   Come for a swim (come for a swim)
   Into this broad old river.
   Bring the family down (bring the family down)
   To the river shore (to the river shore)
   You can see we're winning, just by going swimming
   You can see what we mean 'cause it's
   Cleaner than it was before (than it was before)
   (VERSE BY CAPT. TRAVIS JEFFREY)

7. We're gonna learn the ropes (gonna learn the ropes)
   Out on this broad old river
   We're gonna learn the ropes (gonna learn the ropes)
   Out on this broad old river.
   Bowline and longsplice (long...splice)
   Clove hitch and square (clove hitch and square)
   And when we work together, in all kinds of weather
   Like a lotta little fibers of rope we're
   Gonna hang in there (gonna hang in there).

8. Come fish with me (come fish with me)
   Out on this broad old river
   Come fish with me (come fish with me)
   Out on this broad old river
   And we will see (and we will see)
   What we can hook (what we can hook)
   But if we work together, in all kinds of weather
   We know someday they'll be
   Clean enough to cook (clean enough to cook).

   (VERSE BY DAN EINBENDER)

9. And you can help (and you can help)
   Clean up this broad old river
   And you can help (and you can help)
   Clean up this broad old river
   You'll never know (you'll never know)
   Until you try (until you try)
   But if we work together, in all kinds of weather
   With the power of the people and the river
   We can turn the tide (we can turn the tide).

10. Gotta lift your heart (gotta lift your heart)
    Out on this broad old river
    Gotta lift your heart (gotta lift your heart)
    Out on this broad old river
    Y'gotta understand (gotta understand)
    We got a job to do (got a job to do)
    But if we work together, in all kinds of weather
    Before you know it this mighty river
    Will run clear through (will run clear through).

    (VERSE BY DIGGETT DERMER)

(REPEAT FIRST VERSE FROM TIME TO TIME AS A CHORUS)

The Beacon Sloop Club is a sociable gang that likes to sing at its monthly meetings. It was a pleasant surprise to find others making up extra verses, such as:

   Lotsa songs to sing...
   Lotsa people to meet...
   Be prepared for storms...
   Read the book of nature...
   Gotta lift your eyes...
   Gotta lift your heart...
   Lift your feet...etc.

The second and fourth lines stay the same; the seventh and eighth lines usually also, but change sometimes as in Verse 4.

Clean Up the Hudson

Calypso beat

1. Well, you know it was twen-ty years a-go, In-to New York har-bor there sailed a boat. Peo-ple laughed at such a fool-ish thought, to try to clean up the Hud-son. *("Sing it with me now")*

CHORUS

Clear-wa-ter, da da da da, Clear-wa-ter, da da da da, Clear-wa-ter, you kept your prom-ise to try to clean up the Hud-son!

Words by Pete Seeger (1989) Music by Norman Span ("Matilda")

1. Well, you know it was twenty years ago.
   Into New York Harbor there sailed a boat.
   People laughed at such a foolish thought,
   To try to clean up the Hudson.

   SPOKEN: *"Sing it with me now."*
   CHORUS (AFTER EACH VERSE):
   Clearwater, Da da da da,
     Clearwater, Da da da da,
   Clearwater, You kept your promise
     To try to clean up the Hudson!

2. Some people said we were a bunch of reds
   Some said we smoked dope and were pot heads
   But we ignored them and we pushed ahead
   To try to clean up the Hudson

3. We held festivals in all the river towns
   The young and old would gather 'round
   With food and music to break the barriers down
   And try to clean up the Hudson

4. The beauty was there for all to see
   It broke all resistance and eventually
   Even politicians began to agree
   To try to clean up the Hudson

5. We taught classes in a brand new way
   While floating on the water on a breezy day
   Kids caught fish, 'n' learned that it would pay
   To try to clean up the Hudson

6. To raise the money we invented a way
   The kids sail for free during the day
   But for the evening sail the parents pay
   To try to clean up the Hudson

7. Now so many schools want us to take them out
   From Albany to New Jersey you hear them shout
   Clearwater, you have to build more boats
   To try to clean up the Hudson

8. Think globally, act locally
   Sing and shout for a world that's free
   Of war and toxics and bigotry
   Once more for the Hudson

9. These words were written in Albany jail
   Goddess of Inspiration! You did not fail
   Judge Keegan, send Pete there again without bail
   To try to clean up the Hudson.

Written while I was on a week's vacation, guest of Albany County jail, along with Rev. Al Sharpton and six others, as a result of protesting the Tawana Brawley decision and demanding a special prosecutor in racial bias cases. In jail I had time to write a song. No telephone calls. No mail. No dishes to wash.

One of my favorite American folk songs, learned from Alan Lomax over 50 years ago, was "Long John" — an African-American axe-chopping song (tune is right out of West Africa). With Captain Travis Jeffrey's help, the *Clearwater* got a rope-hauling song.

It's a Long Haul

1. Uh-one day, one day (one day, one day), I was walk-ing a-long (I was walk-ing a-long), I

heard a lit-tle child (I heard a lit-tle child), Just a-

sing-ing a song— (just a - sing-ing a song),—*

CHORUS

It's a long haul,— It's a high haul,—

It's a job for the man-y, Not just for the few,

It's a job for ev-'ry-bo-dy, That's

me and you,— It's a long haul,— It's a

high haul,— It's a hard haul.—

Words & music adaptation by Pete Seeger & Travis Jeffrey (1987)
Adapted from the song "Long John (Long Gone)", collected & arranged by
John A. & Alan Lomax
TRO - © 1934 (renewed), 1993 Folkways Music Publishers, Inc. & Melody Trails, Inc.,
New York, NY.

1. One day one day
   I was walking along
   I spied a little child
   Just a-singing a song

2. About a beautiful river
   Flowing down to the sea
   About getting this world
   In har-mo-ny

CHORUS (AFTER EVEN-NUMBERED VERSES):
   It's a long haul
   It's a high haul
   It's a job for the many
   Not just for the few
   It's a job for everybody
   That's me and you
   It's a long haul
   It's a high haul
   It's a hard haul

3. Now don'tcha get weary
   And don'tcha get tired
   If you don't keep hauling
   You all get fired

4. We're cleaning up a river
   So we all can swim
   Yes the rich and the poor
   Yes the her and the him

5. We got Captain _____
   He's/she's got a sharp eye
   And we all call him/her
   Captain Bligh.

6. Yes Captain _____
   Will make you toe the mark
   If you don't do your job
   You get thrown to the
     sharks

7. It's haulin' all together
   Each doin' what they can
   In all kindsa weather
   Each woman and man

8. It's haulin' in the sunshine
   Haulin' in the rain
   When we haul together
   Then there's no pain

9. So—sail the river
   Spring to fall
   Don't give up the struggle
   For us all

10. Haulin' together
    Keeping in time
    Haulin' on a halyard
    Makin' up a rhyme

11. Yes it's a beautiful boat
    And a beautiful place
    And a beautiful thing
    We call the human race

12. And a beautiful river
    So many beautiful things
    It can make you shiver
    It can make you sing

* This song needs a group, a gang, to repeat each line after the song
leader, no matter what he/she sings. The chorus, sung after every two
or three verses, can use some high harmony.

Variant melodies in subsequent verses:

(repeat)   (repeat)

(repeat)   (repeat)

Harmony ideas:

It's a long haul

This is a *Clearwater* version of a song put together by Leadbelly. He took a field holler with verses about "Old Riley" who escaped (from prison, from slavery) and combined them with a rhythmic axe-chopping song with verses about a man who escaped, even though the hound dogs were hot on his trail. It made a great performance piece for him. After he died, the Weavers used to sing it with full harmony. The slow opening and closing make a framework for the rhythmic center section. The notes here are basically the Weavers' arrangement. I just rewrote the words for *Clearwater*.

Haul, Make Her Go High

Words & music adaptation by Pete Seeger (1978)
Tune: "Old Riley (In Them Long Hot Summer Days)" by Huddie Ledbetter, collected & arranged by John A. Lomax & Alan Lomax
TRO - © 1936 (renewed), 1992 Folkways Music Publishers, Inc. & Melody Trails, Inc., New York, NY.

INTRODUCTION (AND ENDING)::

Clearwater's on the river,
Clearwater's on the river,
And it's a long haul you better believe.

1. Well it's a little piece o' pumpkin, little piece of pie
      Haul, Make her go high!
   I want to see clear water before I die
      Haul, Make her go high!

REFRAIN (AFTER EACH VERSE):
   Well it's hey! Clearwater!
      Haul, Make her go high!
   Hey, Clearwater!
      Haul, Make her go high!

2. Albany's up but the Battery's down (Haul, etc.)
   Now we're headed to Kingston town (Haul, etc.)

3. We'll heist her high without delay (Haul, etc.)
   A few more pulls and then belay (Haul, etc.)

Add more verses as needed. End by repeating the slow introductory verse.

Any experienced arranger of music for choruses will recognize from the above that I am not an experienced arranger of music for choruses. Nevertheless I've helped many to sing in harmony, and have tried to indicate here how adding a few notes above or below the melody can make the music more fun for everybody. The choral music I most admired was that of African Americans — sacred or sinful. It was rarely written down, and it changed from verse to verse.

Nowadays I try and persuade choruses that sometimes they should try and find notes which audiences can sing with them. Bach did it, why can't we?

Words & music by Pete Seeger (1985)
TRO - © 1993 Melody Trails, Inc., New York, NY.

1. Old Father Hudson
   Now we sit us down
   Ye winds and waters
   Come and gather 'round.

2. We've had some good eating
   Now we sit us down
   So let's start the meeting
   Come and gather 'round.

3. Mighty full agenda
   Now we sit us down
   It's quite a mind bender!
   Come and gather 'round.

4. But if we all choose our
      words well
   Now we sit us down
   We'll avoid the too-long-
      talker's hell
   Come and gather 'round.

REPEAT FIRST VERSE

Of course, if this song works, it should eventually get rich harmony on the last four words:

Now We Sit Us Down

A two-part song to pull folks together and get them ready for some sort of meeting.

THE SLOOP *CLEARWATER* WITH SCHOOLCHILDREN

The last song proved hard to teach, so I put similar words to a friendlier melody (see p. 180, where it's given in detail):

Take a Seat, Everybody

Words & music arrangement by Pete Seeger (1986)
Music adapted from "Minuit" by Keita Fodeba & Paul Winter
© 1989 & 1993 Umpawaug Music (ASCAP). All rights reserved. Courtesy of Living Music.

1. Take a seat, ev'rybody, sit down!
    The meeting won't be long, just gather round.
      Oyeh, oyeh, oyeh, oh—oo,
      Oyeh, oyeh, oyeh, <u>oy</u>eh.

2. You see what the agenda will cover
    If we are brief, it will soo...<u>oon</u> be over
      Oyeh, oyeh, oyeh, oh—oo,
      Oyeh, oyeh, oyeh, <u>oy</u>eh.

3. And if we all choose our words well
    We'll avoid the too...oo long talker's Hell
      La la la la, la la la la la
      La la la la la, la la
    (INTERRUPT:) *"OK Let's get started."*

For a century or more there's been a practice with many commercial songs: the well-known performer's name gets added to the unknown songwriter's name, for a share in the royalties. The justification? "This song wouldn't have gone anywhere without my help; I should share in the future profits."

The legal situation is almost the opposite. Singer B changes songwriter A's song, which now "takes off." But the law says that all of B's changes belong to A.

Here's a f'rinstance:

In the 1930's two African-American jazzmen, Slim Gaillard and Slam Stewart, liked to make up scat versions of popular tunes. They'd keep the original chords, and the main outlines of the melody, and add a lot of nonsense words. A popular swing band, Johnny Long's Orchestra, had hit records playing them. In '88 I spoke with Slam Stewart on the phone. "No, we didn't get a dime of royalties. Not even label credit. But that's life." He laughed.

"Slim and Slam" did have one big hit, "Flat Foot Floogie with a Floy, Floy." They've both gone to jazzmen's heaven now. But here's two samples of what they did with pop songs. The first is the 1932 slow, sentimental "Shantytown."

It's on-ly a shan-ty in old shan-ty-town——

"In a Shanty in Old Shanty Town" Words by Joe Young Music by Jack Little & John Siras
© 1932 (renewed) Warner Bros. Music. Used by permission.

They'd first play the song "straight." Then they'd speed up the tempo almost twice as fast for their version.

Shantytown

(In normal slow tempo, finish by singing it the usual way:) It's on - ly a shan - ty in...

Words by Joe Young Music by Jack Little & John Siras
Adaptation by Slim Gaillard & Slam Stewart
© 1932 (renewed) & 1993 Warner Bros. Music. All rights reserved. Used by permission.

Slim and Slam also improvised on Irving Berlin's 1926 hit song "Blue Skies." Here's the original. What a gem!

Blue Skies

Words & music by Irving Berlin

A Clearwater volunteer with a little help from me made up these new words to Slim and Slam's considerably changed melody. Now you can see why this musical digression got put in this chapter.

Blue Skies
(Clearwater Version)

Bye Bye Blues!__ Take it slow, take it slow, and you

nev-er have to go, 'cause it's Blue Skies!__

__ yeah, be-fore long. ("Blue skies") Blue skies... etc.

Words & music by Irving Berlin
Adaptation by Slim Gaillard & Slam Stewart
New lyrics by Pete Seeger & Michael Sherker (1989)
© 1927 (renewed) by Irving Berlin. International copyright secured. Used by permission.
All right reserved.

When Clearwater's Walkabout Chorus does it, we start off singing Berlin's original song, uptempo. Then quite fast, we sing these Clearwater words. Then we sing Berlin's original again real slow, with lots of harmony. I call out the words before each phrase (as shown below), so everyone in the crowd can join in. Ritard at end.

Well it rained all night, I'm feelin' uptight
I face this city feeling kinda gritty, oh
  Blue days
  Do I, do I, do I, do I need a new beginning
Gotta push, gotta shove, scratch around for love,
Squeeze my frame in a slow commuter train, oh
  Blue days
  What else is there to do? I'm bushed.
Then I see that sloop sailin' up stream
Take heart, take heart! It's not just a dream
Breathin' in the breeze, smellin' the air,
Gonna do something, work for what I care

So sing out the good news
  Bye bye blues
Take it slow, take it slow, You never have to go
And it's blue skies for me from now on.

Blue skies!... smiling at me!...
Nothing but blue skies!... Do I see!
Blue birds Singin' a song!...
Nothing but blue birds!... All day long!...
Never saw the sun shining so bright!...
Never saw things!... Going so right!...
Noticing the days!... Hurrying by!...
When you're in love!... My how they fly!...
Blue days... all of them gone!...
Nothing but blue skies from now on!...

Really, if there's a human race here 500 years from now, this will be called an old folksong, just as is "Greensleeves" (which was an English pop song of the 16th Century).

In 1972 shad fisherman Ron Ingolds gave us free shad for *Clearwater*'s first shad festival. Ingolds lives in Edgewater, New Jersey, just south of the George Washington Bridge, and carries on his father's fishing tradition. He introduced me to the wonders of setting the nets at slack tide before flood and taking them in at slack tide before ebb, six hours later. He and a few helpers live on the waterfront for a month, only snatching a few hours sleep at a time. I wrote these words for him and his helpers, using an old German melody.

Of Time And Rivers Flowing

1. Of time and rivers flowing
    The seasons make a song
    And we who live beside her
    Still try to sing along
      Of rivers, fish, and men
      And the season still a-coming
      When she'll run clear again

2. So many homeless sailors,
    So many winds that blow
    I asked the half blind scholars
    Which way the currents flow
      So cast your nets below
      And the gods of moving waters
      Will tell us all they know.

3. The circles of the planets
    The circles of the moon
    The circles of the atoms
    All play a marching tune
      And we who would join in
      Can stand aside no longer
      Now let us all begin.

Here's the German melody, "Es Ist Ein Ros Entsprungen." College choirs know the English translation, "Lo, How a Rose Ere Blooming."

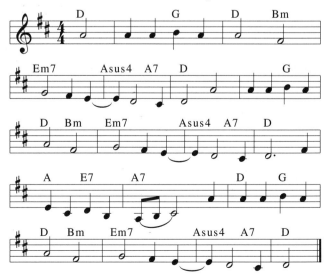

The melody is from an old German christmas carol harmonized by Praetorius — too pretentiously, in my opinion. After 16 years of experimentation, I feel that a driving syncopated rhythm with an audience singalong is the best way to do it — at least for me. I wrote it out for our Clearwater Walkabout Chorus. But as a soloist I call out the words and can get a large crowd to join in.

Twenty years ago when I first wrote the song, I tried singing it slowly. The song was a failure, at least with my voice. About six years ago I started singing it less pretentiously, with a fast rhythm. All of a sudden it "worked" — and I could get a crowd to sing it with me. Again, you'll see how I give these words to the crowd, line by line.

Of Time And Rivers Flowing
(For a Songleader and Group)

La la la la la la,_____ La la la la la
("One more time")

Bm   Em7   A7sus4 A7   D

la la,_____ La la la la la la._____ ("So cast So
your nets below")

A   E7   A   A7

cast your nets be - low,_____ And the
("And the gods of moving waters")

D >   Bm

gods of mov - ing wa - ters_____ ("Will tell us
all they know")

Em7   A7sus4   A7

will tell us   all they know._____

Bm

WOMEN
3. The cir - cles   of the plan - ets,

Em7   A7sus4   A7   D

MEN
The cir - cles   of the moon._____ The cir - cles

Bm   Em7   A7sus4 A7   D

of the at - oms   all play a march - ing tune.

A   E7   A   A7

WOMEN
And we, who would join in,_____

D   Bm

ALL
_____ can stand a - side no long - er,

Em7 >   A7sus4 A7 D   G D

ALL, WITH AUDIENCE
Now let us all be - gin._____ La la la la la
("Sing it with us")

Bm   Em7   A7sus4 A7   D

la la,_____ La la la la la la,_____ La
("One more time")

G D Bm   Em7

la la la la la la,_____ La la la

A7sus4 A7   D   A   E7

la la la._____ And we, who would join
("And we who would join in")

A   A7   D   G D

in,_____ can stand a - side no
("Can stand aside no longer")

Bm   G rit.   A7sus4 A7 D

long - er,_____ Now let us all be - gin._____
("Now let us all begin")

Words by Pete Seeger (1973)
Music: "Es Ist Ein Ros Entsprungen" (Lo How a Rose Ere Blooming)
© 1974, 1993 by Sanga Music Inc.

Drawing by Thomas B. Allen

martha + Hudee   (2)   Somewhere at Sea
                                          Dec 13, 1943

We have been awful lucky in some ways. We have been able to meet thousands of the very best kind of friends and they have always made their home our home, all because they liked the songs we sang and because you people are so nice. We've had some hard knocks and some rough going, but no matter how hard and rocky the road, our friends never quit us, never let us down, and they're the kind of people that will stick with us always. I know you already know this, but I just want you to know how you made me feel tonight when I heard you on the radio. (Of course martha knows that what I say goes for her, too, because she is really what makes Leadbelly keep going.) It is now that we're apart that I really see how close we are together. Your guitar and mine both talk the same language - the language of the working people. When our guitars come in there together they talk their own language. I just wish I could have played my guitar along with you tonight, but I couldn't get to it. You can just imagine how I sweated and shook all over, hearing you play, and not able to play with you. The last time we played together was up at Pete + Toshi's wedding party - we had 3 banjos - boy - we really raised the roof that night, didn't we? I want to say I am speaking for our whole crew here on the ship - we all enjoyed your program. How much, I don't guess I could ever write it down.

        Well, just remember, we're out here listening to you and thinking about you. Here's to a couple of the nicest folks I ever hope to know -
                                your friend as Ever
                                Woody Guthrie

LETTER TO LEADBELLY FROM WOODY GUTHRIE, SOMEWHERE AT SEA, DECEMBER 13, 1943

Chapter X

Time, Home, Family, Friends

I think we judge time by how long we've been on earth. When I was 13, six of us school friends pledged a reunion 10 years later. Those 10 years seemed about as long to me then as the 38 years that have flicked by since I was questioned by the House Unamerican Activities Committee in '55. Which is logical; 10 years then was about half my conscious lifetime.

I told you, as a kid I was a nature nut. Between age seven and twelve I read every single book by Ernest Thompson Seton, the Canadian author of *Wild Animals I Have Known*, *Rolf In the Woods* and others. Then I started reading more widely. Age 16, came a turning point in my life. My mother was teaching violin to the teenagers in a Jewish family (Kantrovich. Some of them later became well-known scientists.)

At a week-end at their house in Connecticut we got in a long discussion on what to do with one's life. I announced that I was going to be a hermit, because in this world full of hypocrisy that was the only way to stay an honest man. They jumped on me like a load of bricks. That's your idea of morality? You're going to stay nice and pure and let the rest of the world go to hell? They posed their traditional Jewish social conscience against my more New England Thoreau way of thinking.

I decided they were right. Started getting more involved, and have been ever since. But still my favorite way to relax is a walk or a work session in the woods.

I've com-mit-ted crimes— a-gainst Na-ture, stay-ing in-doors on sun-ny days.——

And about every April I feel like singing this verse, to the tune of "Midnight Special."

Bright Yellow Forsythias

Strong beat

Bright yel-low for-syth-ias, just pret-ty as you please. Daf-fy-dils and li-lacs, and all the dog-wood trees.— So man-y col-ors,— makes your heart want to sing. You can thank your luck-y stars— for giv-ing one more spring.— Let the mid-night spe-cial shine her light on me,— Let the mid-night spe-cial shine her ev-er-lov-ing light on me

New lyrics & adaptation by Pete Seeger (1980)
Adapted from "The Midnight Special" by Huddie Ledbetter
Collected & arranged by John A. Lomax & Alan Lomax
TRO - © 1936 (renewed) & 1993 Folkways Music Publishers, Inc. & Melody Trails, Inc., New York, NY.

The words of the next song are by that close friend, a Communist poet, now dead, Walter Lowenfels. See p. 95.

Tomorrow's Children

English translation by Walter Lowenfels (from the French of Guillevic)
Music by Pete Seeger (1964)
© 1964 (renewed) by Stormking Music Inc.

1. But you who know days of a diff'rent kind,
   Tomorow's children for whom work is more like play,
   And living is what poems are for me today,
   A passionate utterance carefully designed.

2. Remember us, the lame, the deaf, the blind,
   Not for the stupid things we've done and can't forget;
   Nor the endless dull jobs over which we all sweat,
   Nor all the sad chronicles that we leave behind.

BRIDGE:
But that we loved as much as anyone ever did,
That we knew joys, the little deeds, the grand design.
The dream of changing the world to something new.
Believe us, in our way we loved to live.

3. Know that many, many things we loved,
   and of all of these,
   Our greatest joy was in opening the way for you.

Lest you think all Walter's poems were serious or political here's another of his, a short one.

> These bones you see
> so cold, so white and dead
> Were once a young
> and agile girl in bed.

It was back in the late 1960's the telephone rang: "This is Otto Preminger speaking. (Thick Viennese accent.) Are you the Pete Seeger who makes up songs and sings them?"

"Yes," I reply.

"Well, I want to know if you can write me a song about the will to live."

"Why, that's my business."

"I have a movie which is about the will to live, and I want a song. Can you come to New York? You can see a screening of the rough cut of the movie."

A few days later Toshi and I were sitting in a comfortable apartment eating a very good meal with Hollywood producer Otto Preminger and his wife. He was a heavy-set man, 10 or more years older than I. A direct and honest way of speaking.

We saw the movie screened in his living room. It had been made from a novel, written by a nurse, about three people who leave a hospital at the same time. They decide to pool their meager resources and get a house. One is a young man who will be in a wheelchair the rest of his life as a result of a beating. A young woman has her face permanently scarred because of car battery acid splashed in her face by a man she had spurned and then laughed at. The third is a young man who is an epileptic and will never know when one of his seizures may kill him. The story showed the capacity of ordinary people to survive.

"I need a song to go under the titles of the movie at the beginning of the picture. Will one month be enough for you? Can we set the date now for you to fly out to California for the song to be filmed?"

I said, "Yes," and during the month spent numerous hours trying this idea and that, but not really being satisfied completely with any one idea. Toshi was a little worried. "Do you think you have Preminger's song ready?"

"Yes, I think so." (I lied.)

We landed at Los Angeles to meet Preminger and a camera crew of four or five people. "Can I hear the song now while we are waiting for the plane to Fresno?"

"Well, I have actually several songs. We'll see which one you think is best." I believe I sang three or four to him — some old folk songs with some new verses. I can't remember which ones. They might have been gospel songs or spirituals. "There are still a couple more I have in mind." I could see Preminger was not enthusiastic about any one of them.

We had a one-hour plane flight to Fresno. It was now or never. I borrowed pencil and paper from Toshi. With the airplane drone in my ears, I managed to compose a "new" song. Nothing like a deadline to force something out of you. From the dregs of my subconscious I scraped five verses. Used some repetition, and a melody derived from old ballads.

In the Fresno airport I sang it for Preminger and the rest.

Old Devil Time

1. Old De-vil Time, I'm— gon-na fool you now!—
Old De-vil Time,— you'd like— to bring me down!—
When— I'm feel-ing low,— my lov-ers gath-er round—
And help me rise— to fight you one more time!—

Words & music by Pete Seeger (1969)
© 1969, 1970 by Fall River Music, Inc. & Sigma Productions Inc.

1. Old Devil Time, I'm goin' to fool you now!
   Old Devil Time, you'd like to bring me down!
   When I'm feeling low, my lovers gather 'round
   And help me rise to fight you one more time!

2. Old Devil Fear, you with your icy hands,
   Old Devil Fear, you'd like to freeze me cold!
   But when I'm sore afraid, my lovers gather 'round
   And help me rise to fight you one more time!

3. Old Devil Pain, you often pinned me down,
   You thought I'd cry, and beg you for the end.
   But at that very time, my lovers gather 'round
   And help me rise to fight you one more time!

4. Old Devil Hate, I knew you long ago,
   Then I found out the poison in your breath.
   Now when we hear your lies, my lovers gather 'round
   And help me rise to fight you one more time!

5. No storm or fire can ever beat us down,
   No wind that blows but carries us further on.
   And you who fear, oh lovers, gather 'round
   And we can rise and sing it one more time!

REPEAT THE 5TH VERSE WITH EVERYBODY JOINING IN

"Yes, that will do very well, I think," said he. "Why didn't you sing that one to me first?"

"I only just made it up in the plane."

"Oh, don't tell me that. You had it all along."

Next day we drove out to the sequoia groves in the Sierras, where they filmed me singing the song while tromping through the underbrush around the huge trees, even as a light snow was starting to fall. The next afternoon in Los Angeles with the film fresh from the developers, I recorded it again, "lip-sync," with studio quality. A few months later the film was out: *Tell Me That You Love Me, Junie Moon*, with Liza Minelli. It was not a "hit," but it was a good movie. I am glad it is being seen now on videotape.

Preminger paid what was for me a huge sum — something like $1,500 or $2,000 for the first-rights use of the song, but I have been repaid many times over in getting a good song to sing from time to time in a program. I find I can do without the third verse, but I like to repeat the last verse a couple times so the audience can sing it with me.

I speak, "No storm or fire can ever beat us down." Then I sing it and hope some will sing it with me. "No wind that blows but carries us further on." Then more start to sing it with me.

I keep the soft rhythm going while I speak the next lines, "And you who fear, oh lovers, gather round. And we can rise and sing it one more time." And then the crowd will sing those two lines, and I call out, "And we can rise and sing it." And with a slight ritard at the end, I can usually get nearly everybody to join in.

"And we can rise and sing it — one more time."

I'm a lucky songwriter. Thank you, Otto, wherever you are.

I said the tune was derivative. See its similarity to the famous old English ballad "Barbara Allen," and its first-cousin-melody, "Come All Ye Fair and Tender Ladies."

Barbara Allen

Freely! (notes can be shortened as well as lengthened)

Traditional (English ballad)

Come All Ye Fair And Tender Ladies

I'm glad to see others singing "Old Devil Time" now, but I'm sorry so many seem to miss one of my favorite notes.

It's an old trick of melody writers to outline a chord by the notes of a melody. Hoagy Carmichael's great 1930 song "Stardust" did it.

Fiddle tunes did it all the time. Remember "The Irish Washerwoman"?

Marion Wade added a good new verse.

Old Devil Time, we're gonna fool you now
With words and tunes, the love we leave behind
And before our time is done, we think of those to come
Our voices rise to sing it one more time.

If I'm sitting around, improvising on the guitar, one of my favorite keys is A. That's how "Mexican Blues" was made up, also the next two.

Maple Syrup Time

1. First you get the buck-ets read-y, clean the pans and gath-er fire-wood, Late in the win-ter, it's ma-ple syr-up time.___ You need warm and sun-ny days_ but still a cold and freez-ing night-time For just a few weeks, ma-ple_ syr-up time. We boil and boil and boil and boil it all day long.___ Till nine-ty sev'n per-cent of wa-ter e-vap-o-rates just like this song, And when what is left is syr-up-y don't leave it too long.___ Watch out for burn-ing! Ma-ple_ syr-up time.

Words (1975) & music (1967) by Pete Seeger
© 1977, 1979 by Fall River Music Inc.

1. First you get the buckets ready, clean the pans and
        gather firewood,
   Late in the winter, it's maple syrup time.
   You need warm and sunny days but still a cold and
        freezing nighttime
   For just a few weeks, maple syrup time.
   We boil and boil and boil and boil it all day long,
   Till ninety sev'n percent of water evaporates just
        like this song
   And when what is left is syrupy don't leave it
        too long—
   Watch out for burning! Maple syrup time.

(IF THERE'S ANYONE LISTENING TO ME, I ASK THEM TO MAKE THE SOUND OF MARACAS WITH THEIR LIPS):
   sh-sh-sh-sh—"keep it up through the whole song."

2. I know it's not the quickest system but each year I
        can't resist it.
   Get out the buckets, and tap the trees in time—
   Making it is half the fun, and satisfaction when
        it's done.
   Keep up the fire! Maple syrup time.
   My grandpa says perhaps it's just a waste of time.
   Ah! but no more than this attempt to make a happy
        little rhyme,
   So pat your feet or swing your tail, but keep in
        good time.
   Keep up the fire! Maple syrup time.

3. I'll send this song around the world with love to
        ev'ry boy and girl,
   Hoping they don't mind a little advice in rhyme.
   As in life or revolution, rarely is there a quick
        solution,
   Anything worthwhile takes a little time.
   We boil and boil and boil and boil it all day long.
   When what is left is syrupy, don't leave it on the
        flame too long.
   But seize the minute, build a new world, sing an
        old song.
   Keep up the fire! Maple syrup time.

I got the idea for this tune 30 years ago when trying to help steel bands become better known. No steel band ever picked up my tune, but 15 years later I found words for it, to send as a Christmas present to old friends in Maine.

The original words were, "I'll send this song to Scott and Helen/Up in Maine where they are dwellin'," for Scott and Helen Nearing who wrote *The Maple Sugar Book*, and got me started syruping.

Here's a fun way to play it on the guitar.

Maple Syrup Time
(Guitar Part)

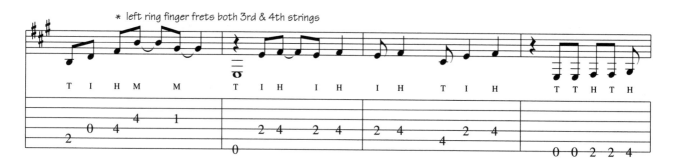

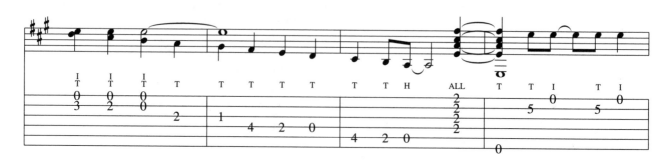

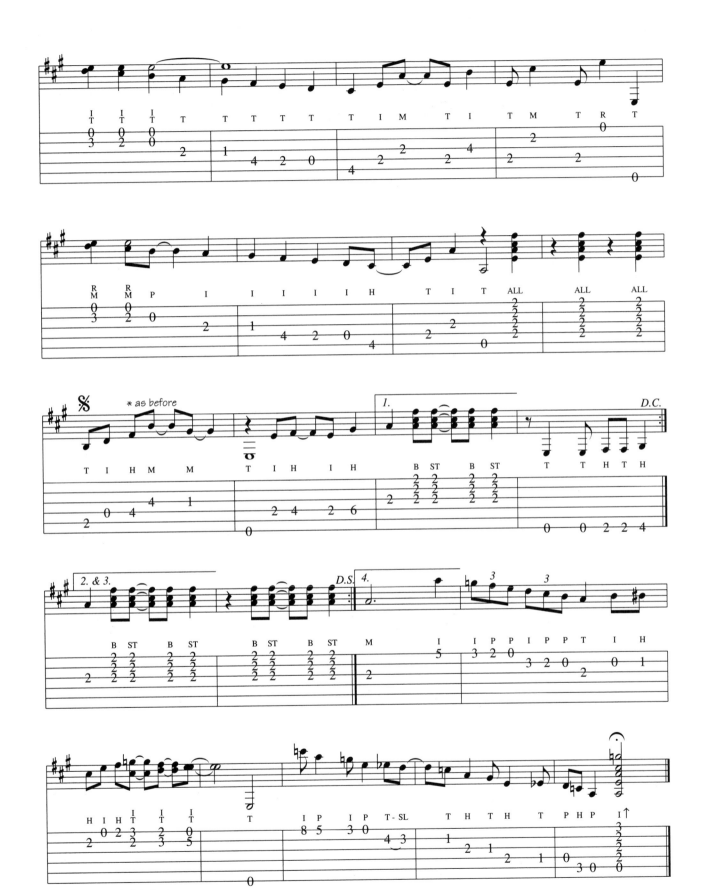

Guitar arrangement by Pete Seeger
© 1977, 1979 by Fall River Music Inc.

This tune I've never played on a stage, but I play it often when riding in a train or waiting in an airport. I can't remember when it began to take shape.

Spring Fever

By Pete Seeger (1973)
© 1993 by Fall River Music Inc.

(The last four measures I usually save for a final ending. Meanwhile I can experiment with variations in the piece. Below are just two possibilities)

* Variant first measure:

**Variant

*** It's less difficult than it looks. The left middle finger frets both the 5th and 4th strings, sliding up and holding it for the next note.

Sour Cream

My name is Pat-rick Spud-nut,* pho-
tog-ra-pher by trade. I
trav-el this world o-ver, some think I got it made.
But while I film the world of fash-ion, I
Yes...
real-ly have a se-cret pas-sion,
I spend all my cash on so-ur cream.

Words & music by Pete Seeger (1976)
TRO - © 1979 Melody Trails, Inc., New York, NY.

1. My name is Patrick Spudnut* photographer by trade.
   I travel this world over, some think I got it made.
   But while I film the world of fashion,
   I really have a secret passion.
   I spend all my cash on sour cream.
       Yes, while I film the world of fashion,
       I really have a secret passion,
       I spend all my cash on sour cream.

2. Sour cream forever, emblazoned on my heart
   You know I can't forget you, I told you from the start.
   But if I ramble now and then
   You know I will return again
   Because I can't forget you, sour cream.
       Yes, if I ramble now and then
       You know I will return again
       Because I can't forget you, sour cream.

3. Sour cream, in salad or in soup
   With you inside me I can really loop the loop the loop
   Civilization will flower
   Black, brown and buff can have cow power
   When we all have plenty of sour cream
       Civilization will flower
       Black, brown and buff can have cow power
       When we all have plenty of sour cream.

* Fake name. No need to libel a good friend. But he did arrive with a whole
quart of sour cream, saying, "I knew you wouldn't have enough."

Variants:

2. So-ur cream for-ev-er, em-bla-zoned in my heart...

3. So-ur cream, in sal-ad or in soup

About 10 years ago, chopping a dead tree down for firewood, I had to face the fact that I was getting more and more out of condition. Getting out of breath. Found myself carrying on a tradition, making up a chopping song — based on an older tune.

Lord Ha' Mercy On Me

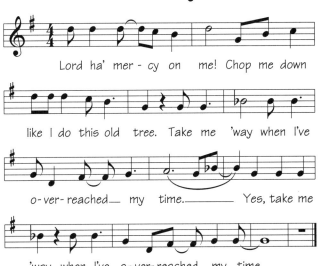

Lord ha' mer-cy on me! Chop me down
like I do this old tree. Take me 'way when I've
o-ver-reached— my time._____ Yes, take me
'way when I've o-ver-reached— my time.—

Words by Pete Seeger (1988) Music: traditional ("Old Reuben")
© 1993 by Fall River Music Inc.

Where'd I get the tune? Alan Lomax heard it from the Golden Gate Quartet, 50 years ago. Taught it to me. It's also similar to "Keep Your Eyes on the Prize."

Old Reuben

Well they got old Reu-ben down and they stole his watch and
chain. It was all that poor boy ev-er had._____ It was
all that poor boy ev-er had. Cry-in' Reu-ben, cry-in'
Reu-ben. Say-in' Where have you been— so long?—

Traditional (U.S.A.)

(European harmonies aren't really needed for this African-American melody.)

In the early 1930's, those deep depression days, Lawrence Gellert came back from a trip down south with some extraordinary songs which were later printed by Communists in a book, *Negro Songs of Protest*. Years later, when he was an old man, I found these lyrics which he'd collected then, now reprinted in Dr. Philip Foner's mammoth volume, *Labor Songs of the 19th Century*. I wrote Larry for the tune, but his notes were indecipherable. I ended making a new tune for them, and was proud when Brother Fred Kirkpatrick started singing it.

The Gainin' Ground

("Nat Turner")   Words: author unknown (1831)   Music by Pete Seeger (1977)
TRO - © 1993 Melody Trails, Inc., New York, NY.

Variants:

Verse 2

Verse 3

THE CAPTURE OF NAT TURNER, 1831

1.   You might* be rich as cream,
     Drive you a coach and a four horse team.

REFRAIN:
But you can't keep this world from turnin' round,
     turnin' roun'.
Nor Nat Turner from the gainin' groun', gainin' groun'.
No you can't keep this world from turnin' roun',
     turnin' roun'.
Nor Nat Turner from the gainin' groun', gainin' groun'.

2.   You might be reader and writer too.
     Wiser than old Solomon the Jew. (REFRAIN)

3.   And your name might be Caesar, sure.
     You got cannon can shoot shoot a mile or more.
     (REFRAIN)

* Gellert's spelling was "mought." A more common southern pronunciation would be "maht."

BROTHER FRED KIRKPATRICK, 1969

At Christmas time I sing carols, but I also sing, "Chanukah, Oh Chanukah" and the song my niece, Kate, named "The Chanukah Chase." I love the few Yiddish folksongs I've heard. "Oyfn Pripichik." "Tumbalalaika." If I have a recorder with me, I may play the Yiddish lullaby written in New York in the late 19th Century, "Rozhinkes Mit Mandeln (Raisins With Almonds)" or the partisan song "Shtille Di Nacht," this last a song I'll never forget. In 1943 Poland, Hirsh Glick, age 19, wrote a song for a girl:

> Shtille di Nacht...
> The night was still
> And the stars shone on the frosty ground.
> Oh do you remember
> I taught you to hold
> A pistol in your hand.

In memory of them, the next song.

Embers of the Martyrs
(The Smoke of Treblinka)

Poem in Yiddish by Ber Green English translation by Martin Birnbaum
Music by Pete Seeger (1978)
TRO - © 1975 & 1993 Melody Trails, Inc., New York, NY.

Those words were written by a man older than I. I put a tune to it after I read his poem in the magazine *Jewish Currents*.

Could a non-Jew presume to add anything to this? Ber Green died before I could show him my second verse. It's for a children's chorus to sing.

1. And still I choke on the smoke of Treblinka.
   Wild winds weep over the bones of the dead.
   In those gray spaces sacred souls are soaring
   The hot ashes of the martyrs rain upon my head.
   Forever these sacred ashes will wail in my heart.
   In their searing my soul forever will groan,
   Endless will be the Kaddish of my song.
   In my blood, forever, a Kaddish will moan.

2. But we are here and we'll not forget you.
   We are here to build and to say:
   The martyrs' ashes circle all the world now,
   And we, yes we will find a way.
   We'll remember; we will build, and you will live on
   And your soul, your soul will mingle with theirs
   Endless will be the brokhe that we bring...
   In our blood, forever, your song will still... sing.

Thanks to Morris U. Shappes, editor of *Jewish Currents* for supplying the word "brokhe." It means "blessing" in Yiddish, derived from the Hebrew. (Harry Schacter thinks "L'chaim," meaning "To Life!" is better.)

People think that what makes America strong is military might, powerful industry, mechanized agriculture. But I think it's the ancient tradition of forming organizations of all sorts, to get a job done. De Tocqueville pointed this out 160 years ago. Put a couple hundred Americans out on a prairie to start a town. Six months later they have religious and social organizations, political and business organizations, sports organizations, educational organizations. Keep in mind: the test of any organization is its ability to renew itself.

I drifted out of the Communist Party in the early '50's when I moved to the country. In the deepest sense of the word, I guess, I'm still a communist. I'd like to see a world without millionaires.

I often joke that I became a communist at age seven when I read about American Indians. No rich, no poor. Life and death decisions made around a council fire. And I've been fascinated to visit communes of one sort or another around the world to see how they attempt to solve problems. Including a kibbutz in Israel, a Christian commune in New York State. I admit, like most book writers, perhaps I'm a capitalist of the imagination, investing time and money to put out a book, then sitting back hoping it sells. Actually, a lot of songwriters look on themselves as gamblers, losing money most of the time, but hoping once in a while to hit the jackpot.

The problem: how to balance the positive values of competition with the positive values of cooperation. Locally, Worldwide. Such thoughts led to the next song. As the Civil Rights coalition started to break up, I was also involved in helping some good people I knew who were in prison.

I still sing this when I sing in prisons.

Walking Down Death Row

Words & music by Pete Seeger (1966)
© 1966 by Stormking Music Inc.

1. Walking down death row,
   I sang for three men, destined for the chair;
   Walking down death row,
   I sang of lives and loves in other years.
   > Walking down death row, I sang of hopes that
   >   used to be.
   > Through the bars, into each sep'rate cell,
   >   Yes, I sang to one and two and three.
   "If you'd only stuck together you'd not
     be sitting here!
   "If you could have loved each other's lives,
     you'd not be sitting here!
   "And if only this you would believe,
   "You still might, you might still be reprieved!"

2. Walking down death row,
   I turned a corner and found to my surprise;
   There were women there as well,
   With babies in their arms, before my eyes.
   > Walking down death row,
   >   I tried once more to sing of hopes that
   >   used to be.
   > But the thought of that contraption,
   >   down the hall,
   > Waiting for whole fam'lies, one dozen,
   >   two or three,*
   "If you'd only stuck together, you'd not be here!
   "If you could've loved another's child as well as your
     own, you'd not be sitting here!**
   "And if only this you would believe,
   "You still might, you might still be reprieved."

3. Walking down death row,
   I concentrated, singing to the young.
   I sang of hopes that flickered still;
   I tried to mouth their many sep'rate tongues.
   > Walking down death row,
   >   I sang of life and love that still might be.
   > Singing, singing, singing down death row,***
   >   To each sep'rate human cell,
   >   One billion, two or three,
   "If we'd only stick together, we'd not be here!
   "If we could learn to love each other's lives,
     we'd not be sitting here!
   "And if only this we could believe,
   "We still might, <u>we</u> might still be reprieved."

Variants:

* Verse 2

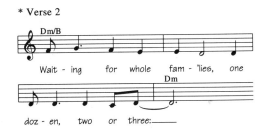

** Verse 2

*** Verse 3

I usually end with a discord:

A couple hundred years ago a shipwrecked sailor drifted for weeks till he saw land. He crawled up the beach not knowing what country or continent he'd landed on. He staggered up the bluff, and at the top found himself in a large field where there was a gallows and a man hanging. He exclaimed, "Thank God! I'm in a Christian country."

Quite Early Morning

1. Don't you know it's dark - est be-fore the dawn,___ And this thought keeps me mov - in' on. If we could heed these ear - ly warn-ings, The time is now, quite ear - ly morn-ing! If we could heed these ear-ly warn-ings,___ The time is now,___ quite ear - ly morn-ing.

Words & music by Pete Seeger (1969)
© 1969 by Fall River Music Inc.

1. Don't you know it's darkest before the dawn
   And it's this thought keeps me moving on
   If we could heed these early warnings
   The time is now quite early morning
   If we could heed these early warnings
   The time is now quite early morning

2. Some say that humankind won't long endure
   But what makes them so doggone sure?
   I know that you who hear my singing
   Could make those freedom bells go ringing
   I know that you who hear my singing
   Could make those freedom bells go ringing

3. And so we keep on while we live
   Until we have no, no more to give
   And when these fingers can strum no longer
   Hand the old banjo to young ones stronger
   And when these fingers can strum no longer
   Hand the old banjo to young ones stronger

4. So though it's darkest before the dawn
   These thoughts keep us moving on
   Through all this world of joy and sorrow
   We still can have singing tomorrows
   Through all this world of job and sorrow
   We still can have singing tomorrows

(PLAY THE TUNE ON BANJO OR GUITAR)

REPEAT FIRST VERSE

I usually strum along quite simply, while singing these verses.

But over the years I've had so much fun picking it three-finger style that for any banjo picker trying to puzzle through this, here 'tis. Don't be scared of the irregular barring of 16th notes. John Roberts, whose computer printed all this music, figured it would be easier to pick the melody out from all those other notes, and I think he's right. John knows a lot more about music notation than I do, and he's been like a consultant on this book.

JOHN ROBERTS, 1993

In 1957, I'm strolling down Chicago's Michigan Avenue, and I hear this song coming out of a loudspeaker — a top hit record by the Ames Brothers. Till this year I didn't know the words, but for 36 years I played it on the banjo, mostly to myself. When a banjo plays softly, you can hear the strings ring out longer, and found I really liked the unison sound of two strings sounding the same note at the same time. Note the unusual tuning. The piece is impossible to play without lowering the fifth string by three frets.

Melodie D'Amour

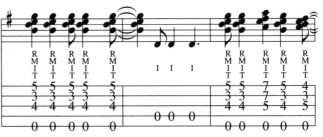

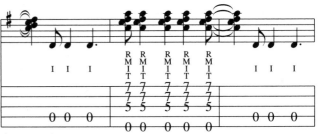

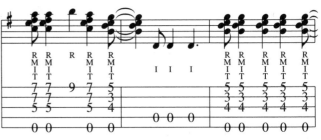

*   If I'm playing soft as I like, I can sound this note by
    hammering on — H

Music by Henri Salvador
Banjo arrangement by Pete Seeger (ca. 1952)
© 1957 (renewed) by Rightsong Music, Inc. and S.D.R.M.
International copyright secured. All rights reserved.

In case you or anyone with you would like to sing the
words to this song. Here they are.

Melodie d'Amour,
Take this song to my lover,
Shoo shoo little bird
Go and find my love.
Melodie d'Amour,
Serenade at her/his window,
Shoo shoo little bird
Sing my song of love.
   Oh, tell her/him I will wait
   If she/he names the date,
   Tell her/him that I care
   More than I can bear,
   For when we are apart   Maladie d'Amour
   How it hurts my heart,   Maladie de jeunesse
   So fly, oh fly away   Si tu n'aimes que moi
   And say I hope and pray   Reste tout près de moi
   This lover's melodie   Maladie d'Amour
   Will bring her/him back   Me fie toi des caresses
      to me.   Si tu n'aimes que moi
Oh, Melodie d'Amour,   Viens, mais prends garde à toi
Take this song to my lover,   Quand l'amour est petit
Shoo shoo little bird   C'est joli, si joli
Go and find my love.   Mais quand il devient fort
Melodie d'Amour,   Me fiez vous mes amis
Serenade at her/his   Cache sous le feuillage
   window,   C'est comme un serpent gris
Shoo shoo little bird   N'allez pas quand il dort
Tell her/him of my love.   Surtout le reveiller
   N'allez pas car il mord
   Si vous le reveillez
Oh, Maladie d'Amour
Maladie de jeunesse
Si je n'aimes que toi
Je reste près de toi
Maladie d'Amour
Qui nous grise et nous blesse
Si je n'aimes que toi
Rien ne m'en pechera
   Quand l'amour est petit
   C'est joli, si joli
   Mais quand il devient fort
   C'est plus beau que la vie
   J'irai sous le feuillage
   Chercher le serpent gris
   Car l'amour c'est la mort
   Mais c'est le paradis
   Car l'amour c'est la mort
   Mais c'est le paradis
Maladie d'Amour...

English lyrics by Leo Johns, French lyrics by Marc Lanjean,
© 1949 by Editions Transatlantiques, Paris, France.

It was a family Christmas party. Some of the crowd were playing Monopoly. Others were off in corners talking. I was sitting on the floor, experimenting with a tune that had just come to me with a nice bass line:

This is actually played in "Dropped D" tuning, again, even though it's in the key of A. You hook your thumb over on the sixth string and play the A chord or the E chord. Arrows point to bass notes plucked by the right hand thumb.

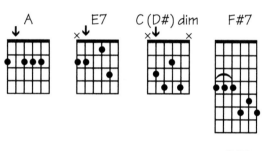

The left thumb solves a lot of problems, but it can't help with the C#7, except to mute the sixth string.

I knew I had a good tune and wrestled with words for it for several weeks, even trying to get friends like Lee Hays to help. No luck. Finally had to be content with one verse. And suddenly realized I was like many another pop song writer—lucky to get one verse which rippled off the tongue nicely. And when I perform it, I usually sing it once myself, then a second time with the crowd (lining out the words, one phrase at a time), then whistling it through once or twice, and finally doing it with the crowd one more time.

Anyway, playing it in A is a little high for some people. This is one reason I use a 12-stringer, tuned two or more frets below normal. The D tuning, as you'll see (note measures marked with an asterisk) is fine for getting barred chords of a certain sort up the neck. Not so good for C#7.

I've put the left hand bass runs in a second staff with a bass clef for the convenience of piano players.

Precious Friend

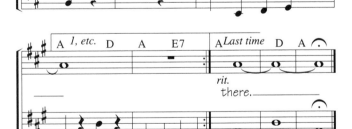

shine through all__ our tears.

And when we sing an-oth-er lit-tle

vic-to-ry song,__ Pre-cious friend,

__ you will be there,__ Sing-ing in har-mo-ny,

Pre-cious friend,__ you will be there._

there._____

Words & music by Pete Seeger (1974)
© 1974, 1982 by Stormking Music Inc.

Just when I thought
All was lost, you changed my mind.
You gave me hope, (not just the old soft soap)
You showed that we could learn to share in time.
  (You and me and Rockefeller)
I'll keep pluggin' on,
Your face will shine through all our tears.

And when we sing another little victory song,
Precious friend, you will be there, singing in harmony,
Precious friend, you will be there.

I'm a lucky songwriter. Till recently I didn't know where I stole the melody from, but Arlo Guthrie discovered one day when we were rehearsing "Precious Friend" that it uses the same chords as "I've Been Working on the Railroad." You can sing both melodies at the same time. So maybe I didn't steal the melody. Just stole the chords.

This is a little like the trick I learned when I was a child. One person can sing, "Way Down Upon the Swanee River" at the same time another sings the melody of "Humoresque" ("Passengers will please refrain from flushing toilets while the train…etc.").

ARLO AT CLEARWATER FESTIVAL, 1983

It was around 1961. Singing in Wisconsin with my younger brother and sister, Mike and Peggy, I found the next verses on the back of the menu of a roadside diner. I had never seen them before except for the first two lines, which I had once seen scrawled on the door of a public toilet.

When I put a tune to it and added a couple lines, I wrote to the hash house. I had stolen their menu. They told me they got the words from a newspaper column in a Milwaukee paper. I wrote to the columnist; he couldn't remember who had sent it to him.

I have since found that the poem has been widely reprinted in different versions. Nobody knows for sure who originally wrote it. It could be from anywhere in the English-speaking world. Probably sometime in the late 19th or early 20th century. I heard from people who remembered it from before WWI. It's sometimes titled "I'm Doing Quite Well For The Shape I'm In."

All I contributed besides the melody were a couple of lines and the idea of repeating the first four lines as a chorus. You'll find that you can do this with many poems that were written originally to be read but need more repetition if they are going to be successfully sung.

Get Up and Go

How do I know my youth is all spent,

My get up and go has got up and went,

But in spite of it all I'm a-ble to grin

And think of the pla-ces my get up has been.

1. Old age is gold-en so I've heard said,

But some-times I won-der as I crawl in-to bed,

With my ears in a draw-er, my teeth in a cup,

My eyes on the ta-ble, un-til I wake up.

*START 3RD VERSE HERE

As sleep dims my vi-sion I say to my-self:

Is there an-y-thing else— I should lay on the shelf?

But tho' na-tions are war-ring and busi-ness is vexed,

I'll still stick a-round to see what hap-pens next.

Words collected, adapted & set to original music by Pete Seeger (1960)
Original poem ("I'm Doing Quite Well for the Shape I'm In") by Ms. A.N. Onymous
TRO - © 1964 (renewed) Melody Trails, Inc., New York, NY.

CHORUS (AND AFTER EACH VERSE):
How do I know my youth is all spent?
My get up and go has got up and went
But in spite of it all I'm able to grin
And think of the places my get up has been.

1. Old age is golden so I've heard said
   But sometimes I wonder as I crawl into bed
   With my ears in a drawer, my teeth in a cup
   My eyes on the table until I wake up.
   As sleep dims my vision I say to myself:
   Is there anything else I should lay on the shelf?
   But though nations are warring and business
      is vexed
   I'll still stick around to see what happens next.

2. When I was young my slippers were red,
   I could kick up my heels right over my head.
   When I was older my slippers were blue,
   But still I could dance the whole night through.
   Now I am older my slippers are black,
   I huff to the store and I puff my way back.
   But never you laugh; I don't mind at all,
   I'd rather be huffing than not puff at all.

(SING TO THE MELODY OF THE LAST 4 LINES OF THE VERSE:)

3. I get up each morning and dust off my wits
   Open the paper and read the obits
   If I'm not there I know I'm not dead
   So I eat a good breakfast and go back to bed.

Eleanor Walden of Berkeley sent a new ending for
"Get Up and Go" to me in 1990.

I get up each morning and dust off my wits
Open the paper and read the obits
If I'm not there I know I'm not gone
So I eat a good breakfast and plan to go on.
For life is a blessing and love is a hope
There's too much to do now to sit here and mope
So I tie my Adidas and answer the call
I'll die in the struggle or I won't die at all.

How do I know I'm ready to fight
My get up and go is still within sight
In spite of my body my spirit is strong
And I'm passing the torch from the old to
   the young.

In 1958 I sang at the funeral of John McManus, co-
editor of the radical newsweekly, *The Guardian*, and
regretted that I had no song worthy of the occasion. So this
got written. I print the song here as I do if I send it to the
family of someone who has died — with a hand-colored
flower alongside it.

To My Old Brown Earth

Freely—slowly

To my old brown earth

And to my old blue sky

I'll now give these last few mol-e-cules

of "I"

And you, who sing,

And you who stand near - by,

I do charge you not to cry:

Guard well our hu-man chain,

Watch well you keep it strong,

As long as sun will shine,

And this our home,

Keep pure and sweet and green,

For now I'm yours

And you are al - so

Mine.

Words & music by Pete Seeger (1958)
© 1964 (renewed) by Stormking Music Inc.

You could enlarge it on a photocopy machine so it would fit on an 11" by 17" piece of paper. Then color it or make your own picture. Trim off these paragraphs of type before enlarging. Note that I wrote the words "Freely-slowly" at upper left. So while I've tried to give the time value to the notes as I sing them — purposely irregular in length — you sing it like you feel it.

A little old lady in New York took her dog out for a walk every night. As a good citizen she always obeyed the law that says, "Scoop up your dog's poop; don't leave it sitting on the curb.

One evening as she and the dog were returning after their evening stroll, she had a small suitcase with her. She was walking close to the curb when a car slowed down beside her. An arm reached out and grabbed her suitcase. The car zoomed off into the city traffic.

And the little old lady laughed and laughed and laughed, just to think what the people in that car thought when they opened that suitcase and saw what was in it.

"If you're in a coalition and you feel comfortable it's not a broad enough coalition."
— Bernice Reagon

"Steal from one person, it's plagiarism; steal from ten, it's scholarship," a girl at Oberlin College told me in the '50's. Added her friend, "Steal from a hundred, it's original research."

"I came to America from Italy," said the old man. "Through Ellis Island. I came because I was told the streets were paved with gold. I found out three things. One, they're not. Two, they're not even paved. Three, I'm expected to pave them."
— learned from Rande Harris

An old woman had lost almost all her teeth. But she said triumphantly, "I got two left. Thank God, they're hitters."
— from Lee Hays

"At times I cannot decide on a tune to use with my words for a song. Woe is me! I am then forced to use some old family style tune that hath already gained the reputation as being liked by the people."
— Woody Guthrie

"Anything too stupid to be said, can be sung."
— Voltaire

"Plagiarism is basic to all culture." (CLS)

Well May the World Go

Well may the world go, the world go, the world go, Well may the world go, When I'm far a-way.

Well may the ski-ers turn, the swim-mers churn, the lov-ers burn, Peace, may the gen-'rals learn When I'm far a-way.

Words & music by Pete Seeger (1973)
© 1973 by Stormking Music Inc.

CHORUS (AND AFTER EACH VERSE):
Well may the world go,
the world go, the world go.
Well may the world go,
When I'm far away.

1. Well may the skiers turn,
   the swimmers churn, the lovers burn
   Peace, may the generals learn
   When I'm far away.

2. Sweet may the fiddle sound
   The banjo play the old hoe down
   Dancers swing round and round
   When I'm far away.

3. Fresh may the breezes blow
   Clear may the streams flow
   Blue above, green below
   When I'm far away.

Here's 5 different ways you could sing that first line:

These new words to a traditional English song occurred to me one day, and in a few hours I'd got the verses set. It was such an easy song to write, I was surprised to find how usable it is.

The "original" song was "Weel May the Keel Row" (well may the boat row) from Newcastle-on-Tyne, northeast England. Different rhythm.

The Keel Row

As I went thro' Sand-gate, thro' Sand-gate, thro' Sand-gate, As I went thro' Sand-gate, I heard a las-sie sing. Weel may the keel row, the keel row, the keel row, Weel may the keel row, that ma— lad-die's in.

Traditional Geordie song, Newcastle-on-Tyne, England

I now give tablature for the tune as played on a five-string banjo "double thumb." Later I speed up, strum it or frail it. I play it in the G tuning, although G is an impossible key to sing it in, except for a low alto or high tenor. What to do? Capo up or tune down. My friend Lois Pinetree, an alto, sings it in the key of A. I pitch it in E which is where my long neck banjo is in G tuning. Southern fiddlers know the tune as "Bile Them Cabbage Down." It's also a cousin of "Hard, Ain't It Hard," "Bury Me Beneath the Willow" and "Woody's Rag." Same chords suit 'em all. Just different speeds.

Well May the World Go
(Banjo Arrangement)

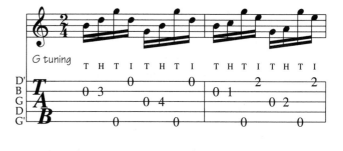
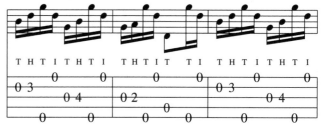
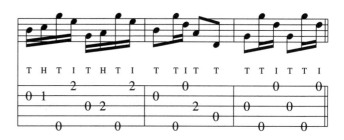

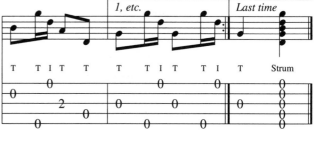

Rockin' Solidarity
(A Chorus Version)

Dave Welsh of San Francisco is a barrel house piano player with a high tenor voice. He worked out new ideas for melody and rhythm to this famous old song. All I contributed was the choral arrangement and the idea that new verses could be added (and got some women to work on 'em). The key of G is fine for altos. A few tenors can reach it. The key can be made higher, A or even B, but beware of making it as low as E or F. The larger crowd will growl the famous chorus too low.

If the men shout out the third verse and the women a new fourth verse, then as large a gang as possible should do the fifth verse together.

Any hand clapping should be on the "offbeats."

(clap)　　(clap)

The reason I put some words for the chorus to shout is that the whole audience should be singing the famous old melody, while the high voices are singing the new melody.

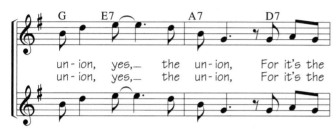

Words by Ralph Chaplin (1916) Tune: "Battle Hymn of the Republic"
New music & additional words by David Welsh (1987)
Choral arrangement by Pete Seeger
© 1988 & 1989 David Welsh. Used by permission.

1. When the union's inspiration
   Through the workers' blood shall run
   There can be no power greater
   Anywhere beneath the sun
   Yet what force on earth is weaker
   Than the feeble strength of one
       But it's the union, yes, the union
       Makes us strong.
       ("Everybody sing it out, Sing it with us")
CROWD (CHORUS AFTER EACH VERSE):
Sol-i-da-ri-ty For-e-ver ("Gotta have it now")
Sol-i-da-ri-ty For-e-ver ("Ev'rybody's talkin' 'bout")
Sol-i-da-ri-ty For-e-ver
For it's the union, yes, the union
Makes us strong.

2. They have taken untold millions
   That they never toiled to earn
   Yet without our brain and muscle
   Not a single wheel would turn
   We can break their haughty power
   Gain our freedom when we learn
       That it's the union, yes, the union
       Makes us strong,
       ("Got to have it, Everybody's got to have it.")

(SUNG BY MEN:)
3. It is we that plowed the prairies
   Built the cities where they trade
   Dug the mines and built the workshops
   Endless miles of railroad laid
   Now we stand outcast and starving
   'Midst the wonders we have made
       But it's the union, yes, the union
       Makes us strong,
       ("Sing it over, Everybody sing it over.")

(SUNG BY WOMEN:)
4. It is we that raised the families
   Scrubbed the floors and chased the dirt
   Fed the kids and sent them off to school
   And then we go to work
   Where we work for lower wages
   With a boss that likes to flirt
       But we will make it
       Yes, we'll make the union strong.
       ("Everybody join in, join in now.")

This fourth verse by Marcia Taylor, Faith Petric, and others. Whatever other verses you add, have the entire chorus sing this famous last verse together:

5. In our hands is placed a power
   Greater than their hoarded gold
   Greater than the might of armies
   Magnified a thousand fold
   We can bring to birth a new world
   From the ashes of the old
       'Cause it's the union, yes, the union
       Makes us strong,
       ("Sing it once more, Sing it once more now.")

       Sol-i-da-ri-ty For-e-ver   (A GOOD PLACE
       Sol-i-da-ri-ty For-e-ver   FOR SOME
       Sol-i-da-ri-ty For-e-ver   JAZZ BREAKS)
       For it's the union, yes, the union
       For it's the union, yes, the union
       For it's the union, yes—
       The union makes us strong.

Here's a sample of a piano part. I'm no piano player but I know that anyone who can play jazz piano would feel right at home here. The left hand does some sort of "walking bass," the right hand gets the offbeat chords. And if there's trumpet players around, this song can use 'em.

Frank's Yodel

By Pete Seeger (1975)
© 1993 by Sanga Music Inc.

My brother Mike has recorded southern farmers who do extraordinary yodels when in the fields. Here are two of my own favorite yodels — a quiet one I used to hum to myself, and a loud one for ship to shore or vice versa. The small ○ over a note indicates falsetto.

Can't remember when I made that yodel up. For 20 years I've yodelled it at the beginning of concerts. And from ship to shore and shore to ship. The harmony works.

Frank Morrison was my neighbor, a teenager. We'd yodel to each other, across 500 feet of wooded mountainside.

Now that my voice is mostly gone, I more often whistle. Artists, professional and amateur, will doodle on paper napkins and scratch paper while telephoning. Musicians play similarly at odd times. I whistle. There are now whistler organizations. They whistle parts to concertos, symphonies. But one of the best whistlers I ever heard was a woman who whistled pop tunes to herself as she cooked or cleaned house.

(Whistle is 2 octaves higher)

By Pete Seeger
© 1993 by Fall River Music Inc.

But one "whistler" I really couldn't get out of my head. I thought I'd swiped it from an old pop tune. Ended up putting a story to it and performing it on stage in the 1980's.

Whistling Past A Graveyard

*mouth click

A few years ago I found how to perform this on stage. I pitch it in F because that's the best key for me to whistle it in. But guitarists will know it's easier to play in G, C or D. Use a capo! I play it first, then start talking:

For 20 years I've had this tune in my head. I can't find where I stole it from. I whistle it in the streets of New York. People look at me and grumble, "What you so happy about?" I finally decided what to do with it. It'll be a music video! The scene is a dirty city street. Trash in the gutter. Boarded up buildings. Down the sidewalk come two people whistling. A kid is sitting on the steps. "Joe, want to learn to whistle?" They take his hand.

Another kid is sitting on the curb. "Hey, Maria, want to learn to whistle?" So now there are four of them, dancing down the street. Kicking at the garbage cans! Suddenly they come to something you can see in an old city: a little graveyard between two buildings. The camera zooms in between the iron fence and you see a gravestone.

"Catherine Johnson, born 1890, died 1895." The kids grow silent, thinking of a little girl that only lived five years. But the grown-ups turn to the kids and sing:

Whis-tl-ing past a grave-yard is not a

fool-ish thing, When all o' the world ap-pears to be

com-ing a-part at the seams. And

who can tell for sure what-'ll be

next to go?__ Did you ev-er think that

Trick-y Dick* would leave like he did?

Whis-tl-ing past a grave-yard, I'll keep on whis-tling.

And if you want, you can whis-tle a-long.__ For

who knows just how man-y more__ might

like to try the mel-o-dy and whis-tle

a sim-i-lar song? (answer back) and

whis-tle a si-mi-lar song.

* This refers to past President Richard Nixon and Watergate.

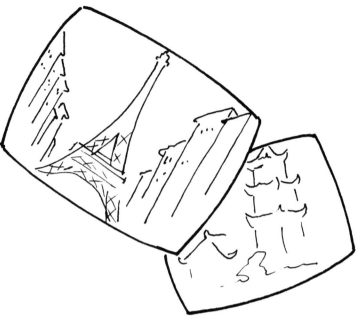

Now the kids are smiling again. The four start down the street once more, whistling. But in only a few seconds (this needs trick camera work) they see the Eiffel Tower in front of them.

Some French kids come out to join 'em. A few seconds later there's the pyramids of Egypt. Some Egyptian kids come out to join them. All of a sudden there's a pagoda, and some Chinese or Japanese kids come to join them. Suddenly there's the pueblos of New Mexico, and some Native American kids come out. All of a sudden there's palm trees, and Sugarloaf Mountain in Rio de Janeiro, some Brazilian kids come out, and everybody's on a beach, that famous beach. There's high surf, spray blowing. Whshhh…whshhhh!

The two grown-ups sing:

Whistling by the seashore
Upon a windy day
Look at the breakers trying to
Drown out the song!
The seagulls laugh as they glide past
And sandcastles all around
Come tumbling down
Whistling by the seashore
We'll keep on whistling
And if you want you can whistle along
The ocean may be wide but on the other side
There lot's of people
Whistling a similar song.

All of a sudden on the screen is a woman in Japan, in ancient costume, kneeling on the floor playing the koto.

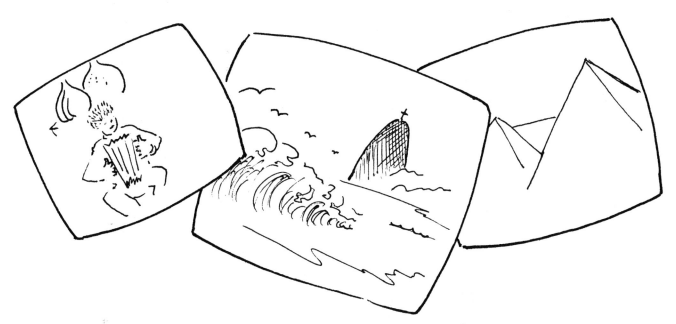

Back on the beach the crowd is singing

Whis - tling   a si - mi - lar   song.

On the screen is a family from Guatemala, playing the xylophone.

(SING)   Whistling a similar song.

(ON STAGE I MIMIC EVERY INSTRUMENT PLAYING THE SAME SHORT PHRASE)

On the screen is the whole Vienna Symphony in white tie and tails, fiddling.

There's Mount Kilimanjaro in East Africa, and someone playing the thumb piano.

There's a rock band with an electric guitar. Ka-twee, ka-twee.

There's the Taj Mahal in India, and a fellow play-ing tuned teacups. Tinkle tinkle.

There's St. Basil's Cathedral in Moscow and an accordion player.

We end up with the birds in the tree overhanging the beach all whistling.

And the last thing you hear is the ocean surf: whshsh... whshsh...

That's the end of my music video.

But, now, if you'd like to try whistling that tune, it's not hard to get that flutter:

You don't raise your tongue. You should push your tongue forward till it touches all the lower teeth. Try it.

AUDIENCE TRIES IT. I NOW WHISTLE THE WHOLE TUNE THROUGH ONCE, WITH THE AUDIENCE AND AT THE END GO BACK TO SINGING.

We're   on   the   beach   to-geth-er

We're on the beach together
Whistling a similar song
Come on and pucker up now (SAME TUNE)
Whistling a similar song
We won't be drowned out if we (SAME TUNE)
Whistle a similar song. Whshsh...whshsh...

Words (1984) & music (1965) by Pete Seeger   Second verse by Lorre Wyatt
TRO - © 1987 Melody Trails, Inc., New York, NY.

And right while this book was in preparation, came a song for a family birthday party. Strictly speaking, this song should have been in Chapter IV. If all goes well while the presses are printing this book, Toshi and I will have a golden wedding.

Only in my 60's did I realize I was carrying on an old family tradition of living in a three-generation family. I was close to grandparents as a kid. Our own children knew grandparents well. Now Toshi and I live 100 feet from our daughter Tinya's family. Modern industrial society has done many bad things, and one of them has been to take children too far from their grandparents. But I confess, in the old pre-penicillin days, there weren't so many of us grandparents still alive and kicking.

GRANDMA TOSHI & MORAYA, 1988

A Little a' This 'n' That

1. My grand-ma, she can make a soup,— with a lit-tle a' this 'n' that.* She can feed— the whole sloop group, with a lit-tle a' this 'n' that.

Stone soup! You know the sto-ry. Stone soup!— Who

needs the glo-ry? But with grand-ma cook-ing, no need to wor-ry. Just a lit-tle a' this 'n' that.

2. Grand-ma likes to make a gar-den grow,— with a lit-tle a' this 'n' that. But she likes to have the ground just so, with a lit-tle a' this 'n' that.

Not too loose— and not too firm.— In the spring, the ground's— all got to be turned.— In the fall, lots of com-post, to feed the worms,— with a lit-tle a' this 'n' that.

3. Grand-ma knows we can build a fu-ture, with a lit-tle a' this 'n' that. And a few ar-gu-ments nev-er ev-er hurt ya, with a lit-tle a' this 'n' that.

True, this world's___ in a hell-u-va fix, And

some say oil and wa-ter don't mix. But

they don't know___ a sal-ad-mak-er's tricks,___ with a

lit-tle a' this 'n' that.

4. The world to come___ may be like a song,___ with a

lit-tle a' this 'n' that. To make

ev-'ry-bod-y want to sing a-long, with a

lit-tle a' this 'n' that. A

lit-tle dis-so-nance ain't no sin,** A

lit-tle sky-lark-ing to give us

all a grin. Who knows but God's got a

plan for the peo-ple to win,___ with a

lit-tle a' this 'n' that.

1. My grandma, she can make a soup,
     with a little a' this 'n' that.
   She can feed the whole sloop group,
     with a little a' this 'n' that.
   Stone soup! You know the story.
   Stone soup! Who needs the glory?
   But with grandma cooking, no need to worry.
     Just a little a' this 'n' that.

2. Grandma likes to make a garden grow,
     with a little a' this 'n' that.
   But she likes to have the ground just so,
     with a little a' this 'n' that.
   Not too loose and not too firm.
   In the spring, the ground's all got to be turned.
   In the fall, lots of compost, to feed the worms,
     with a lit-tle a' this 'n' that.

3. Grandma knows we can build a future,
     with a little a' this 'n' that.
   And a few arguments never ever hurt ya,
     with a little a' this 'n' that.
   True, this world's in a helluva fix,
   And some say oil and water don't mix.
   But they don't know a salad-maker's tricks,
     with a little a' this 'n' that.

4. The world to come may be like a song,
     with a little a' this 'n' that.
   To make ev'rybody want to sing along,
     with a little a' this 'n' that.
   A little dissonance ain't no sin,
   A little skylarking to give us all a grin.
   Who knows but God's got a plan for the people
       to win,
     with a little a' this 'n' that.

* I know this measure would be easier: But it isn't right.

The tempo is ♩ = **120**. Those six notes should be *fast*.

**I usually strike the most dissonant chord I can, at this point. Banjo tuning, GCGBD.

Sometimes I repeat the 1st verse. However you decide to end it, take advantage of the fact that your listeners now are comfortable with the little phrase, and with a bit of encouragement can repeat it several times before a nice abrupt ending, a bit like "All Mixed Up" in Chapter I.

Melodies? #3

Continuing the discussion from p. 89, how *does* one learn to make up melodies? Inspiration surely has a part to play, but I think, as in any other field of endeavor, whether cooking or carpentry, one starts by imitating. Using recipes. Later one starts making small changes according to one's own personal likes and dislikes. Then with luck comes the wonderful discovery that there is no great crime in making bigger changes.

Keep in mind that one tradition's "good melody" is another tradition's pain-in-the-ear. A melody can be:

Short (3 seconds) or long (3 minutes)
Much repetition — or none
3 note range or 30 note range
Major, minor scales of several kinds
Many different kinds of rhythm - or none

Think of the wide varieties of melodies in one country — France, for example. Melodies with a range of five notes, like "Go Tell Aunt Rhody" (originally French):

And another famous French tune with a range of five notes — "A La Claire Fontaine."

Compare the above two conservative melodies to this adventurous one ("La Marseillaise").

Well, now I give you a melody with only one adventurous note. But it works. Elsewhere in the song are 17 notes in a row that don't change pitch, but changes in the accompaniment make them meaningful, just as on p. 123 changes in harmony give meaning to a Beethoven melody (12 notes the same).

I read the words in *The Nation* magazine, summer '92. Rearranged them slightly so people could join in more easily. And surprised myself with finding a tune which did justice to them. I think the ghosts of Gilbert and Sullivan would be amused.

I do it in Dropped D tuning. The chords are not that difficult. Check the Appendix.

The Ross Perot Guide to Answering Embarassing Questions

Words by Calvin Trillin Music & adaptation of lyrics by Pete Seeger (June 19, 1992)
The poem originally appeared in *The Nation.*
Words © 1992 by Calvin Trillin Music © 1993 by Sanga Music. Inc.

1. When something in my history is found,
    Which contradicts the views that I propound,
    Or shows that I perhaps am not the guy
    I claim to be, here's what I usually do:

CHORUS (AFTER EACH VERSE):
I lie.
I simply, boldly falsify.
I look the other feller in the eye,
And just deny, deny, deny.
I lie.

2. I don't apologize. Not me. Instead,
    I say I never said the things I said.
    Nor did the things some people saw me do
    When confronted by some things they know are true,

3. I hate the weasel words some slickies use
    To blur the past or muddy up their views.
    Not me. I'm blunt. One thing that makes me great
    Is that I'll never dodge, or obfuscate.

Admittedly, no music school teaches students how to write a good melody. To write a half-good melody is easy. But writing one that people cannot forget; that's something else.

I asked a number of musicologists how one could define a good melody; they all shrugged. "It depends upon the culture." I've always admired the slow Irish airs — the tradition that gave us "The Londonderry Air," "The Minstrel Boy," "My Lagan Love," (p. 87) "Hills of Glenshee" (p. 87) and countless others.

So when I found the next tune taking shape I wrote it down. Tried to get words for it. (See below).

The Autumn Wind

By Pete Seeger (1980)
© 1993 by Sanga Music Inc.

Later, I realized I'd swiped most of the second line from my brother-in-law, Ewan MacColl. See the second line of "The First Time Ever I Saw Your Face." When my sister Peggy heard me play this, she laughed to recognize an old folk tune Ewan borrowed from to write his song for her.

I thought__ the sun_____

rose__ in your eyes_____

By Ewan MacColl © 1962 (renewed) Stormking Music Inc.

Of course I never play it twice exactly the same. I tried making up words, but with my wobbly 74-year-old voice, I've never sung it in public.

D is a fine key to play it in on an alto recorder. A soprano recorder would find it best in the key of A.

The au-tumn wind whis-pered, Don't

be a-fraid. Though win-ter snows will

soon__ be here. If you stick to-geth-er,

work to-geth-er, sing to-geth-er now. When__ spring comes

'round a-gain you will still__ be here.

Words & music by Pete Seeger (1980)
© 1993 by Sanga Music Inc.

As a child I played a pennywhistle by ear, any tune that struck my fancy. Age 17, I switched to the English recorder, with greater range and slightly different fingering. Started discovering a wider range of melodies. Age 30, met an Israeli, Ilka Raveh. As I told you, he learned from Arab shepherds how to make and play an open end reed flute called "nai" in Arabic. Ilka adapted it to western scales and called it a "chalil."

Ilka is one of the world's greatest masters of this difficult instrument. I never became very good at playing it, but I found myself making up tunes on it which I would not have made on the recorder. The chalil has a smaller range — about 12 notes, for the average player — but you can make the high notes soft, the low notes louder. That's impossible on the recorder.

So on the next page is the last tune in the book, a free, rambling little tune for a bamboo flute, which I made up 43 years ago. On p. 43 I told you how it got its title. Every time I play it I think of Ilka Raveh and his Arab friends. If you have a blue pencil in the house, color the little globe bluish. The title is

How Soon?

By Pete Seeger (1950)
© 1993 by Sanga Music Inc.

Free — imperiodic rhythm

Extroduction

In May 1968 I got a phone call from poet John Beecher. "Pete, I'm down at Duke University, North Carolina. A thousand students are having a sit-down strike demanding some changes be made. Can you come down and sing them a few songs?"

It seems that in April, when Martin Luther King was assassinated, a group of white students at this conservative institution of the Solid South had visited the college president, demanding he give more scholarships to black students, also start negotiating in good faith with the union of maintenance employees, mostly black. And he should resign from his white-only country club. The President said, in effect, thank you for your advice, but I'm running this university. The president went to bed; in the morning the students were still in his living room.

"We don't think that's a good enough answer. We're staying here till we get a better one." After a week the president moved to the college infirmary. The students moved their protest to a large quadrangle and their numbers grew to over a thousand; I sang to them as they were sitting on the grass.

"You young folks are risking your scholarships, your college careers. This kind of thing has never happened at Duke. How come I haven't heard of it in the media? This is news."

"Oh, we called up the New York Times. They gave us a couple inches on the back pages. We called NBC and CBS, and they said they couldn't spare any cameramen. But they said, '*Let us know if there's any violence; we'll send somebody down.*'"

I felt the blood rushing to my head. This is how our country is misgoverned. I picked up a small stone the size of a golf ball, started shouting (unwise any time). "I've never thrown a stone at a person; I've had stones thrown at me and it's no fun. But I'm going to carry this in my banjo case; some day there could be some glass broken."

A stone's still in my case, 25 years later. The problem is still as big as ever. In a world of misinformation what do you do? It's like being at a noisy cocktail party, trying to get a sensible word in edgewise. In any given minute any day, about $130,000,000 are spent on armaments in the world, and in that same minute some 30 children in the world die of malnutrition.

Back in the 1950's there was a tiny peace demonstration in Times Square. A young Quaker was carrying a sign. A passerby scoffed:

"Do you think you're going to change the world by standing here at midnight with that sign?"

"I suppose not," said the young man. "But I'm going to make sure the world doesn't change me."

* * * *

I've been surprised by some good things happening in my lifetime. Sometimes quite suddenly.

Imagine a big see-saw, with a basketful of rocks sitting on one end. That end is down on the ground. At the other end, up in the air, is a basket half full of sand. Some of us are trying to fill it, using teaspoons. Most folks laugh at us. "Don't you know the sand is leaking out even as you put it in?"

We say, that's true, but we're getting more people with teaspoons all the time. One of these days that basket of sand will be full up and you'll see this whole see-saw just tip the opposite way. People will say, "Gee, how did it happen so suddenly?" Us, and our goddamn teaspoons.

Will there be a human race here in another 200 years? Yes, it's a possibility. If so, it will be partly because songwriters of many kinds used whatever talents they were born with or developed.

And used them to help their fellow humans get together. Their closer neighbors. Their distant cousins in the wider world. These pages show some of the mistakes made and some of the small successes of one songwriter and his friends in the 20th century.

Here's hoping that readers will find a few ideas worth stealing.

Still rockin' and reelin',

Pete Seeger

Appendix
Music Notation — A Kind of Shorthand

Can you carry a tune in your head? If your eyes can focus on a page, you can probably learn within a few weeks or months how to pick up average tunes out of a songbook.

You'll find it a handy skill. And you'll be able to write down new tunes when you think of them, before you forget them.

At right are two NOTES, the most common kind. The first one is called a QUARTER NOTE, and the one on its right is a HALF NOTE, and lasts twice as long. The STEMS can point up or down. Put a note on a line or a space of a STAFF (plural, STAVES).

The vertical BAR LINES mark off the rhythm.

The spiral thingummy at left is called a TREBLE CLEF sign, or a G CLEF, because it's an ancient way of writing the letter "G." Yes, every line and space has a letter. Before long you'll have 'em memorized, just as you can memorize a typewriter keyboard or the calendar.

To memorize the spaces try "FACE." For the lines, try "Elsa Gobbles Butter Down Fast," or "Even Government Bureaucrats Deserve Food."

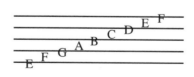

Seven letters, and they repeat themselves over and over. With short LEDGER LINES you can add more notes below or above the staff:

The PITCH of a note can be raised a HALF STEP (or HALF TONE) by putting a SHARP SIGN ♯ in front of it. Pitch can be lowered a half step by putting a FLAT SIGN ♭ in front of the note. To get back to the regular pitch in the same measure, use a NATURAL SIGN ♮ before the note. (After a bar line, the pitch reverts to what it was anyway.) Next time you're in a music store check out Irving Berlin's famous song "White Christmas." You'll see sharps, flats, naturals in the very first line, such as:

...dream-ing ♭ of ♮ a...

All this is why pianos have black keys. You'll find out later why each black key can be called either a flat or a sharp.

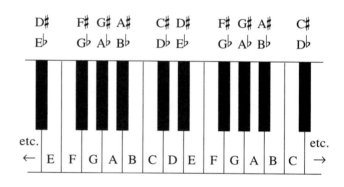

Here's a more complete list of notes:

A WHOLE NOTE ○ has 4 beats

A HALF NOTE ♩ has 2 beats

A QUARTER NOTE ♩ has 1 beat

Two EIGHTH NOTES ♪ ♪ = ♩

Two SIXTEENTH NOTES ♬ ♬ = ♪

And a dot after a note increases its length by 50%.

Thus: ♩. = ♩ + ♩   ♩. = ♩ + ♪   ♪. = ♪ + ♬

Short notes can have BEAMS instead of FLAGS, thus:

(A "BEAT" is like one tap of a foot, or one bang of a drum when you're marching, or one step when you're dancing.)

Sometimes there's a moment of silence, so you put a REST on the staff:

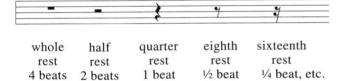

a "quarter rest"

Shave and a hair-cut, two bits!

Here's all the rests of different lengths.

whole rest	half rest	quarter rest	eighth rest	sixteenth rest
4 beats	2 beats	1 beat	½ beat	¼ beat, etc.

(And each rest can also be made 50% longer by adding a dot to it.)

You may have wondered what the $\frac{4}{4}$ next to the clef sign meant.

It's a TIME SIGNATURE. As written here, both "Yankee Doodle" and "Shave and a Haircut" have four beats in each MEASURE. The space between bar lines is called a "measure." Most of our songs are like this, in "four-four" (4/4) time.

There's other TIME SIGNATURES, like 2/4 ("two-four") or 3/4 ("three-four" — that's like a waltz), 6/8 ("six-eight" — like an Irish jig) and 12/8 ("twelve-eight"). In the last two rhythms *three* eighth notes add up to *one* beat.

4/4 time is sometimes written as **C** ("common time") but if it's fast it might be written as **₵** ("cut time") or as 2/2 ("two-two"). And there's other less common rhythms and time signatures.

Now would be a good time to go through any songbook that has in it songs that you know. Follow the notes up and down on the staff. Note the time signature of each song, and see how each measure has the correct number of beats in it, whether of notes or rests.

But before you can read unfamiliar melodies, you need to know what KEY it's in. The same tune can be written high or low on a staff, that is, in different keys. If you're a guitar picker, the chords will help you find the key. But between the clef sign and the time signature you'll often see one or more sharps or flats on the staff. These are known as the KEY SIGNATURE. Here's old "Shave and a Haircut" in six common keys (there's six more, less commonly used). And a faster speed, 2/4.

When will you *not* see a key signature next to the clef sign? Answer: when you're singing a song in the key of C. On a piano, you can play in C without having to play any of the black notes.

And if a song is in A minor (Am) you also don't need a key signature. Minor scales have a flatted 3rd, and usually flatted 6th and 7th notes of the scale. Do you know any of the following songs? They're all in minor:

Volga Boatmen
God Rest Ye Merry, Gentlemen
Greensleeves
Hey, Ho, Nobody's At Home
Hatikva
House Of The Rising Sun
Bei Mir Bist Du Shayn
Go Down Moses
What Shall We Do With The Drunken Sailor?

Here's the first line of "Drunken Sailor" written out for several common minor keys:

But for reference only, here's most of the possible key signatures:

Sharpening or flattening a note becomes more complicated when you're in some other key than C. Here's "Down By The Old Mill Stream" in the key of C and then the key of F. The FERMATA ⌢ ("eyebrow") means "hold this note longer."

Down by the old mill stream where I first met you,

With your eyes of blue, dressed in ging-ham too. It was...

By Tell Taylor, 1910

Down by the old mill stream where I first...

At last! Test your knowledge. Open some of those songbooks again. Before you try reading the melody of any song, check the key signature as well as the time signature. But you may be wondering about some curved lines:

I - rene, good - night,_____

I - rene, good - night,_____

Those curved lines are called SLURS (where a voice slurs from one note to another) and TIES (which makes two notes into one longer note).

In general, it helps to learn to recognize the 1st, 3rd, and 5th notes of any scale. They make a bugle call. Here's "Taps" in G:

An assignment: write down "Taps" in all the keys you can think of.

When a melody takes a big jump, you may be uncertain what note it's jumping to. So try counting up or down one step at a time.

Now you'll recognize this tune:

Twinkle, twinkle, little star

In time you'll get to recognize and hear in your head how far apart any two notes are. And if you want to study music further, you'll learn that the different INTERVALS between any two notes all have names. But for now, if you can find what key a song is in, and you can sing the scale to yourself, major or minor, you can feel your way up or down the staff to any note in the song you're trying to learn. Just make sure you know where the first note of the scale is on the staff.

I first learned how to read music better by whistling my way through a book of fiddle tunes.

Getting used to hearing the pitch of a note in your head is usually easier than getting to hear the rhythm in your head. It's especially hard when it comes to blues and gospel songs, which have such a liquid flow, such a syncopated rhythm. "Syncopated" means that the note is advanced or delayed, not right on the beat. In learning to read music,

RHYTHM IS USUALLY A STUMBLING BLOCK.

On the next few songs, try tapping your foot regularly, four beats to the measure. Note the arrows. But sing the melody like you remember hearing it. Remember, a tie makes two notes into a longer one.

Note that each of the two words "his hands" started *before* the foot-tap came down: "his__↓__hands__↓__." Try reading the two well-known songs below:

Words and music adapted by Lee Hays
TRO © 1951 (renewed 1979) Folkways music Publishers, Inc., NY, NY.

And I hope you know this one:

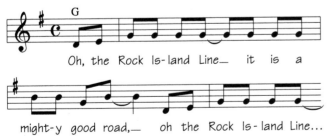

New words and music arrangement by Huddie Ledbetter Edited with new additional material by Alan Lomax
TRO © 1959 (renewed 1987) Folkways music Publishers, Inc., NY, NY.

And you can try looking at some of the songs in this book, such as "Kisses Sweeter Than Wine," (p. 64), or "Both Sides Now," (p. 139), or "Proud Mary," (p. 138).

If by now you say, "This is an awfully complicated way of writing down a simple tune," — I agree with you. This kind of music notation was first put together by European church musicians in the Middle Ages. It's not as good for writing down the music of Africa, Asia, or Latin America. And a good opera singer wouldn't think of sticking to the bare bones of a melody. Yes, a tune on paper, compared to a recording of it, is like the stick figure at left, compared to the silhouette at right.

It's a shorthand; it can't really show the liquid flow of a human voice. It tends to put everything into steps, as on a keyboard instrument. But it's the main system of writing music we have right now. Any music store can sell you books about it. I even wrote one years ago (see bibliography). But no matter what instruction book you get, the best way to learn to transfer the music from the page to your throat or your hands is this:

GET A SONGBOOK WITH SONGS YOU KNOW AND LOVE TO SING. FOLLOW THE NOTES UP AND DOWN ON THE STAFF. GET TO RECOGNIZE DIFFERENT KEYS, DIFFERENT RHYTHMS.

Like anything else in the world, you do it over and over and you get better at it.. I'll close by giving a few more musical terms you may run into:

RITARD (or "rit.") means "slow down."

⟍ means to get softer.

⟋ means to get louder.

8va (8va) means "sing or play these notes an octave higher."

Dots under or over a row of notes means to cut the notes very short ("staccato").

At the end of a song is always a double barline. A double barline with dots is a REPEAT sign. Two of these bracket the section to be repeated:

D.C. means "Repeat from the beginning," and D.S. means "Repeat from the sign." Rove your eye over the song till you see a fancy cross: 𝄋
That's where you repeat from.

Repeat signs are used to save space, but often there's a different ending the second time through. So above the staff you'll sometimes see a horizontal line with a number. This means to repeat the chorus, or whatever it is, and on the second time through you have the final ending:

...way, Oh what fun it is to ride on a

one-horse o-pen sleigh,— one-horse o-pen sleigh.

The sign 𝄎 means "Repeat the previous measure." A number over it tells you how many times to repeat it.

In this book you'll often see the number 3 over three notes. They're called TRIPLETS. The three notes take up the same amount of space as two notes normally would.

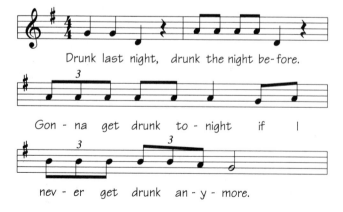

Drunk last night, drunk the night be-fore.

Gon-na get drunk to-night if I

nev-er get drunk an-y-more.

And maybe that's the best place to end this awfully incomplete discussion on how to read music.

Tablature...

...is a form of writing for stringed instruments first developed by lute players in 16th Century Europe. The horizontal lines stand for the strings of the instrument, six for a guitar (even a twelve-stringer with its double strings), five for a banjo.

I give the tuning for the instrument at left of the letters "TAB." The numbers on the lines tell at which fret the fingers of the left hand stop the string. "O" means to sound the open string, not fretted at all. Here's tablature for two scales in E:

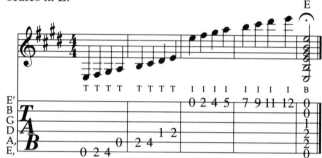

Have you a guitar, mandolin or banjo handy? Put your fingers where the arrows point and you'll hear a major scale.

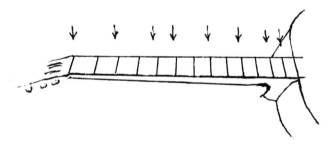

Put your fingers where the arrows point and you'll have a natural minor scale (there's other minor scales, too).

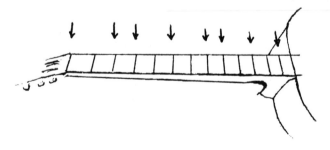

Above the TAB, but below the music, sometimes is indicated how the string is sounded:
T - right thumb, plucking down
I - right index finger, plucking up
M - right middle finger, plucking up
R - right ring finger, plucking up

L - right little finger, plucking up

B - brushing *down* across the strings, with thumb for a guitar, with back of fingernails for banjo.

ST - the index finger strums *up* across the strings

H - "hammering on" - a finger of the left hand frets a string so forcefully that it sounds

P - "pulling off" - a finger of the left hand plucks a string, or several strings. I'm quite proud that the last two terms, which I invented in the 1940's for my banjo book, are now in general use. Violinists call pulling off "left hand pizzicato."

SL - the left hand slides from one fret to another, the instant after the string is plucked, keeping the pressure on the string

CH - the fretted string is plucked, and immediately the finger fretting it pushes it to one side, stretching it and raising its pitch. It's a tradition when playing blues or rock. Sitar players in India do it too.

Dropped D Tuning

If any guitar picker has struggled through this book, he or she will have learned about the Dropped D tuning, D A D G B E. I use it to play mostly in D, G, or A, capoed up or down. My 12-string guitar has very heavy strings, tuned lower than normal. Without a capo my strings sound C F B♭ E♭ G C. No buzzing. LaBella makes them for me. The gauges I use are as follows, in inches/millimeters: 1st pair, .011/0.279 and .010/0.254; 2nd pair, both .018/0.457; 3rd pair, .024/0.610 and .010/0.254; 4th pair, .034/0.864 and .017/0.432; 5th pair, .046/1.168 and .023/0.584; 6th pair, .067/1.702 and .032/0.813. (Thanks, Bruce Taylor!) 90% of the time my capo is at the 4th fret — concert pitch.

If I play in E or C, and sometimes A, I'll use standard tuning. To play in F, B♭, A♭, or B or F♯, I always capo up or down. I like the ring of open strings; you tend to lose that when you use a lot of barred chords.

I got into using Dropped D in the mid-1950's when I visited the great folk guitarist Joseph Spence, carpenter, in Nassau, Bahamas. Before then I'd only used it occasionally.

Some chords become difficult to play in Dropped D. But a batch of new ones become possible. Here's a lot of chords for you to try out. Use a left thumb when necessary to fret the 6th string.

Well, after all this technical talk, I guess we need to remind ourselves that to make good music you have to put the paper down, and let the melodies, rhythms, harmonies flow out from your heart, to your throat, to your hands. May the muse smile on you.

"Can you read music?"
"Not enough to hurt my playing."
— overheard in Nashville

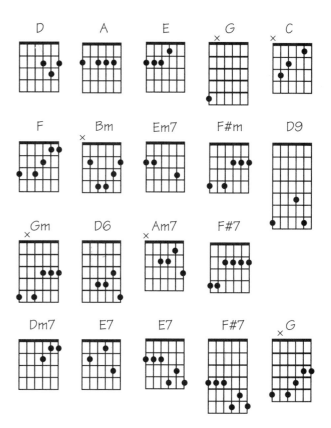

Photo by Thomas Neuman, Berlin, 1988

"OH MY GOD, DID I SAY THAT?"

Key: Where Have All the Flowers Gone

KEY: WHERE HAVE ALL THE FLOWERS GONE

1. Waist Deep In The Big Muddy
2. Skip-a-Rope
3. Vietnamese Woman & Baby
4. José Marti
5. Paul Winter
6. Keita Fodeba
7. Oscar Brand
8. Calixa Lavallée
9. Solomon Linda
10. African Dancer
11. Old Granny
12. Grandbaby
13. Mike Seeger
14. Bob Killian
15. Charlie King
16. Lorre Wyatt
17. Ewan MacColl
18. Joni Mitchell
19. The Byrds
20. Peggy Seeger

21. Victor Jara & Family
22. Joe Hickerson
23. Moses Asch
24. Johannes Brahms
25. Nicolo Sacco
26. Lord Invader
27. Lisa Kalvelage
28. Cole Porter
29. Ruth Rubin
30. Bartolemo Vanzetti
31. "Slam" Stewart
32. "Slim" Gaillard
33. Irving Berlin
34. Sonny Terry
35. Noriko Ibaraki
36. John Jacob Niles
37. LeRoy Carr
38. John Fogerty
39. Buffy Sainte-Marie
40. Ernie Marrs
41. Brownie McGhee
42. E.B. White & Friends

43. Charlotte & her Web
44. Zilphia Horton
45. Paul Robeson
46. Ho Chi Minh
47. Malvina Reynolds
48. William Shakespeare
49. Mika Seeger
50. Model of the "Clearwater"
51. Toshi Seeger
52. Bernice Johnson Reagon
53. Jewish Prisoner at Treblinka
54. Johann Sebastian Bach
55. Marlene Dietrich
56. Alan Lomax
57. Charles Seeger
58. John Lennon
59. Yoko Ono
60. Rachel Carson
61. Pete Seeger

62. Lee Hays
63. Ronnie Gilbert
64. Fred Hellerman
65. John A. Lomax
66. Blacksmith
67. Slave
68. Rev. Charles Tindley
69. Ecclesiastes
70. Henry Crowdog
71. Ludwig van Beethoven
72. Noel "Paul" Stookey
73. Mary Travers
74. Peter Yarrow
75. Welch Coal Miner
76. Aunt Molly Jackson
77. Blind Lemon Jefferson
78. Huddie Ledbetter
79. A.N. Onymous
80. Woody Guthrie
81. Arlo Guthrie
82. Where Have All the Flowers Gone

BIBLIOGRAPHY

SONGBOOKS AND INSTRUCTIONAL GUIDES BY PETE SEEGER

American Favorite Ballads, Tunes and Songs as Sung by Pete Seeger. New York: Oak, 1961.

Bantu Choral Folk Songs. New York: G. Schirmer, 1959.

The Bells of Rhymney and Other Songs and Stories. New York: Oak, 1964.

Bits and Pieces. New York: Ludlow Music, 1965.

The Carolers Songbag - see Weavers

Carry It On; The Story of America's Working People in Song and Picture (with Bob Reiser). New York: Simon and Schuster, 1985; Bethlehem, PA: Sing Out Publications, 1991.

Everybody Says Freedom (with Bob Reiser). New York: W.W. Norton, 1991.

The Folksinger's Guitar Guide (with Jerry Silverman). New York: Oak, 1967. [originally published as booklet accompanying Seeger's 1956 guitar instruction album on Folkways]

The Goofing Off Suite. New York: Hargail, 1961.

Hard Hitting Songs for Hard Hit People (compiled by Alan Lomax, notes on the songs by Woody Guthrie, music transcribed & edited by Pete Seeger). New York: Oak, 1967. [originally compiled in 1940]

Henscratches and Flyspecks: How to read melodies from songbooks in twelve confusing lessons. New York: Berkeley Books, 1973. [watch for forthcoming reprint]

How to Make and Play a Chalil. Self-published, 1955.

How to Play the Five-String Banjo. Self-published, 1948; New York: Oak, 1962.

Oh Had I a Golden Thread. New York: Sanga Music, 1968.

Pete Seeger Sings Songs of American People (compiled by Grigory Schneerson, translated into Russian by Samuel Bolotin & Tatyana Sikorskaya). Moscow: State Publishers Music, 1965.

Songs for Peace (edited with Jeff Marris & Cliff Metzler). New York: Oak, 1966.

The Twelve-String Guitar as Played by Leadbelly - see Leadbelly

OTHER PETE SEEGER BOOKS (AND BOOKS BY OTHER SEEGERS)

Abiyoyo, by Pete Seeger. New York: Macmillan, 1985.

American Folksongs for Children, by Ruth Crawford Seeger. Garden City, NY: Doubleday, 1948.

American Folksongs for Christmas, by Ruth Crawford Seeger. Garden City, NY: Doubleday, 1953; New York: Oak, 1990.

Animal Folksongs for Children, by Ruth Crawford Seeger. Garden City, NY: Doubelday.

The Foolish Frog, by Charles Louis Seeger and Pete Seeger. New York: Macmillan, 1973.

How Can I Keep from Singing: Pete Seeger, by David King Dunaway. New York: McGraw-Hill, 1981. [biography, includes an exhaustive discography and bibliography up through 1980]

The Incompleat Folksinger, by Pete Seeger, edited by Jo Metcalf Schwartz. New York: Simon & Schuster, 1972.

Pete Seeger on Record. New York: Ludlow Music, 1971.

The Steel Drums of Kim Loy Wong, by Pete Seeger. New York: Oak, 1961.

Studies in Musicology, by Charles Louis Seeger. Berkeley, CA: University of California Press, 1977.

AFRICAN-AMERICAN MUSICAL TRADITIONS

Everybody Says Freedom - see Pete Seeger songbooks

Negro Folk Songs as Sung by Leadbelly - see Leadbelly

Sing For Freedom: The Story of the Civil Rights Movement Through Its Songs. Edited by Guy and Candie Carawan. Bethlehem, PA: Sing Out Publications, 1990. [Combined edition of two collections, long out-of-print: We Shall Overcome (1963) and Freedom Is a Constant Struggle (1968).]

We'll Understand It By and By: Pioneering African American Gospel Composers, edited by Bernice Johnson Reagon. Washington, DC: Smithsonian Institution Press, 1992.

APPALACHIA

Voices from the Mountains, by Guy & Candie Carawan. University of Illinois Press, 1982.

CHILDREN

Abiyoyo - see Seeger books

American Folksongs for Children - see Seeger books

Animal Folksongs for Children - see Seeger books

The Foolish Frog - see Seeger books

The Raffi Singable Songbook: A Collection of 51 songs from Raffi's first three records for young children. Don Mills, Ontario: Chappell, undated.

Tweedles and Foodles for Young Noodles - see Malvina Reynolds

CHRISTMAS

American Folksongs for Christmas - see Seeger books

The Carolers Songbag - see Weavers

CLEARWATER / ENVIRONMENTAL SONGS

The Clearwater Songbook, edited by Ed Renehan, introduction by Pete Seeger. New York: G.Schirmer, 1980.

For the Beauty of the Earth: An Environmental Songbook to Benefit the Hudson River Sloop Clearwater, by Liza DiSavino. 1993. [available from Clearwater, 112 Market Street, Poughkeepsie, NY 12601]

Songs and Sketches of the First Clearwater Crew, edited by Don McLean, forward by Pete Seeger. NY: North River Press, 1970.

The Survival Songbook, edited by Jim Morse and Nancy Mathews, introduction by Pete Seeger. San Francisco: Sierra Club, 1967.

WOODY AND ARLO GUTHRIE

Bound for Glory, by Woody Guthrie. New York: NAL Dutton, 1983. [autobiography]

California to the New York Island, by Woody Guthrie, introduction and music editing by Pete Seeger. NY: Oak, 1958.

Pastures of Plenty: A Self-Portrait, by Woody Guthrie, edited by Dave Marsh and Harold Leventhal. NY: Harper Collins, 1990.

Roll On Columbia: The Columbia River Collection, by Woody Guthrie, edited by Bill Murlin. Bethlehem, PA: Sing Out Publications, 1991. [26 songs about the Northwest written by Woody while under contract to the Bonneville Power Administration in June of 1940.]

Songs by Woody Guthrie. New York: TRO Ludlow, 1992.

This Is the Arlo Guthrie Book. New York: Amsco Music Publishing Co., 1969.

Woody Guthrie: A Life, by Joseph Klein. New York: Ballantine, 1980. [biography]

Woody Guthrie and Me, by Ed Robbins, introduction by Pete Seeger. Berkeley, CA: Lancaster House, 1979.

Woody Guthrie Folk Songs, edited & compiled by Pete Seeger. NewYork: Ludlow Music, 1963.

Woody Sez, by Woody Guthrie. NY: Grosset & Dunlap, 1975.

Woody's 20 Grow Big Songs, by Woody Guthrie and Marjorie Mazia Guthrie. New York: HarperCollins, 1992. [written and illustrated by Woody in the 1940's - available with a cassette of all 20 songs performed by Woody, Arlo and other Guthries]

JEWISH SONGS

Treasury of Jewish Folksong, by Ruth Rubin. New York, Schocken Books, 1950, 1964, 1967.

LABOR SONGS

Carry It On - see Pete Seeger songbooks

Labor Songs of the Nineteenth Century, by Philip S. Foner, University of Illinois Press, 1975.

Songs of the Workers to Fan the Flames of Discontent. Chicago: Industrial Workers of the World, 1973. ["Little Red Songbook"]

Songs of Work and Protest, by Edith Fowke & Joe Glazer. Dover, 1973.

LEADBELLY

The Leadbelly Songbook, edited by Moses Asch and Alan Lomax, introduction by Pete Seeger. New York: Oak, 1962.

The Life and Legend of Leadbelly, by Charles Wolfe and Kip Lomell. New York: HarperCollins, 1992. [biography]

Negro Folk Songs as Sung by Leadbelly, by John A. and Alan Lomax. New York: Macmillan, 1936.

The Twelve-String Guitar as Played by Leadbelly, by Julius Lester and Pete Seeger. New York: Oak, 1965.

JOHN A. AND ALAN LOMAX

Adventures of a Ballad Hunter, by John A. Lomax. New York: Macmillan, 1947.

American Ballads and Folk Songs, by John A. and Alan Lomax. New York: Macmillan, 1934.

Cowboy Songs, by John A. and Alan Lomax. New York: Macmillan, 1938. [original 1910 version by John A. Lomax]

The Folk Songs of North America in the English Language, by Alan Lomax. Garden City, NY: Doubleday, 1960; Dolphin Books, 1975.

Folk Songs: USA, by John A. and Alan Lomax. New York: Duell, Sloan & Pearce, 1947.

The Land Where the Blues Began, by Alan Lomax. New York: Pantheon, 1993.

Negro Folk Songs as Sung by Leadbelly - see Leadbelly.

Our Singing Country, by John A. and Alan Lomax. New York: Macmillan, 1941.

EWAN MACCOLL

Journeyman, by Ewan MacColl. England: Sidgwick & Jackson, 1990 [autobiography]

PEOPLE'S SONGS AND SING OUT!

[Note: Pete is listed as an associate editor for all of the titles below.]

Collected Reprints from Sing Out!, Vols. 1-6 (1959-64). Bethlehem, PA: Sing Out Publications, 1990.

Collected Reprints from Sing Out!, Vols. 7-12 (1964-73). Bethlehem, PA: Sing Out Publications, 1992.

Lift Every Voice and Sing: A Second People's Songbook. Edited by Irwin Silber. New York: People's Artists, 1953; Sing Out!, 1957; Oak, 1962.

The People's Songbook, edited by Waldemar Hille. New York: Boni & Gaer, 1948; People's Artists, 1956; Sing Out!, 1959; Oak, 1960.

Reprints from the People's Song Bulletin, forward by Pete Seeger. New York: Oak, 1961.

Rise Up Singing: The Group Singing Songbook. Edited by Peter Blood and Annie Patterson, introduction by Pete Seeger. Bethlehem, PA: Sing Out Publications, 1988.

MALVINA REYNOLDS

Little Boxes. New York: Oak, 1961.

The Malvina Reynolds Songbook. Berkeley, CA: Schroder Music (1450 6th St, Berkeley, CA 94710), 1984.

There's Music in the Air. Berkeley, CA: Schroder Music, 1976.

Tweedles and Foodles for Young Noodles. Berkeley, CA: Schroder Music (1450 6th St, Berkeley, CA 94710), 1961.

[Watch for the forthcoming biography by Ellen Stekert!]

THE WEAVERS

The Caroler's Songbag, by Pete Seeger (with the Weavers). New York: Folkways, 1952.

Lee Hays: Lonesome Traveller, by Doris K. Willens. Lawrence, KS: University of Nebraska Press. [biography]

Traveling On with The Weavers. New York: Harper, 1966.

The Weavers Sing, by Ronnie Gilbert, Fred Hellerman, Lee Hays, and Pete Seeger. New York: Folkways, 1951.

Weavers Songbook. New York: Harper, 1960.

WOMEN

Here's to the Women: 100 Songs for and about American Women, by Hilda Wenner and Elizabeth Frelicher, introduction by Pete Seeger. Syracuse, NY: Syracuse University, 1987.

For more information on Woody Guthrie, Lee Hays and The Weavers, write Harold Leventhal, 250 W. 57th Street, New York, NY 10107.

DISCOGRAPHY

The following list indicates where specific songs in this book can be found on the author's recordings, as well as on selective recordings by other artists. Songs not listed have not been released on any recordings to date (to our knowledge), although the author intends to issue a new set of recordings to include all the titles in this book which are not recorded or available elsewhere at this time.

The author's recordings (as well as those of the Almanac Singers and Weavers) are listed by title only. A listing of these recordings with catalog information can be found at the end of this discography. Note that this discography lists *only* the Pete Seeger recordings which include one or more songs from this book. A more complete Pete Seeger discography (through 1980) can be found in Dunaway's biography, *How Can I Keep from Singing* (see Bibliography).

Although many of the recordings included in this discography are out of print, a number have recently been reissued on compact discs by Folkways, Columbia, Vanguard, and others. Bear Family Records is issuing a 6-CD set comprising much of the early material found in Chapter 2 (see below under Almanac Singers recordings). In addition, *all* recordings on the Folkways label can be purchased on cassette directly from Smithsonian Folkways. For ordering information and a catalog, contact: Smithsonian Folkways Records, 414 Hungerford Dr, Suite 444, Rockville MD 20850. Phone: (301) 443-2314; FAX 443-1819.

Abiyoyo
PS: Abiyoyo, Bantu Choral Folksongs (song only), Children's Concert, Family Concert (video), Greatest Hits, If a Revolution Comes, Sing-a-long Demonstration Concert, Sleep-time, on Folk Festival at Newport Vol.1
Robbie Clemment: Jubilee (Tomorrow River 1004)
Bill Harley: Monsters in the Bathroom (Round River 101)

Aircraft Mechanic Song
tune: (Lincoln & Liberty Too) Songs of the Civil War (Folkways 5717)

All Mixed Up
PS: Strangers & Cousins
Peter, Paul & Mary: Flowers & Stones (Warner 45069), Peter Paul & Mommy Too (video Warner 38339-3)

All My Children of the Sun
PS: Young vs. Old

Andorra
PS: The Bitter & the Sweet

As the Sun - see The Emperor Is Naked Today-o

Ballad of Harry Bridges
Almanac Singers: Ballad of Harry Bridges (78rpm: Keynote 304)

Ballad of October 16th
Almanac Singers: Songs for John Doe

Ballad of the Sloop Clearwater
PS: Rainbow Race

Barbara Allen
PS: The Bitter & the Sweet, God Bless the Grass, Sings American Ballads, World of

Bells of Rhymney
PS: Essential, Greatest Hits, I Can See a New Day, Sings & Answers Questions, World Of, PS & Sonny Terry, 12 String Guitar (instrumental), on Folk Festival at Newport V.1, on Live Hootenanny

The Byrds: The Byrds (Columbia 46773), Greatest Hits (Columbia 9516)
Cher: All I Really Want to Do (Imperial 9292)
Judy Collins: #3 (Elektra 7243)
Also recorded by Chad Mitchell Trio, John Denver, Phil Ochs, The Oyster Band, Gram Parsons, Serendipity Singers, and others

Both Sides Now
PS: Young vs. Old, World of
Joni Mitchell: Clouds, Miles of Aisles, on Troubadours of the Folk Era, Vol. 2 (Rhino OPCD 1620)
Judy Collins: Wildflowers (Elektra 4012), First 15 Years
Dave Van Ronk: And the Hudson Dusters (Verve/Forecast 3041), A Chrestomathy (Gazell 2007/8)

Bright Yellow Forsythias
tune ("Midnight Special") on PS: Amer. Fav. Ballads Vol. 2, Folk Music Blues, Big Bill Broonzy & PS in Concert

Bring 'Em Home
PS: Young vs. Old

Broad Old River
PS: With Hudson River Singers (Clearwater Records 300CR)

Business
Broadside Ballads Vol. 2 (Broadside 302)

C for Conscription
Almanac Singers: Songs for John Doe
tune: ("T for Texas") on PS: Cumberland Mountain Bear Chase (1948 78rpm single, Charter C-500), Almanac (Folkways)

The Calendar
Short Sisters: A Planet Dancing Slow (Black Socks Press 8654-12) [Black Socks Press, Box 208, Harrisville NH 03450]

Come All Ye Fair & Tender Ladies
PS: Essential, Sing Out! Hootenanny

Dear Mr. President
Almanac Singers: Dear Mr. President

Deck the Halls
PS: Indian Summer (listed as "Many Colored Paper")

Deliver the Goods
Almanac Singers: Dear Mr. President

Djankoye
PS: as "Zhonkoye" (1948 78 rpm single - Charter 30A), We Sing
    Vol.1 (as "Hey Zhankoye")

The Emperor Is Naked Today-o (As the Sun)
PS: Circles & Seasons, on What Now People? V.3 (Paredon 2003)

Empty Pocket Blues
PS: Goofing-Off Suite (as "Barrel of Money Blues")
Weavers: At Home

Estadio Chile
PS: Banks of Marble, If a Revolution, Together

Everybody Loves Saturday Night
Alex Campbell: on Tønder Musik Festival 1976 (Rica 4511)
The Spinners: Carribean Sunshine Hits (One Up 2235)

False from True
PS: Pete Seeger Now

Filksong Ole Time Religion
PS: Sing-a-long Demonstration Concert, Together

The Foolish Frog
PS: Live at Newport, Story Songs, Three Saints
Dave Van Ronk: Peter & the Wolf (Alacazam 1004)

Frank's Yodel
PS: Banks of Marble, Together, Franklin D.
Almanac Singers: Songs for John Doe
tune ("Ida Red") on PS: Amer. Fav. Ballads Vol.5, Darling Corey,
    Essential

From Way Up Here
PS: Broadsides, God Bless the Grass, We Shall Overcome
Malvina Reynolds: Malvina Reynolds (Cassandra 5100) [available
    from Schroder Music, 1450 6th St, Berkeley CA 94710]

Full Fathom Five
PS: Dangerous Songs

Garbage
PS: Banks of Marble, Circles & Seasons, Visit Sesame Street
Bill Steele: Garbage (Bay 202)
Peter Alsop: Peter Alsop (Moose School P5, orig. Flying Fish)
Guy Carawan: My Rhinoceros (Gentle Wind 1023)
Rozenshontz: Share It

Get Up and Go
PS: Broadsides, Together, Young vs. Old
The Weavers: Together Again, Wasn't That a Time (video)

Give Peace a Chance
John Lennon: Imagine (Capitol)
Plastic Ono Band: Live in Toronto (Capitol)

Guantanamera
PS: Canto Obrero (Americanto 1004), Greatest Hits, If a Revolution,
PS & Bro. Kirk Visit Sesame Street, Together, We Shall Overcome,
    World of, Family Concert (video)
The Weavers: Greatest Hits, Reunion at Carnegie Hall, Traveling
    On, Wasn't That a Time On video: Wasn't That a Time
Joan Baez: Gracias a la Vida (A&M 3614)
Paul Winter Sextet: Jazz Meets the Folk Song (Columbia 2155)
Also recorded by Celia Cruz, Jose Feliciano, Julio Iglesias, Trini
    Lopez, Tony Martin, Roger Williams & many others.

Haul, Make Her Go High
Hudson River Sloop Singers (includes PS): (Clearwater 300)

He Lies in the American Land
PS: Amer. History in Ballad & Song Vols. 1 & 2, Amer. Industrial
    Ballads, Carry It On, on Live Hootenanny, PS in Concert Vols.
    1 & 2 (Folklore F-Laut-1, Vox 1.580)

Here We Are in Madison Square
tune ("New York City") on PS: At the Village Gate Vol.1

Here's to the Couple
PS: Bantu Choral Folk Songs

Hold the Line
PS: Gazette Vol. 1
Weavers: Almanac (Fontana/Topic 6028), also as "The Peekskill
    Story" (1949 78rpm single Charter 502)

Hole in the Bucket - see There's a Hole in the Bucket

How Soon? (Chalil instrumental, Hillel melody)
PS: Big Bill Broonzy & PS (as "Chalil melody")

I Come and Stand at Every Door (Girl of Hiroshima)
PS: Gazette Vol. 2, I Can See a New Day, on Swords Into
    Ploushares (Folk Tradition S005,006)
The Byrds: Fifth Dimension (Columbia 9249)
Sally Rogers: Generations (Flying Fish 493)
Sands Family: Now & Then (Spring 1008)

If a Revolution Comes to My Country
PS: If a Revolution, on What Now People? Vol. 2 (Paredon 2002)

If I Had a Hammer (The Hammer Song)
PS: Love Songs for Friends & Foes, Precious Friend, Sing Out with
    Pete, Sing-a-long Demonstration Concert, Strangers & Cousins,
    Wimoweh, World of, Peace Is the World Smiling (Music for
    Little People D-2104)
Weavers: 1949 orig. single ("The Hammer Song" - Hootennany
    H-101), Reunion at Carnegie Hall, Wasn't That a Time (the
    4CD set & the video)
Peter, Paul & Mary: Peter Paul & Mary (Warner)
Arethra Franklin: Yeah! (Columbia 9151)
Gretchen Reed: Come Holy Spirit, Freedom Ministries
Also recorded by: Eddy Arnold, Anita Bryant, Ray Coniff, Senator
    Sam Ervin, Percy Faith, Waylon Jennings, and others.

I'm Gonna Sing Me a Love Song
PS: Love Songs for Friends & Foes

I Wonder, I Wonder, I Wonder
PS: Song & Play Time

In Dead Earnest (Lee's Compost Song)
PS: Precious Friend

In the Evening
PS: At the Village Gate Vol. 2, (with Memphis Slim & Willie Dixon), Bawdy Songs & Real Sad Songs, Folkpeople (Time Wind F 5000), If a Revolution Comes, PS Concert

Jacob's Ladder
PS: HARP, Hootenanny at Camegie Hall, Sing-a-long Demonstration Concert

Jesu, Joy of Man's Desiring
PS: Folk Music Blues, Goofing-Off Suite, Live Hootenanny, PS in Concert Vols 1-2 (Folklore/Topic F-LAUT-1, VOX 1.580), Studs Terkel's Weekly Almanac

Kayowajineh (Seneca Canoe Song)
PS: Champlain Valley Songs, Circles & Seasons, Family Concert (video), Fifty Sail on Newburgh Bay

King Henry
PS: Dangerous Songs

Kisses Sweeter Than Wine
PS: Love Songs for Friends & Foes, On Campus, Precious Friend, on A Tribute to Leadbelly (Tomato R2-70665)
Weavers: orig. 1951 single (Decca 27670), At Camegie Hall, Best of, Greatest Hits, Reunion at Camegie Hall Part 2, Together Again, Wasn't That a Time (CD set & video)
Jimmie Rodgers: The Best of (Rhino 70942)
Peter, Paul & Mary: Album (Wamer 2-26653)
Kate Smith: The Golden Voice of (Good Music KSK)
Also recorded by Marlene Dietrich, The Lennon Sisters, Rod McKuen, Piano Roll, Andy Williams, and many others
Also recordings in French ("Ses Baisers Me Grisaient") by Zack Matalon, in Swedish ("Vuddet Elamaa On") by Reijo Taipale

Kuroda Bushi
Myrdhin & Pol Huellou: Harp & Shakuhachi (Goasco 027)

Last Train to Nuremburg
PS: Rainbow Race, World of

Leatherwing Bat
PS: Amer. Fav. Ballads Vol. 5, Birds Beats Bugs

Letter to Eve
PS: Pete Seeger Now
Magpie: Living Planet (Collector 1948)

Lisa Kalvelage (My Name Is Lisa Kalvelage)
PS: Sings & Answers Questions, Waist Deep in the Big Muddy
Charlie King: Food Phone Gas Lodging (Flying Fish 70536)

Little Boxes
PS: Broadside, Little Boxes & Other Broadsides, We Shall Overcome
Malvina Reynolds: Malvina (Cassandra 2807), Sings the Truth (Columbia 9414 / mono: 2614) [for ordering info see p.107]

Little Girl See Through My Window
PS: Love Songs for Friends & Foes
tune ("Little Bird Fly Through My Window") on PS: Birds Beasts Bugs, Children's Concert, Sing-a-long Demonstration Concert

Living in the Country
PS: Bitter & the Sweet, Family Concert (video), Greatest Hits, If a Revolution Comes, Nonesuch (as "Singing in the Country")
Arlo Guthrie: Running Down the Road (Wamer 6346, Rising Son 903)
Leo Kottke: My Feet Are Smiling (Capitol 11164)
Kevin Roth: Mt. Dulcimer Instrumental Album (Folkways 3570)
George Winston: Summer (Windham Hill 11107)

Lonesome Valley (Guthrie version)
PS: Family Concert (video), Hard Travelin' (album and video), Sing-a-long Demonstration Concert, Together
Woody Guthrie: Library of Congress
[Original version on Joan Baez: Very Early; Carter Family: The Famous]

Lulloo Lullay
Weavers: We Wish You a Merry Christmas

Maple Syrup Time
PS: Circles & Seasons

Melodie d'Amour
PS: Waist Deep in the Big Muddy
Original single by the Ames Brothers (1957)

Mexican Blues
PS: Circles & Seasons, The Folksingers Guitar Guide

Minuit (Sower of Seeds)
Paul Winter Consort: Common Ground (A&M 3344), Icarus (Living Music 0004), Wolf Eyes (Living Music 0018).

Mrs. Clara Sullivan's Letter
PS: I Can See a New Day, We Shall Overcome

My Dirty Stream - see Sailing Up My Dirty Stream

My Father's Mansion
PS: Banks of Marble, Essential, Waist Deep in the Big Muddy

My Rainbow Race
PS: Family Concert (video), Rainbow Race, World of
The Bergerfolk: Sing of Sunshine & Rainbows (Folkways 32417)
Judy Gorman-Jacobs: If Dreams Were Thunder (Icebergg 102)
Peter La Farge: Sing Women Blues (Folkways 2534)

New York Town
On Woody Gutherie: Hard Travelin' (video & album Arloco 284)
O Sacred World Now Wounded
tune ("Chorale from Beethoven's 9th Symphony") on PS: Goofing-Off Suite

Ode to Joy
PS: Goofing-Off Suite
Ed Sweeney: The Times They Are Something Like They Used to Be (Old Harbour 001)

Of Time and Rivers Flowing
PS: Fifty Sail on Newburgh Bay
tune ("Lo How a Rose E'er Blooming") on PS: The Nativity

Oh Had I a Golden Thread (Golden Thread)
PS: Essential, Live at Newport!, Rainbow Quest, Strangers &
     Cousins, Where Have All the Flowers Gone
Also recorded by Judy Collins, Nana Mouskouri

Oh How He Lied
PS: Amer. Fav. Ballads Vol. 4

Old Devil Time
PS: Rainbow Race, Sing-a-long Demonstration Concert, Tell Me that
     You Love Me Junie Moon (Columbia 3540)
Jay Mankita: Jay Mankita (Low Budget Butterfly 1)
Claudia Schmidt: New Goodbyes Old Helloes (Flying Fish 305)
Rosalie Sorrels: Report from Grimes Creek (Green Linnet 2015)

Oleanna
PS: Folksongs of 4 Continents, With Voices Together
In orig. Norwegian by Lille Bjorn Nilsen (Scandisk Music)[7616
     Lyndale Ave. S, Minneapolis MN 55423]
Kingston Trio: At Large / Here We Go Again (2 CD set, Capitol
     96749
Also recorded by Theodore Bikel, Gene Bluestein

One Dime Blues
Blind Lemon Jefferson: One Dime Blues (Rounder 2112)

One Grain of Sand
PS: Abiyoyo, Dangerous Songs, Folk Festival at Newport Vol. 1,
     Sleep-time, on Equilibrium (Audubon's Album of Nature &
     Humanity - Folkways 37305)
Carolyn Hester: on Kerrville Folk Fesvital 1977 (PSG 77)
Odetta: Odetta (Vanguard 222060)

One Man's Hands
Carolyn Hester: on Kerrville Folk Festival 1977 (PSG 77)
Also recordings by Chad Mitchell Trio, Odetta, Jackie Washington

Only Remembered
Bill Shute & Lisa Null: American Primitive (Green Linnet SIF
     1025)

Our Generation
PS: Rainbow Race

Over the Hills
PS: Love Songs for Friends & Foes, Waist Deep in the Big Muddy
Weavers: On Tour

The People Are Scratching
PS: God Bless the Grass

Plow Under
Almanac Singers: Songs for John Doe

Precious Friend
PS: Banks of Marble, Precious Friend
Bright Morning Star: Live in the USA (Rainbow Snake 008)

Proud Mary
Creedence Clearwater Revival: Bayou County, Chronicle, Concert,
     Gold, Live in Europe, 1968-69 (all on Fantasy)
Elvis Presley: On Stage, Live at Madison Square Garden (RCA)
Ike & Tina Turner: Ike & Tina Turner (EMI)
Tina Turner: Alone (Capitol)

Quite Early Morning
PS: Banks of Marble, Essential, Together, Feeding the Flame (gay
     liberation compilation - Flying Fish 70541), Songs for Peace
     (Rounder 4015)
Guy Carawan: The Land Knows You're There (Flying Fish 391)

Rainbow Race - see My Rainbow Race

Reuben James (The Sinking of the Reuben James)
PS: Folk Music, Gazette Vol.1, Sing with Seeger, Sings Woody
     Gutherie, World of, on Hard Travelin' (album & video)
Woody Gutherie: Greatest Songs of (Vanguard 35/36)
Almanac Singers: Dear Mr. President

River of My People
PS: Love Songs for Friends & Foes

Rockin' Solidarity
Dave Welsh & the Rockin' Solidarity Band: Rockin' Solidarity
     [write PO Box 26581, San Francisco CA 94126]
Also on: This Line Is Singin' (Freedom Song Network)
Original version on PS/The Union Boys: Solidarity Forever (1945
     single with Tom Glazer & Burl Ives - Stinson 622) and
     Almanac Singers: Talking Union

Round and Round Hitler's Grave
Almanac Singers: Dear Mr. President, on The Unforgotten Men
     (National Guardian album from early 1950's)
tune ("Old Joe Clark") on PS: Bitter & the Sweet, Darling Corey,
     Essential, Folk Music Blues

Sacco's Letter to His Son
PS: on Ballads of Sacco & Vanzetti, on Folk Song America Vol.4
     (Smithsonian Collection 0464)
Magpie: If It Ain't Love (Philo 1112)

Sag Mir Wo Die Blumen Sind
Joan Baez: Farewell Angelina (Vanguard 9200)
Recorded by Marlene Dietrich

Sailing Down My Golden River
PS: Circles & Seasons, Rainbow Race, on Bread & Roses Festival
     of Acoustic Music Vol. 1 (Fantasy 79009)
Arlo Guthrie: Outlasting the Blues (Wamer 3336, Rising Son)

Sailing Up My Dirty Stream (My Dirty Stream)
God Bless the Grass, on Clearwater II (Sound House 1022)

Seek and You Shall Find
PS: Rainbow Quest, Waist Deep

Seventy Miles
PS: God Bless the Grass
The Coachmen: The Coachmen (Fantasy 2482)

Snow, Snow
PS: Rainbow Race
The Short Sisters: A Planet Dancing Slow (Black Socks Press
     8654-12) [write: Box 208, Harrisville NH 03450]

Sour Cream
PS: Circles & Seasons

Sower of Seeds - for original version see Minuit

Strange Death of John Doe
Almanac Singers: Songs for John Doe
tune ("Young Man Who Wouldn't Hoe Corn") on PS: Frontier
    Ballads, Songs to Grow On Vol. 3

Step by Step
PS: Carry It On, Rainbow Quest, Songs of Struggle & Protest, on
    Can't You See the System Isn't Working (Paredon)
Laura Burns & Roger Rosen: on Swords into Ploughshares (Folk
    Tradition S005,006)
Ronnie Gilbert, Earl Robinson & Chet Washington: Songs of the
    Working People (Flying Fish 483)
Joe Higgs: Triumph! (Alligator 8313)
John McCutcheon: Step by Step (Rounder 0216)
Sweet Honey & the Rock: The Other Side (Flying Fish 366)

Sweepy, Sweepy, Sweepy
PS: Abiyoyo, Sleep-Time

Sweet-a-Little Baby
PS: Abiyoyo, Sleep-time, Take a Seat Everybody
tune - see Minuit

Talking Blues (original version)
PS: Amer. Fav. Ballads Vol. 5
Weavers: On Tour

Talking Union
PS: Carry It On, Greatest Hits, Hootenanny NYC (Topic 37),
    Hootenanny Tonight!, Songs of Struggle & Protest, on The
    Unforgotten Men (National Guardian album in early 1950's)
Almanac Singers: Talking Union

Teacher Uncle Ho
PS: If a Revolution Comes, Rainbow Race

Theme from the "Goofing-Off Suite"
PS: Big Bill Broonzy & PS in Concert, Goofing-Off Suite, PS &
    Sonny Terry, on Raising Arizona (original soundtrack album)

There's a Hole in the Bucket
PS: Amer. Fav. Ballads Vol. 4, Sing-a-long Demonstration Concert
Faith Petric: Sing a Song / Sing Along (Gentle Winds 1015)

This Is a Land
PS: Banks of Marble, Fifty Sail on Newburgh Bay

This Land Is Your Land
PS: Children's Concert, Family Concert (video), Folk Music, I Can
    See a New Day, Live at Newport!, Visit Sesame Street, Sing
    with Seeger, Sings Woody Guthrie, Song & Play Time, Songs
    to Grow On Vol. 3, World of, Hard Travelin' (album & video)
Weavers: Greatest Hits, At Home, Songbag, Wasn't That a Time
    (album & video)
On Folkways / A Vision Shared / A Tribute to Woody Gutherie &
    Leadbelly (Columbia recording and video). Woody Gutherie:
    Greatest Hits, 1940-46
Flatt & Scruggs: Changing Times
Peter, Paul & Mary: Moving (Warner 1473)

This Old Car
PS: Young vs. Old

Times A-Gettin' Hard, Boys
PS: At the Village Gate Vol. 1, Goofing-Off Suite
Harry Belafonte: Scarlet Ribbons
Kevin Roth: Somebody Give Me Directions (Folkways)

To Everyone in All the World
PS: Rainbow Quest
Raffi: Baby Beluga (MCA, in Canada: Troubadour)

To My Old Brown Earth
PS: Broadsides

Tomorrow Is a Highway
PS: Gazette Vol. 2

Tomorrow's Children
PS: Broadsides

The Torn Flag
PS: Pete Seeger Now

Turn, Turn, Turn
PS: Bitter & the Sweet, Greatest Hits, World of, on Troubadours of
    the Folk Era Vol. 2 (Rhino 70263)
The Byrds: The Byrds (Columbia 46773), Greatest Hits (Columbia
    9516), Original Singles Vol. 1 (1965-1967 - Columbia 37335),
    Turn Turn Turn (Columbia 9254)
Judy Collins: #3, Recollections (Elektra)
Mary Hopkin: Post Card (Capitol 97578)
Also recorded by Theodore Bikel, The Lettermen, Gordon Lightfoot,
    Mitch Miller, Dolly Parton, Nina Simone, and many others
Recorded in French ("Tourne le Temps") by Gerard Melet, in
    Spanish ("Todo A Su Tiempo") by Las Cerezas.

Visions of Children
tune on PS: Goofing-Off Suite (as "Duet from Beethoven's 7th
    Symphony")

Waist Deep in the Big Muddy
PS: Waist Deep, Sings & Answers Questions, original 1967 single
    on Columbia

Walking Down Death Row
PS: Dangerous Songs

The Water Is Wide
PS: Amer. Fav. Ballads Vol. 2, On Campus, PS Now, Sing-a-long
    Demonstration Concert, Twelve String Guitar
Joan Baez: Very Early (Vanguard)
Ronnie Gilbert: The Spirit Is Free
Carolyn Hester: Carolyn Hester
Buffy Sainte-Marie: Little Wheel Spin & Spin
Jackie Washington: Volume 2

We Shall Overcome

PS: Bitter & the Sweet, Broadsides, Carry It On, Complete Carnegie Hall Concert, Greatest Hits, Sing Out! Hootenanny, We Shall Overcome, on Dogfight (original soundtrack - Nouveau 10082)
Louis Armstrong: What a Wonderful World (Bluebird 8310)
Joan Baez: In Concert (Vanguard 113/114)
Guy Carawan: Songs of Struggle & Celebration
SNCC Freedom Singers: on Evening Concert/Newport Folk Festival 1963 (Vanguard 77002), on Sing for Freedom/The Story of the Civil Rights Movement through Its Songs (Smithsonian Folkways 40032 - companion recording to the book by Guy & Candie Carawan, see Bibliography)
Mahalia Jackson: Let's Pray Together (Columbia 8930)
Odetta: In Japan (RCA 3457)
Paul Winter Sextet: Jazz Meets the Folk Song (Columbia 2155)
On Voices of the Civil Rights Movement (Smithsonian Institution)
Also recorded by: James Cleveland & the Troubadours, Eileen Farrell, Roberta Flack, Huntley & Brinkley, Bernie Sanders, and many others
Videos: We Shall Overcome (1989 PBS special)
Eyes on the Prize (6 part PBS series on the history of the Civil Rights Movement, Blackside Productions, 1986)

We Wish You a Merry Christmas

Weavers: We Wish You a Merry Christmas (1951 single, Decca 27783), We Wish You a Merry Christmas (1952 Decca LP), At Carnegie Hall, Best of, Greatest Hits
Kingston Trio: The Last Month of the Year (Capitol 93116)
Peter, Paul & Mary: A Holiday Celebration (Warner 9-45070-2), A Holiday Concert (video - Rhino 1951)

Well May the World Go

PS: Banks of Marble, Together
New Lost City Ramblers: Second Annual Farewell Reunion (PS plays & sings - Mercury 1-685), 20th Anniversary Concert (Flying Fish 090)

When I Was Most Beautiful

PS: Young vs. Old

Where Have All the Flowers Gone

PS: 1963 single (Columbia), Bitter & the Sweet, Essential, Greatest Hits, Live at Newport!, Rainbow Quest, World of
Kingston Trio: Best of, College Concert, 25 Years (Capitol)
Joan Baez: Very Early (Vanguard 79446)
Earth Wind & Fire: The Eternal Dance (Columbia 42439), Last Days & Time (Columbia 31702)
Flatt & Scruggs: Changin' Times
Peter Paul & Mary: Peter Paul & Mary (Warner 1449)
Also recorded by: Bobby Darin, Marlene Dietrich, Richie Havens, Huntley & Brinkley, The Lennon Sisters, Gordon Lightfoot, and many others

Where's My Pajamas

PS: Abiyoyo, Sleep-time, Stoney Plain (Smithsonian Folkways 45001)
Joanne Olshansky: Pizza Boogie (JHO 101)

Whistling Past the Graveyard

PS: Love Songs for Friends & Foes

Who Killed Norma Jean?

PS: Little Boxes, We Shall Overcome

The Whole Wide World Around

PS: On People's Songs for National Maritime Union (soundtrack for filmstrip, People's Songs, 1947)

Wimoweh (Mbube)

PS: Amer. Fav. Ballads Vol. 3, Essential, Greatest Hits, HARP, Hootenanny at Carnegie Hall, Hootenanny Tonight!, Precious Friend, Sing Out with Pete, With Voices Together
Weavers: orig. 1952 single (Decca 2792), At Carnegie Hall, Best of, Greatest Hits, Reunion at Carnegie Hall, on Dogfight (soundtrack from the film - Nouveau 10082), Together Again, Wasn't That a Time (video)
Chet Atkins: The RCA Years (RCA 61095)
Nanci Griffith (with Odetta): Other Voices/Other Rooms (Elektra 61464)
Kingston Trio: From the Hungry I (Capitol 96748)
Miriam Makeba: Miriam Makeba (RCA 2267)

Words, Words

PS: Rainbow Race

The following lists catalog numbers for Pete Seeger albums which include one or more songs from this collection:

Abiyoyo & Other Stories and Songs for Children - Folkways 1500, 7525, 45001
Almanac - Folkways (early 1950's)
American Ballads - Folkways 2320 (1957)
American Favorite Ballads, Vol. 2 - Folkways 2321 (1959)
American Favorite Ballads, Vol. 3 - Folkways 2322 (1960)
American Favorite Ballads, Vol. 4 - Folkways 2323 (1961)
American Favorite Ballads, Vol. 5 - Folkways 2445 (1962)
American History in Ballad and Song, Vols. 1,2 - Folkways 5801, 5802 (1961)
American Industrial Ballads - Folkways 5251 (1956)
At the Village Gate, Vol. 1 (with Memphis Slim & Willie Dixon) - Folkways 2450 (1960)
At the Village Gate, Vol. 2 (with Memphis Slim & Willie Dixon) - Folkways 2451 (1962)
Ballads of Sacco and Vanzetti (with Woody Guthrie) - Folkways 5485 (1963)
Banks of Marble - Folkways 31040 (1974)
Bantu Choral Folk Songs (with chorus) - Folkways 6912 (1955)
Bawdy Songs & Real Sad Songs (with Betty Sanders) - Charter (1947)
Big Bill Broonzy and Pete Seeger in Concert - Verve Folkways 9008 (1965)
Birds, Beasts, Bugs and Little Fishes - Folkways 7610 (1954)
The Bitter and the Sweet - Columbia 8716 / mono: 1916 (1963)
Broadside Ballads, Vol. 2 - Broadside Records 302 (1965)
Broadsides - Folkways 2456 (1964)
Champlain Valley Songs - Folkways 5210
Carry It On (with Si Kahn & Jane Sapp) - Flying Fish 104 [companion recording for Seeger's book of labor songs, see Bibliography]
Children's Concert at Town Hall - Columbia 8747 / mono: 1947 (1963) [reissued as Harmony 30399]
Circle and Seasons - Warner 3329 (1979)
Clearwater II - Sound House Records 1022 (1977)
Complete Carnegie Hall Concert (June 1963 - 2 CD set, Columbia 45312)
Dangerous Songs - Columbia 9303 / mono: 2503 (1966)
Darling Corey and the Goofing-Off Suite, Folkways 40018

The Essential Pete Seeger - Vanguard 97/98 (1978)
Fifty Sail on Newburgh Bay (with Ed Reneham) - Folkways 5257 (1976)
Folk Festival at Newport, Vol. 1 (various artists) - Vanguard 9062 (1959)
Folk Music - Folkways 9013
Folk Music Blues - Folkways 3864
Folksongs of Four Contients - Folkways 6911 (1955)
Frontier Ballads, Vol. 1 - Folkways 2176 (1954)
Gazette, Vol. 1 - Folkways 2501
Gazette, Vol. 2 - Folkways 2502 (1961)
God Bless the Grass - Columbia 9232 / mono: 2432 (1966), Folkways 37232
Goofing-Off Suite - Folkways 2045 (1954), reissued in 1993 on CD - Folkways 40018
Greatest Hits - Columbia 9416 / mono: 2616 (1967)
HARP (with Holly Near, Arlo Guthrie & Ronnie Gilbert) - Redwood 409 (1985 live concert recording at Universal Ampitheater, Los Angeles)
Hard Travelin' (with Arlo Guthrie, others) - Arloco 284 [original soundtrack recording from the film on Woody Gutherie's life and work]
Hootenanny at Carnegie Hall - Folkways 2512 (1960)
Hootenanny Tonight! - Folkways 2511 (1959)
I Can See a New Day - Columbia 9057 / mono: 2252 (1965)
If a Revolution Comes - Oktober 508
Indian Summer (soundtrack of the film) - Folkways 3851 (1961)
Little Boxes & Other Broadsides - Verve/Folkways 9020 (1963)
Live at Newport! - Vanguard 77008 (1993)
Live Hootenanny - Aravel 1006
Love Songs for Friends and Foes - Folkways 2453 (1956)
The Nativity - Folkways 35001 (1964)
Nonesuch (with Frank Hamilton) - Folkways 2439 (1959)
On Campus - Verve/Folkways 9009 (1965)
Pete Seeger and Brother Kirk Visit Sesame Street - Children's Records of Merica 22062 (1974)
Pete Seeger and Sonny Terry - Folkways 2412 (1958)
A Pete Seeger Concert - Stinson 57 (1954)
Pete Seeger Now - Columbia 9717 (1969)
Precious Friend (with Arlo Guthrie) - Warner 2-3644
The Rainbow Quest - Folkways 2454 (1960)
Rainbow Race - Columbia 30739 (1973)
Sing Out! Hootenanny (with "The Hooteneers")- Folkways 2513 (1959)
Sing Out with Pete! (with group) - Folkways 2455 (1961)
Sing-a-long Demonstration Concert - Folkways 36055 (1980) [live concert recording includes Pete's teaching and coaching the audience]
Sings and Answers Questions at the Ford Hall Forum in Boston - Broadside 502 (1968)
Sing with Seeger - Disc 1101
Sings Leadbelly - Folkways 31022 (1968)
Sings Woody Guthrie - Folkways 31002 (1967)
Sleep Time: Songs & Stories by Pete Seeger - Folkways 7525 (1958)
Song and Play Time with Pete Seeger - Folkways 7526 (1958)
Songs of Struggle and Protest - Folkways 5233 (1965)
Songs of the Civil War - Folkways 5717 (1960)
Songs to Grow On, Vol. 3 - Folkways 7027 (1951)
Story Songs - Columbia 8468 / mono: 1668 (1961)
Strangers & Cousins - Columbia 9134 / mono: 2334 (1965)
Studs Terkel's Weekly Almanac on Folk Music Blues on WFMT (with Big Bill Broonzy) - Folkways 3864 (1956)
Three Saints, Four Sinners & Six Others - Columbia 160266

Together in Concert (with Arlo Guthrie) - Warner / Reprise 2R5-2214 (1975)
Traditional Christmas Carols - Folkways 32311 (1967)
The Twelve-String Guitar As Played by Leadbelly - Folkways 8371 (1962)
Waist Deep in the Big Muddy - Columbia 9505 / mono: 2705 (1967)
We Sing, Vol. 1 - MDH records ("bootleg" album recorded live at Reed College, 1950)
We Shall Overcome (1963 Carnegie Hall concert - Columbia 8901 / mono: 2101, reissued on CD as 45312)
With Voices Together We Sing - Folkways 2452 (1956)
The World of Pete Seeger - Columbia 31949 (1974)
Young vs. Old - Columbia 9873 (1971)

Seeger recordings with the Almanac Singers:

Dear Mr. President - Keynote 111 (1942)
Songs for John Doe - Keynote 102 (1941)
Talking Union and Other Union Songs - Keynote 106 (1941), Folkways 5285 (1955)
Note: the above albums are being reissued with other material from the period on a new 6 CD set issued by Bear Family Records, PO Box 1154, 2864 Vollersode, Germany - phone: 011 (49) 4794-1399.

Seeger recordings with The Weavers:

At Carnegie Hall - Vanguard 6533 / reissued as CD: 73101 (1957)
At Home - Vanguard 2030 / mono: 9024 (1958)
Best Of - Decca 7173 / mono: 8893 (1959), MCA 4052
Greatest Hits - Vanguard 15/16
On Tour - Vanguard 6537 / mono: 9013 (1958)
Reunion at Carnegie Hall - Vanguard 2150 (1963)
Reunion, Part 2 - Vanguard 79161 (1965)
Songbag - Vanguard 73001 (1967, from earlier albums)
Together Again - Loom 10681
We Wish You a Merry Christmas - Decca 5373 (1952)

Videos which include the author:

Pete Seeger's Family Concert - Sony Kids Video 49550 (1992)
The Rainbow Quest - Central Sun Video [10 videos of Seeger's television series, each featuring a guest artist including Doc Watson, Woody Guthrie, Leadbelly, Donovan, Judy Collins, Sonny Terry & Brownie McGhee, etc. - write: Box 3135, Reston VA 22090]
A Tribute to Woody Guthrie and Leadbelly: A Vision Shared (various artists) - CBS Music Video (1988)
The Weavers: Wasn't That a Time - Warner Reprise Video 38304 (1981)
Woody Guthrie: Hard Travelin' (with Arlo Guthrie) - MGM/UA Video 600884 [soundtrack from the film]

See also: Love It Like a Fool [16mm film on the life and of work of Malvina Reynolds. Forthcoming in video format. Contact: New Day Films, 121 W. 27th Street, #902, New York NY 10011, (212) 645-8210.]

INDEX

This index encompasses the subject matter of the songs and photographs in this book as well as the text. People listed include composers of songs (usually co-composers with the author--who are usually discussed in the text accompanying each song). Separate listings for text references and songs are provided only for those individuals with many songs in this collection (Woody, Lee, Leadbelly, Malvina, the Lomaxes, and The Weavers). Songs and text are also indexed by events, musical genres and issues, and for songs in languages other than English. Explanatory information about individual listings is given only when it is not provided in the text and to help readers sort out the various members of the author's family.

Titles of songs which are only excerpted or referred to in the text are included in this index. The titles and first lines of songs which are reprinted as complete songs can be found in the Song Index at the end of the book.

SONG INDEX

This index includes song titles, listed here in **Boldface**, alternate titles, listed in Regular type, and first lines, listed in *Italics*. First lines of choruses are included where appropriate. Also please note: only complete songs are included in this index, song fragments and song references are included in the preceding regular index.

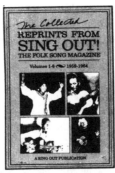

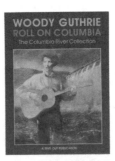

How To Become A Member Of Sing Out

Dear friend of folk and acoustic music,

You may wish to know about the organization that has made this songbook available. The Sing Out Corporation, a not-for-profit tax-exempt organization, was formed to preserve the cultural diversity and heritage of all traditional folk musics; to support creators of new folk music from all countries and cultures; and to encourage the practice of folk music as a living phenomenon. Major emphasis is placed on multi-cultural, rooted music which does not receive serious attention from the commercial media and the music industry. Sing Out! is:

SING OUT! The Folksong Magazine — Since May of 1950, Sing Out has been sharing songs in the pages of the longest continuing folk music publication in the world. Along with the twenty (or more) songs in each fat issue of **Sing Out!**, you'll find feature articles, news, and reviews covering the broadest possible definition of folk music. Regular columnists in each quarterly issue include Ian Robb ("The British-North American Act"), Sandy Byer ("Kidsbeat"), Dan Keding ("The Endless Tale"), as well as Sing Out founder Pete Seeger ("Appleseeds"). All free to members!!

THE SING OUT RESOURCE CENTER — Housed at our Bethlehem, Pennsylvania main office, the Resource Center is a public access folk music center concentrating on materials relating to the folk music revival from the 1930s to the present. It is a multi-media library containing thousands of recordings, books, periodicals, photographs, video tapes, and ephemera. This is a free resource for members!!*SUSTAINING MEMBERS receive up to $50 worth of copies or printouts free each year.*

SING OUT PUBLISHING — Sing Out is releasing a series of folk music songbooks. A catalog listing of books currently available and their prices can be found on the preceeding page of the insert. We will be releasing more songbooks and learning aids over the next couple of years. Members get special advance discounts and information. *SUSTAINING MEMBERS revceive an additional 5% discount on all Sing Out Publications and "Marketplace" purchases.*

If you'd like to become a member, we've included a handy return card below. Simply fill it out and send it with your check or money order (or credit card information) to:

Sing Out, P.O. Box 5253, Bethlehem, PA 18015-0253 or call: **(215)865-5366** (MasterCard or Visa accepted!)

If the card is missing ☞ don't fret!

Simply send your name & address with your check or money order (or call, if you'd prefer to use your credit card!)

Basic Membership:

$18.00 1-year
$32.50 2-years
$45.00 3-years

Sustaining Membership:

$30, $50 or $100 /year

Outside U.S.:
Add $3.00 per year;
U.S. funds only!

Sing Out Membership Order Form

Yes! I'd like to become a member of Sing Out. **Sign me up** as a:

Basic Member: ❏ 1-year; $18.00 ❏ 2-years; $32.50 ❏ 3-years; $45.00
Sustaining Member: ❏ $30 ❏ $50 ❏ $100 for 1-year

❏ *Institutional rate:* $25 per year

Outside U.S.: *Please add $3.00/ year. U.S. funds Money order or check from U.S. bank only!*

Name:_____

Address:_____

City:_____ **State/Prov.:**_____ **Zip:**_____

Country:_____

This is a ❏ **new** ❏ **renewal membership**

❏ **This is a gift. Please send a gift card from:** _____

Payment : ❏ Check or Money Order enclosed
❏ Visa/MasterCard *(circle one)* Signature:_____

card#:_____ Exp. Date:_____

Sing Out, P.O. Box 5253, Bethlehem, PA 18015-0253

Offer subject to change Free recording deal ends with supply.

FROM:

_____

_____

_____

TO: **SING OUT!**
P.O. Box 5253
Bethlehem, PA 18015-0253